BECOMING YOURSELF

BECOMING YOURSELF

Overcoming Mind Control and Ritual Abuse

Alison Miller

Routledge
Taylor & Francis Group
LONDON AND NEW YORK

First published 2012 by Karnac Book Ltd.

Published 2018 by Routledge
2 Park Square, Milton Park, Abingdon, Oxon OX14 4RN
711 Third Avenue, New York, NY 10017, USA

Routledge is an imprint of the Taylor & Francis Group, an informa business

British Library Cataloguing in Publication Data

A C.I.P. for this book is available from the British Library

ISBN: 9781782200765 (pbk)

Edited, designed and produced by The Studio Publishing Services Ltd
www.publishingservicesuk.co.uk
e-mail: studio@publishingservicesuk.co.uk

CONTENTS

This book is dedicated to those who have died as a result of mind control and/or ritual abuse, and those who have lived when they would rather have died.

ACKNOWLEDGEMENTS

First of all, I want to thank all the clients who, over the past twenty-three years, have shared with me their painful stories of mind control and ritual abuse. They have been my most important teachers, and without them I would not have been able even to conceive of writing such a book. Some of them will recognise themselves in these pages, and I know it will be important to them to know they have helped point the way to freedom for many other survivors who have had experiences similar to their own.

Beyond that, words cannot express how grateful I am to those courageous survivors who have provided original contributions for this book: Jen Callow, Adriana Green, Wendy Hoffman, Sally, LisaBri, Arauna Morgan, and Meredith Sharman. Their bravery in facing their experiences, their hard-won internal co-operation and maturity, and their willingness to speak up constitute a unique contribution to our understanding of both these abuses and their healing process. Trish Fotheringham, Aurora Levins Morales, and Jean Riseman have also graciously allowed me to reprint their writings from elsewhere (in Jean's case, after her editing), and Stella Katz, before she died, gave me permission to use anything she had written or told me. One reason these survivors have had the courage and motivation to tell their stories is a desire to speak for those who cannot; another is to expose what the criminal groups do so that others may become free of those groups' control.

Therapists Gaby Breitenbach, Heather Gingrich, and Steven Frankel have also contributed techniques they use to help survivors. We therapists who have not personally experienced mind control or ritual abuse have, nevertheless, been touched by these horrors, through caring for clients who have gone through them. We cannot turn our backs on those who come to us, or fail to hear their stories simply because there is no external verification of the cause of their suffering. (Of course, some therapists are also survivors.)

I asked four survivors and three therapists to read this book chapter by chapter and provide feedback regarding whether each part would be helpful for survivors, and whether it could trigger programming. Survivor therapists Arauna Morgan and Wendy Hoffman, survivors LisaBri and Sally, and psychologist and lawyer Steve Frankel put in long hours reading the book chapter by chapter for conceptual clarity, accuracy, and safety, and I thank each of them from the bottom of my heart. You will see their own creative ideas in the book, not only in the longer pieces they wrote, but they are also quoted here and there in my text. All my readers put their hearts into this task because they want to help and empower survivors to overcome mind control.

ABOUT THE AUTHOR

Alison Miller is a clinical psychologist in private practice in Victoria, British Columbia, Canada. She worked for many years in child and youth mental health services, treating children and families. She is the original developer of the Living in Families Effectively (LIFE) Seminars (www.lifeseminars.com), and has co-authored two books on parenting with Dr Allison Rees. Since 1991, Dr Miller has been treating and learning from persons with dissociative disorders, in particular survivors of ritual abuse and mind control, and has developed a protocol for effective treatment. She is a Fellow of the International Society for the Study of Trauma and Dissociation. Her previous work on this subject is: *Healing the Unimaginable: Treating Ritual Abuse and Mind Control* (London, Karnac, 2011).

FOREWORD

This is Alison Miller's second book on mind control. To take on the task once is brave, but to take on the challenge of mind control twice is like professional suicide. Yet, without people like her speaking out, the cycle would continue, children and adults would be no more than puppets on a string, unaware of their lack of control. As survivors, we can hide behind anonymity, but for a professional this is not acceptable. Yet, it is the professionals who are attacked time and time again on our behalf and I would like to thank Alison and all the professionals that speak out.

I am pleased to have the opportunity to write something for this book as a mother, an artist, an author, and a main person of a programmed dissociated identity disorder (DID) system. This is the first time I have publicly given up my anonymity and stated that I am a mind control survivor. This book helped me decide to do that. Thank you again to Alison and our therapy for giving me the strength and support to do this.

I was introduced to mind control slowly and sensitively by our therapist, but went off on a false sense of strength, denial, and power and searched the Internet only to find our paintings were all over the mind control sites, being ripped apart and analysed. It was shocking and frightening to read about all the mind control symbols different people saw in our art, both rightly and wrongly. When I first came across this, I was not ready to hear what I read. As a survivor with DID, it is hard enough to get used to being in the public eye as an artist, and with my autobiography I allowed more of my life to become public. However, that was not about mind control. Reading the words written about our paintings and the different language used to describe programmes was indeed shocking. This made me realise how careful we survivors must be in how we time ourselves for such journeys.

With Alison's book, you are able to take one step at a time, read through it slowly and digest it chapter by chapter. It might not relate to you or it may be similar to your experiences. It might even be you to a T, but we are all different. It matters that we realise there is no single key to unlock each of our unique systems. We have to be honest with ourselves. It might help to take it to therapy, as I did, and it opened up new discussions and learning.

This book is carefully written with understanding of, and sensitivity to, the reader. From the beginning it slowly prepares one for the tragic truth of the damage one human being can do to another and the frightening world we live in. It is not only from one human being to another adult. It is, of course, what full-grown adults can do to tiny people, from babyhood onwards. Alison Miller is careful not to traumatise.

One important issue Alison's book highlighted for me was the difference between DID and mind control DID. Now there is more understanding that DID exists and survivors are communicating with each other on social networks, and through books and art, a difference needs to be noted between these two very different conditions.

DID as a creative defence against trauma is not the same as programmed DID, DID that is deliberately created through abusers deliberately torturing babies and young children with the aim of creating alters with particular tasks and identities. In the early days, professionals were not even trained to understand, recognise, or treat DID, so it did not seem that important to know the difference, but now the significant difference needs to be noted as there are different treatment implications.

It has been of concern to me, as the main person of a programmed DID system, to have some professionals lack knowledge of the severity of my condition. As an individual from such a programmed system, I can manage competently in certain areas, much to the disbelief of some professionals. Many feel DID means dramatic public switches of state which everyone can see all the time.

In addition, it needs to be stated that just as each human is different, each person with DID of any kind is also different, and we do not all fit into a square box. To have DID, we have all suffered in one way or another and the healing process is a very long, difficult journey made easier by the dedicated professionals who speak out on our behalf.

Kim Noble

Introduction

As a therapist working with survivors of mind control and ritual abuse, I became acutely aware of the need for a book to guide me, and for twenty years I waited for that book to appear, while struggling to learn from my survivor clients. Two years ago, I wrote the book that I had wanted to have. I hear from therapists all over the world that it is helping their understanding of how to work with survivors.

In that book, I included survivors' writings which detailed some of the abuses which mind-controlling and ritualistic abuser groups perform. I wrote "A word to survivors" in which I suggested they not read my book, but instead recommend it to their therapists. The reasons I gave were:

1. "You do not want your memories to be contaminated by reading the details contained on these pages about what ritual abusers and mind controllers do. Genuine survivors have difficulty in any case believing their memories, and it is easier to believe what comes up from within you if you do not have other people's information to confuse you.
2. "There are some graphic details of abuses here, and they can trigger flashbacks or trained behaviours in people who are actually survivors of such abuses. This can be unpleasant and destabilising for you."

After the book came out, I heard that some survivors complained about these cautions. They felt, quite rightly, that it was up to them to read it and judge whether or not it was appropriate. I have been told that survivors did read it. But because that book had a lot of "therapist language" as well as potentially upsetting details of abuses, I came to realise that perhaps I should write a book specifically geared to survivors. (If you want those gory details, you can read the other book, *Healing the Unimaginable: Treating Ritual Abuse and Mind Control.*)

Shockingly, at present, the self-help literature for persons suffering from complex dissociative post trauma conditions makes little or no mention of mind control or ritual abuse, despite the fact that many such persons have had those experiences, which are the strongest reasons to dissociate.

There are historical reasons for this omission. When therapists began to talk about the disclosures they were receiving, some of the leaders in the field were slapped with lawsuits, and a very well organised media campaign was orchestrated to convince the general public that most mind control and ritual abuse stories came straight from the mind of the therapist, and that survivors were gullible enough to believe anything a therapist would tell them. That concept is, in my opinion, an insult to survivors as well as to therapists. No one would deliberately make up such horrifying stories, and no one who had not undergone such experiences would claim them for their own and terrorise themselves with false memories of sadistic abuse, when they could just live a "normal" life.

Be that as it may, you can still receive some help from some of this literature, just as long as you do not expect it to do what it cannot do. The index of Boon, Steele, and van der Hart's otherwise excellent *Coping with Trauma-Related Dissociation* (2011) does not even mention the words *mind control*, *programming*, or *ritual abuse*, and neither does the text, despite the fact that for many people these abuses are the basis of the symptoms which the authors are trying to address.

However, that book, which has received much praise, does have many helpful exercises to help you cope with everyday life. It is based on a day treatment programme, and the authors recommend it be used only as part of work with a trained and skilled therapist. Unfortunately, not all survivors can afford therapy, or can find a safe therapist who understands and is willing to face what they are dealing with. Other self-help books, especially for survivors of sexual abuse, can also be helpful, particularly for dealing with the effects of abuses which were not deliberately orchestrated to create mind control.

In reading *Coping with Trauma-Related Dissociation*, as well as many books for therapists about trauma and dissociation, I keep recognising the effects of programming in the case examples. I see the experts making up complex intrapsychic motives for survivors doing things which have a very simple explanation: young inside parts of them doing jobs they were trained to do. In my opinion, trying to fight programmed urges can be a constant losing battle, and there are much more effective ways to deal with these once you recognise that they are programmed (which means they are driven by the terror of young child parts of you).

There are several first-person accounts of mind control and ritual abuses, but not many books that point the way to recovery. I know of two: Chrystine Oksana's *Safe Passage to Healing* (1994) and Emilie P. Rose's *Reaching for the Light* (1996), both of which take a very gentle and compassionate approach but are aware of the mind control through which cults control those they abuse. At the time these books were written, non-religious military/political and organised criminal abuses had not yet come to light, but still much of what they say is applicable to survivors of non-religious mind control abuse.

What is different about my book? It is compassionate, but it is not gentle. It tackles the problems head-on. I believe that people who have survived horrendous childhood abuse can be strong and courageous in finding out the truth of what happened to them and doing the necessary work to achieve safety and healthy lives.

I do not believe that survivors are more suggestible than other people. This is a cover-up lie disseminated by abusers to make therapists afraid to ask survivors what happened to them. Certainly, the young child parts of you might have been fooled by stage magic and adults' lies, but you are now old enough to put two and two together and make four, not a hundred. If you are a mind control survivor, even your desire to deny the facts of what happened to you is not just coming from your own wish to have had a happy childhood and to continue to have a happy family, it is programmed—that is, it was drummed into you—by abusers.

So, much of this book is about how you can overcome the lies that your young parts were told, and might be continuing to be told. In order to do this effectively, you need to involve all parts of you in the process of assessing reality. When you read survivors' stories, you need to say within yourself: "This is that other person's experience. If it resonates with mine, perhaps something similar happened to me. But if it doesn't resonate, then perhaps my experience was different." Mind control is complicated, and different groups do different things. What is important is that you find out what was done to *you*, and what you were forced to do, and find ways to reverse the effects of these experiences. It is possible that things do not resonate because your system is blocked or closed down by the abusers, but it is also possible that they do not resonate because those things did not happen to you. Only your insiders can tell.

What about triggering, the second concern I expressed in my introduction to the book for therapists? Well, if you read this book, you are going to be triggered. There is no way around that. The destabilisation caused by beginning to remember is temporary, however. There are two kinds of triggering. The first kind is when something in the present reminds you of a past trauma, and sets off flashbacks. If you are a survivor, you have parts inside who already know how to shut that down. The second kind of triggering is when some part of you sets off a programmed emotion or behaviour, usually as a warning or punishment when you are coming to know or tell something which is supposed to be a secret of the perpetrator group. You have parts who know how to turn that off, too, but they have to decide to do so. You can also refer to Chapter Ten, which gives more detailed information on dealing with triggering.

Every chapter in this book is potentially triggering. One survivor therapist I know says "Triggering is good, and it gets you out of your stupor." She sees it as a way to access her inside parts and her memories.

The other way in which this book is different from other self-help books is that I am writing to you as if you are multiple, because whether you know it or not, if you are a survivor, you are. This just means that you have different inside parts who know and feel different things and have different "jobs". I am writing to all parts, at least, to all parts who are old enough to read and understand what I am saying, not just to the part of you who goes to work or takes care of your children. That part has a specialised job in the present-day world. For most survivors, that part has to be protected from the knowledge and feelings of the mind control abuse. So, I am inviting other parts, particularly those who were trained and indoctrinated by your abusers, to participate in learning from this book. Do not leave it to the adult who has to handle daily life. You can heal if you all choose to take part. You can even read portions of the book out loud or internally to child parts who cannot yet read. Yes, the material is not suitable for children—but neither were the experiences you underwent when you were in the hands of your abusers.

Finally—this is only a book. I am not exercising any control over you. I am not telling you what to feel or think or believe. I am only laying out things that I have learnt from the survivors

I have known, in order to help you engage in your own healing process. You are not "telling" me anything, so there is no need to turn on punishments for telling or talking! You are only reading.

I chose *Becoming Yourself: Overcoming Mind Control and Ritual Abuse* as the title because that is what this book is about. Mind controllers do not recognise a child's right to become himself or herself. Rather than recognising their children's innate abilities, interests, and choices, they attempt to turn children (and the adults they become) into mind-controlled slaves who serve someone else's purposes. Yet, valiant survivors all over the world are struggling to reclaim their true identities, overcoming the effects of all the atrocities that they have endured to claim their true selves. Some have already succeeded.

Although this is a tough book, I am hoping it is a compassionate one. Indeed, it is a love letter to survivors. (Yes, love, *not* sex.) I was fortunate enough not to have to endure mind control or ritual abuses. My personal acquaintance with a number of survivors who have been brave enough to pursue healing has given me great admiration for them. I care about those who have endured these horrendous experiences, and I want to provide you with as much help as possible to enable you to engage in and complete your own healing. I hope that as survivors come to recognise what has happened to them, and to heal, they will transform "civilised" society from one which permits the existence of mind control abuses by denying or dissociating its awareness of them into one which recognises, rejects, and combats these evils. Your first step to becoming yourself is awareness of what is inside you and what happened to you.

Only the small secrets need to be protected. The big ones are kept secret by public incredulity.
(*Marshall McCluhan*)

The most authentic thing about us is our capacity to create, to overcome, to endure, to transform, to love and to be greater than our suffering.
(*Ben Okri, Nigerian poet and novelist*)

Our sorrows and wounds are healed only when we touch them with compassion.
(*Mohandas Gandhi*)

CHAPTER ONE

Symptoms, memories, and evidence

This book is written for survivors of mind control and ritual abuse. Perhaps you know beyond a doubt that you are such a survivor, because you have clear memories of childhood abuse that involved attempts to split and control your mind through occult rituals, torture, and deception. If so, you are in a minority.

Over centuries, organised perpetrator groups have observed and studied the way in which extreme childhood traumas, such as accidents, bereavement, war, natural disasters, repeated hospitalisations and surgeries, and (most commonly) child abuse (sexual, physical, and emotional) cause a child's mind to be split into compartments. Occult groups originally utilised this phenomenon to create alternative identities and what they believed to be "possession" by various spirits. In the twentieth century, probably beginning with the Nazis, other organised groups developed ways to harm children and deliberately structure their victims' minds in such a way that they would not remember what happened, or that if they began to remember they would disbelieve their own memories. Consequently, the memories of what has happened to a survivor are hidden within his or her inside parts.

My purpose in writing this book is not to suggest to you anything that could have happened to you, but to help you know how to work with those inside parts (if you have them) to help them deal with their own experiences. They, rather than any book, outside group, or even therapist, know the ultimate truth about your life. If something in this book resonates with you, check with your inside parts who know what did and did not happen, recognising that no one of them knows the whole story. If you do have separate inside parts, some of them will not know what happened to others of them. This can be a lengthy process, and we shall spend several chapters on it.

My other purpose is to help you heal from whatever happened to you, as survivors of these unimaginable abuses usually, and quite naturally, suffer from quite a few debilitating symptoms.

The human brain is very complex, with many component circuits that communicate with one another through electrical and chemical signals. In traumatic dissociation, those parts are kept separate by strong barriers, so that one part is not aware of the content or feelings held by the other parts. The child who attends school does not remember the abuse that happens at home or via the family; those memories are held in another part of the child's mind. The child does not even remember abuse that happened the preceding night. When the child grows up, he or she might not consciously remember the abuse, but might experience flashbacks and other symptoms related to it.

Although a body has only one brain, the circuits in that brain can operate relatively independently, so that people with very separate brain circuits experience themselves as more than one person, multiple. Dissociative splitting is an adaptation which enables a child to live with ongoing trauma, in many or most cases involving his or her own parents or care-givers, with the "normal" parts of that child being unaware of the things that happened to the other parts. (When I speak of "parts", I do not mean to imply that any internal identity is less important than the identity who manages everyday life; it, too, is a part of a complex brain.) Dissociative splitting is a defence against post traumatic stress disorder, in which flash-backs, nightmares, "body memories", and overwhelming emotional states can make life unbearable.

Dissociative separation of brain circuits does not always work perfectly. Because the different parts are located in the same brain, emotions or impulses can "leak" from hidden parts into the "front person" who manages everyday life, and can give rise to a large number of psychiatric symptoms which affect the person's physical health, interpersonal relationships, ability to manage emotions, ability to control behaviour, beliefs and thinking, and self-concept.

Amnesia for the traumatic events which cause the symptoms and the dissociation is very likely if care-givers, such as parents, are involved in the abuse, and if it has to be kept secret, as Jennifer Freyd points out in *Betrayal Trauma* (1996), and has demonstrated in many research studies. This is true for survivors of incest, for children beaten by their parents, and, most of all, for children whose parents are involved in an organised perpetrator group. With mind control, which includes ritual abuse, the dissociation is deliberately created and the secrecy enforced through "programming" the child never to speak of the abuse, and sometimes never to remember it. (I use the term "mind control" to mean any attempt to deliberately control the mind. Ritual abuse is one type of mind control, but not the only kind.)

Finding out what happened to you

If you do not remember what happened to you because of dissociation, what evidence can you find to discover it? There are now checklists for formal assessments of childhood trauma history by professionals, notably Briere's and Runtz's "Trauma Symptoms Check-list" (see www.johnbriere.com/tsc.htm), which includes measures of dissociation, anxiety, depression, sexual abuse trauma, sleep disturbance, and sexual problems. A high score on this checklist will tell you that something happened, but not *what* happened to you.

Some of your experiences, however, can give you clues about what actually happened.

Evidence in flashbacks

Since "flashbacks" are episodes during which survivors re-experience parts of traumas they have undergone, they serve as indicators of experiences that are hidden from consciousness. Flashbacks are especially likely to happen when triggered by some kind of reminder, such as a smell that reminds someone of an abuser. They can be like "waking dreams". Flashbacks can be pure emotion, or body sensations, or pictures, or sound. You might hear someone calling your name or feel as if someone is there behind you. Sometimes flashbacks are difficult to interpret, as they only give part of the whole experience.

Evidence in body memories

Certain aspects of your experience are hard to disbelieve. Your body can give you important clues. "Body memories" are flashbacks of physical trauma that are experienced as pain or other bodily symptoms. One client of mine had small sores appear on his body before he actually discovered the story behind them—cigarette burns used as punishment during his childhood. Another had body sensations of being raped, and recognised that she must be a survivor of childhood sexual assault. She also had different sensations, for example of her hands being pressed together painfully, and she did not know the meaning of these sensations until some of her inside parts were able to provide the visual and auditory parts of the memory, in which a man was behind her pressing his hands around hers while she held a knife. The original reason she began therapy was because of an obsessive fear of harming someone with a knife.

It is harder to disbelieve body memories than narrative memories. They are involuntary. They cannot really be influenced by television shows or books; if you have not experienced something in your body, you do not know what it feels like. So, body memories are evidence that cannot be discounted. They simply must be "heard" and respected.

Evidence in dreams

Freud called dreams "the royal road to the unconscious". When we dream, the material that affects our life, of which we might not be aware in our everyday consciousness, comes to the surface and makes stories. Dreams can represent our wishes, and our fears. They can also represent our past experiences, known or unknown to us. All of this is commonly known. They can also represent people's internal parts and the relationships between them.

One client of mine had spent many hours interpreting her dreams symbolically with her Jungian therapist. This interpretation, based on someone else's theory, was misleading. When I saw the dreams (written out), I saw the stories of conflict between her dissociated inside parts, and of happenings that looked a good deal like ritual abuse. And, sure enough, when I got to know the younger parts, very slowly over about four years, a ritual abuse history, from a period very early in her life, emerged. This client has never heard the term, and still does not use it. Nevertheless, her dreams told her story.

Another client meets her inside parts only in dreams, where they appear as children or teenagers with whom she is spending time, or whom she is helping.

Dream content is mixed and distorted, so you can never say that a dream has definitely shown you what happened to you. You cannot be sure about the meanings of dreams. They are influenced by everything that happens to us, including games, television shows, and the news. But if we do have hidden abuse memories, or hidden parts of ourselves, these are likely to show up in dreams. Since dreams contain helpful clues, some abuser groups tell the children, when they ask about things they remember, that it must have been "only" a dream.

Recurrent dreams are especially significant and, in my experience, they continue to recur because they are conveying an important message, and may not stop until they are acknowledged.

Evidence in artwork

If you make spontaneous art, you might find that indications of your trauma surface in your artwork. Interpreting your art is similar to interpreting your dreams. The content might be mixed and distorted, but it can tell your story.

An activity that helped one survivor was drawing an outline of her whole body, and colouring the areas of it where she felt violated and where she had felt pain. This was the beginning of her discovery of what had happened to her.

Throughout this book, you will find exercises to help you apply the book's material to your own life. Here is the first one.

Exercise 1. Writing down your possible experiences

Do you have conscious memories of events which appear to have been mind control or ritual abuse? (Mind control and ritual abuse will be explained in Chapter 2.)

Do you have flashbacks? What does their content suggest might have happened to you?

Do you have body memories which seem to go with physical or sexual assaults which your conscious mind does not remember?

Do you have dreams of traumatic events which you do not consciously remember happening to you? What could have influenced these dreams (TV, reading news, others' stories-or your own dissociated memories)? Are there recurrent themes in your dreams?

If you make artwork, have any of your works suggested any specific kind of trauma? Are there recurrent themes in your artwork?

When you look at your flashbacks, body memories, dreams, and artwork, what clues do you see about what might have happened to you?

Write a brief description of each of the events you have remembered or encountered in dreams or flashbacks. Try to put them in chronological order, by how old you believe you were when these things happened. If some events, especially very early ones, cannot be put into words, try drawing them.

Do you remember other children, such as your siblings, being present at any of these events? (Note that if they were present, it is not wise to ask them about it, since they might alert abusers to the fact that you are remembering. See Chapter Nine for more information on this topic.)

Is there any part of the events that could possibly be validated by physical evidence? Are there places that you remember and could visit with a safe companion? Do you have scars on your body that could be evidence of something that happened to you?

Dissociative conditions as evidence

One of the best indicators of the possibility of a mind control history is the presence of traumatic dissociation. Unfortunately, dissociation itself functions by hiding. Not only does it hide the material, but it hides *the fact that the material lives somewhere out of awareness.* Therefore, while some people seek help because of overt and disconcerting symptoms of dissociation, the average dissociative person is no more aware of having it than the average mind control or ritual abuse survivor is aware of what has happened to him or her.

At present, psychiatry and the other mental health professions define dissociation as a disorder, and the two major dissociative disorders they currently recognise are dissociative identity disorder (DID) and dissociative disorder not otherwise specified (DDNOS). A person is considered to have DID when different parts of the mind take over the body at different times, with the main person not remembering what has happened when he or she is not consciously "out" in the body. DDNOS is an overly inclusive diagnostic category covering many types of dissociation other than DID—essentially, a situation in which a person meets some but not all of the criteria for DID.

In what I believe is the most common form of DDNOS, the main person is only a "shell" through whom the inside parts come. The visible personality differs depending on which combination of inside parts is near the surface, temporarily blending with the "front person". This condition is the intended goal of mind controlling abusers. In mind control created DDNOS, the parts live behind the scenes, and only take over consciousness, or executive control, when "triggered" to do so, either deliberately by the abusers, or accidentally by someone else, or by an event that resembles the abuse. The "front person" is not supposed to know about the other parts.

Mind control builds on the natural, reactive dissociative fragmenting caused by childhood trauma. The trauma-based developing of many separate part-selves that begins in early childhood and results from extreme (often life-threatening) trauma is not merely psychological. It is also a biological process in the brain. It is not something that the person chooses, and it cannot begin in adulthood. Although the parts are all in one body, they represent different brain circuitry that appears to have been separated by some biological process that we do not sufficiently understand. Brain imaging studies show different brain pathways activated with different parts, and other studies show physiological differences between different personality states.

DID used to be called MPD (multiple personality disorder). I shall, at times, use the old term "multiple" in this book, in respect for the internal experience of people whose psyches have been split in childhood, as those who are aware they are multiple often feel like a "we" rather than an "I". The term "multiplicity" is usually assumed to describe DID alone, but it also applies to DDNOS, which, for the purpose of this book, is even more important. The psychiatric community calls multiplicity a "disorder", but it is a valuable, creative asset that has served the person well. It is not an inferior way of being.

I like to tell my clients something that I learnt from one of my first survivor clients: that a dissociative disorder is mental injury rather than mental illness, and, therefore, requires a different treatment. For a broken leg, you would put the bone parts back together and keep them connected so they could heal, even though it might be painful. Similarly, with a broken mind, you bring the parts back together by introducing them to one another, and you clean the wound by helping the person resolve what happened to make the parts split from one another.

Singletons (non-multiples), being conscious of everything that happens to them, are well adapted for living in safety. They do have different parts, adapted for different situations, but there are not strong barriers or amnesia between those parts. They are unable to "go away" from the body if they are afraid or in pain.

A person who is multiple, on the other hand, is well-adapted for living with ongoing trauma. I once heard a prison psychologist say he would not treat multiples, because prison is so traumatic that you need to be multiple to survive well. Certainly this is also true of the early life years when the divisions first develop, as this is a time of relative helplessness and dependence on others. The barriers that separate the parts of a multiple are what enable a child to tolerate, and so survive, unavoidable abuse or other trauma.

Even in an adult life that is not challenged by ongoing trauma, there are sometimes advantages to being multiple. In some cases, it permits heightened abilities. I knew a multiple whose internal part called "Brain" (not *Brian*!) memorised all her textbooks and was able to remember everything word for word for exams, and another who had insiders with all kinds of special savant abilities. Without the distractions of emotions, everyday life, and other thoughts, a part with a singular focus can sometimes do amazing things.

Some multiples are consciously aware of their dissociative personality systems. Others are not, especially if they have deliberately structured personality systems which are designed so that the person who lives the regular daily life is unaware of the other inside parts and their activities.

Someone who is multiple experiences life through a series of different selves. Just as a singleton cannot become a multiple at will, a multiple cannot become a singleton, until and unless the barriers between the parts of the self are removed. Those barriers were put up to enable the child to tolerate and so survive unavoidable abuse or other trauma. Someone who was not multiple might not have been able to survive those overwhelming experiences.

If you are multiple, you are probably a survivor of some kind of severe and prolonged trauma beginning in early childhood, perhaps right from birth or even in the womb. This might or might not have been deliberate mind control or ritual abuse. It could be from physical or sexual abuse by a family member, or from living in a war zone, or from a prolonged painful illness.

Whether or not people understand that they have been through severe and prolonged childhood trauma, they might experience the signs of a dissociative disorder, even without identifying them. There are a number of excellent books and other resources that can help you work out whether or not you could be diagnosed with a dissociative disorder.

There are also several good assessment tools for professionals. However, if you have a formal assessment, make sure that the person who conducts it is aware of dissociative disorders and the tools necessary to diagnose them, as many psychologists and psychiatrists have not yet been educated about the dissociative disorders (which some dissociative people would argue are not "disorders" at all, since they are normal adaptations to abnormal situations).

Whether you have DID or DDNOS, you can only find out what traumas happened to you and resolve them by communicating with your inside parts and working through the memories they contain.

Exercise 2. The Dissociative Experiences Scale

The Dissociative Experiences Scale (DES) is a well-known quick instrument for assessing dissociation. It covers a number of experiences that are common to persons with dissociative disorders. It is not a substitute for a professional diagnosis, however.

The DES is available online at www.serene.me.uk/tests/des.pdf. Take the test and see how high your score is. Remember that people with DDNOS might not score as high as those with DID, and that if you have dissociative parts who were designed to be well hidden, you might have a low score. Some of the items also reflect "normal dissociation", the ability to be so absorbed in thought or in what you are doing that you do not notice what else is happening, as in "highway hypnosis", when you do not notice the landmarks and drive past your destination.

How high is your score? What does this tell you about yourself?

Many persons doing this test are struck by how well some of the items capture experiences which they thought were unique to them. Did this happen for you? Which items were significant to you?

I have observed that when clients with dissociative disorders do the test in my presence, they often "switch" during the test, so that they will say no to the first few items and then begin to say yes more frequently as different internal parts of them recognise the experiences on the test. Did this happen to you? If so, you might want to deliberately do the test in different states, or, if you know you are multiple, with different parts of you "out". This shows how different the experience can be from one internal part to another.

Deliberately structured dissociative personality systems are designed to hide the dissociation, so it is possible to get a low score on the DES and have a very complex personality system.

Mind control and ritual abuse indicators

Some survivors do not have any concrete memories, but suspect mind control and/or ritual abuse because of specific symptoms they are experiencing. Ellen Lacter provides a current, and comprehensive, list of indicators on her website (www.endritualabuse.org). Lacter's list for adult survivors of ritual abuse has forty-three items, many of which resonate with my experience of ritual abuse survivors. She also has a separate list of indicators of mind control by groups other than religious ones.

In Exercise 3, I have put together a list of symptoms that are common in survivors of mind control and ritual abuse. Some items are drawn from earlier lists developed by Pamela Reagor and Catherine Gould, as well as Lacter; others come from my own experience of dealing with survivors.

As you check off the list items, remember that individual items can be explained by a variety of experiences. For example, difficulties around birthdays or holidays could come from childhood participation in a cult that celebrated birthdays and holidays with abusive rituals. Or they might indicate a family history of alcoholism, with drunken violence at those times. Other items are more specific for mind control and ritual abuse—such as ritualistic chants in your head, or patterned self-mutilation.

In medicine, the same symptom might be indicative of a number of different conditions, some serious and some benign. Items on this checklist, like those on symptom lists for cancer or other diseases diagnosed by physicians, are not intended as individual indicators. It is the configuration and pattern of the symptoms that make a difference. When all the items are taken together, they accurately present a profile that can alert you to the possibility of a mind control or ritual abuse history.

The following exercise looks at symptoms that are common in survivors of mind control and/or ritual abuse.

Exercise 3. Symptoms of mind control and/or ritual abuse

Tick each item which applies to you.

- You have been diagnosed with DID or DDNOS;
- You have made drawings characterised by ritual-like features, for example, lots of red and black, knives, fire, cages, robes, body parts, blood, etc.;
- You find yourself preoccupied with or needing to avoid newscasts, magazine articles, or conversations, about mind control or ritual abuse;
- You have worse psychiatric symptoms around your birthday, family members' birthdays, Christmas, Easter, Halloween, May Day, and early September;
- You have cut patterns, shapes, or letters on your own body;
- You have unexplained scars on your body, or scars for which the explanations you were given do not make sense or seem right;
- You have intrusive thoughts or impulses regarding violent sex, sex with children, or sex with animals;
- You find odd, ritualistic songs or chants running through your head, sometimes with a sexual, bizarre, or "you'd better not tell" theme;
- You hear voices ordering you not to talk or to be quiet;
- If you talk about what might have happened to you, you experience symptoms like bodily pain, nausea, a severe headache, paranoid thoughts and fear, or flashbacks of violent events;
- You get spontaneous spasms or head jerks as if you are receiving an electric shock;
- Sometimes you feel that there is something foreign inside your body which can do harm to you or others, or can signal your location or your thoughts to abusers;
- Sometimes you worry that you will harm or murder someone or that you have done so;
- Sometimes you feel that your energy will poison those you are close to;
- You have dreams which seem to describe mind control or ritual abuse experiences;
- You have fears, phobias, and nightmares associated with the following:
  - religion and church;
  - Christmas and Easter;
  - going to the doctor or the dentist;
  - bodily fluids and excretions;
  - injections and needles;
  - weapons;
  - birthdays and weddings;
  - police, jails, and cages;
  - baths and drowning;
  - insects, snakes, spiders, and rats;

(continued)

- cameras and being photographed or videotaped;
- specific colours or shapes;
- ropes, being tied up, being hung;
- confined spaces, basements, crawl spaces, pits;
- death and burial;
- red meat and/or certain other foods;
- harm being done to your loved ones or your pets.

Some of the fears (such as needles or insects or the dentist) are common. If you have ticked these, do you have a way to account for them in your life history?

Some of the fears, and the non-fear items, are uncommon. Have you ticked any of the uncommon ones? Do you have a way to account for them in your life history?

Look at the entire pattern of your answers. No single one of these items means you have a history of mind control or ritual abuse. However, if you say yes to a large number of them, especially the uncommon ones, you might suspect such a history.

The real life conscious fears, feelings, and reactions that survivors of mind control and ritual abuse experience are not the only or deepest indicators of such a history. In Chapter Four, we shall look at a checklist which goes deeper, covering the characteristics of a personality system designed by mind controlling abusers.

"Maybe I made it up"

If you are having memories indicating mind control or ritual abuse material, and have tried talking to friends or to authorities about them, you have probably had a frustrating experience. Many people do not want to listen to such things. They might question your truthfulness. They might tell you to "grow up and get over it". They might wonder whether you are imagining things. Even people who are genuinely interested just cannot grasp the meaning; they cannot believe that such things happen.

Child abusers exploit such reactions when they tell their victims things such as "No one will believe you". It is not true. True friends can, and will, honour what you share with them, although it might be a struggle for them to hear that such awful things happened to someone they care about. Competent, empathic therapists are also capable of knowing how difficult it is to talk about these things, and being open to hear horrendous truths, though, sadly, there are not many therapists who can tolerate hearing about this level of abuse. If someone cannot hear what you have to say, you should not continue to disclose your experiences to that person; seek out someone else.

But survivors of mind control and ritual abuse usually have a more serious problem: they have difficulty believing themselves. Many times I have had survivors come into my office the week after disclosing a particularly horrendous memory and say, "It didn't happen, I made it all up." Or "There are no younger parts inside me holding memories; I just wanted attention." Or (my favourite) "We are not multiple." Why does this reversal or denial happen?

Survivors who are discovering apparent memories of mind control or ritual abuse often struggle with the question, "Could this really have happened?" and insist that none of it is true.

They struggle to find excuses to dismiss it, such as that they made it all up, they got it from television shows or the Internet, or they have vivid imaginations.

Some survivors do have vivid imaginations; some do not. Some like to read and research, others do not. In fact, others deliberately do not read or watch anything related to what they are remembering so that they do not contaminate their memories. If you do have such an imagination, you might want to be careful about what you read and watch, so that you cannot be accused, or accuse yourself, of making things up. My concern here is mainly so that you can reassure yourself about this. I do not believe that non-survivors, even imaginative ones, are easily able to make up the kinds of memories which survivors have. I myself have listened to literally thousands of narratives of mind control and ritual abuse experiences—and I am still convinced that I have never personally experienced such things. I do not even dream about them.

One of my clients had flashbacks of ritual abuse, and her mother informed her that certain neighbours who used to look after her were the perpetrators. The client now doubts both whether she was ritually abused, and whether those were the real perpetrators, just because it was her mother who told her this. Outside influences can be very confusing for people with these memories.

Many things that happen to persons with a dissociative disorder feel as if they happened to someone else. This is because those things happened to another part of the person, and the information about them "leaked" into the "front person" who lives most of daily life. In addition, events that are remembered at one time might not be remembered at other times, and this leads to confusion. (Such people have been described as having "multiple reality disorder".)

There are many reasons that someone might insist that what they are remembering cannot be real. One obvious reason is the bizarre and horrific nature of the flashbacks that survivors experience. If you are seeing such things in your head, you do not want to believe they are real, or even possible.

Inside parts may "recall" different realities and maintain different beliefs about abuse. One survivor I know has a group of little child parts inside who have horrible memories of abuse outside the family that began early in her life (via a babysitter). At the same time, another group of parts, comprising adults and teenagers, has no conscious memories of this abuse. They tell her that they have been having awful nightmares of things which cannot be real. Some of their "nightmares", they say, are during the day. The little ones told me about the "line" down the middle of their head that separates those who lived inside the home from the ones who remember the early abuse outside the home. So the older parts are unaware of the little ones and what happened to them. However, pictures and emotions leak through this dividing line and are interpreted by the older parts as signs that they must be either crazy or evil to invent such horrible things.

In Chapter Five, we shall look at mind control "programming", which is the deliberate training of inside parts of a person to produce automatic beliefs, emotions, and behaviours which the perpetrators want them to have. This training gives each part or group of parts a specific job. Many jobs serve the purpose of security and secrecy for the perpetrators of the abuse. Mind control training involves various kinds of deception, including stage magic and technology.

One category of training is denial training, designed to make the "regular" everyday life person disbelieve any memories of the abuse that might leak into consciousness. Denial of mind control material is not just the natural product of human nature. Most mind-controlled children are trained in denial and disbelief of their own memories and their own internal multiplicity by mind controlling abusers, who have studied the processes of remembering and forgetting, and how dissociation works.

Types of denial training that I have heard about include:

1. Training that makes survivors unaware of their dissociation by creating "walls" between the inside parts or using anti-psychotic drugs to suppress internal voices.
2. Simulated murders of people who later turn out to be alive. These memories are designed to pop up if the person starts to remember other secret events, and if they are disclosed, investigators find out the victims are alive and then disbelieve other disclosures. Needless to say, the survivors who remember these supposed murders become very confused, and begin to doubt everything they have remembered.
3. Deliberately designed "cover memories" that are impossible, such as alien abductions. These memories, like the simulated murders, are supposed to come up if other things are remembered or disclosed.
4. False but reasonable explanations for scars or particular memories that come up for a survivor.
5. Built-in denial training during rituals, such as people chanting, "This is not real, this is a dream."
6. Training that discourages telling the truth because of survivors believing that the abusers know what they do and say, and/or young parts of them believing something horrific will happen if they tell.

Validation and proof

Many survivors feel they would believe their own memories if they only had some proof other than their own memories. Unfortunately, most of the time this proof is hard to come by. Organised groups who abuse children are very careful to remove all evidence of their crimes.

Sometimes there is cross-corroboration by other survivors or family members who were actually present during the abuse. (However, even if this exists, not all who shared mind control or ritual abuse experiences might be ready to deal with them at the same time.) The similarity of survivors' experiences in different locations is well documented. The Extreme Abuse Survey (see http://eassurvey.wordpress.com/extreme-abuse-survey-final-results/) asked questions about quite a number of different experiences, and found large percentages of those reporting extreme abuse had similar experiences.

If survivors of ritual abuse find it difficult to be believed, it is even more difficult for someone who was abused and mind controlled by his or her own government. Fortunately, however, these survivors potentially have available to them the most substantial documentation of these acts having been committed. Mind-control survivor Carol Rutz, in her book, *A Nation Betrayed*, has described some of the validation that she obtained through her Freedom of Information Act submission in the USA (although other survivors have more recently been unable to find their own records this way).

Look for your internal truth

All your feelings are real and are based on your life experiences, including those you do not yet remember. There is a reason for any dreams, flashbacks, or body memories, or other symptoms you are having. Whatever is in your head and causes emotional responses or flashbacks deserves to be investigated.

The truth about the specifics of what has occurred to you might take a lot of time to unravel, but you need to keep the question open, and explore it as best you can. Do not make premature conclusions. I once counselled a teenage girl who was very upset because she was having feelings of having been sexually abused, along with an image of her father's face. When the memory finally emerged, it was her father rescuing her from abuse by the boy next door. Thank goodness she did not accuse her father of abuse! On the other hand, one of my first ritually abused clients thought that her grandfather was the only safe person in her life, and that he never abused her. After he died, memories of very sadistic abuse by him began to come up. You might want to be very cautious if you find yourself idealising someone.

I tell my clients that they can talk with me about whatever they need to talk about, regardless of whether or not at this moment they believe that their memories or the images in their head represent real experiences. That gets them "off the hook" of having to tell "the truth" (actually a lie) which their abusers wanted them to tell. So, I now tell you the same thing: find out first what is in your head; you can decide later whether it is true or false. You have a right to know what is in your head. You can work out later what is real and what is not.

If you are having memories that seem impossible, remember that mind-controlling abusers engage in a lot of deliberate deception. You may be remembering real events, but events that are not what they appear to be. *There is a difference between believing that bad experiences happened, and believing what your child parts were led to believe.* For example, a woman recently disclosed to me a memory in which a group of her child parts who believed they were boys were anally raped by a group of priests, who told them that this was a special honour and a spiritual experience which was only given to boys. It is not necessary to believe that they were actually in a boy's body or that it was a spiritual honour in order to think that my client's memory could be valid. Similarly, when I meet an insider personality who informs me that he or she is not part of the body and would not die if they killed the body, I acknowledge that they had some experience which led them to believe that, but I do not accept their belief at face value; I search for what was done to make them come to this conclusion, and I attempt to unmask the trick. You can do the same.

Respect your parts, and validate their experiences as well as their right to believe what they believe as a result of those experiences. As you put the memories together with all the parts of you who were involved, you and all your parts will come to see the truth.

When everything seems to fit together, your symptoms, your insiders' stories of what happened, your body sensations and emotions, and any external corroboration (although this is rare), over time you may come to the reflective belief that certain experiences must have happened to you. Or, of course, the reverse, if it does not fit together.

Mind control and ritual abuse often reveal themselves in stages. It is possible for a dissociative person to completely work through his or her non-mind-control trauma memories without touching the parts of the personality system who have experienced mind control or ritual abuse. It is also possible to remember ritual abuse without accessing the memories of other kinds of mind control (we shall look at these kinds in the next chapter). A ritually abused client of mine with whom I have worked for many years recently discovered a new group of inside parts who believe themselves to be intelligence officers of the Gestapo, the Nazi secret police.

No matter who your abusers were or are, or what tactics they used or are using, your recovery goals will be the same: freedom, healing, and empowerment: taking back your own life from those who robbed you of it, and becoming yourself. That is what the rest of this book is about.

CHAPTER TWO

The struggle for healing

What is mind control?

I had difficulty finding a definition that, in my view, best described mind control, but Wikipedia defines it as involving "a broad range of psychological tactics able to subvert an individual's control of his or her own thinking, behavior, emotions, or decisions . . . The goal is to have those individuals carry out actions which ordinarily would go counter to human nature. This training involves physical, sexual and emotional torture, the use of drugs, and, in some cases, the use of technologies which directly affect brain function". One implication of this definition is that victims are not responsible for having been mind controlled, even if they have done things that they would not otherwise do.

Popular media representations of mind control involves trained spies or assassins working for the CIA or other military/political groups, or even companies, without their conscious knowledge, because they have other "personalities" who engage in these activities. Think of Jason Bourne, or the hero of the film *Conspiracy Theory*, or Echo in television's *Dollhouse*, among other American television shows and films. The fictional stories concocted about these mind-controlled special agents suggest that they are recruited in adulthood, even making a conscious choice to participate. Once they have been recruited, the story goes, their previous memories are erased and new "personalities" created with special skills and manufactured memories.

However, there is only one stage of life during which mind controllers can create persons who will engage in these activities without *any* conscious awareness, or resistance, throughout their days, and only one way to do so: that is, through the abuse and torture of small children. The awful reality is that there is no adult who volunteers loyalty to such a group because of thought-out endorsement of its goals. There are only tiny victims.

The mind control discussed in this book achieves its power over victims through programming. Survivor therapist Arauna Morgan (see Chapter Eleven) defines programming as

> the act of installing internal, pre-established reactions to external stimuli so that a person will automatically react in a predetermined manner to things like an auditory, visual or tactile signal or perform a specific set of actions according to a date and/or time.

Programmes are implanted lessons that serve as the workhorses—perhaps we should say Trojan Horses—of the abusers. Implanted within the victim through hypnotic suggestion reinforced with torture and terror, they are designed to exploit victims' natural trance or dissociative response to trauma.

What is ritual abuse?

The first form of mind control to be disclosed by survivors to their therapists was ritual abuse, abuse by occult religious groups. In the 1980s, therapists rediscovered dissociation, which had been forgotten by psychologists when Freud reneged on his brilliant original discovery of sexual abuse, and decided that his patients must have invented it. As they explored the other selves of their dissociative clients, therapists in the 1980s and 1990s discovered that many of them had experienced ritual abuse.

In 1991, a report by the Los Angeles County Commission for Women's Ritual Abuse Task Force reflected their early enlightenment regarding the mind control aspect of ritual abuse, including how it is created, and for what reason. It stated,

> Mind control is the cornerstone of ritual abuse, the key element in the subjugation and silencing of its victims. Victims of ritual abuse are subjected to a rigorously applied system of mind control designed to rob them of their sense of free will and to impose upon them the will of the cult and its leaders . . . The mind control is achieved through an elaborate system of brainwashing, programming, indoctrination, hypnosis, and the use of various mind-altering drugs. The purpose of the mind control is to compel ritual abuse victims to keep the secret of their abuse, to conform to the beliefs and behaviors of the cult, and to become functioning members who serve the cult by carrying out the directives of its leaders without being detected within society at large.

The term "ritual abuse" is not *literally* accurate in describing all similar abuses. Although other labels are also used, such as "ritual abuse torture," "RA/MC", the term "ritual abuse" has come to be applied generically, both to abuses contained in the classic, religiously based abuse and to non-religious forms of mind control; however, I find it more accurate to use "mind control" for this purpose, as mind control is what all these organised perpetrator groups have in common.

Whichever term is used, what I am talking about in this book is the organised abuse of children by secret groups for the purpose of mind control. The tactics of hidden groups are violent, extreme, and sophisticated, and many survivors experience ongoing abuse. As a result, the consequences of those tactics are more complex. The groups' invisibility to everyday society makes them particularly dangerous, and this combination of violence, sophistication, and secrecy makes recovery more complicated for their victims/survivors. For one thing, in order to keep their existence secret, members have to maintain "normal" lives while continuing to be involved with these groups. This requires the segmentation of consciousness that we call dissociation: survivors have different internal parts with different awarenesses. We shall return to dissociation in Chapters Three to Eight, because it is the keystone of mind control.

Kinds of abuser groups

Ritual (religious) abusers

Most of the religious ritual abuse seen in Western society occurs in the context of occult religions, primarily the worship of either Satan or Lucifer, or both. (Although some such groups, such as traditional Christians, see Satan and Lucifer as a single entity, most treat them as separate beings and prefer to worship one or the other, whichever they believe is the most powerful. See cult trainer Stella Katz's description of Satanic *vs.* Luciferian religion in Miller, 2012, p. 93.) Organised religious groups meet in covens (of thirteen "adults"—over thirteen years old—plus their children), and on special occasions hold a much larger gathering. They celebrate both Christian and pagan (Wiccan) holidays by reversing the worship of those benign groups. There are also groups who believe in making the good and evil in the world equal; they abuse in the names of God and Jesus as well as Satan and Lucifer. There are also Jewish ritually abusing groups. Other deities worshipped through rituals include such ancient gods and goddesses as Isis and Tiamat.

All these groups abuse children in the following ways:

- breaking the mother–child bond;
- lack of nurturing or comfort;
- terrorising through costumes and robes, horror films and videos;
- lavish use of blood;
- sexual abuse in rituals and orgies;
- sexual abuse by parents and relatives (if they belong to the group);
- use of psychoactive drugs to create altered states;
- use of high voltage electricity applied to various parts of the body;
- punishment for disobedience by confinement, isolation, starvation, burial, physical and sexual abuse, and other forms of torture;
- simulation of religious figures, and heaven and hell, to destroy the child's belief in a loving God and to control the "soul" or "spirit" of the child;
- forcing children to participate in actual and/or simulated sacrifice of animals and (at special gatherings) of human beings (the children believe the killings are real);
- forcing children to participate in real or simulated cannibalism, that the participants believe is real, at the black mass and other events;
- developmental rituals such as Satanic baptism, Satanic rebirth (after "death" and burial), and marriage to Satan (including consummation through rape);
- "programming" of various inside parts of the person to believe what the abusers say and to do the "jobs" assigned to them (see discussion in Chapter Five);
- creation of parts of the person who believe themselves to be demons or animals, and supposed "attachment" of evil spiritual beings to parts (see discussion in Chapter Twenty).

Child Abuse Wiki says of ritual abuse,

> It usually involves repeated abuse over an extended period of time. The physical abuse is severe, sometimes including torture and killing. The sexual abuse is usually painful, sadistic, and humiliating, intended as means of gaining dominance over the victim. The psychological abuse is devastating and involves the use of ritual/indoctrination, which includes mind control techniques and mind altering drugs, and ritual/intimidation which conveys to the victim a profound terror of the cult members and of the evil spirits they believe cult members can command. Both during and after the abuse, most victims are in a state of terror, mind control, and dissociation in which disclosure is exceedingly difficult."

Because Satanic cult abuse was the first type of mind control to surface, the first people to discover it focused on its religious—specifically Satanic—aspects. In fact, for a long time all of it was referred to as "Satanic ritual abuse" (SRA). Over time survivors reported that in the religious form of the abuse, other deities besides Satan are worshipped, and that the religious form was not the only kind of mind control practised on children.

Initially, most of the survivors who disclosed these abuses appeared to have been taken into these groups by their parents; these were intergenerational cult groups that involved many generations. But children of innocent parents were also recruited through day care settings, without their parents being a part of the abuse. Once they became aware of what was happening to their children, these parents often became dedicated advocates on their children's behalf, at great personal and emotional expense. Neighbours, business associates, well respected doctors or lawyers, and often religious and political leaders in their communities were often reportedly involved as abusers. Sometimes whole communities were involved. Adults raised by group members were expected to continue to participate in the groups, and not break the cycle.

Government and military/political experimenters

During the Second World War, Nazi doctors studied mind control in unethical experiments in their concentration camps. After the war, the Americans recognised that these Nazi doctors (as well as other German scientists) could be of use to them in their next conflict, the "cold war" with the Soviet Union. Hence, they imported some of these doctors to continue mind control experiments in North America.

The USA's government, through various secret projects, used the Nazi doctors to teach their own operatives how to conduct mind control. They wanted to create a spy who did not know he or she was a spy, and a "sleeper" assassin whose killer personality would only emerge under very specific conditions. They wanted to create what was then known as "multiple personality disorder"—persons with different identities who emerged under different circumstances and were largely unaware of one another. The Nazi doctors were happy to oblige. They not only created personality systems for the USA's government, they put in some sections of their own, loyal to the Aryan race. The Ku Klux Klan co-operated with this manipulation.

Other political systems have also engaged in mind control, including at least the Soviets and the Stasi (East German intelligence). Any country wanting to engage in espionage and assassination is aware of the value of mind-controlled unwitting "soldiers".

Where did these military and political groups access the children on whom they experimented and whom they trained? We can speculate that groups who use children in child pornography often borrow them from multi-generational incestuous families, such as are found in organised cults. Military mind-control trainers have easy access to children who reside on their own bases, and find cult children a bonus as they are readily trainable as potential spies and killers because a dissociative foundation has already been created in them. If the parents are dissociative and are being accessed in the military or by any cult, the children will most likely be accessed and trained by special trainers, without parental conscious knowledge. Whether criminal, religious, or political/military, abusers on an international scale are aware that dissociation is the linch-pin of power and secrecy. What better source of already dissociative children than the parents who themselves are members of abusive cults? The parents might or might not be directly abusing their children, but by being members of an abusive cult, they make sure that their children *will* be abused.

Survivor therapist Arauna Morgan writes,

> In the groups I was involved with, adults were asked to join a secret, benevolent society, backed by rich anonymous backers who want to reward virtuous people for their good deeds. The one requirement, besides being virtuous, is that they are allowed to question your children, unescorted, to see if they will be making the same offer to them when they become old enough. If the adults are not dissociative, a relationship will be established with them for the sole purpose of gaining access to their children. If the adults are dissociative and/or are programmed, then the system will be mapped and exploited and programmes will be exploited or created, as needed.

According to survivors, during the second half of the twentieth century there appears to have been some collaboration between the secretive military and political organisations and the occult religious groups who were already engaging in deliberate systematised child abuse, as well as organised crime. These groups apparently share children, strategies, and even trainers. Many survivors report being abused by religious groups, more than one military or political group (for example, CIA and neo-Nazis and Ku Klux Klan), and also organised criminal groups. In the Extreme Abuse Survey (http://eassurvey.wordpress.com/extreme-abuse-survey-final-results/), of 987 self-identified survivors of extreme child abuse, 19% stated they experienced ritual abuse, 7% stated they experienced mind control, 52% stated they experienced both ritual abuse and mind control, and 22% stated they had experienced neither. These statistics are probably underestimates because of dissociative amnesia in the subject population, and because many, if not most, survivors did not participate in the survey because they had been "closed down" by their perpetrator groups. The definition of mind control used was ". . . all mind control procedures designed to make a victim follow directives of the programmer without conscious awareness including, but not limited to, government-sponsored mind control experiments". There have been assassins who claim to have no memory of the killing they performed.

All these groups employ the same torture, interrogation, and training techniques used on adults by military and police all over the world. According to the *Guardian* (2009) there is evidence that many of the techniques of mind control and ritual abuse are used for child pornography, the training of child soldiers (notably in Africa), and the human trafficking of sex trade workers. The beliefs of at least some suicide bombers and terrorists are consistent with that found in young parts of some mind-controlled survivors who present for therapy.

Survivors of abuses by military and political groups first disclosed their horrendous experiences to therapists. Subsequently, evidence was made available to all of society regarding mind control abuses designed and perpetrated by USA intelligence agencies and those of other countries. These activities were assigned such names as MK-ULTRA, BLUEBIRD, and PAPERCLIP, which involved the Nazi doctors and scientists who had been given asylum in the USA. The Cold War was used as justification for these mind control abuses, intended to create spies or assassins who lacked conscious awareness of their involvement.

Described in CIA documents that became available through the American Freedom of Information Act in the latter part of the twentieth century, these activities have been the subject of senate hearings in the USA and much media attention. Colin Ross documented them in his 2000 book, *Bluebird,* now republished as *The CIA Doctors*. There is clear documentation that some mind control abuses that we identify as government based were designed, promoted, and executed by the most respected psychiatrists and psychologists of the day, in the most revered learning and behavioural health institutions. Some perpetrators have been exposed for practising such techniques on persons who came to them for help. For example, Canada's Dr Donald Ewen Cameron was a leading Montreal psychiatrist who, in the 1950s and 1960s, with the support of CIA funding, engaged in unethical experiments on people who sought help for run-of-the-mill emotional difficulties, destroying memories of their entire previous lives, and thereby ruining their brains and their future.

It is not generally known that some of these projects involved experimentation on children in an attempt to create a perfectly controllable spy or political assassin. It is suspected that most documents regarding this were destroyed. In her book, *A Nation Betrayed: The Chilling True Story of Secret Cold War Experiments Performed on Our Children and Other Innocent People* (2001), survivor Carol Rutz describes the years of government mind control experiments to which she was subjected. Her memories of sexual abuse, hypnosis, drugs, ESP, and other experiences were specific and meticulous, but she wanted more proof and documentation. In 1999, at the age of fifty-two, after submitting a Freedom of Information Act request, she received the validation she had been waiting for. It came in the form of three CD ROMs:

> Forty-eight years after I was first experimented on, I found solid proof of my memories—proof that was in the government vaults of the nearly 18,000 pages of declassified documents from the Bluebird/Artichoke and MKULTRA programs. One of the documents specifically stated that experimental studies of the postulated abilities of a few specially gifted subjects would be conducted. . . .
>
> The document states 'that in working with individual subjects, special attention will be given to dissociative states which tend to accompany spontaneous ESP experiences. Such states can be induced and controlled to some extent with hypnosis and drugs . . . The data used in the study will be obtained from special groups such as psychotics, children and mediums . . .'
>
> The document continues, 'Learning studies will be instituted in which the subject will be rewarded or punished for his overall performance and reinforced in various ways by being told whether he was right, by being told what the target was, with electric shock etc.' The proposal then goes on to say, 'In other cases drugs and psychological tricks will be used to modify his attitudes. The experimenters will be particularly interested in dissociative states, from the abaissement de niveau mental (reduced concentration and attention and loosening of inhibitions), to multiple personality in so-called mediums; and an attempt will be made to induce a number of

> states of this kind, using hypnosis.' The government had finally handed me the validation I had been searching for. To say my heart stopped that day is almost true. (Rutz, 2001, p. xviii)

Many ritual abuse survivors, including Rutz, report "doctors" at their cult training centres who assisted with their training.

One of the declassified documents from MK-ULTRA describes two experiments in 1951, in which, after being taught to respond to code words which would function as post-hypnotic suggestions, two girls were successfully trained to place an incendiary device or steal a person's belongings while in a trance state, and then be amnesic for doing it. Ross quotes similar documents in *The CIA Doctors* (pp. 46–47).

Below is an account from Wendy Hoffman, a survivor of this early training, who may possibly have been one of the two girls referred to in the above document, although in all probability many girls had such training. In this account, a Nazi doctor (Mengele) collaborates with a cult trainer (Mrs Twartsky).

Wendy Hoffman: "Creating a government robot"

"Now, Mrs Twartsky, I will show you how to construct a government bureaucrat.

"For males, we build on their capacity for violence. For females, we build from their capacity for sexuality and seduction. The formula is that simple, sterling and simple.

"We divide these programs into age categories: 18–22, 22–26, 26–31 (especially if the girl looks young); After that, we close the program down. No age group knows about another. No function within a category knows about another.

"Ingenious, isn't it?" Mengele said.

"Brilliant," Mrs Twartsky said.

"With her (meaning me), "we will make her a sexual robot. She has a good body and we will use it.

"We use the obedience drug. We show her the card. We tell her to sit in the chair. We tell her to put her own helmet on.

"We strap her in.

"'You are now being made a criminal. Do you agree?'

"Shoot her with electricity.

"'Nod when you agree.'

"Keep shooting her, Mrs Twartsky.

"That's all for today. We want to make her agree, not kill her," Mengele said.

This went on for consecutive days until I started to die. No food, water or sleep.

On the 5th day, some part of me nodded and I agreed.

> "When you are beckoned, you come out. The maitre d' will point. Next person inside sits on designated man's lap. Next person dances on his lap. Next person gets two pills from purse. Next person leans breasts into man's face covering his eyes. Next person drops both pills in his drink. Next person slips out documents from pocket in jacket. Next person slips in replacement document. Man should pass out by now. Next person slides away from man. Next person exits room. Exiting, next person hands maitre d' in doorway papers taken from passed out man. The assistant will help girl take off her costume. She will return to her home and remember nothing. No person will feel anything—no fear, pleasure, shame, victory—nothing. She will perform her sequence of tasks like a puppet with no emotion, an emotionless puppet. A puppet of the state. Herr Hitler wanted a country filled with these people. Controllable people doing the right thing for the welfare of the government."

When Mengele said "next person", he meant parts within Wendy. Survivor accounts such as this are corroborated by others who indicate that governmental groups wanting to create mind-controlled spies used not only hypnosis, but also electroshock, torture, and complex technology.

Organised crime

Almost every survivor of organised abuse whom I have treated has reported being used as a child in both prostitution and pornographic filming. This is true whether or not they were part of a religious ritually abusive group or indoctrinated into the beliefs of one or more military/political groups. Other therapists report the same thing. In many (but by no means all) cases, it appears that Satanic rituals were staged for the purposes of filming, even those involving actual murders. Persons in uniforms or costumes (soldiers, generals, doctors, Ku Klux Klan members) have also been reported as involved in sadistic abuse, but, again, in some cases, it appeared that these costumes might have been for film purposes rather than genuine. Some survivors' evidence suggests that even when a person is abused in military locations, pornographic filming occurs. Trish Fotheringham and others also report trafficking of overseas children:

> Often, I was taken to the yacht by my grandfather when he delivered newly acquired trainees. These were usually missing or unregistered children of all races and ages, who had been transported from other places in North America and were being readied for shipping and sale in other countries. (Miller, 2012, p. 82)

Mind control has evolved significantly since the 1940s. Most survivors now do not have flagrant dissociative identity disorder (visible switching between personalities); their switches are beneath the surface and difficult to detect. Technology has improved, and every kind of new relevant technology is being used. So, survivors from different generations might have had somewhat different experiences. As technology becomes more sophisticated, it is entirely possible that the techniques that were used in the beginning will be replaced by technologies that we cannot imagine. But at the core, the goal will be the same: to control and violate children and thereby create an invisible slave labour force for financial, political, and hedonistic purposes.

What they have in common is having had their minds split through torture in childhood, and their hidden young insiders deceived by the abusers into love and loyalty to the very people who hurt them. To maintain the security of their horrendous crimes, these abuser groups have implanted various paralysing beliefs in their victims, via torture and trickery, so that the victims will not tell, and will almost never remember, what they have experienced. That is what you must undo, if you are a survivor, so that you can regain ownership of your own life.

Healed cult trainer Stella Katz wrote, in *Healing the Unimaginable* (Miller, 2012, p. 116), "The rewards of ordinary life can seem very mild compared to those given in the cult. But I know the value of what I now have: freedom of body and soul. I am no longer a trapped soul; that is worth it".

The history of disclosures

Therapists (and society) did not understand what mind control and ritual abuse were, or even recognise their existence, before the early 1980s. When significant amounts of this material first began to be revealed, therapists and researchers did not even know much about child abuse, especially that by trusted care-givers. No one understood how widespread it was, or that abuse memories would not always be maintained in the forefront of victims' consciousness. When the issue of "forgotten" childhood trauma was first confronted in therapy offices around the country, therapists called it "repressed memory", since most therapists had barely any understanding of the workings of dissociation. Therefore, most therapists did not know what they were seeing when clients presented with amnesia and other signs of divided minds. This ignorance and naïveté left survivor clients feeling invalidated and not helped.

In the beginning, most of us therapists dismissed our survivor clients as psychotic. The material they were disclosing certainly sounded "crazy". I remember a client in the late 1980s telling me about attending a church service in which everything was done backwards, and about her child seeing "demons" move in a picture on her wall. It did not occur to me that she could have been involved in a group which celebrated the Black Mass and conjured demons. This woman had been diagnosed as "manic-depressive" (now known as bipolar disorder) by the psychiatric system, and, as any conventionally trained psychologist would do, I told her to get back on her medication because she was having a breakdown. For years I observed this woman's "mood swings" and did not recognise the clues which pointed to ritual abuse, because I was uninformed.

It is easy to see why so many therapists resisted their clients' disclosures. We had been taught a model of mental illness which suggested that the problem was in the mind, or brain, of the afflicted person, not in what had happened to them. Those of us who grew up in safety had accepted the myth that "civilised" Western society did not engage in the torture of children. It was only in the 1980s that spousal abuse and child sexual abuse began to be accepted as realities, but even then they were thought of as very rare.

However, courageous survivors persisted in telling their stories, in spite of all the fail-safes their abusers had put in their minds to prevent this from happening, and in spite of therapists not deciphering what they were reporting.

Around 1992, when I had just begun working with my first (known to me) survivor clients, the politics surrounding mind control and ritual abuse erupted with the "memory wars", a well-orchestrated, well-funded political effort to silence survivors and destroy those who would seek to help them. A group in the USA called the "False Memory Syndrome Foundation" was the cornerstone of a variety of organisations that declared war on therapists, authors, and others who advocated the reality of incest, dissociation, and, especially, ritual abuse. Their illogical claims and theories suddenly filled the headlines under the guise of "science". They said they had valid research proving that something called a "false memory syndrome" of childhood trauma could be, and was being, implanted by unethical therapists (and books). They claimed that there was no research establishing that memories of childhood trauma could be or were being "forgotten". But, in fact, there were dozens of such studies (now there are even more) which showed that not only are memories dissociated, but that forgotten and retrieved memories are just as likely to be proved true as those always remembered. (See http://ritualabuse.us/research/memory-fms/recovered-memory-corroboration-rates/.)

Trauma professionals were totally unprepared for this political attack. A leading journal, *Treating Abuse Today*, was forced out of business when its editor was harassed by picketers representing supposedly innocent accused parents. Leading therapists in the dissociative disorders field, such as Bennett Braun, Judith Peterson, and Kathy Snowdon, were targeted for lawsuits and, in Peterson's case, even criminal charges. Insurance companies chose to settle most lawsuits out of court—this is their usual policy—but the enormous amounts of money they gave in settlements, along with some of their actions, gave the impression that the therapists were guilty. Some therapists were doubtless foolish and did unethical things, but most were not, and the evidence against those who were sued has been discredited.

The false memory movement was taken at its word by the press, despite its lack of scientific credibility and the fact that those involved could hardly be considered objective. Many of the founders and declared membership of the American group were accused, convicted, and confessed perpetrators and their spouses. Its advisory board included not only a married couple with documented child sexual abuse activities (such as the publication of a child pornography magazine called *Finger*) but also a minister and his wife who made statements in an interview for a paedophilia magazine about how paedophilia was an expression of God's love. Books by the minister, revered as significant and scientific, were found to include countless errors, including the fact that many of the studies they claimed supported their theories actually either proved the opposite, or did not address the issue at all.

None of the scientific advisers of the group had ever treated, or even interviewed, any survivors. In fact, almost none of the advisers had ever done any psychotherapy at all. What some of them did have was documented involvement as researchers in some questionable government mind control experiments of previous years. Most people knew nothing of their dual roles. Neither the media coverage of the claims of these spokespeople, nor the attention they received in mainstream psychological literature, nor the courts that welcomed their "expert testimony" ever addressed their duplicity.

The false memory movement devoted considerable attention to ritual abuse, which it dismissed as "hysteria". Many of the lawsuits were about cases where ritual abuse was alleged. With their speciality under attack, a significant shift occurred among the remaining leaders in the field of dissociation, the therapeutic arena where these abuses were most often addressed. They pulled back, taking a sceptical—even hostile—position regarding the existence of ritual abuse.

Eventually, not only were mainstream books and other media presentations of the issue skewed or silenced regarding ritual abuse, but the psychotherapy professions were as well. No one talked about the phenomenon except to challenge its existence. The topic was driven totally underground. Therapists discussed it in the hallways at conferences, but there were no formal presentations on the subject.

The survivors, however, remained. Only now it was even harder for them to find help.

Some of we therapists were still working with ritual abuse survivors, but we were isolated. We watched the leaders and pioneers in this work being publicly ridiculed and humiliated, or worse, destroyed. We were attacked by sceptics when we mentioned ritual abuse in online discussion forums. We had no local colleagues who understood what we were dealing with. No textbooks to guide us. No professional conferences. Isolation and paranoia ruled the day. In response, many of us simply stopped doing this work. Others, like me, continued quietly, in private. Our isolation and fear were a pale shadow of what survivors live with day in and day out, from their birth onwards.

My introduction to ritual abuse was abrupt and extreme. In the early 1990s, I acquired no fewer than four survivor clients at virtually the same time, through my work at a government mental health clinic. The first was a young mother, Teresa, who sought parenting help. She was followed by a teenage girl, Jennifer, who had disclosed sexually abusing her younger brother. Next was a young man, Tony, who had been diagnosed with schizophrenia, who called the centre when I was on telephone duty. Teresa's best friend, Lorraine, came to see me after Teresa begged her to because many years of the hospital's revolving door had not helped her significantly. (I have changed the names and some details to preserve confidentiality.)

It was not long before I discovered that these young people all knew one another. In fact, they were members of the same coven of a local Satanic cult. Teresa and Tony were the same age and had been reared together in this group, while Lorraine and Jennifer had moved to town from elsewhere. Their work on recovery brought on severe harassment by the cult group, including repeated abduction and torture of those survivors, and threats against my life.

All this was new to me. I reached out to local colleagues, many of whom were sympathetic but knew nothing to help me. Those I communicated with online who were working with dissociative disorders were embroiled in the "false memory" controversy and reluctant to even entertain the idea that my clients' past and current abuses could be real. One leader in the field actually suggested that perhaps my clients met and created their stories in my waiting room (as if they had been all coming to see me at the same time!). I experienced a small part of the invalidation that survivors must feel when told they are inventing their experiences, as well as disgust that someone so well respected lacked the courage to face reality.

So I was left to learn from the real experts in the field—my survivor clients. Eventually, both Teresa and Jennifer made significant recovery and moved to distant locations. Lorraine, crippled by severe osteoarthritis from her abuse, and unable to keep herself safe, was freed from her ongoing abuse only by death, an alleged suicide by a method which would have been very difficult, if not impossible, for her to accomplish, and which I believe was murder. Tony left town but was recaptured by his cult-involved family members.

I learnt as I treated; I treated more clients with this kind of history, mostly referred to me by other therapists, and I worked out what helped and what did not. I have written about these experiences and discoveries in my book for therapists, *Healing the Unimaginable: Treating Ritual Abuse and Mind Control* (Karnac, 2012).

Many of the early therapists working with survivors believed what their clients believed, that the abusers were terrifyingly omnipotent, and that they had sophisticated ways of tracking survivors' activities and disclosures and exerted control over them no matter how far away they got. We had not yet come to understand the importance or purpose of the most salient feature, and ultimate goal, of this kind of abuse: mind control. We and our clients had no idea of the sophisticated lies and tricks abusers were employing, or how they embedded these lies in parts of survivors' shattered brains. Now we have learnt one important fact—that it is trained parts of survivors who disclose their activities to their abusers. Certain insiders have the job of reporting any disclosures or relocations, believing that the abusers already know what they tell and that the reporting parts will be severely punished if they do not do their jobs. Now, having learnt this, we can pass this information on to the courageous survivors who are struggling to get free.

Over time, as survivors continued to disclose their experiences, abuses experienced in secretive military/political and organised criminal groups came to light. Experiments or military training predominated. Some Satanist scenarios seem to be staged for the purpose of controlling and frightening the children or for use in pornography rather than as part of genuine occult worship. However, other survivors continued to speak of their experience in Satanic and other occult groups who practised ritualistic child abuse, dressing up in robes, torturing and raping children in rituals, sacrificing animals and what the children perceived to be human beings, and celebrating the Black Mass.

The therapeutic situation is somewhat better now. Because mind control and ritual abuse have not gone away, and clients continue to dare to disclose, many more therapists know about it. Therapists are once again sharing their knowledge widely, and some excellent websites have developed over the years. There is a large special interest group on ritual abuse and mind control within the International Society for the Study of Trauma and Dissociation (ISST-D), the main professional organisation for therapists in that field. Professional texts, such as my book for therapists (Miller, 2011), Valerie Sinason's 2012 *Trauma, Dissociation and Multiplicity: Working on Identity and Selves*, and *Ritual Abuse and Mind Control: The Manipulation of Attachment Needs* (Epstein, Schwartz, & Schwartz, 2011), are once again being accepted for publication.

Survivors who have discovered what was done to them have never stopped teaching us. It is no small act of bravery that they have continued to speak out and share their stories. One such survivor has sent me a list of qualities of those survivors who are on the road to healing:

- resilient;
- spunky;
- intelligence and personal abilities shine through despite abuse and programming;
- kindness despite . . .;
- humanity despite . . .;
- ability to be in relationship despite . . .;
- desire to be free;
- keeping on living even though their lives were essentially stolen;
- crave justice even though they have had none;

- capable of not being loyal to perpetrators and abusive families;
- able to see the world from many different perspectives;
- realistic about the evil in the world;
- empathic.

If some of this describes you, I hope this book will help you in your healing journey. It is worth the fight. Even a day of freedom is better than a lifetime of slavery.

Everything I share here I have learnt from survivors.

CHAPTER THREE

Dissociation, multiplicity, and personality systems

Almost all survivors of mind control and ritual abuse have a dissociative mind, even if the dissociation is hidden from public view and perhaps from the survivor him- or herself. Dissociative states of being are necessary adaptations to having to endure ongoing life-threatening trauma in childhood. Organised child abuser groups know about this adaptation, and deliberately structure their victims' dissociative disorders so that their awful secrets will be kept, not only from the authorities and the outside world, but from the main "front person" inhabiting the victim's body in everyday life.

If you are such a survivor (and that is who this book is written for), I invite all internal parts of you who are old enough to understand it to read this chapter, so that you will understand yourself—or your selves—better.

Who am I really?

A child who is being abused on an ongoing basis needs to be able to function despite continuing hidden trauma. He or she has to eat breakfast with parents who might be abusers, to attend school and not appear to be in pain, and to present as relatively "normal" to persons outside the abusive situation. So, the child has at least one part whose job consists of that daily functioning.

When DID was still officially called MPD, the person who primarily lived life on the outside in the real present world was known as the "host" personality, and the other parts were known as alters (short for "alternates"). Unfortunately, the word "alter" can be upsetting to ritual abuse survivors, who remember altars being used for sacrifices. (Note the different spelling.) The term "host", unfortunately, implied that all the parts other than the host were guests, and, therefore, of less importance than the host. They were somehow secondary. They are not.

Another kind of terminology used by therapists, coming from the theory of "structural dissociation", distinguishes between the "apparently normal personality" (ANP) and the "emotional personalities" (EPs). While I think that "apparently normal personality" describes the everyday person quite well, the term "emotional personality" does not fit many of the inside parts, since quite a few are not emotional at all, and the everyday person can also be emotional.

In this book, I shall use the term "front person" to describe the primary identity who lives everyday life, and the word "insiders" to describe the inside ones who hold different aspects of the traumatic memories. Sometimes, I will call the insiders (as well as the front person) "parts", "states", or "identity states", as they are parts of a single brain. But I do respect their sense of being themselves, in their own experience separate people, as they have lived separately from the rest of that brain and often they do not know what happened to the others or that the body has grown up, and other parts do not know about them.

Front people are created to be unaware of the abuse and also of the multiplicity, and to "pass for normal" in the real world. A front person is actually just another part—one who is specialised for handling the normal (non-abusive) world. Most people assume that the adult who functions in the world is the "real" person, and the other personalities, or ego states, whether or not they come out and take over conscious awareness, are less real. This assumption is a misunderstanding. All the parts reside in the same brain and the same body, whether or not they believe they do, and all are real and important.

Many people (at least, their front parts) have a great deal of difficulty accepting that they are multiple. If you know or suspect that you have insiders, you need to face the reality that they hold not only some of your hidden memories, but also many of your potential abilities, emotions, and desires. Rather than being "more" than the others, the front personality who deals with daily life is generally very limited, with little power in the personality system, little memory of what happened, limited emotions, and not much depth. Many front people have very little energy or strength and are chronically depressed. Others are really "apparently normal personalities", function well, and are even vital.

The present-day main person is almost never the original person, especially if the person has an extensive abuse history. In my experience, the front person who handles most of adult life is usually formed when the person first moves away from home, cannot remember his or her childhood, and adapts quickly to "normal" adult life.

It is unlikely that one front person will serve as a constant throughout the life of someone who is multiple. Dissociative adults often have several front people from earlier stages of life inside. They usually have the same name, but are of different ages. Sometimes, there are several current front people. Each assumes he or she is the "real" person and has amnesia for the existence of the others. Their current knowledge and experience might overlap, while their other characteristics differ somewhat. This makes them glide easily from one to the other, and even people who know them can easily miss the switch.

One client of mine has four front people by the same name who alternate with one another and with some teenage parts at the workplace. One of them is severely depressed and suicidal, another is just a functionary who does her job, another loves music and art and nature, and another is an investigator who wants to know what has gone on in her life to create her symptoms. What they all have in common is their ignorance about the abuse the client suffered and their ability to function somewhat in the adult world. They are not unemotional, although they do not necessarily know the sources of those emotions or recall what they relate to. Emotions from the inside parts leak into the suicidal one more than into the other front parts.

In most cases, the front person is replaced for each new stage of life. For example, one survivor was doing well at her workplace until the employers changed the computer system to a more complicated one, so a younger front person had to come out in order to learn it. Another survivor had a front person who was becoming increasingly overwhelmed with emotions coming from the hurt insiders, so his system decided to put out a tougher part as the front person. Another survivor's front person began to recall sexual abuse from the age of three, and blended with the three-year-old part from which she had been split, so a teenage insider had to take over as the front person.

So, who is the real person? Well, it depends on what you mean by "person". If a person is the contents of one brain, then all of your parts together constitute a person. On the other hand, if a person is a well-organised "self" with a sense of personal identity, an age, beliefs, and emotions, then perhaps many or most of your insiders qualify as people. Even parts who are just memory fragments often see themselves as people (unless they have been told they are puppets, or robots, or computer chips). What is clear is that all parts, whether or not they are front people, are parts of a greater being, whether they know it or not. You all live in the same brain, and in the present-day outside world you all share the same body, regardless of whether or not you experience yourselves as having "inside bodies". What you cannot say is that the person who handles everyday adult life is more "real" than the other parts. He or she just has a different job.

It has been my experience that the only multiples in whom there is one strong main person are those who were abused or traumatised for only a brief period of time, usually outside the home. Their long period of safety has allowed them to build a strong "outside world" personality. However, they still have hidden split-off parts who come out only occasionally, or never come out but influence the person's behaviour and feelings from time to time. In the kind of personality system deliberately created by mind controllers, the front people are merely shells through which the other parts are manifested without visible switching. This structuring makes the multiplicity much less obvious. Successfully created mind-controlled persons never recognise that they are multiple (at least, their front people do not).

Wendy Hoffman: "Discovering my multiplicity"

Moments in life are indelible and do not wash away no matter how many years have passed. Those moments can derail the stream of a life and put one on a different path. I was in bed in my co-op on 108th Street near Amsterdam Avenue. I can't remember whether I was about to sleep or wake up. It was as if a curtain ripped open within me from the bottom up. Many people inside came to the surface and told me they existed. That was the worst and best moment of my long life.

"No, I am not multiple," the surface me or me's screamed back. "These things did not happen to me. Multiplicity is a hoax," I flailed. The force of my recoil from my own being alone could have right there shredded me into fragments. I refused to be multiple. Anything was better, I thought, not knowing that only multiplicity had so far saved my life.

> I had already written, performed and toured with my multi-media performance *Incest: Remember & Tell*, mounted art exhibits on sexual abuse and given lectures to survivors and professionals around New York City on incest and what we then called satanic ritual abuse. But I hadn't yet known the most important part, that I was multiple. Other survivors talked about their multiplicity in 12-step meetings around the city, but I had not acknowledged mine. I didn't mind exposing society's abuses, but I couldn't get a hold on my own internal system.
>
> The people and voices who had come to the surface began telling me horrendous stories, even worse than I had heard in meetings. The list of my perpetrators kept growing longer. But slowly, breath by breath, thought by thought, eye lash by eye lash blink, I accepted my selves. I didn't know them yet or the structure they lived in. That would take years. But I came to know that my mind was a tangled web of serious despair. I had to face that multitudes lived under my surface and I had to meet everyone.
>
> Despite my initial rejection, I learned that the parts I avoided are the strongest, most selfless and the real me. Anyone could live regular life. Not everyone could swim through a constant river of double binds and life or death decisions. Survivors of multiplicity are brave people, trying to go on without being aware of major parts of ourselves and now trying desperately to dig through fragmented memories of abuse to find what remains of who we are.

Problems of front people

You might need to read this section more than once. When your "main personality" (current front person) who deals with everyday life reads it, you can see whether or not your symptoms and problems fit what is described here, and perhaps get some insight into why these things happen. When your insiders read it, they can perhaps gain some understanding of what life is like for the front person, and develop more empathy for that part.

Amnesia

Dissociation becomes a disorder when the activities or behaviours of the usually hidden parts result in problems for the adult survivor. When a person has DID, the front person may suffer from amnesia not only for past abuse, but also for pieces of everyday life. Sometimes nothing happens during a period of amnesia; the person just sits there, "spacing out". Sometimes the amnesia is caused by inner parts of the person coming out into the world and taking over the body for a period of time. A child part of a person with DID might come out when the person is at work, or driving, or during sex, or at a doctor's office. This can cause very concrete problems, even life-threatening ones. A client of mine came home from a business meeting to find that a child part of her had begun to cook something and then left the pot on the stove, almost burning her house down. A forty-year-old married woman discovered her multiplicity when a teenage insider took over the body and developed an online romance with a young man in another part of the continent. Believing herself to be a teenager, she made arrangements to fly to his city to meet him. Needless to say, the trip was a disaster. Some people with DID lie to cover up for their periods of amnesia. Their own lives feel like a television series in which they have missed some of the episodes. Persons with DDNOS do not experience this kind of upheaval; they are more likely to just feel unreal, as hidden inside parts influence their behaviour.

Hearing voices

Hearing voices is another one of the most important parts of the experience for most multiples. The voices are usually the sound of the other inside parts attempting to talk to the front person or to one another, arguing or giving orders. They can easily be misunderstood as signs of a psychotic disorder or as "possession" by external entities. Multiples who do not understand their condition frequently seek out help from churches who perform exorcisms or mental health facilities who diagnose psychosis, medicating heavily and inappropriately.

Many therapists believe that these voices are distinguished from the voices of schizophrenia by the fact that they are experienced as coming from inside the head. But this is not always the case. One of my first DID clients, diagnosed with schizophrenia, heard the insiders' voices coming out of his television set. I asked one of the main insiders why this happened. "If we talk inside his head, he thinks we're demons and doesn't listen to us. But he believes everything he hears or sees on TV." This person was a ritual abuse survivor, as well as a very religious Christian, and had probably been trained to believe his insiders were demons. The insiders called him "religious Tony".

The voices might sound to the main person like background noise in a crowded place, or they might stand out individually. In some cases, they are just experienced as thoughts rather than heard as voices, but they still feel alien to the person experiencing them, and contribute to the person feeling that he or she is going crazy. They might be strong thoughts that come "out of nowhere" and do not really seem to belong to the person. "Thought-snatching", having your thoughts disappear as inside parts take them away, is also common.

Often, the voices are critical. Everyone has an "inner critic", of course, which shows up in self-critical thoughts, but the inner critics of multiples are generally very unpleasant, and are internally audible to the person who is trying to accomplish things or carry on a conversation. No matter what one of my clients does, he hears some insiders complaining about it, usually in foul language. He used to speak to them out loud, and nastily. He appeared psychotic. He has now learnt to "think" to them, and, since he realises they are small child parts, to reassure them and tell them he loves them. As a result, they are more co-operative, but they still complain in the only kind of language they know, the foul language they heard at home while attempting to grow up.

You might notice that some voices often tell you to shut up or be quiet, call you a liar, and say that certain events never happened. Others might suggest self-harm or suicide. These parts, who have been called persecutor–protector parts or trauma-bonded parts, try to protect you from the abusers by acting like the abusers. They are common in mind control created personality systems, as they have been given the jobs of making sure the secrets of the abuse do not leak out. They are also usually present if abusers have made threats to the child, and they repeat those threats. They often engage in more severe reprisals if they are not heeded.

It is common for multiples—DID and DDNOS—to hear the sound of infants or small children crying. Abusers often punish children severely for crying (suffocation is the treatment of choice for many cult children being trained not to cry), so the crying goes "inside". An inside child part who never comes out into the world holds the tears and the crying sound.

Above all, remember that when you hear your insiders' voices, they are *communicating*. They need you to communicate with them. This might be quite difficult, at first. You begin by listening.

In many mind-controlled personality systems, the person on the outside is not designed to communicate directly with the insiders, just to be influenced by them without knowing it, thinking their voices are demons or hallucinations or crazy thoughts, and their emotions are just moods, or that everyone has a "busy mind". This is how the abusers maintain control of children, and of the survivors they become.

There are some multiples who do not hear voices at all, even when they try to. That is the experience of one of my clients who has only four insiders (she did not experience mind control or ritual abuse). It is difficult for the front person to communicate with the inside parts, because they are unable to hear one another, so they have to write in a book or give me messages to pass on.

Sometimes, the voices being heard are not those of the other insiders, but pieces of traumatic memories being played back, such as the voice of an abuser telling the child not to talk about what happened on penalty of death. This is particularly true with mind-control survivors. If you have this experience, it is actually being created by an insider who is trying to frighten you away from remembering or telling what happened by showing you the threat that was made.

Seeing insiders

Many multiples not only hear, but also see their insiders. Even if your outside person does not see them, it is common for insiders to see one another. You might be afraid of those who resemble your perpetrators, or demons, or monsters, or animals. Although it might be hard for you to believe, these insiders are also hurt children who were deceived into believing they were these beings. You might be afraid to go near those insiders who appear hurt, or dirty, or in the conditions in which they were abused. And in some cases, going near them means you begin to feel their pain or see their memories.

Some multiples see their insiders' faces in mirrors, which is part of why they often avoid mirrors. Fake mirrors (with pictures glued on to them) are used by abusers to deceive children into believing they are something they are not.

A sense of unreality

Particularly with DDNOS, the person often feels as if he or she is no longer himself or herself, or feels that familiar places are strange. When insiders first appear, the person might have the experience of watching himself doing things he has no control over, such as harming the body. Another part is actually "out" and is doing it, and the usual main person is relegated to a "back seat". This situation can make the world feel unreal to the person who is not fully present. It can be quite frightening.

Flashbacks and nightmares

Dissociation protects the front person against overwhelming trauma. Still, sometimes the traumatic memories come back via flashbacks, nightmares, anxiety, or depression, or body memories. All these things are known as post trauma intrusive symptoms. They can be visual, auditory, or tactile (including physical or emotional pain). Small things in the present environment could trigger flashbacks and feelings of being overwhelmed and an inability to cope. Intrusions are more common than we generally realise: depression, anxiety, panic attacks, obsessions, and compulsions are often emotional intrusions from past traumatic memories that are not recognised as such.

Emotional numbness

Many survivors of severe trauma have periods of emotional numbness, in which they feel very little, to balance out the times when they have intrusive symptoms of flashbacks and nightmares. If the person is multiple, the front person is often numb and feels unreal, except when the feelings and memories leak through from inside parts.

Ignoring, or conflict with, insiders

Since the purpose of the adult front person is to deal with everyday adult life, and since insiders cause all the problems we just discussed, it is tempting for the front person to just want the insiders to go away and not exist. If you think the voices are signs of psychosis, or, even worse, intruding spirits or demons, you obviously want them gone. It is common to be afraid of, or hostile to, those insiders who are rude, impulsive, or threatening. You might fear those parts doing things that will get you into trouble.

You need to know three things about such parts:

1. They helped you survive in childhood when your survival was at stake, physically or emotionally, so they deserve your respect, compassion, and gratitude.
2. It is their disconnection from the rest of you (the parts of you who have a conscience or empathy or "common sense") that permits them to have the attitudes or perform the behaviours that you worry about. They are not balanced, because they are disconnected.
3. You cannot get rid of them—but if they become connected to the rest of you through sharing memories, they will change. Those who have appeared the most hostile or dangerous can often become the most helpful.

I have known survivors to try to get rid of their inside parts or voices by drowning them in liquor, throwing out their toys and stuffed animals, and answering the voices with angry threats or "spiritual" rebukes. Doing such things will only make your internal conflict worse.

Insiders and their origins

Because it is so overwhelming, clear conscious memory of childhood sexual and betrayal trauma does not develop, at least in a front personality, who is designed to deal with ordinary life and not know about anything else. This process is both psychological and organic. From the organic perspective, the different aspects of the traumatising experience are stored in separated circuits of a single brain.

When the trauma is extreme and complex, begins in early childhood (under the age of six), and involves pain, betrayal, and threats to life, the various aspects of the overwhelming traumatic memories and their responses are divided between different internal personalities. For a single memory, one insider might be aware of the first piece of the story, another insider of the next segment, and so on. Or one insider might hold the pictures, another the "sound track", another the feeling of sadness, another the anger, another the fear, another the physical pain, another the tastes and smells, and another the sexual arousal. If there are repeated traumas of a particular kind, these aspects of experience go into the same brain circuits that held them previously.

Over time, insiders develop who specialise in certain emotions or physical sensations, and hold these from many different memories. Mind controllers, aware of this process, utilise it to control their victims.

Regardless of how they view themselves, if you are a multiple, you are likely to find within your mind the following categories of insiders:

1. *Parts from before the trauma*: relatively untraumatised child insiders who hold positive or neutral memories. They stop growing and are put away when they experience trauma or serious deprivation. (There are some survivors who do not have such a base of non-traumatised being.)
2. Parts created during the trauma:
   (a) *Hurt children* who have unfulfilled needs and/or hold traumatic pain or emotions. They often still "live" in the experience of their trauma.
   (b) *Protectors* (including internalised perpetrators). Like the hurt children, these parts generally live in the past and think the trauma is still happening. (In some cases, it might be.)
   (c) *Observers*, recorders, watchers, parts in the sky, etc.—parts who "left the body" when the trauma was happening. Some might be aware of what happened, others live in a cloud, or some such place where they could be unaware. Perpetrator groups call these "floaters", and try to get rid of them or lock them up, as they often know secrets the abusers do not want known.
3. *Parts from after the trauma*: survivors, usually the body's chronological age. They have to deal with everyday life, so must not be affected by the trauma, which they often do not remember. They may be high-functioning, or they may be weary and empty, and they might have post traumatic stress disorder. Front people belong in this category, as do those who were previous front people at different ages.

It helps to think of the needs and purposes of each of these categories as you get to know your parts. Frightening or angry parts are often protectors. Observer parts can be helpful for putting memories in order and knowing what really happened (*vs.* what illusion the abusers created). Parts from after the trauma might need to be protected from much of the trauma until it has been worked through by those parts who actually went through it.

As I mentioned in Chapter One, being dissociative (or multiple) is mental injury rather than mental illness, and, therefore, requires a different treatment. For a broken leg, you would put the bone parts back together and keep them connected so they could heal, even though it might be painful. Similarly, to heal a broken mind, you bring the parts back together by introducing them to one another, and you clean the wound by resolving what happened to make the parts split from one another. Marlene Steinberg's book *The Stranger in the Mirror* (2000) can help you and your support people understand your experience, and so can a newsletter by and for multiples such as "Many Voices" (http://www.manyvoicespress.org/).

Understanding internal parts

The main front person in a personality system generally has continuity of memory for most of his or her current life, and hears only some of the parts as voices or thoughts, or feels their experiences as body memories. It is uncommon that the front person knows much about the insiders, unless he or she has deliberately worked on it.

The situation is reversed with the insiders. They often do not know much about what is going on in current everyday life, but at least some of them have much more awareness of the other insiders, and are likely to recognise that they are part of a "personality system".

Although all the selves of a multiple are really separated circuits of a single brain, in most cases they experience themselves and one another as separate people. They are just as real to one another as people on the outside. They might actually see the other selves in locations in the inner world. In addition, when mind control has been involved, some of the selves might believe things about their identities and purposes (and those of other parts) that were deliberately taught to them by their abusers.

Insiders have separate and different memories, feelings, and approaches to life, and a sense of separate identity and agency. Although they feel themselves to be complete persons, each tends to have a specific function and a certain typical emotional state.

The front person is generally orientated to time and place, knowing accurately the details of present life. However, many of the insiders might not be. They generally believe it is still the year and place where their abuse happened, sometimes the very moment the abuse happened, and they interpret all current events in terms of the experience of that time and place.

Beginning to communicate with your insiders

It is essential for the front person to learn to communicate with the other parts. Many multiples lack this skill. A lifelong habit of looking outward and not speaking with the voices is difficult to overcome for the front person. But it can be done. And if, for some reason, your front person cannot do it, some older insiders can learn to get communication happening internally. So, this section is directed to either the front person or any other adult or teenage parts who are prepared to learn inner communication.

Listening

In many cases, the insiders do not really know the front person (the part who handles everyday adult life), and might not even like him or her. If you are a front person, you may have to earn their trust. If you have spent the past twenty, forty, or sixty years ignoring them, it is no wonder they do not trust you and do not ask your advice. So, when you first approach them, be gentle and try to learn from them rather than bossing them around. If they will not speak with you, ask your therapist or best friend to help by speaking with them first. Then treat whichever parts try to communicate with you with respect, kindness, and gentle curiosity, even if they are swearing at you. Do not shut them out; they need to be heard, and if they are not heard they might find other ways of getting your attention, such as giving you pain or making you feel sick.

Do not ask your parts too many questions at first; it might feel like interrogation, and they might have been interrogated as part of their abuse. Just be open and sympathetic, until they are ready to talk.

If you hear a voice, listen to it and treat it with respect. If it says "Don't talk", for example, you can ask it why not. Listen to what it is saying, and then talk with it. If it is swearing or threatening you, this is its way of trying to protect you from the abusers, just as other parts protect you by holding pain or rage, or withholding traumatic knowledge from you. Listening to, and dialoguing with, your insiders will make a difference in your life which you will see and feel.

Note that "listen" does not mean "obey", as it frequently does to adults who abuse children. When I say "listen to the voices", I just mean try to understand them. It will take time to determine how much you can trust them, since some of them might have been deceived by abusers.

Looking for the source of symptoms or emotions

When you want to know something about, for example, the source of a symptom you are experiencing, think your question to the insiders, and see what words or thoughts come to you. You might be surprised.

Parts often make themselves known by exerting influence on the "outside", or presenting, part. This (called "passive influence") is common, and can be detected simply by asking internally about it. If you have a feeling or an impulse that you do not understand, someone inside might really be experiencing the feeling which is "leaking through" to you. You can follow the feelings to find who inside is their source. Ask, for example, who is feeling depressed, or who is crying internally, and why. Or ask who has the impulse to buy that chocolate bar, and what it means to them. Do not insist on knowing internal names, as some parts might feel that this gives you or hostile parts power over them. Abusers use names to call them out for torture or punishment, or to give an assignment, or make them do a job. Your insiders might have no trouble giving names, but do not assume they want to.

Any symptom can be dealt with by communicating with the insiders. If you are having flashbacks, seeing pictures of frightening events, you can ask who inside is seeing these pictures, and who is making them see them, and why.

Once you talk to the right inside "person", often a simple explanation of reality can lead to big changes. In every case, the key is communicating with the insiders responsible. You and the rest of the personality system have the opportunity to introduce these parts to the safe present (assuming you have got away from your abusers; these issues will be discussed in Chapter Nine). They can tell you the false beliefs the abusers put into their heads, and you (or other parts who know more than you do) can explain the truth, or show them the trickery involved.

Matching your communication to the insiders

It is important to match your communication to the kind of part you are talking with. Some use strong, challenging language, and will respond to dares and challenges and humour. Other parts are terrified and just need listening. They might be dealing with dire threats about what will happen if they talk to anyone, especially about their experiences at the hands of the abusers.

Some cannot speak and might need to communicate through writing, through drawing, or through another part. Some insiders might believe that they cannot talk because their tongues were cut out (a common deception used by abuser groups). Some might be too young to have words; they can draw, or older parts can speak for them. Others might speak different languages, and you can find an internal translator for them.

Be careful with your language. Innocuous words have often been given sinister meanings by the perpetrator groups. If you experience distress when you use words like "love", or "safe", or "feel", you can ask your parts what the word in question means to them, and you can train yourself to substitute another word when you speak with that particular part. (Did any part of you have a reaction to the words I just wrote?) With one survivor I know, I have to substitute "believe" for "think", and "sense in your body" for "feel", since the original words were used by the perpetrators as part of torture.

Do not show favouritism

Remember that it is very important to treat all parts with equal kindness; do not pick favourites. Every part is there for a purpose, and is an important part of the system. So, for instance, do not be afraid of hostile parts. It has been said that every persecutor is a misguided protector. Its protector job was important and necessary when it first developed, but it can be a handicap later in life when your needs are different. Most hostile insiders are using anger to protect vulnerable parts inside, usually younger children. If they seem dangerous, talk with them at first through another part. But if you act scared, you will create a self-fulfilling prophecy. Watch out for good kid–bad kid dichotomies. You need to appreciate all your parts, just as they all need to accept one another. Sometimes, an internal part unknowingly makes trouble for the front person and feels bad about it, for example, if a child comes "out" at the wrong time or in the wrong place. In the end, remember they (*and you*) are all parts of one person (or at least, of one brain), so it is important to accept all your selves, including the parts that you or others do not want or like.

Do not hurry to change things

Personality systems structured by perpetrator groups tend to be better organised than those spontaneously created, but they usually operate through a military-style hierarchy where everyone obeys his or her "boss" out of fear of punishment. It is wise not to interfere with this hierarchical organisation at first, but get to know the leaders, and, over time, you can help them change the governmental system to a more democratic one.

Talking with your insiders pays great dividends. As soon as one part is persuaded to work together with you for healing, another will appear who is supposed to stop this process, *but secretly wants you to help them, too.* You might have to work your way through many layers, but you will get there.

Eventually, it can be helpful to ask insiders to help you map the system if they are willing. But if you are a survivor of mind control or ritual abuse, you should not do this too soon, as it is breaking the rules of the insiders' training, and they could be punished (by insiders or by the perpetrator group, if they know what is happening) for doing it.

Communicating with child parts

In most personality systems, many, usually a majority, of parts feel themselves to be children or teenagers. There might be some who are too young to talk or to understand language, or who can only speak a language which has not been spoken since childhood. I believe that the child parts of any multiple split off during childhood, not later, and remain developmentally children. They are not ordinary children, however. They are child parts who have been assigned jobs, and who hold knowledge or feelings that would be too overwhelming for the front person to handle. Sometimes, children can handle what adults cannot.

Child parts believe themselves still to be children, and if they take over the body, they behave and think like children. I am currently looking at four different handmade birthday cards given to me by the same survivor: one with beautiful sophisticated artwork done by her older parts, one with a cute picture done by those around age six, one with simple drawings of themselves made by the parts around age three or four, and one with scribbles done by the infants. They are just like the drawings my own children made at those ages. Before I understood multiplicity, a child part of one of my first survivor clients stole an electric wheelchair from the hospital where I worked, and rode around the hospital grounds on it. When she was caught, she said she was my employee. Another survivor in a child state sat on the floor and put out her feet for me to tie her shoes, assuming she was in preschool. I have been in session with an adult man when he stood on his head on my office couch, because the child that he "was" at that moment preferred that position. I have met with adults whose "out" personalities knew no English, but spoke languages the main person had learned in early childhood and then forgotten. And one woman shocked and frightened me by falling down my office stairs because a baby part who did not know how to walk came out at the top of the stairs. When you begin communicating with the children inside you, it is important not to let them out to drive the car or take on other adult tasks!

The thinking process of child parts is like that of actual children of those ages. They might not understand long words or sentences. They might not grasp abstract concepts. When you speak with an insider, one of the first things to ask them is their age. This will help you use language that they understand. It is easy to talk "above their head" in adult words, if you do not realise that their life experience was cut off in childhood and they have not grown since then. Talk as you would to a "real" child, no matter how articulate the front person may be. You will find that as they become comfortable in the present world, they will begin to grow up gradually.

Child parts will often echo the words of their adult abusers. I frequently have to remind my client with the foul-mouthed critical parts to ask them their ages. There is a pause while he asks internally, then, "Oh." The one who believes herself to be his abusive mother (who had to be his father's sexual partner) is four. She understands things like a four-year-old, but she swears like an old pro.

Parts with different identities

As you meet your insiders, you are likely to find parts who believe they are older than the body's age, parts who believe they are of the opposite sex to the body, and parts who believe they do not belong to the body at all.

Although I believe that a child part is really a child and thinks like a child, I also believe that a part who says he or she is older than the body is not really older, but, rather, is a child's, or a young adult's, conception of an older person. And an opposite-sex part (a male in a female body, for instance) is more like a young girl's idea of what a boy is like than like a "real" boy. Boys in women's bodies usually represent the part of the person who has traits that are traditionally considered masculine, such as bravery, or anger, or stoicism; girls in men's bodies often have supposedly "feminine" traits, such as fearfulness, or are the ones who were raped. Insiders who believe they do not belong to the body might have been deliberately made to believe this (through drugs) for the abusers' purposes, or might just believe that by not identifying with the body they will not be hurt.

It is unwise and disrespectful to argue with parts about what they are, even though you must keep in mind that they are all just parts, they do all belong to the brain of the present body, and the body they are in (in the real, present-day world) is actually an adult male or female human being.

What newly discovered parts do not know about the present

Many insiders have not come directly out into the world since childhood, so they know nothing of the present. They are often terrified or hostile if they actually come out into the body. Their past experience could be that they did not emerge directly into the world unless called out by a perpetrator. I encourage newly discovered parts to look around my office and see that it is daytime, and we have our clothes on, and there are no weapons or programming chairs.

You can do the same in the safety of your present home. Your young insiders can notice that they have control over their environment; they can stand up or sit down when they want, and they can choose to open the door or to lock it and keep it locked. All this is very different from the time when the abusers had control of them.

Here is what inside parts do not know.

1. They can be mistaken about the date, especially what year it is. Often, they believe it is the year in which they stopped growing, that is the year of their own last remembered experience, which was, of course, when you (they) were still being abused. So it helps to have a calendar and a recent newspaper or magazine handy to show them the date. You can also show them things that have changed: for example, a personal computer and a mobile phone rather than a typewriter and a rotary dial phone.
2. They are often mistaken about their location, where you live, and whether you are still near the location where the abuse occurred. If you are no longer living there, you need to help

those parts recognise that. A map will help, on which you can point out the location of where the abuse happened and where you are now. You might need to tell them how you got to where you are now, and also where the abusers are currently, especially if the abusers are dead.

3. They might have difficulty recognising the fact that the body has grown up. Insiders who come out into the body will often discover that they are in an adult body, for example, noticing they have breasts or they are bigger than they believe themselves to be, or that they have a full set of teeth, or wrinkles, or bags under the eyes. It takes work to help parts adjust to the fact that they live in an older body who looks like the adult front person, not the way they believe they personally look. In many cases, the parts (except for the front person) "see" one another in the inner world, looking just as they looked when the body was a child or a teenager. Parts discovering the adult body might say things such as "This isn't my body." You can ask them to come out and move their hand, while looking at it. You can offer to use a mirror so they can see what their body looks like now, but be careful, since mirrors are used by organised groups of abusers to deceive parts about their nature (such as showing a child a "mirror" which has on it a picture of a scary creature).
4. They might have difficulty accepting the fact that they all inhabit the same body, which is now that of an adult. It takes time for parts to accept this reality. You can tell them that their inside bodies are different, but that in the present, real world, of this year in the twenty-first century, they are all in the same outside body.
5. They might not be aware that some places, and some other people, are safe and will not harm them. They might believe that every adult will hurt them, especially if you (and they) are a mind control survivor and your insiders have been taught that "outsiders" (ordinary people) are all dangerous. You might need to fill them in on who your therapist, your spouse, your children, your doctor, and your friends are; they do not automatically know.

And here is what you, the front person (if that's who is reading this), need to know: those voices, except for the ones that are flashbacks of memories, are all parts of the same brain that you are a part of. They are not outside influences. They are not psychotic hallucinations. And you, too, are a part. A very specialised part, with an important job: to handle real everyday adult life.

The suggestions in this chapter are only the beginning of getting to know your internal parts. In the following exercise, you will have the opportunity not only to describe what you are experiencing, but to try to deliberately communicate with inside parts of you. If you already know how to do this, feel free to skip this exercise.

When I ask you to talk to the parts, you can do it by thinking; you do not need to talk out loud. If you are not able to hear the voices of your parts but are pretty sure they exist because you are missing time, or you have been told of doing things you do not consciously remember, you might need to communicate in writing, allowing the parts to write back to you some time later.

If you have an inner world, see whether you are able to enter this inner world and meet the parts. If you can, that is a huge step forward. If you find this impossible, you will have to rely on thinking or writing to the parts.

Exercise 4. Beginning to know your insiders

Do you have missing periods of time? If so, think of the most recent period of amnesia, and gently enquire by thinking to the inside of your head: who was in charge of the body when you lost that time, and what were they doing? Write the answer down in a notebook. It might be in the form of a thought, or it might sound like a voice. (Remember to write the question if thinking gets no result.)

Do you hear voices? If so, what kind of voices? Adults or children? Male or female? If they are children, ask their ages, and be sure to talk with them at a level of language they can understand.

Do you hear crying or shouting in your head? If so, can you visualise the person who is crying? How old does he or she seem to be? Try to speak to that person, imagine him or her as a hurt child, and tell that child you want to help him or her.

Do voices criticise you or call you names? If so, does what they say remind you of anyone in your earlier life, or do they actually sound like those people? (Voices can be parts of you who have learnt from your parents or others, they can be parts who imitate those people, or they can be "tape recordings" of what those people actually said.) You might want to ask who they are, and why they criticise you like this.

Do any voices tell you to be quiet? How do they say it? Again, do they sound like adults, children, or tape recordings of someone unpleasant? Are there specific threats?

Ask the voices who tell you to be quiet why they want you to be quiet. Ask them what you did wrong, and listen to what they say.

Can you categorise the voices you hear into: happy kids, hurt kids, protectors (who might threaten or criticise), or observers?

Do any of the voices have names? Or titles? Do any of them say they are not human, or make noises which do not sound human? Make sure you take what they say seriously even if their names or titles or what they believe about themselves seems strange to you.

Introduce yourself to your insiders by thinking or writing to them. Tell them who you are, how old you are, what year it is, where you live, and facts about you such as your job or your present family. Let them know that you are in control of the body most of the time and you want to get to know them. Try some of the suggestions I gave earlier for updating parts on present life.

If you suddenly get a symptom such as a flashback or a strong emotion that seems inappropriate to the present, enquire inside your head about who this comes from. If you can, reassure them that the danger they sense is no longer there, but something in the present reminded them of it. Tell them you will keep them safe, and if they are not safe, you will find a way to make them safe. Listen to their response, and stay in dialogue with them.

You can find more exercises in getting to know your insiders in some of the self-help books for multiples, such as *Got Parts?*, by ATW (2005), *Amongst Ourselves*, by Tracy Alderman and Karen Marshall (1998), and *Coping with Trauma-Related Dissociation*, by Boon, Steele, and van der Hart (2011). In the next chapter, we shall look at the special characteristics of mind-controlled personality systems.

Be assured that discovering, listening to, and dialoguing with your insiders will make a difference in your life, and you will see and feel that difference.

CHAPTER FOUR

Engineered multiplicity: personality systems created by mind control

The personality systems of mind control and ritual abuse survivors are different from those of dissociative individuals whose abuse has been less systematic, such as in severe physical or sexual abuse by a family member. The definitive clues to what happened to you will be found within your personality system, even though people who have experienced organised criminal abuse have often also experienced abuse within the family.

Now, there is abuse that can technically be called "ritual abuse" but does not really involve systematic mind control—for example, by teenage Satanic dabblers. Personality systems created spontaneously in response to abuse do not manifest the degree of internal organisation seen when a person's insiders have been deliberately split off and trained by an organised group for the purpose of achieving mind control. Without the mind control, healing can proceed in much the same way it does for someone who has undergone abuse that is not systematic.

What I shall tell you in this chapter and those that follow is based on my experience of survivors I have known, as clients or colleagues. So, when I make a statement of what I believe to be the case, you can preface it with an "in my experience . . ." even if I do not say that every time.

Mind-controlled, deliberately created personality systems do have certain identifiable characteristics, which only the insiders within that system can know about. If you have most or all of these characteristics, you might suspect that you have been abused by an organised criminal group. When I say "criminal", I include religious (pseudo-Christian) and governmental groups, because even if they say they are doing it for a good cause, they engage in criminal practices of child abuse, and keep it secret. If those in charge of your personality system do not allow your front person to know about these things, you can have some of your knowledgeable insiders read this chapter. It is a good idea for those in charge to read it, because the abuser groups hide things from you as well as from the front person, and you have a right to know what has been done to you and the others inside you.

Markers of mind control

A front person who is a shell

In my experience, organised perpetrator groups often (not always) design their trainees to have a front person who has little or no real "self" of his or her own that the inside parts can speak through. The shell on the outside bridges the transitions (internal switches) smoothly so the individual does not appear multiple at all. He or she switches as different parts or groups of parts come to the fore, but the switches are subtle and hard for others to detect, as the voice is always the same. When the front person is a shell, his or her awareness, memory, and behaviour vary according to which other parts are conscious at any given time. Shell personalities themselves feel hollow and empty and are often depressed.

Trish Fotheringham gives an example of how her system was designed to work (Miller, 2012, p. 84):

> In order to give my personality system a new structure, a combination of four alters were to be simultaneously present in my consciousness at all times, though only one could actually be out at any given time. This would ensure two things: that I would always appear normal (not multiple) to the world, and that only the appropriate skills and knowledge base would be accessible in any given situation. A young alter called Pat memorized patterns for who should be out in each situation, and conveyed them to a Controller alter. The controller alter flipped the right combination of switches to bring the correct alters to "just below the surface" where they could then take their turns out as the situation warranted. Songs and rhymes continued in my head as instructions to the alters who were out.

This might seem strange, and even shocking, to you, especially if something similar is how your own system works. Front people are designed by abuser groups to not know about the others who fill them from within, and change places. Sometimes, they are aware to some degree. I remember one client telling me that, when in a meeting, she actually saw one of her insiders get up and go out the door, leaving her without the knowledge and skills that this insider held.

Deliberately placed triggers for learned behaviours (programmes)

Although all abuse and trauma survivors may be "triggered" into intrusive flashbacks by present-day experiences that remind them of the trauma, the triggers deliberately installed by mind controllers are different, in that they are cues for conditioned behaviours. Some of these are behaviours such as going home, going outside (where someone is waiting), coming to the person who uses the trigger, or switching to a particular insider. Others are psychiatric symptoms such as flashbacks, self-harm, or suicide attempts, which are actually punishments given by insiders for disobedience or disloyalty. For many survivors, every trigger causes a switch to a part programmed to perform a particular behaviour associated with that trigger. For others, the front person remains present in the world but has an irresistible compulsion to perform the behaviour.

Most organised abuser groups call each particular training a "programme", as if you were a computer. Many specific trained behaviours have "on" and "off" triggers or switches. Some personality systems are set up with an inner world full of wires or strings that connect switches to their effects. These can facilitate a series of actions by a series of insiders. For example, one part watches the person function in the outside world, and presses a button if he or she sees the person disobeying instructions. The button is connected to an internal wire, which rings a bell in the ear of another part. This part then engages in his or her trained behaviour, opening a door to release the pain of a rape, or cutting the person's arm in a certain pattern, or pushing out a child part. So the watcher has no idea of who the other part is or what she or he does. These events can be quite complicated. You can see another example in Trish's description, above, in which Pat provided the patterns for who should be "out", the Controller flipped switches to bring certain insiders out, and some other part played the songs in the head to guide those insiders' behaviour.

Triggered behaviours can sometimes be temporarily stopped if you can speak with those responsible and get them to agree to turn off the programmes that have been triggered. In some systems, it is possible to explore the whole chain of planned events from an outside perspective so that all parts can be shown how the situation was set up. Once the insiders see how they were tricked, they can agree to stop their trained behaviours, particularly if their perpetrators are no longer in their lives.

On and off triggers include sights or sounds or touches. For example, one survivor had a habit of pushing on the fingers of her left hand with her thumb. This turned out to be the inside copy of an abuser (a child part who had been told to "be" that abuser) warning her not to talk by doing what the real abuser had done. Although many triggers are particular to the person, like that one, others are used widely. One common trigger looks like a reassuring rub on the crown of the head, to silence a child. The husband of one client of mine discovered that this calmed the client down when she was upset. He had no idea he was using a pre-installed trigger. The Satanic "horned hand" (so often used by heavy metal musicians) is a common sight trigger to identify survivors to cult members, although it is widely used by other kinds of groups, both benign and evil. Beeping sounds on the telephone, or beeping of a car horn, or wind chimes (a gift from a family member) convey particular messages, such as "go outside". Not every such sound is an intentional trigger, of course. However, if you are programmed to be triggered by something, then you will go through the paces you were taught, whether the perpetrator group did the triggering or whether the trigger was accidental, just part of everyday life.

One of my early clients compiled a catalogue of "touch triggers" and what they meant. I have discovered that many of them are familiar to other clients, including unrelated people from very different geographical locations.

I want to emphasise once more that you are not really a computer or robots or inanimate object of any kind. You are a person, or a community of persons, no matter what you were told. When someone inside responds to a trigger, it is because they were hurt in the past to make them do so, and they are living in the memory of that hurt.

Booby traps or fail-safes

Booby traps or fail-safes are dangerous internal events that are triggered to happen if the survivor investigates too much of his or her own training, and/or talks about or becomes aware of memories he or she (the front person) is not supposed to know. The effects of booby traps include such things as suicide attempts, serious self-harm, or falling into terrible depression. It is important to know that the overwhelming emotions experienced when a booby trap is set off actually belong to real, specific memories.

A booby trap can be set off without the knowledge of the main outside personality. Because of such traps, *it is very important to go very slowly in discovering what happened, if you are a survivor of this kind of abuse*. Even though parts of you are involved in setting off the booby traps, they may not know the effects of what they are doing (pushing buttons, turning switches, and so forth), and it might be difficult to anticipate what will happen.

Internal calendars with jobs to be done on certain dates

If the perpetrator group has a long-term agenda—and most ritual and political groups do—there are insiders who memorise a "calendar" which lays out the "jobs" to be done on certain dates. Regular ritual dates are part of the calendar for any ritual abuse survivor, and have been learnt by insiders in a normal everyday way, just as we learn the dates of our birthdays and Christmas. Some survivors also have parts who hold significant future dates, such as the anticipated return of Satan, or the date of the political group's planned battle to take over the world.

In addition, some groups implant personal dates, which are years in which survivors are to return to the group, integrate real-life parts with cult-loyal parts, commit suicide, or become ill. Young adult survivors are frequently let go in their twenties to create an identity in the world, then recalled to the group at a certain age in their late twenties or early thirties. During this "growing up" period, the main identity is usually unaware of the mind control or of the other internal identities. There are often internal punishments, such as a very annoying sound, spinning, or a sensation of being shocked if the person does not return to the group when he or she is supposed to. At this time, the survivor might be told that a significant family member or friend is seriously ill, forcing the survivor to return and be re-accessed. If a member has become established in a strategic position in society, then he or she will be allowed to return to that position and contact with the original cult will be maintained along with returning to, starting, or joining a cult group where the member now lives.

When an important date is near, the personality system may be trained to "turn" and bring to the front a group of insiders who have jobs connected with that date. These insiders are generally not aware of what has gone on in the world or in the body's life between this date and the last time they were "out", which might have been many years ago.

An internal structure (or structures) and/or a complex inner world where insiders live

Many ritually abusive cults deliberately divide the personality system down the middle of the head, making sure that there is no communication between the two sides. (This is not a literal physiological fact, since inside parts occupy brain circuits rather than specific sites in the brain, but it is a belief system common to ritualistic mind controllers and their victims.) "Left side" parts might be instructed to speak to no one other than the perpetrators. Although emotions might leak out from these parts, the person could go through years of therapy without the survivor or the therapist ever suspecting that they exist.

For many years, therapists and survivors have been aware of ritualistic (religious) abuser groups, but not of other groups who engage in mind control. Thus, they have tried to work with the ritual abuse, not realising other groups of insiders were present but hidden. For instance, after many years of therapy for ritual abuse, one of my clients has discovered that she not only has the left side–right side division, she has Ku Klux Klan parts hidden "beneath the ground" in the "right side" of her inner world and Nazi parts "up in the sky". Many survivors have groups of parts hidden in this way, and often these parts are only found when the survivor looks for the part that does a particular job, such as flooding the system with emotions.

When you look inside your mind, do you see an internal geometric structure or set of structures? This is a "red flag" for organised perpetrator group abuse. The insiders are mentally located in an internal structure with a particular shape. A typical structure might be shaped like an upside-down pyramid, or a prism, or a tetrahedron, or a spider web. Many MC survivors have an internal world that contains several or many structures or "worlds". There are also systems where mountains, rivers and lakes, trees, or other "natural" structures contain programmed insiders. When you search internally, the part who is searching needs to "look" and feel inside of virtually everything to see whether there is someone hidden inside.

These structures are neither random nor merely created for the purpose of organisation. They are used by perpetrating groups to locate specific inside people, and to call out specific combinations of them for certain tasks. The adults who deliberately create these structures or inner worlds do so at a stage of the child's development when the child is able to internalise things he or she sees in the outside world. They use stage settings in the real world that they want replicated in the inner world of the child's mind. Or they might use a combination of drugs and hypnosis while describing the inner world, or showing films. Often, there is both a structure and an inner world.

Very young children are often taught to create their inner world or structure. The child builds an actual, real life, physical structure, while the child's trainer explains that this structure is to be replicated inside the child's mind as a place for the parts to live. The building materials vary according to what is available at the time of building: Tinker Toys, Lego, or blocks. According to the late Stella Katz, a former trainer in a Kabbalah based cult training centre, each child's builder part was trained to build a structure with building blocks of varying colours, and to place dolls of the same colours representing the inner children in their proper places in the structure. The builder part was instructed that everyone must be kept in their places.

The structure is gradually developed and elaborated over the years. Walls between the parts or groups of parts prevent their communication. Taking down the walls will allow parts to integrate, after memories are shared, or to become co-conscious with one another if they are not ready for integration. Often the builder is supposed to take down certain walls when the survivor gets to a certain age; for example, some survivors are programmed for their everyday life parts to integrate with the cult-loyal ones, leaving out the pain holders. When this happens, the everyday life parts become "conscious", that is, they come to know that they have been involved in the cult or group, but since the pain is being held by hidden parts, the person does not realise how gruesomely they have suffered.

Knowing the nature of the structure(s) you have, if you have any, will help you discover how many insiders there are and which ones are most important to work with. It does not matter much what kind of structure or structures exist; the approach to dealing with them is still the same: explore each part of the structure and its purpose and who lives there. It is important to note that parts might not just be in an empty space within the structure, but are also the structure itself; these parts are often not aware that they are part of a living human being, because as soon as they were created they were made to believe that they were inanimate objects. See Arauna Morgan's story in Chapter Eleven for an example of this.

Outlier parts (my name for them) are located outside the structure that houses the main personality system. Their job is to keep those in the main personality system in line. They might be located in a structure separate from the main structure. For example, two of my clients programmed in Ontario had their main parts in an inverted pyramid, and their outliers in rings around the outside of the pyramid. As you have seen, survivors of ritual abuse often hear the voices of parts who appear to be demonic beings, ghosts, or other evil and generally non-human entities. (They might also purport to be other people, living or dead, or God or Jesus.) These identities give them more power over the parts who are supposed to run the system. However, they are just parts like everyone else, with a job to do; their job is to keep those in the main personality system in line.

Mind controllers encourage children to create, either instead of or in addition to a structure, a complex inner world in which the parts live. It is often based on fairy tales, stories, or films that have been shown to the child. It might have frightening places in it, some copied from the outside world (such as a pit or a torture chamber) and some created by suggestion. The trainer gives the child suggestions about the appearance of the internal world, through showing the child a picture of a tree, or a pyramid, or a house, or a box, and telling the part who is out that he or she lives, for example, in the roots of the tree, or in the upstairs bedroom of the house.

Trish Fotheringham's account in *Ritual Abuse in the 21st Century* describes the way in which she was taught to construct her inner world. In her case, an actual theatre with a stage was used, enabling the abusers to create the "stage of life". When Trish first worked on her recovery, she believed that her parts and her own imagination had created the inner world in which the insiders lived. She engaged actively with this world, going "inside" to see how each of the parts was doing and adding things to the inner world to make it more comfortable for them, such as a healing hot tub for those who were in pain. It was only after many years of therapy that she came to recognise that most of the features of the inner world had been deliberately installed by the abusers.

If your internal world is frightening, you can use your own imagination to redesign it to your liking and put the parts in safer places. The people who placed them in the first place will not know that anyone has been moved unless your reporter parts (see Chapter Nine) tell them.

A survivor of childhood trauma whose parts were not deliberately created by an organised group might also have an inside structure, but it is usually only a place for the parts to "live" inside, such as a house. One of my ritually abused clients has cult-trained parts housed in an upside-down pyramid, and abused-at-home parts living in an internal house.

Sometimes, places or structures that have been installed inside are copies of outside places, including places where abuse happened. This is true for both structured (deliberately created) and reactive (self-created) multiples, but many whose abuse was not perpetrated by an organised group have no inner world at all, and parts, when not "out", simply disappear into blackness or exercise an effect on the person's emotions without being internally visible.

In "Simplifying complex programming" on the Survivorship website, Jeannie Riseman states,

> Often the alters [parts] are arranged in complex patterns—sometimes geometric patterns (as in Cabala-based or matrix programs), sometimes patterns based on things or communities. Some people have systems that replicate an organizational structure, with a CEO, advisory boards, etc. Sometimes the pattern is more like a video game, with castles and dragons and all sorts of tricks and booby traps for the unwary.

There are some organised perpetrator groups who do not create inner structures or worlds, but still install cues to bring out different insiders to do their jobs.

Internal filing systems for memories, especially of training sessions

Many survivors of organised abuse have internal filing systems, usually with a "control room", files, a file manager or controller, and labels on the files which refer to such things as the type of training, age, and place where it was done. When you come to working with the memories, it is very important to work with the file managers. In some cases, there are "programme codes", which, when said in the right order, will make certain programmes or pieces of training cease to work.

Usually, a type of training session, or "programme", is repeated at different ages, so that by the time the person reaches adulthood, the training is well established and the conditioned response automatic. All the times this particular training was given will be noted in the internal files, as well as which insiders were involved. These files make it easy to access the memories, once you have got by the security systems and gained the co-operation of the insiders in charge of the system.

By now you might be alarmed, overwhelmed, and perhaps frightened by the complexity of all this. Do not worry; I am going to explain it all to you, and it will come to make sense gradually, particularly to those parts of you who were assigned by the abuser group to be internal leaders. Feel free to reject anything which does not apply to you; each personality system is unique. However, this chapter is focusing on the characteristics that systems set up by abuser groups have in common.

Tricks and technologies used for deception and training

The mind-controlling perpetrator groups use stage magic extensively to create non-human parts and simulate various false scenarios, such as murders or alien abductions. They wear costumes and dress children in costumes to make them believe they are demons, or animals, or robots. They put a bag of blood on top of a drugged person's body, and force a child to stab that bag, making the child believe he or she has murdered that person. Dentists numb children's tongues and then tell the children in the chair that their tongues have been cut out. Survivor therapist Arauna Morgan writes,

> The group that I was in was all about trickery . . . Resuscitation dummies, combined with drugging the children who were supposed to kill someone, cows' internal organs to simulate human

> internal organs, dye to simulate blood, pretty much anything that could be faked was faked. However, the drugs that were used knock people out, put them to sleep, cause blurred or double-vision, cause hallucinations or increased suggestibility, were real and used extensively.

I remember one of my first ritually abused clients confessing to me that for a long time she had remembered being abducted by aliens, but had not told me because she did not want me to disbelieve her other memories because of it. We worked through the "alien abduction" memory and discovered that the "spaceship" was parked in the courtyard of the cult training centre. An insider had been instructed that if the survivor began to remember the ritual abuse, she was to make her remember the alien abduction, so that nobody would believe her account of the ritual abuse. This programme did not work in this case, but you can imagine the larger consequences of such a ruse.

You might have noticed my mention of the training centre. Yes, cults have training centres; Stella Katz worked in one, which I accidentally discovered years before I knew about mind control or ritual abuse. With my family (including a furiously crying baby), I was trying to find the way to a summer camp, but we took a wrong turn. We drove down a long winding road through tall dark trees, and began to encounter strange road signs. When we came to "Trespassers will be shot", we turned back (thank goodness!) because it was beginning to feel quite frightening. Years later, Stella mentioned to me the location of the training centre, and I recognised it.

Besides stage magic props and settings, perpetrator groups use technology. Military and political groups have the most sophisticated technologies, and much training or programming is now done with virtual reality equipment. Films and holograms are used to deceive a child into believing in things that are unreal. For example, survivor Sally (see Chapters Six and Eight), as a Nazi-trained child, was shown many films of Hitler, suggesting he was alive and ready to take over the world. Her insiders did not know that he lost the war or that he committed suicide. I asked whether the films were in colour or in black and white. "Black and white, of course. All movies are black and white." I had to explain to the trained insiders that if a film is in black and white it is usually a very old one, from the time when people did not know how to make colour films.

A hierarchy of trained insiders with "jobs"

Most deliberately created personality systems are hierarchically organised. Each system has levels or layers, and each level has a boss, who reports to someone on the next higher level. There are often several parts with the same name but different functions, usually on different levels. The ones in charge usually have titles representing their authority. In military or political systems there are captains, leaders, and soldiers; ritual systems have demons, Satans, Lucifers, and high priests or priestesses, as well as representations of family members who have authority in the person's life. Each layer in a Satanic system usually includes a Satan, a few demons, a high priest or priestess, a copy of the primary trainer, and various guards. Authoritative insiders have the job of disciplining others under them for disobedience (such as talking about the abuse.) If the disciplinarian on one level fails to do its job, the discipline moves up to a higher level.

Abuser groups also place fail-safe parts outside the "layers", and these parts have the job of dealing with the problem if the ones in charge prove disloyal. They have been told they are such entities as ghosts, chameleons (who can impersonate other parts), jokers, deceivers, and spiritual guides.

Not all systems are equally complicated. Some complicated systems might have several different groups of parts, each with its own layers, trained by different perpetrator groups or for different purposes. A "criss-cross" security system might have parts from one group disciplining those from the other groups. Those in charge of the system are usually aware of what goes on in the outside world, but rarely intervene directly at first. You can talk to them; they are usually listening even if they do not speak to you.

All parts in a deliberately created system have jobs to do, and doing one's job is the most important expectation after compliance and silence. The first parts of this kind of which you are likely to become aware are the ones who punish others for disclosures. If you have frequent bodily pain or flashbacks, ask your insiders whether it is someone's job to punish you for some misbehaviour or disloyalty.

Many dissociative persons have experienced some degree of mind control, even done individually by, for example, an abusive parent. They might have internal punishers who replicate the behaviour of their abusers, even in the absence of organised group abuse, but their inside parts are less likely to refer to what they do as a "job". If you hear about your parts having assigned jobs, you are probably dealing with mind control by an organised perpetrator group.

Most insiders are created and trained in childhood. Different job training is given to each part or group of similar parts. The more complex the abuse and mind control training the child has experienced, the more complex the personality system. In this way, the perpetrator group can create the ideal sex slave, drug courier, and/or cult priest or priestess, who does not know he or she has been victimised or committed a crime, and, thus, will genuinely and convincingly claim innocence if caught. This structuring of the personality system allows perpetrator groups to continue abusing and training children without those children breaking the secret.

Abusers purposefully design systems where additional personalities are created and stored so that they can be programmed for specific uses at later dates; when these new personalities show up without memories of early abuse, the front person of the victim often believes that these personalities were created in adulthood and never looks for the intensive and complex splitting and programming of youth. In their everyday lives, child victims will be unaware that any of this has happened. Later, neither will the adult survivors.

Typically, some parts will interact with the "normal" world, and others will perform functions only for the perpetrator group as a result of being cued or "called out". Some of those can take over executive function of the body. Identity states will have no access to, or memory of, the thoughts and activities of the other states. Only those who know how to activate a particular trained identity state will be able to talk to the person in that identity state. This is one thing that differentiates such structured systems from the more organic form of multiplicity that comes from non mind-control based, albeit severe, child abuse. Sometimes, the group hides parts within other parts, and you can only get to the second part by accessing the other part. It can be quite complicated.

Many of the states, even in adults, will continue to experience themselves as young children, and believe their only choice is to remain loyal to the group in order for themselves, or others, to stay alive.

Trainees discarded by the perpetrator groups because they are rebellious or security risks often have parts who are programmed to self-destruct with drugs and alcohol and other risky behaviours. Successfully programmed survivors are reported to be highly functional in the identity states that perform cult rituals or other tasks required by their group.

Basic rules and arrangements for insiders

The internal parts (personalities) are arranged in a hierarchy, and all who were designed to be useful to the abusers have jobs. To help you understand, I have divided the kinds of jobs into three categories: organisers, enforcers, and discards.

Internal organisers

Gatekeepers and switch controllers. Most mind-controlled personality systems include gatekeeper parts, often but not always called by that title. I have encountered gatekeepers who hold back memories or permit them to surface, and gatekeepers who hold back parts, only permitting certain ones to come out into the body or to influence those out in the body. Some insiders have the job of controlling switching—that is, controlling who is "out" in the body or coming through the presenting shell person.

Higher-ups with impressive names and titles. Depending on the kind of perpetrator group, the higher-ups in the hierarchy may have different titles. In religious ritually abused systems there will be high priests or priestesses and deities such as Satan and Lucifer (and sometimes God and Jesus). In military/political systems you will find great leaders, generals, and people with specific names, such as Hitler.

Introjects (inside copies) of perpetrators are also common in personality systems that are not created by organised abuse. The internal punitive "mother" or "father" warns the child not to perform behaviours which will get the child punished by the real external mother or father, often by giving a reminder of the pain of the real parent's punishment. Leaders of organised abuser groups have capitalised on this natural phenomenon by deliberately creating (and, therefore, controlling) these copies of themselves. It is important to realise that these copies are not really identical to the perpetrators, but are child parts who were instructed to play back or imitate the sound of the perpetrators' voices.

Many perpetrators put their own stamp on to a personality system by putting "themselves" inside it. This is often done by splitting off parts during a rape, and instructing those parts that they are the perpetrator, or "born from his seed", and have to do what he does (usually, bring on the pain of that rape) if the person is disloyal. A child might be tortured until a part emerges who agrees to "be" the perpetrator in the inside world, reminding everyone inside of the pain the perpetrator gave them. In less cruel groups, a cardboard cut-out of the perpetrator is placed in the model of the internal world or structure, so that the insiders will always "see" the perpetrator. This is not an actual personality, just a trick to scare the young child parts.

File keepers and internal programmers. Training events are not only recorded by the perpetrators; an internal record is kept by trained insiders. This record contains information about each type of training, when it was given, and what signals can be used to activate or de-activate it. The insiders in charge of this tend not to know much about everyday adult life, having been kept in a place where they only saw switches or control panels.

Recyclers of memories and programmes. A recycler (or reactivator) is an insider who has been trained to keep a small piece of each training memory, so that the survivor will be unable to recover the entire memory and thereby undo the effects of training. The recycler might be given a name like Piece Keeper, Puzzle Maker, Collector, Juggler, or Key Holder, and will be instructed to do something with the pieces, which are not kept in the files with the rest of the memories.

No doubt the development of Recycling programmes was based on the observation that a partially known traumatic memory creates flashbacks more than a completely dissociated traumatic memory. Because these recycling parts exist, it is important to enlist their co-operation before you start working through the traumatic memories, especially those of training or programming events. That way, the recycling pieces can be put in with the memories the first time you work on them, and the programmes will not reappear.

"Blank slate" parts can also be stored, split off, then kept for future programming or for reinstituting a damaged programme.

Internal enforcers

Observers, recorders, and reporters. Survivors of organised abuse generally have observers or watchers inside who are trained to be aware of, and remember, everything that happens. These parts are often told that they can see everything but cannot and must not act in the outside world. They may have been taught (through trickery) to believe they are non-human, for example, aliens, or whales, or spirits. They can be very helpful in accessing memories for processing.

The observers and recorders are often the reporters who have the job of telling the person's handler what the person has said or done, or sometimes even thought. Getting them to co-operate is essential to maintaining your safety during the recovery process.

Also, look for *"floating parts"*. These are not deliberately created parts of the system, but parts that were accidentally split off at the same time as others. They may be escapees, in a way, parts who intentionally left the body when it was being harmed, and watched instead of feeling the pain. They are able to float around the system, learning everything they can, often unnoticed by the other insiders. Since the perpetrating group is unaware of them, they do not get hurt unless they get in the way accidentally or they choose to take someone's pain. They can be an incredible source of information about the system and about what has happened and of great assistance in recovery, as they have not been instructed by the abusers. Organised perpetrator groups try to find the floaters and assign them to the dump, but if the floaters are able to hide effectively, they can be the key to undoing the programming. One of my clients has one such part who calls himself "The Observer"; he detected many of the tricks which deceived the trained insiders, and when we process their memories he chimes in with his observations about what was really going on.

Threateners and punishers. The structured personality system of a mind control survivor is always protected by a security system. The observers and reporters watch any parts who are "out" in the body, and sometimes those who speak to one another internally. They report to others in the hierarchy, who then issue threats and order punishments to be administered by those parts who are trained to punish. Punishments include such things as flashbacks, flooding of unbearable emotions, painful body memories, self-harm, suicide attempts, and flooding of memories in which the survivor perpetrated against others. Each insider who punishes has his or her place in the hierarchy, and if he or she fails to do the assigned job, a backup will do it while the disloyal punisher himself experiences punishment or is banished. Parts who believe themselves to be soldiers or guards are common in mind-controlled (including ritually abused) systems, and, like real soldiers, they are trained to both obey the abusers' instructions and enforce obedience in other parts.

Spinners. Cults and mind control agencies often use physical spinning of the child, using devices such as baby scales and spinning chairs. Some survivors report having been spun on a huge catherine wheel, sometimes going in and out of water. This is also known to have been used in political torture, and has been shown in films. Spinning is not a programme. It is a means to that end. It is used very generally, in many kinds of training, just as torture and rape are.

Spinner parts, who do not themselves become dizzy, have the job of spinning internally to send out feelings or impulses to all the other parts, the main person, or a group of selected parts. Many of the "booby traps" or "fail-safe" programmes involve spinning. Often, when a programme (that is, a particular training) is in operation, the survivor feels dizzy, as though something or someone is "spinning" inside his or her head. If this is happening to you, you can speak to the spinner and ask that part to stop spinning or to slow down the spin. If this does not work, ask to speak with whoever is making the spinner part spin. This strategy, of working up through the chain of command, applies to mind control treatment recovery in general. Another tactic you can use is to ask the spinner to spin in the opposite direction, which will often put away whatever is being spun. If permitted by those in charge, a spinner can also replace whatever lesson is being spun with something positive, such as a feeling of calmness, taken from a positive memory.

For a complicated target behaviour which must not be set off by accident, some military/political mind-control groups use a sequence of parts rather than a group who are spun together. For example, some parts are trained to sing the songs on a record in the head to get out one insider after another in a sequence until the final one performs an assassination.

A dump containing discarded insiders

"*Garbage kids*" are child parts that were discarded because they either would not comply in training, or could not learn quickly enough. Often, garbage kids are hidden pain-holders, and continue to participate in some memories. If they have been "killed", they are stuck in the memory of being unconscious, and have not actually been destroyed. I believe that it is important to find these parts, and process their part of any traumatic memories that need to be worked with. Often, they have the most resistance to the perpetrators, and can become helpful allies in healing. However, they have usually been severely traumatised. Sally (see Chapters Six and Eight) refers to her dump of discarded parts as "the blue pile". The pile is blue because these inner children are black and blue with bruises. As long as your garbage kids remain hidden, the trauma cannot be worked through thoroughly, because their parts of the memories are missing. The training of the other parts will still have some power in your life, even if you are working hard to resist the pull of the abusers' instructions. Survivor therapist Arauna Morgan says, "To me, these parts are pure gold: they are the ones that the cult could not tolerate and so are the best ones to help the person break free."

These are the primary characteristics I have seen in personality systems created by organised mind controllers. I know it looks complicated, but actually its organisation makes it possible for the survivor to find an organised route to healing, since so many things about it are predictable. In the next chapters, we shall look at how you can work with your structured personality system towards recovery.

Exercise 5. Symptoms of a structured personality system

You might or might not be aware of the following indicators of mind control within your personality system. The more of these you agree with, the more likely it is that you are a survivor of mind control. As with other diagnostic questionnaires, a "yes" to one of these questions means very little, but if you say yes to most of them, it might indicate that you have a structured (mind-controlled) personality system.

Caution: For some survivors, just thinking about some of these questions could trigger insiders to do the jobs the questions represent. Please do your best to make sure that all your parts know that you are only imagining responses to these questions; these things are not actually happening, so no one inside you has to take action.

- Do you sometimes feel empty, as if you have nothing inside? And at other times, have differing sets of emotions and beliefs? Is it possible that you (the front person) are a shell through which other parts operate?
- Are there sights, sounds, or touches to which you have immediate, strong reactions which you cannot stop? If so, what are they? Could they be cues for trained behaviours?
- Have you had a strong impulse to do something such as return home to your family at a particular time, even if they live far away?
- Have you suddenly fallen into a strong suicidal depression without knowing why? If so, ask your insiders (by thinking to them) what it is about, and whether it could be a booby trap.
- Are there certain dates which trigger fear in you? If so, what are they? Do you know why? Do they match any regular or cult holidays, or family birthdays?
- Do you feel as if your head has a division between the right and left sides?

The part of you who lives your everyday life should only be permitted to do the rest of this exercise when your inside parts are ready to let that part have hidden information. If you are a mind control survivor and your front person explores these questions too soon, it could trigger some strong conditioned reactions from trained insiders.

However, if you are not ready for the front person to find out these things, perhaps one of the parts in charge would like to take over and ask these questions to the rest of the system. Mind-controlling abusers hide a lot of information from the parts who believe themselves to be in charge, and the parts put in charge do have a right to know what has been hidden from them.

(continued)

- Where do your inside parts live? Is there a structure of some kind where they are located? If so, what does it look like?
- Do you have an inner world where your parts live, and can you explore it, or can insiders draw parts of it?
- How are your traumatic memories stored? Are there files? Who is in charge of those files? Are there inside people such as file keepers and librarians?
- Are there internal programmers who keep the records of the programmes and turn them on or off or down low in response to triggers?
- Are there gatekeepers inside who keep the insiders in their places, or control who is "out" in the body?
- Is there anyone inside who has the job of keeping a piece of each memory separate from the rest of it (so that if you recall the memory this piece will not be included, and the programme it controls will continue to function)?
- Do you have flashbacks which could involve technology, such as virtual reality or an electrified chair or a helmet?
- Do you have memories which appear to be impossible, such as alien abductions?
- Do some of your insiders have jobs?
- Is there a hierarchy inside (parts having bosses and underlings)? Do some of your insiders have titles connected with their place in the hierarchy?
- Do you "see" the perpetrators of your abuse (if you remember any of it) in your inside world? If so, do their actions seem to be flashbacks of what they did in the past, or new actions? Or do they just stand still and look scary?
- Do you have inside parts who believe they are other real people in the outside world?
- Is there anyone inside who has the job of watching everything you do and say, and reporting it to an outside person?
- Do you have secret parts who watch everything but are not controlled by people who hurt you? (Do not ask them to identify themselves, or they will not answer.)
- Do you hear threats of punishment in your head for disclosing secrets?
- Do you have insiders who believe they are computers or machines? What are their jobs?
- Do you have insiders who believe they are animals? What are their jobs?
- Do you have insiders who believe they are demons, devils, Satan, Lucifer, or other such entities? What are their jobs?
- Do you have insiders who believe they are structures, such as buildings or bridges, etc., or who believe they are features of the internal landscape, like trees, mountains, lakes, or rivers?
- Do you have insiders who are underground and hidden in your internal landscape?
- Do you have insiders who believe they are wired to bombs and/or booby traps?
- Do you sometimes get a sense of spinning and vertigo, combined with some other symptom such as a strong feeling or belief or flashback?
- Is there an inside place where "garbage kids" or others who would not obey abusers are kept?

CHAPTER FIVE

Indoctrination

The most obvious evidence of mind control is the existence of insiders who believe what they were indoctrinated to believe. This is central to understanding mind control, and to no longer being controlled by the abusers. If you have experienced mind control, you, or many of your insiders, believe things that the mind controllers want you to believe.

In this chapter, we will look at the basic beliefs and the deceptions involved. In subsequent chapters we shall look at specific lies which mind-controlling abusers use to maintain control over their trainees. Encourage your higher-ups to read this section even if the adult who handles the outside world does not.

Psychologist and lawyer Steve Frankel read this chapter and responded, "Abusers have two goals: (1) to do whatever they want (to hurt children) and (2) to get away with it." All the deceptions are for the purpose of these goals.

The most important thing for you to know is that the foundation of the mind control created in children, whether by cults, military or government groups, or organised criminal groups which use children as sexual slaves, is one of carefully designed and meticulously executed deceptions. Mind control is produced through a combination of hypnotic suggestion, drugs, torture, threats, and double binds (choices where there is no good option).

If you are a survivor, members of the abuser group created false beliefs in your insiders while you were a child through staged scenarios, films and videos, stories, pictures, costumes, puppets, and other techniques of "stage magic". Many of your insiders remained children even while your outside person grew up, and those children continue to hold the beliefs implanted in them in childhood through this trickery. Any parts you might have that were fooled should not feel bad about this, because all the trickery was only done after torture that even strong grown men have been unable to resist; you were only a child when this happened and the trauma from that torture is why those parts of you stop getting older and stay "stuck" at that age, and often still believe themselves to be with the abusers in the places where the abuse occurred.

Some of those beliefs (such as that the abusers always know where you are) might have been actually true in childhood, but are no longer true. Others were never true. The indoctrination of mind control consists of lies reinforced by tricks. But when you were a child you did not know that these were lies and tricks, and probably most of your insiders still do not know that. The emotions resulting from these experiences are just as strong now as they were in childhood.

The most crucial lies are those that create lifelong obedience and loyalty in every survivor, and those that maintain the secrecy and security of the perpetrator group. Other lies are told to get inside parts to do their "jobs". Even your ability to accept the truth of your life is affected by this training or "programming".

Each of your deliberately created insiders began at a certain age, when he or she was split from a previously existing insider through torture. The programmers might have permitted some parts to grow up with the body, but they provided most parts with their own torture/traumas, which made those parts stop maturing. They have been unable to grow up since then, and remain at that age. Each insider has a "start" point and a "stop" point at which he or she stopped growing. The abuser groups know this because they created it deliberately.

Abusers tell parts of different ages lies that are believable for children of those ages. So, for instance, four-year-olds will be told about the "magic" powers of the group members, and will see these demonstrated; eleven-year-olds could be told about the extensive power of the group to infiltrate every organisation, spy on everyone, and use sophisticated technology that has not yet been released to the general public. Both these lies serve the purpose of causing the child, and, later, the adult survivor, to believe there is no way to escape the perpetrator group. An adult survivor might have many different parts who believe the lies they were told at the ages when they were trained.

The fact that there are parts (front personalities) who live most of their daily lives and function socially in the outside world, parts who often do not know of the beliefs, training, or even the existence of the other parts, allows for the lies and tricks to be effective. In my experience with survivor clients trained by different groups, I have found that there are many lies and tricks that might be called "standard".

Before I tell you the kind of things these abuser groups tell children, perhaps you would like to ask your own insiders what they were told, and what they believe. Then you can compare your own answers to what I have heard from other survivors.

Exercise 6. *What your insiders were taught*

Ask your insiders each of these questions. You may receive more than one answer, since many survivors have been involved with more than one group.

Do your insiders think or know that a group created and trained them? What do they believe about the group who trained them? What were they told? How is this group different from any other group in society?

Do your insiders believe the group's teachings were right, or superior to what your front person may have heard elsewhere? If so, why?

Do your insiders believe they can trust the group? Why?

(continued)

Do your insiders believe that the group did things for their (the insiders') own good? Did the group hurt them for their own good? What were your insiders told about this?

What were your insiders told about people who are not part of the group? Whst do they believe?

What do your insiders believe will happen if they talk to anyone outside the group about what occurred or occurs in the group?

How important is obedience to the group, according to your insiders?

What were your inner children told about being good?

How important is loyalty, according to your insiders?

Do you have insiders who had to make vows of loyalty, or sign agreements?

What do your insiders believe they should do if they are disloyal.

What do they believe will happen to them if they are disloyal?

Do you have insiders who believe their only purpose in life is to do the jobs the group gave them?

What do they believe about the group's power in the world? What were they told about this?

Do your insiders believe your abusers can locate you through magic or prayer or sophisticated technology and can know what you say or think? (Note: such sophisticated technology might be available now, but it was not at the time most survivors were abused and trained.)

Do you have soldiers inside? If so, what is their duty?

How old are the insiders who believe they are soldiers? What kind of training did they go through?

Do you have robots inside? If so, what is their duty?

What were your insiders told about thinking for themselves?

What were your system leaders taught to believe? What would they need to know in order to agree to work towards healing and freedom?

Teachings about the abusers' correctness, superiority, and wisdom

Right, now that you have given your own private answers to the questions, I will tell you what I have learned from survivors about the teaching of the groups within which they grew up.

Here is what these groups tell children. The words are slightly different depending on which group is saying them and what they are doing to the children. Compare these statements to what you wrote.

"Our way (the way of the Family, or the Luciferians, or the Third Reich, or the Illuminati, or Satan, or the white American way of life—or whoever the group that trained you was) is the only right way. Our leader (or our deity) deserves your complete obedience and loyalty."

"You can trust us because we are your family and we act in your best interests. You can't trust anyone else."

"We do these things for your own good. Taking pain without crying makes you strong. Harming or killing inferior beings gives you power. All this training makes you one of us and permits you to rise to the top."

Do your insiders believe things like this? Often children believe things that adults say, because adults are supposed to know better than children. And the adults who say these things may themselves truly believe them. But that does not make what they say true.

Methods of indoctrination

If these are the beliefs of some of your young insiders, what was done to force the abusers' belief system into their minds? Intense, abusive, religious or military indoctrination. These beliefs were hammered into each part of your young mind over and over, through religious ceremonies, military drills, songs and chants and rhymes, severe punishments, and rewards for compliance or memorising the correct beliefs. You may have been forced or coerced into making vows of loyalty and signing official documents, sometimes in blood, swearing allegiance to the group.

At night or during breaks from real school, you might have attended special schools or camps run by the abuser group. If you were part of a military-style group, you may have been dressed up as a soldier, given weapons, and made to engage in military exercises. If you were in a religious group, you would have taken part in rituals and were taught how to kill and dissect sacrifices. You may have been trained in the various kinds of sexual behaviours desired by the group, especially if organised crime was involved and you were used for prostitution and/or pornography. You might have been trained and used by more than one group, since many of these groups are connected and use the same children.

Obedience, loyalty, and betrayal

Again, here is what the group leaders might have told you about *obedience*. They tell different things to different insiders in the same body. See whether what you wrote down about obedience is similar to these abuser statements:

"You're good if you obey us, and you're bad if you disobey us."

"You have to be loyal and obedient to us, because you made vows or promises to be loyal."

"If you disobey us, someone you love or another kid or a pet will be punished or will die, and it will be your fault."

These statements twist the meaning of words. I believe that every child has an innate sense of what is good—kindness to all living creatures. But "good" to the abuser groups means doing what they tell you to do, even if it is harming or killing another living being.

It is not surprising that they say obedience is good, since for many years Western society believed children are supposed to be obedient to their parents, who know better than they do. But persons whose beliefs and life goals are dedicated to harmful values will try to make their children adopt those beliefs and their lifestyle. It is obedience that has enabled dictators in many countries to exercise power over the people, and made them fight to keep those dictators in power, even when those rulers clearly did not have the best interests of the people at heart. When children are taught to obey, they can be manipulated easily by bad bosses and rulers when they grow up. So, parenting experts now recommend that children be taught to think for themselves and develop their own values rather than obey adults without question. (I consider myself a parenting expert, as parent education was my earliest speciality, and I have co-authored two books on parenting—see the References section.)

Within the personality system of a child being trained and/or abused in a mind-controlling group, there is a hierarchy, and lower-down insiders (usually younger) are told to obey the higher-ups. Adults in these groups tell the higher-ups (those insiders they have put in charge of the others), "You must always make the others obey, and punish them if they disobey, or we will find you and punish you severely." They tell them, "If you do as you're told, you'll rise to be the highest members of the coven or to be generals in the army." And they give them "promotions" to make them feel important.

Loyalty is a rather strange value. It has been used by military organisations, companies, schools, and various other institutions to get people associated with them or in their employ to put the organisation first. But, in my opinion, it has been misused. Yes, it is important not to sell out your friends for money, and when a person has treated you with kindness and respect they deserve the same back. But this is earned loyalty.

In team sports, it helps a team to have loyal fans who cheer for them. But experiments show that people assigned to different teams who are rivals will quickly come to believe that their team is superior to the other team, even though they did not choose the team in the first place. When you were a child, you did not choose your parents. You did not choose the groups to which your parents belonged. They have not earned your loyalty unless they treated you, all parts of you, with kindness and respect.

I have frequently heard of mind control groups punishing "traitors". What is a traitor? Someone who is disloyal, or someone who betrays. Someone who belongs to one side in a war, but sells secrets to, or spies for, the other side. If you are a traitor to your country, you are helping a country who wants to harm your country. But all this assumes there is a war, and there are the good guys and the enemies, and if you choose to belong elsewhere you are betraying your side.

Children in perpetrator groups do not get to choose sides, unless it is a false choice to give them the illusion of choice. For example, a little girl was placed between two groups of people, one in hooded black robes and the other in ordinary clothes. She chose the ordinary looking ones, and they abused her. She was given the choice again, and this time she chose the robed ones. She chose them only to avoid being hurt, not because she truly believed that they were good people. Of course, both groups of people were really part of the larger perpetrator group.

Perpetrator groups talk a lot to children about loyalty and about traitors.

"If you fight back against us you are a traitor and will be punished."

"Traitors deserve punishment [by the rape or torture or even death of themselves or others]."

Punishment and reward

Note: Some of these examples might be triggering, in terms of bringing up unpleasant memories, so your system needs to prepare to put memories away as soon as they come up. (See Chapter Ten about triggering.)

Children being shaped to a group's beliefs are punished for minor mistakes. Children have to watch a supposed "traitor" being tortured or apparently killed in a particular way, and are told this will happen to them if they become traitors. They are given a sample of what this feels like, such as being stretched on a rack, or severely electroshocked. This is very terrifying, especially if the "traitor" suffers a great deal.

One survivor wrote, "We were severely raped, over and over for any infractions. We were held underwater in the river until we desperately struggled to get loose to breathe, then raped again. We were electrocuted then raped again. If we still resisted we were told that our whole family would be killed and with the earlier punishment, this was very believable. This treatment started at FIVE YEARS OLD."

Those parts of a child who will become the higher-ups are also rewarded for doing what they are told. Simple rewards are candy or sweets, drugs, and pleasurable sex. Children are also rewarded by being allowed to harm someone else instead of being harmed themselves. For some children, this is a reward, but some experience it as worse punishment. When they obey, they gain the respect instead of the disdain of the community, although there is still disdain because they caved in, could not take the punishment, and chose to punish others instead. They are given "promotions" in the cult or the military organisation, with stripes, or rings, or medals, or some kind of token of the increased status. Of course, this is all fake, but the children do not know it. They are told they can rise to be the highest members of the coven, or to be generals in the army.

So, if you have insiders who (at least when questioned by group members) demonstrate unquestioning loyalty and obedience to the group, this is a sign that you have experienced mind control. Groups that are not involved in mind control do not demand such loyalty and obedience, and do not indoctrinate so brutally.

The power of the group

Perpetrator groups lie to children about their power. They tell children such things as "We can kill you or take you away at any time and no outsider can stop it from happening, because we have infinite power." When children are small, and large adults have power over them, and especially when parents are involved, it is easy to see that these adults can actually do such things. But when the children have grown up, the situation is different. The trainers know that children will grow up and move away, and they do not have infinite power and resources to track them down. (Chapter Nine, on "Safety", will go into more detail regarding this.) They also have to be careful not to alert the authorities. So, their power in survivors' lives is much more limited. Therefore, they make sure that all the child parts inside each survivor continue to believe in the group's infinite power.

The adult parts in you need to let the inside children know that the group does not really have infinite power. Abusers have jobs and families like anyone else; their resources are not unlimited, and they do not have the time to track people down. In the chapter on "Safety", we shall look at what they actually do to keep survivors connected with them. It is not magic; it is mind control. They actually rely on the survivor's trained insiders to keep in touch with them.

Soldier training

Many mind-controlling perpetrator groups, including even the religious ones, find it useful to create insiders who believe themselves to be soldiers. They are usually children, of various ages.

In regular life, all armies exert some degree of mind control over their soldiers, because their commanders need bodies willing to go to battle and obey without question. Foot soldiers have been called "cannon fodder" because they fight and even die for the goals laid out by the people in power, regardless of whether those people are good people trying to stop a vicious dictator or evil people seeking to dominate the world and acquire land and property. In regular societies, people are not allowed to join armies until they reach a certain age. Children are not allowed to become soldiers. The Lord's Resistance Army in Africa has been condemned by all societies because it forces children to be soldiers.

To make children believe they are soldiers, abuser groups dress them up in uniforms, and uniformed adults who call themselves generals, or commanders, or captains use their power, their size, and their loud voices to frighten the children and make them obey. The children are forced to engage in training just like adult soldiers, often with weapons. In some of these exercises, they believe they are killing enemies; in others, they are instructed to pretend to be killed. They might have to fight one another. If you have insiders who believe they are soldiers, this is what they might have gone through.

The "generals" make the children watch films of soldiers marching or fighting. They talk about pride in fighting for their glorious cause, and dying for it. They give fake promotions. They shout at the children and tell them to obey and not think for themselves. They punish severely those who cry, vomit, show fear or sadness, or show compassion for others who are being hurt.

Soldier children are taught "You are a soldier and your duty is to obey without thinking. Don't think, just act. It's wrong to think." If you have soldier insiders, they were taught to despise weakness, which includes emotionality, fear, sadness, loneliness, nausea, disgust, or any other human feelings. In particular, they are not to show empathy for animals or people being tortured or killed. Hidden parts hold all these emotions and sensations for them, because the soldiers are punished severely if they show humanity.

Child parts, especially those who have been designated "soldiers" by the perpetrator group, are fed many lies regarding those they are to harm or kill. These are similar to those lies taught to actual adult soldiers in training, told because it is not natural for any person to harm or kill another human being. You might have been told that the people you were hurting were subhuman, or did not feel anything, or were just inferior animals, or were dangerous enemies who must be exterminated or they would pollute the whole world. Children believe what adults tell them, and even though your whole insides revolted against the actions, the insiders who did these things might have believed they were doing it for a greater good. Parts who have to do these things are often given contracts to sign, in blood, to prove their loyalty to the group, who are presented as righteous and good.

Military/political groups train their little assassins using standard military indoctrination and training, praising children for being skilled "soldiers". However, these children are generally tortured to produce these soldier insiders, who are then forced to commit acts of extreme cruelty. We can see this kind of training in the Ugandan "Lord's Resistance Army", known to engage in both mind control and ritual abuse, though these terms are not always used in news reports. Much of soldier training is about dehumanising the enemy as "inferior" and "deserving to die", and about being "tough" and not showing feelings such as nausea, sadness, and empathy while harming others.

Similar training is given to those children in religious cults who have to do the killing and dissection of the sacrifices.

These are not real soldiers or priests; these are *children* who have been deceived into believing they are adults doing important jobs. What they have been through is heartbreaking—and they themselves are not allowed to experience their own heartbreak; it has to be hidden inside. If you have parts like these, treat them with compassion, no matter how tough they seem to be. Their hearts *are* broken, and often they have other parts within them who hold their pain.

When it comes time to look at their memories, do not forget the hidden ones, often "garbage kids", who hold the feelings. For every "tough" insider, there are usually several feeling-holders, some of them children who refused to obey and were punished, others parts who feel strong emotions or horrible physical sensations which could not be shown by the visible part. They have never been thanked for their work or relieved of their suffering.

You might want to take a moment now and notice how your insiders are feeling, both the "tough" ones and the ones who hold the different kinds of pain for them, as you read this.

Non-human insiders

Sometimes parts (originally, actual small-bodied children) are taught that they are not human at all. They may be *robots or computers*, not permitted to have any feelings. Or sex machines, or killing machines, that just perform their functions without any emotions. But they are actually parts of a human brain, and, as with the soldiers, other parts hold the feelings for them. Sometimes, robotic parts are only fragments, not full-fledged insiders; they understand very little. A fragment is an internal part that is split off through trauma and has only one small piece of life experience and perhaps a skill it learned during that experience, such as a particular sexual behaviour or use of a particular weapon.

Animal parts, who are usually young children, are used for jobs similar to the abilities of the animals they believe they are. Dogs keep watch at rituals or come when called. Cats sneak out at night.

Demons and beast parts are very young children who are led to believe they are entirely evil and are therefore not loveable by anyone except Satan. They also believe they are very ugly so that anyone from outside will be afraid of them. They are given the job of frightening other internal children.

Aliens, ghosts, spirits, and deities are parts whose job is to keep the higher-ups in line. Because these parts typically believe they do not belong to the body, they do not feel the body's pain because they are created while the child is under the influence of a strong pain-killing drug. This makes them very useful to the perpetrator group when the person requires punishment, such as self-harm or suicide attempts. They might have been taught that they will live on if the body dies, since they think either that their "internal bodies" are the real ones, or that they do not have bodies at all. The following is my own story.

The Woo-Woo Kids

My client left me a message: "I went to bed really early and woke up at 12.45 a.m. and can't get out of my head. I keep replaying everyone I know who is dead and they are taunting me, telling me that I'm making it all up and they are watching me and know that I'm a liar." She managed to calm herself with medication until our next appointment.

I know this client pretty well, and we have worked through much of her training and abuse memories. So I did as I usually do with her. I requested that the client ask High Priestess 9, who was the main insider in charge of the system, whether she knew who inside was making my client hear these voices. I was assuming that the voices were neither real dead people nor memory fragments, but something some insider had been trained to do.

The reply was that High Priestess 9 was also affected by hearing the voices of the dead, as was Satan 9. It had taken me about a year to work my way up to High Priestess 9 and convince her that I wanted to work with her, rather than against her. The left side of this client's system had nine layers, and each one had a high priestess, a Satan, and a number of deliberately created parts.

I remembered a group of three parts I had worked with about a year ago, the Big High Satan and two others called the Entities. This little group functioned to keep the parts in charge of the system in check by frightening them, Big High Satan frightening the rulers on Level 9, and the Entities in turn frightening him. It had taken some convincing for this client's system to let me actually meet the "Big High Satan". Didn't I know he was the real Satan, implanted in her at a ritual? The parts knew by now that all the other Satans from ages three to twelve were just inside parts like them. But this one was the *real thing*. That was in line with what many survivors and therapists believe, that somehow real demonic entities are attached to the personalities within a ritual abuse survivor.

I reminded my client that little Satan One had thought Satan Two was the real Satan, and Satan Eight had thought Satan Nine was the real Satan, and so on. Why should this new situation be any different? And, sure enough, it was not. The Big High Satan, who was all of eleven years old, boasted about how he was the one *really* in charge. The system had worked through some of his memories, and he became, for the most part, a co-operative part of the system.

I thought, "This new problem sounded as if it might originate with our young Big High Satan." So I asked to speak to him. He came out. "I'm the only one who can make those voices," he bragged. I asked why he was doing it. He said it was because Stan was telling him to.

The problem with this was that Stan was not a part. He was an actual high priest and the uncle who had abused my client. And he had died of cancer several years ago.

I asked the Big High Satan whether he thought anyone inside could be impersonating Stan, since he himself was impersonating several different dead people. He was indignant. No, he was the one really in charge, and he was the only one who could do the voices realistically. I reminded him that the Entities had been split off from him in order to control him, just as he was supposed to control the rest of the system. Oh, yeah, then, he guessed it could be them. I asked him to check it out. He reported that he heard laughter. They were laughing about how they had fooled him.

Then we all laughed together about how Big High Satan went "Woo woo" and scared the rest of the system, and how the Entities had done the same thing to him. We decided to call them "the Woo Woo Kids" from then on.

Although cults in particular take great pains to convince certain deliberately created parts, like the "Woo Woo Kids", that they are non-human or demonic entities, they are not. They are all insiders like everyone else.

If abusers want to teach you as a child that you are really a killing machine or a robot, they put you in a position where you lack control over your own body (for example, because of a paralysing drug, or strong arms moving your arms, or electroshock making your body jerk). Your body is made to perform the actions the group wants even against your will. After this training, those parts continue to believe they cannot choose what they do, even when it is no longer true.

Stella Katz, a former Kabbalah programmer, wrote about the creation of demon and animal parts in the training centre where she worked.

Warning: this account is very graphic.

Stella Katz: "How non-human parts are made"

It is important to remember that not all of what is seen or believed by members of these groups is real. For instance, you know there are alters who believe they are cats or dogs or snakes or demons, although you also know they cannot possibly be real. But to the alter, they are as real as you or me. Tricks, technology and "stage magic" are used to deceive the child. These are regarded as legitimate parts of magik . . .

For demon and animal alter creation, puppets are used to simulate demons. The puppets are operated from above, and some are spiked. Some are hand puppets; others are on strings and fly in the air. They come at the child, who then gets a shock. The child is strapped down and wired. Probes are used to create pain. Some demons appear to fly right through and inside the child. This is done in an empty room with white walls on which the demon pictures can be projected. Finally, the "Granddaddy of All Demons", a man or teenage boy in a costume, rapes the child. Little girls are raped anally as well as vaginally. Little boys are raped anally while the penis is manipulated, and then they are raped orally. The rapist is using a drug which maintains his erection.

This takes place during a long session, lasting through the night. More than one perpetrator is present. One operates the puppets. The trainer does all the vocalisations—making demon sounds, and giving each demon a name and a job. As many demons and animals are made as possible, from two to twelve.

After the rape, while still heavily drugged, the child is decorated with theatrical makeup and corresponding tail and horns. When he or she "comes around", the child alter is told that it is a puppy, pussycat, or snake, or a demon, gargoyle, or devil. The alter might be a demon in the shape of an animal, or just an animal. The child is shown a small "mirror" that is painted with the image of an animal or a demon, and told that it is them.

For example, the "cats" are kept in a dark room, until their eyes become accustomed to the darkness. Objects are coated with neon paint. The children are then told that cats can see in the dark. A black light is turned on, and the objects glow in the dark, making the children believe they can see in the dark like cats do. When the child has been shown that he or she is a demon, an image of fire is projected on to a screen hidden behind a wall of smoke. The smoke has been created by dry black ice that has a red lamp shining on it. These children are told the fire will not burn them because they are from hell. In their drugged state, they are walked through what they perceive as fire. "Snake" children are bound with gauze and plastic wrap so they cannot move their arms or legs, then are placed on the ground and told to slither like a snake.

The purpose of the demon alters is to keep the child in line and in constant fear of being grabbed and harmed by a demon. They represent actual demons, just as idols may represent deities in the Hindu faith. A total of thirteen demons are wanted, including the original one, and six animals. The job of demons is to come up during rituals and during times of potential disloyalty. If the child is about to disclose something to an outsider, a demon will come up and scare him, so as to ensure compliance. The demons are set up in a hierarchy. They are given names of actual demons. Animal alters are used for purposes consonant with that animal's nature, such as a cat for going through the bushes at night. The large animals, such as dogs, are also used for sexual intercourse with real animals. The child usually gets to pick their own animal names.

None of the children who are programmed to believe they have animal or demon alters are beyond the age of five years. This appears to be the best age in which to create these kinds of illusions. The group will be very careful to maintain the age of these alters. Beyond that age they would tend to question, and the illusion would be broken. If you come across a cat or dog or snake or demon . . . remember that it is not likely to be more than five years old.

* * *

So, approach your non-human insiders as you would any other insider. Get to know them, ask their ages, ask about their jobs, help them achieve and maintain present-day safety, and eventually you will be able to work with them in the recovery process.

Trainers say to the insiders, "You were created only to do the job we gave you, and if you don't do it you won't exist any more." This is a lie. Everyone inside is a part of a greater whole, split off and separated in childhood. Everyone inside contains real human emotions and needs and abilities. As you reclaim them for your own purpose rather than that of the abuser group, you will become stronger and more whole.

Trainers also say, "All you inside people must stay in your places in the inner world (or structure)." This is simply for the convenience of them finding the parts they want. It does not benefit you. There might, of course, be chaos, if everyone inside moved out of their allotted places at the same time. But if you choose to alter your inner world to make it a comfortable living space for your insiders, and then move them gradually into better places, it will benefit you. We shall talk more about this in Chapter Twelve.

In later chapters, I shall address some of the more specific types of indoctrination, about such topics as the group knowing where you are and what you say, about your being evil, about people outside the group, especially professionals, being dangerous to you, and about what you have to do to prove your loyalty.

Different lies for different parts

One of the things that mind-controlling groups do is tell different things to different groups of insiders. So, even though you all share the same body and live in the same head, some of you were told that your body is a girl, and others that it is a boy. Girl insiders receive different training from boy parts. Some parts might have been told they are not human, are immortal, and can never die, but they do live in the same body with the rest of you. Some parts were dressed up in costumes, or shown "mirrors", which were actually pictures, to make them believe they were adults, or midgets, or animals, or non-human beings.

The way you can find out the truth about your life is through internal sharing, finding out what different insiders experienced and were told. Then you can make up your own mind(s).

Look again at your answers to Exercise 6, about what the abusers taught you. What do you now think about these things? Would it help you to take the questionnaire again?

Regaining your own mind

I believe strongly that your mind is your own, and that no one, whether they are your actual family, your cult "family", your country's military or intelligence service, or your "owners", has the right to dictate what you believe and what you do. In order to take your own mind back, you need to discover what is in it, what experiences your different parts have had and what those experiences have made them believe about life and about you. Then, between all of your parts, you can form an identity which was not programmed for you in childhood, but is your own chosen path in life.

CHAPTER SIX

Sally from three perspectives

In order to help you understand the varying perspectives of the different parts inside a survivor of mind control and ritual abuse, I asked Sally to tell the story of three years of her life from three perspectives: that of the adult, Sally, that of the younger insiders ("the Kids"), and that of the higher-ups inside her. This story is in their words. You will notice that the insiders refer to Sally as "Old Lady" rather than by her name. Perhaps some of your own insiders have had the experience of looking in a mirror and being shocked to see an adult man or woman there.

A note from me: Sally's higher-ups use the word "programmes". It is the word the abuser groups used to describe the specific kinds of trainings they gave to her insiders. Some mind-controlling perpetrator groups see the mind as a kind of computer in which they can place programmes. What they actually do is train inside children to obey particular instructions, using behavioural conditioning and torture and hypnosis. These are the insiders' "jobs". Sometimes, there are internal "switches" in the inner world which insiders (internal "programmers") use to turn programmes on or off. When a programme is turned on, the insiders with that particular training do their jobs. (I have put their descriptions of the programmes and their purposes in endnotes to this chapter, so that explanations will not interrupt the flow of ideas.)

Sally and her insiders also use the word "littles" to refer to the younger insiders. This word will be familiar to those of you who are involved in online support groups and websites.

Sally

In my mid-thirties, I took a leave of absence from my place of work and moved across the continent to attend university with the idea of graduating and applying for another position within my place of employment. Aside from the ongoing memories of being molested by an "uncle" during childhood, I had forgotten about being raped and tortured by a female room-mate nine years earlier, and had no conscious memories of surviving ritual abuse/torture and mind control. I had told my father when I was ten about my uncle's abuse, and I believed it had stopped at that point, as my family had ended the connection with that "uncle." This uncle was actually a major leader of the group who abused me throughout my childhood, including after the disclosure.

The stress of trying to complete a fast-tracked university programme within a year without any family support triggered me into a self-destructive lifestyle. I was a "Christian" who feared God and eternal damnation, so, during the early spring of that year, I chose to abuse alcohol on a daily basis instead of committing the unforgivable sin of suicide. This triggered the emergence of PTSD symptoms: I became distant, anxious, hyper-vigilant, enraged inside, depriving myself of sleep. I experienced continuous nightmares and flashbacks relating to an experience of rape and torture by a female room-mate as well as incest. I kept seeing "snapshots" of my father, uncle, mother, and aunt.

By the next summer, my erratic behaviour caught the attention of the campus security guards. Their concern for my safety increased when they searched my dorm room and found evidence (piles of empty beer cans, dark notes) of suicidal behaviour. They called the police, who said I could either go with them or with a counsellor. I feared what would happen to me if the police took me, so I chose to go with the counsellor instead.

Once I was packed, the counsellor drove me to a government-funded transition house. I was allowed to stay there for ninety days while attending AA meetings and a twenty-day course of treatment for women. My family would not let me return home when I fell apart and failed my courses, so I had to quit university, leave the dorm, and go on social assistance while getting treatment. I was ashamed of getting myself into this predicament. I almost wished I had succeeded in killing myself via a more immediate means, such as hanging, stabbing, or drowning. I hate making a fool out of myself, especially in public. I couldn't move out of the university dorm fast enough. I was also still in shock that my entire family had abandoned me—especially my mother. I was always loyal to her, and had been there for her 24/7. I couldn't believe she had betrayed me like this!

I was diagnosed with PTSD and depression. For two years a newly certified counsellor tried to help me work through emerging body memories of being tortured and raped by a woman when I was a young adult. I was always anxious before seeing her. She was nice and caring, but did not have much confidence and was not sure how professional she was supposed to be yet with her clients. I could see her being warm and understanding and then there would be a shift in her attitude, and she would become more professional in her stance and the words she used.

Whenever I went to take the bus to see her, my right leg would start to shake uncontrollably. It would start again when I sat down in her office. My upper body would tense up, my head would suddenly turn towards the left, my whole body would shoot back towards the back of the chair, and my head would hit the wall behind me. I didn't know what was going on. It all happened within seconds. I would lose my vision and then come to, drained and exhausted, either leaning to one side of the chair or on the floor near her desk. I could not comprehend anything the counsellor said to me until she helped me to ground myself by looking at five different objects in her room and/or feeling my feet flat on the floor and/or standing up for a few minutes to reorientate myself. Every session was basically the same, going through body memories without understanding them.

I signed up for three correspondence courses. At first, I was managing all three fairly well. Signs of a learning disability began to emerge, but I shrugged it off. Then it became more and more difficult to comprehend, process, and articulate information for my courses. I had to write and rewrite what I was reading so that I could retain the information for exam time. However, when exam time came, I was not able to understand the questions on the exam, and I couldn't organise or articulate my thoughts. Sometimes I would go into a trance-like state and just stare at the paper until a sudden noise or something triggered me out of it again. I barely managed to complete the courses.

Then I went back to university, but attending school on campus became increasingly difficult for me. I felt like a freak. I was afraid of being asked a question or participating in group work because sometimes a student's or a professor's voice sounded garbled to me and I could not make sense of it. Or, even though I understood the question, I began to talk like someone having a stroke. Sometimes the content of the course (sociology of religion, criminology, psychology, social issues) would trigger flashbacks of being molested, raped, killings, and fires. The campus psychologist referred me to a psychotherapist.

For seven years, the psychotherapist tried everything she knew to help me heal and do well, but she became literally exhausted. My insiders increasingly harassed her and the counsellors at the university. In the therapy office, we would hit our head, and she would get mad at us, and yell at us to stop. I started drinking heavily again, and had constant thoughts of suicide. I used to hit myself in the head a lot, or take scissors to the stomach or punch/cut the left arm. I later realised that these were programmes, in which robotic insiders obeyed instructions to self-destruct or die. Finally, we made a serious suicide attempt. One of my insiders called the university psychologist and told her that we had just drunk coolant. I ended up in hospital for three days.

When I got out of hospital, three years ago now, my psychotherapist finally gave up on me, and referred me on to my present therapist, who understands survivors of mind control and ritual abuse. Everything changed for the better. My crazy symptoms came to an end, and I completed my degree within a year. I began to practise my innate right to think for myself. I am now doing what I have longed to do and thought was impossible: I have been volunteering for over a year now, helping others through an organisation that values a person's innate right to live as a peaceful, unique, free-thinking, and respected human being! And I now have part-time paid employment there.

* * *

Note: Sally's experience with the new therapist will be shared in Chapter Nineteen.

The kids

We be on the bad people's side and believed what they told us and was really scared of them too (not supposed to say we scared but we were). We didn't like Old Lady [Sally] because she be stupid and a traitor. It be the higher ups who make us turn the programmes on and off to hurt Old Lady, make her feel stupid, crazy, or want to kill herself. Because it be the higher ups' job to protect us and keep us loyal to the bad people and we just robots and do what we told. We do a really good job with the programmes to make Old Lady drink and get caught by the police. We so happy because we knowed we do a good job and that mean that the higher ups be happy with us and we don't get pain to make us obey them better. But we get scared too because we not like the police because some of them bad people who could hurt or kill us. And we really scared of going to crazy land and that might be what happen if we get taked to the hospital by the police or the doctor or the therapist so we be really scared. We also supposed to kill ourselves because that show we be honoring our cult family so we happy we doing our jobs good but we scared about dying too.

The counsellor Old Lady have to see after the police were called not know about us because we still be trapped in memories. Old Lady just goed through body memories and the counsellor only watch, write, and be there in case Old Lady fall down or something when in the memory. We do a really good job of making our body look dead in a body memory. The counsellor be scared and picked up her phone to call emergency but we not want the police to come so we wake the body up and it make the counsellor happy again. That funny we think.

Our reporters make sure Old Lady tell our mum and dad everything that happening with counselling so they be informed. We do this till Old Lady tell the police in 2006 to not allow our dad or family to speak to us no more.

We like to be out in the body sometimes so we feel like real people instead of being treated like its or nothings or parts or stupid mental cases because we not mental cases or retards, we real kids who have feelings and thoughts and like to do things too, but we never be heard by Old Lady or be heard very good by our counsellors. We start to use the body's mouth and speak with the psychotherapist, but she don't understand us.

Then, the higher ups get mad at us and at our psychotherapist when she asks Old Lady (because she thinks it's her sometimes when it really is us) or us not to do our job. So, if we do our job, we get in trouble or make our psychotherapist mad or worried about us and if we don't do our job then our higher ups get mad at us and give us and Old Lady head pain or stomach pain,[1] or high-pitched sound in her head like she going crazy, or make her get flashbacks, or make her get really angry and feel like she being tortured, or make her want to kill herself.

Then some of us littles who scared of the higher ups and dark insiders ask our psychotherapist to put those ones up on the moon or Mars before we go home so we not be scared of them. So she do this but it make our higher ups and Darks really mad and then we get really scared and we start to feel the pain of being tortured again or we think we gonna be sent to hell again. It make us want to cut the arm so she remember who she belong to. We supposed to be loyal to them for they are our only family.

When the psychotherapist didn't help us, the higher ups were looking for excuses to get mad and walk out, or to push the therapist over the edge instead of us. We sent the therapist lots of emails, one after the other to get her mad, up to 100 in a week. We would also leave a lot of messages on her office and personal phone.

Then after we drank the coolant and went to hospital, we find out that our psychotherapist fired us and we have to see our present therapist instead. We littles were really sad and confused and felt betrayed and some of us were really mad at her, too. Our higher ups were happy because it worked, we got fired. But they didn't expect us to be alive and especially to see another therapist. And so, they were going to give the new therapist a hard time too.

The higher-ups

We were created to keep everyone in line so that they would remain loyal to the Luciferians, KKK, SS, Freemasons, GI and Green Beret organisations. They were our family, not the parents, and we owed our lives to them; they were our leaders, fathers, mothers, military trainers, confidantes and family. They told us: "Obey or be killed. Obey or suffer. Obey and do. Do not think—just do it. Do not listen to outsiders, they don't understand, they are stupid and naïve, they are tools to be used and are worthless. They have no worth, no rights and are full of lies. They will not help you, they will mess with your head and confuse you and make you feel bad and unworthy. They will contaminate your mind and your soul. They are toxic and not one of us. You belong to us, you are ours, you are property, to be owned only by us and for our use and no other. We will tell you what to do and when, and you will listen or be punished and sent to hell, for God is not the leader here, we are—the Luciferians, SS and KKK. Do not deceive us or we will find you and bring you back or dispose of you or make you self-destruct." These are our powers, the higher-ups, that were instilled in us by our leaders and family, the "cults" and military.

"For your work, little ones, you will be rewarded by not being harmed, thrown into prison, into caves or coffins, or killed or tortured or have your friends killed or sacrificed. Obeying and being able to take pain via training makes you stronger and more determined to follow our light, the light of darkness, the way of truth, of light, of power and superiority over all humans and life. Heil the Aryan race, heil Hitler, hail God on high, hail Lucifer the almighty and the devil his superior, then Satan—the 'father of lies,' the father of the true light not lies.

"The father of lies is what the counsellors will tell you but this is not true, for we are the light. We light the way of the truth, of the power of the Aryan race, and this is your purpose little ones, so obey us and be strong and do not let any outsider fool you into believing their lies. You are free with us, not with them, you don't need to think, for we think for you and for your safety and your power, so that you may have power over life itself, and the blood of all humanity, and animals, for you are superior and will honour us till death or be called a traitor and die with the outsiders in mind, spirit and body. We will make it so."

From the body's first anointment at birth until age fifteen, when the body betrayed us for a second time by leaving the "cults", we were in full control and then, slowly we began to lose our grip on the body. The body was not obeying. It never did to the fullest and thus was always a problem, so we had to keep it in line with the turning on and off of switches via the little ones being told to follow commands, acting like robots for us, and thus not asking or whining or thinking, just doing regardless of the consequences.

The underlying programme we used to control Old Lady was Snakes and Ladders®.[2] It gives Old Lady a sense of hope (ladder) and then, there is a sudden drop (snake): suicidal thoughts, she freezes or collapses and fails an exam. All the other programmes are "snakes." Whenever Old Lady feels like she is doing well, she will feel that she has been humiliated in public and has made a fool out of herself. Then look out, a trip wire is set off for the snake pit, and she falls hard towards self-harm and suicide.

In addition, the Submissive programme was always on. It caused fear, sensations of electric shock, flashbacks and a need to submit to the abusers whenever we heard any of the following words: light, truth, trust, touch, free, feel, and think. It is still at work in us today, but not as strongly, as we have worked through some of the memories behind it.

Old Lady had another underlying programme running, which started when she was three and has never been fully turned off. It is a spiritual programme to make her fear God. She gets flashbacks of God looking down at her, remembers scripture, feels unworthy, and needs to live as a perfect, God-fearing Christian.

Soon after Old Lady started university, we told the littles to turn on the Self-Destruction,[3] Dead Head,[4] and Scramble[5] programmes so it would make it hard for her to think, and make her feel stupid and think she is no good and needs to escape being at school and in this world. And we had the littles turn on the memories of her being molested by her uncle and wondering if her dad molested her too via the Fear Family[6] programme. We deprived her of sleep by haunting her with nightmares of being molested, hearing her father and uncle knocking on her dorm door, and sensing some adult being in the room ready to grab her and calling out her name for her to come to them.

The snake pit gave Old Lady a sudden drop as the Suicide/Self-Harm[7] programme was turned on. She hated herself and life, period. She wanted to escape this life, to die. She felt abandoned and alone with no support, stranded 3,000 miles away from home. She didn't know anyone, had no income now, and knew for sure that she was not going to be able to complete the fast-tracked university programme; she was going to fail.

We took this and ran with it. Time to turn up the heat. The Fear God programme influenced Old Lady to choose abusing alcohol and cigarettes over killing herself with a knife, drowning or hanging herself, because she knew from reading the New Testament that committing suicide was an unforgiveable sin. (Committing suicide confuses us because we were told that this was an honourable act which shows our loyalty to all of our cult families.) Old Lady didn't want to upset God and be damned to hell. She felt like she was already living in a torturous hell, but this would be worse and for eternity.

When Old Lady started to see a counsellor to help her with her nightmares and memories of being molested, this upset us because you are not supposed to see a therapist, that's against the rules. Old Lady was a traitor and we needed to honour the code: Once you leave the cult family, if you share anything about us or seek outside help, you will either be tracked down and killed, will be killed by us insiders, or driven insane and useless and be institutionalised. That was where Old Lady was heading, but she didn't know that.

We knew that the first counsellor was inexperienced so we could have some fun with turning various programmes on and off. We needed to maintain control and so we turned on Shield[8] and Enemy[9] programmes to make sure Old Lady kept her distance with counsellors and other people trying to heal. We didn't want her to get close to anyone and become weak. Ugh! Old Lady is so weak and stupid sometimes we think. She's not like us, that's for sure. She would try to trust people or help them. The littles loved to help people and longed to trust others or find a mother-figure, but we didn't want that. Old Lady was supposed to be loyal to the cult and not think or help others. We couldn't trust Old Lady or those she mingled with.

None of us higher-ups wanted the first counsellor's help. She was the enemy, but we were confused. She wasn't shocked or scared when the littles came out and she was willing to talk and help them through the memory. We were jealous and scared and mad. We wanted to talk too and be heard, but were scared because that was not what we were supposed to do and mad because our family secrets might be found out.

In our therapy sessions, Old Lady was only going through the motions of parts of memories, and the emotions and pain were not being processed by all of us who were involved in the memory. This caused Old Lady to struggle with a rage that was unbearable and could not be controlled. We now know that when only part of a memory is experienced, the rest of it can flood the system. It was connected to the memory of the blue pile (black and blue) insiders who were tortured and the beasties who felt the rage against the bad people. Old Lady didn't know how to work with this rage or help it to go away.

However, once she left the counselling office and was out in public, she would switch into a strong disbelief/denial about what happened and would switch into a polite demeanour so that she would not be conspicuous in public. When she got home, the strong disbelief/denial programme[10] took over to the point of her being unreceptive to her littles and any of us. She went on about her daily business as if nothing had happened. She couldn't relate to her insiders, not realising that they were really littles (younger parts of "her"). She also didn't know she too was a host, just another part, and not the whole person or a singleton.

Old Lady had to go to a daily treatment programme for her alcohol abuse. The head counsellor there could see right through Old Lady and knew somehow that Old Lady had been involved in more than what she was sharing. We feared her and so, one time we turned on a Suicidal and Trance[11] programme when Old Lady was near the ocean outside the treatment centre. She just stood near the water and looked out, ready to walk in the water to her death. This daily drug and alcohol treatment programme Old Lady attended was disturbing because it made Old Lady use her mind. She had to think back to childhood and we didn't know how to think. We'd always been told "Don't think—just do." We didn't like this and so we made it easy for Old Lady to stay clean and graduate and get out of there.

When Old Lady started the correspondence courses, we wanted to give Old Lady some hope of being able to go to school and graduate again. But we knew we were also going to turn the Snake part of the programme on so that she would begin to struggle again and fail. She needed to be taught a lesson: that we, not her, were in control of her life (even if she didn't know about us; she would know that she doesn't have any control over her life). So, we let Old Lady get into the correspondence courses at first and then, within a couple of months, we started to turn on the Scramble, Dead Head and Smoke Bomb/Mist[12] programmes. She struggled. It took her a long time to understand the questions and answer them correctly. She would start to go off track with her answers, write partial sentences, or misunderstand questions. She would write and rewrite her answers and worry about completing all three courses on time.

By the time of the final exams, Old Lady could not remember what she was studying and had to write out what she was reading to retain the information. Her confidence level was starting to sink, but she persevered and went to the college to write the exams. It was then that we turned up the heat: we kept the Scramble, Dead Head, Smoke Bombs programmes going, and added the Trance, Confusion,[13] and Will Fail[14] programmes so that it would be difficult for her to find where to write the exams and she would feel even more self-conscious and stupid when trying to understand the exam questions.

She passed anyway.

When Old Lady started school again, we initially turned off the Suicide programmes. We kept the Shield, God-Fearing, Family-Fearing, Self-Hatred, Will-Fail programmes going and then turned the Denial, Dead Head, Smoke Bombs, Drugged,[15] Trance, Scramble, Garble,[16] Confused, Robot,[17] Crazyland,[18] and Voice Over[19] programmes on and off so that she would increasingly struggle with school and therapy.

We knew now that the most honourable thing to do was to kill ourselves and we were prepared to do this if we had to because we didn't like Old Lady and some of us (the Lights and littles, not the Darks; the Darks could only go to hell not heaven) also wanted to be with our best friend and the others who were killed/sacrificed when the body was six.

The most debilitating programme was the Denial programme because it played with Old Lady's emerging and overwhelming emotions. The programme would cause Old Lady to think she was going crazy to the point of wanting to die. She would believe the bits and pieces of memory that she had consciously remembered in the counselling office, and felt overwhelmed, shocked and angry at the abusers for what they did.

We were around too many people so we got scared ourselves. We would see someone who looked like our uncle, dad, aunt, or mother. When we saw rabbits, dogs, kids, or babies we would have flashbacks and be confused. Were we still in the barn, church, coffin, tunnel of death, or were we in another world, Old Lady's world? The body would even react and feel sick, want to vomit, gag, choke or be unable to breathe. The angrier we got, the more destruction we would cause. We would have our littles send the professors and/or therapists numerous emails that were full of anger, apologies and/or suicidal thoughts. We would even set off physical symptoms of head pain, headaches, muscle spasms, stomach aches, vomiting, gagging and choking, shortness of breath, dizziness and depression.

The psychotherapist used to say Old Lady was "ambivalent" when that wasn't true. It was because we were fighting inside and she didn't know that it was us who were mad. The therapist didn't ask us what we wanted or why the littles were afraid of us; she just pushed the memories back and put us up on the moon and Mars. This made us mad. We are kids too; we were not being heard and were being treated as if we were bad for just doing our jobs; we felt like we were being punished. Sometimes the therapist would get mad—you could hear it in her voice—so we would ask her if she was mad at us and she would say no, she was mad at the people who did this to us and was frustrated that she couldn't help us. She tried to help us, but she wasn't; she was making it worse. We didn't know that each other existed and definitely did not know that the Lights were the Darks' enemy and the Darks were the Lights' enemy. We were starting to fight with each other on the inside and hated Old Lady. Old Lady didn't understand us either and didn't want to know us or get to know us. She was ashamed of us and wanted to be classified as a person with mental illness.

By this time, we had taken over. All the programmes were running, including the Suicide programmes. Old Lady started drinking heavily again and then we ordered the littles to drink poison. Old Lady, in a trance-like state, went to the store, bought the coolant, and hit the conscious point of knowing that there was no going back, this was what she was going to do.

She felt no emotion at this time (Shield programme); the Robot programme was engaged and she drank the coolant. We didn't expect one of our littles though, a six-year-old, to panic and call for help. And we didn't expect what happened next: the psychotherapist fired us and sent us on to a therapist who actually knew how to help us! And now we are healing.

* * *

I have edited Sally's original story only for clarity and to reduce its length. Her original description showed even more of her anguish, confusion, and anxiety. It is a testament to her that she accomplished so much despite her internal conflict and sabotage. I should note that Sally had strong programming to be dysfunctional and addicted. Some survivors are designed to be much more functional than Sally was during these years, and some even hold very high positions in government or professions.

As you read about Sally's experiences from each of these different viewpoints, we can see how differently each event in the life of a mind control or ritual abuse survivor is viewed by different parts of the whole person. The main adult suffers from symptoms and often does not know their cause. The little insiders are confused and upset by various triggers in daily life. They are also aware that they have to obey orders from the higher-ups, even though they often do not know what it means when they obey in this manner.

From the disclosures of the higher-ups, you can see that the abuser groups deliberately create "programmes" which are trainings for little insiders to do their "jobs" of creating symptoms and problems, and for higher-up insiders to order the little ones to perform this sabotage of the person's life. You can see how complex and numerous these programmes can be. You can see a little about the training of the insiders, the ways they have been deceived, and the lies that they were told by the abuser groups.

You can also see what therapy can be like for a survivor of mind control and ritual abuse. The usual methods that survivors are taught to deal with their symptoms are unlikely to be effective. What good will it do for the front adult to try to calm herself down by mindfulness, or relaxation techniques, or rational thoughts when her head is filled with insiders doing their jobs of creating symptoms in fear of being tortured or killed? You can also see how difficult it is for survivors to engage in therapy, and to trust a therapist, and how difficult it is for a therapist to know how to help a survivor. (See Chapter Nineteen.)

Sally was fortunate to eventually find a therapist who did understand mind control. Not all survivors have that chance. If you have a therapist now, you need to be realistic about that person. Is he or she sincere and caring? Does your therapist listen to all of you? And if your therapist does not have the understanding of mind control that Sally's final therapist had, is he or she willing to learn? Your own higher-up insiders will tell you that no therapist can be trusted. That is a lie they were told.

Even if you do not have a good therapist, because no one is available or because you cannot afford one, you can make a lot of progress on your own in understanding all your insiders, how they were abused, trained, and deceived, how they are behaving now, and how they, as well as the front person, can heal.

Exercise 7. Learning from Sally's story

Think about your life over the past year or two, and write down what activities you have been involved in, such as education, work, housing, parenting, relationship, friendships, counselling, treatment programmes, and therapy. List each of these activities with lots of space after it.

For each activity, write down what it has been like for your main adult, "apparently normal personality" or "host" (front person.) How has it been helpful or unhelpful? If it has gone wrong, in what ways has it gone wrong?

Now, for each activity, ask your insiders, kids and higher-ups, to write down what that experience has been like for them? What has gone well? What has not gone well, and why? What programmes have been operating, and why?

Do you have any decisions to make about your healing process? What needs to change to make your healing more effective?

You will have noticed how Sally's counsellors, though sincere and well meaning, were unable to help her. If you are in therapy, are there any things you need to tell your therapist so that he or she can be a more effective helper for your healing? Do you need to find a new therapist? (Read Chapter 19 first.)

Notes

1. *Body Illness Programmes*: Sally's body illness programmes included stomach ache, headache, head pain (from vice grips or electricity applied to the head), gagging/vomiting, tiredness, and eye pain (being hurt by the light). Other survivors have had ear and nose and dental pain from needles.
2. I have encountered this programme in other survivors. It is first taught to the child through playing the game Snakes and Ladders® or "Chutes and Ladders".
3. *Hate Self Programme*: She wants to cut and/or stab herself, drink alcohol, hang or drown herself, neglects to eat or eat well, smokes, punches herself.
4. *Dead Head Programme*: Sally is unable to think at all, as if her head is full of cement.
5. *Scramble Programme*: Sally cannot understand words or numbers because they seem scrambled. Note that some other survivors have different learning disability programs, like training to write letter or numbers backwards.
6. *Fear Family Programme*: She sees flashbacks of abuse by family members.
7. *Suicide*: She wants to die and/or sees herself committing suicide.
8. *Shield Programme*: She has no emotion, is detached. This helps to protect herself, or hurt herself and push people away, or hurt other people.
9. *Enemy Programme*: An enemy is any outsider, especially those outsiders who are genuinely nice or trying to help us, in particular, "friends", counsellor, doctor, spiritual people, teachers, and people in authority; she is to make them hate her, leave her, abandon her, fire her. Or she is to go crazy and kill them.
10. *Denial Programme*: She does not believe that the mind control or ritual abuse really happened, despite her memory flashbacks.
11. *Trance Programme*: This puts Sally in a trance, such as we were in during rituals.
12. Smoke Bombs/Mist Programme: Sally's mind goes foggy, and she cannot see the truth or reality of the situation.

13. *Confusion Programme*: Sally is spatially disorientated or mentally confused, and does not know what or whom to believe.
14. *Will Fail Programme*: She thinks she is stupid; cannot do anything right; believes that eventually something will go wrong and she will fail.
15. *Drugged Programme*: She has the sensation of being drugged or poisoned, and is unable to focus, groggy, slow to act, and weak, just wanting to sleep.
16. *Garbled Programme*: Voices sound garbled so that Sally cannot comprehend what is being said.
17. *Robot Programme*: This makes her "Just do it; don't think".
18. *Crazy Land Programme*: She gets lost in the maze at the back of her mind, or driven crazy via a high-pitched sound in the head, or feels electricity or a scared feeling of "losing it'".
19. *Voice-Over Programme*: When a person (a therapist, friend, or person in authority) talks, Sally hears one of the abusers' voices instead.

CHAPTER SEVEN

Internal hierarchies

I begin this chapter with another survivor's story, which illustrates important mistakes made by her first therapist (and, therefore, by her) in her journey towards recovery. (The names of the therapists have been changed.)

LisaBri: "Mistakes my therapist made"

In childhood, severely abused emotionally, physically, and sexually, I refused to die. My perpetrators, including my own mother and father, did not mildly abuse; they subjected me to the horrors of incest and satanic ritual abuse on a continual basis.

I was fearful of the slightest noise at night—beds creaking, house settling, pipes banging or a door opening left me cowering in the corner of my bedroom. I knew they would be back to twist and warp my mind for their sadistic purposes. They always knew where to draw the thin line between death and sanity. I always waited in fear, with my heart pounding through my chest and cold, sweaty, and clammy hands.

At the age of twenty-five, I ran across the continent. I arrived battered and worse for wear, ready to do anything, especially continue to drink, to curb the intense feelings I was experiencing. When I looked for help, I was diagnosed with everything from schizophrenia to premenstrual syndrome. I was told to get a hobby and to not drink in the evenings. One psychiatrist pulled a packet full of white pills from his desk drawer every time I showed any kind of emotion. Every doctor and psychiatrist I saw wanted me to stuff the feelings away. But where could they go? The more I "stuffed", the worse I became. For five years, I was hospitalised two weeks of every four, until I landed in a locked ward of a psychiatric hospital when I hit bottom. Soon afterwards, I was diagnosed with a dissociative disorder (having inside parts) and I finally sobered up, threw away the drugs and alcohol, and looked for a therapist to talk to.

Three thousand miles from home, in hiding, I approached my first therapy appointment. I was about to break one of the cardinal rules of the cult—you do not disclose to outsiders. Body shaking, icy, freezing hands and feet, knees feeling like they would buckle with every step, I reached "Linda's" home office—scared but alive. She would guide me through the next five years. I left my car on the road and thought of a hundred reasons why I should not continue and each was just as feeble as the last. During that two-minute walk, I convinced myself I had not escaped and behind that door lay my abusers ready to punish me for my indiscretion. As I stood at the door, ringing the bell, hearing the sudden bark of dogs and what sounded like a thousand troops pounding down the stairs ready for battle, it took all my inner reserves not to take flight as the internal pull to run or stay clashed in my brain.

With Linda's help, I discovered that I had been ritually abused. I soon learned to substitute the process of stuffing feelings away with stuffing away "bad" inside parts. This was what my left side (cult) parts were labelled—evil. They needed to be dealt with harshly, I was told. They were "sabotaging" therapy by creating chaos in the system, preventing any healing. Today, we bear the scars caused by these early misinterpreted inner parts, who were just doing the jobs assigned to them by our abusers.

When we discovered an inside part whose main function was to hold pain arising from both the present day and past traumatic memories, Linda felt it only right for her to be banished and isolated from the rest of the system. Miss Pain was sent away to an internal imaginary beach, alone with all her pain. She had no one to talk to, cry with or hold.

In order to make our right side more strongly defended against the left side, Linda attempted a forced integration between the front person, Lisa, and the strongest defender of our system, Brian (Bri), by creating a hypnotic integration ceremony which took place in an imaginary forest. It appeared to work, and Linda was ecstatic, but it was too confusing inside. I tried to talk, but I couldn't find the proper words. Julie, a five-year-old part from abuse by my father, had appeared just as we joined. At that moment, we were a threefold being who had no idea how to live in this singleton world. I tried to convey that there was a complication, but Linda didn't listen. We finally made it out to the car and stalled it all the way home as we couldn't operate the gearstick. It felt as if our core strength, Bri, who had been the basis of our survival for so long, almost crumbled because of a botched attempt by an outsider to gain control of our personality system. After three days of not being able to function and carry out simple tasks such as unlocking a door or preparing a meal, we broke apart, but not before deciding never to integrate again.

Those first few years with Linda were turbulent, with many valleys and hills. I would reach the crest of one only to fall down the other side. Linda did more than guide me; she broke her own ethical rule of conduct by laying no boundaries. She spent one-on-one time with me in her home. I would have lunch with her family. She spent her time off frequently having coffee at my house. I could call her twenty-four hours a day, seven days a week, and she bought me presents. Within four years, I had moved from the city to the small town that she resided in. I became part of Linda's other life away from therapy. Playing to my constant insecurities, Linda consistently told me, "I will never hurt or leave you," and I believed her.

Looking back upon it now, telling me this was as cruel as it was kind. With no set therapeutic boundaries I had no sense of myself. I was living Linda's life and I was bound for hurt or betrayal. Instead of helping me find independence and growth, I grew increasingly dependent on her and when the blow came, it hit the core of my being.

The telephone message I received in the midst of intensive memory work told me Linda had renewed her faith in God, and overnight had come to believe that only God could save me. She would no longer work with non-Christians. Scared, hurt, disbelieving, and having been so dependent on her, I could not comprehend life without her. Desperately not wanting to lose Linda, I ignored my own instincts and the daily growing knot of uncertainty in my stomach. I went to her now Christian counselling and to her church for a year, until the fear completely overwhelmed me. Coming from such a horrendous background had left me spiritually raped and unable to cope with any religious denomination. When I stopped going to her church, she never contacted me again. I finally had to accept that I had lost Linda in more than a therapeutic way.

I began work with a new psychiatrist who also set the goal of banishing the "bad" parts. He had the strongest right side parts gather all the left side parts, many times forcibly, put them into a rocket, and send them over the highest imaginary mountain into space. We did this routine with him once a week for over three years.

After shopping around for almost a year, I found "Christyne", but with a different resolve. I chose her, not from an overwhelming sense of urgency and neediness, but from an educated place of having learnt a harsh lesson. I talked to Christyne on the phone prior to making an appointment and she said, "I can guide you, I can help you find yourself and what that means, but first we have to set boundaries." I made an appointment.

I must have reached for the phone twenty times from that day to the date of my appointment to cancel. I didn't. I arrived at my appointment with Christyne, weak-kneed, with a parched mouth and throat, and feeling as if I could not string two words together.

Our first session scared the hell out of me. She said, "I will work with your right side; however, we need to do a lot of healing with the left side parts. This is going to be my starting focus." She wanted to *work* with the left side, my inner cult parts. Was she crazy or what? After spending almost a decade with doctors and therapists doing all they could possibly do to get rid of those parts, this took me by complete surprise. But, that's what I needed. Finally, I could heal.

With boundaries set by Christyne, I embraced my inner world. I stopped letting others make decisions about my inside parts, no matter how honourable their intentions seemed to be. Labels were discarded. Each now had a say. No inside part was ever hidden or banished again. As a result, I broke free from my abusers and we have become a self-sufficient community with the capability to ask for outside help when needed. Every inside part is loved and respected for his or her unique contribution to our survival and healing. We strive to meet the needs of fulfilment, hunger and safety for all.

With a sense of pride, I used what I had learnt about boundaries and the therapeutic process to help others by creating a website for survivors. Christyne taught me to "listen inside." All survivors could benefit from those two words.

* * *

LisaBri's experience with Linda reflects two important mistakes that are easy for survivors, as well as their therapists, to make. The first one is a lack of boundaries. The child parts of most survivors do not even know what boundaries are, since theirs were never respected. We shall look at boundaries in more depth in Chapter Eighteen. For some reason, perhaps the existence of child parts, many therapists do not maintain firm boundaries with survivors. They become over-involved, make promises they cannot keep, and then abandon the survivor when it becomes too much for them.

The second mistake is that many survivors and their therapists or helpers focus on helping one side of the personality system and battling with the other side. This is because the moment a survivor of mind control or ritual abuse begins to remember, and particularly to disclose, memories of that abuse, the insiders who are part of the internal security system go into action and do their jobs. It begins with warnings: "Don't talk." "You can't trust her." "You'll be killed if you talk." If the survivor continues to talk to an outsider, the insiders with security jobs (assigned by the abuser group) begin to administer flashbacks or other kinds of punishments.

The enforcers—the key to unlocking the system

In his study of the features of DID, Colin Ross (1997) found that 84% of 236 DID patients said they had internal persecutor parts. As he describes them, "On first meeting they will be fearsome, loathsome, demon-like entities totally committed to the malicious harassment and abuse of the patient". These parts are aggressive exaggerations of the more common "inner critic" which almost everyone experiences. They tell you not to talk, they threaten consequences for disobedience, they alienate your friends, and they might harm or even attempt to kill the body.

In your inner world, these parts might look like demons, or they might look or sound like some of your actual abusers, so that your scared inner kids believe either that you have these abusers in you or that they abusers are somehow magically contacting you and speaking to you. The fact is, these parts are not actually demons or abusers, and usually they know it. But they are doing their jobs of impersonating them because of their fear of the consequences if they do not keep on doing those jobs.

When "Satan" or some similar part talks in a deep scary voice to you, it is easy to think this is a nasty perpetrator or a supernatural being; it is natural for you and/or your therapist to want to oppose it or fight with it or try to banish it. It is unwise, and damaging to you, to avoid dealing with the insiders who issue the warnings. To battle with them is even worse. These insiders have probably already been badly hurt by the abuser group, and have been told that anyone to whom you talk about the abuse will also hurt them and you. So fighting with those parts will only make them angry, which is not a good idea because they have the capacity to punish the front person and other insiders through using feelings, pictures, or scary sounds from horrible traumatic memories.

In my experience, front people and other insiders can be very afraid of these parts, leave them alone as much as possible, and do what they say, such as stopping talking about forbidden topics. Unfortunately, this is exactly what the real life abusers want; that is why they designed your personality system this way. Getting free of the abusers begins with communicating with the parts who are scaring you, coming to understand them, and forming an alliance with them. No matter what they might look like in your inner world, they are really just scared insiders, children and teenagers. It takes patience to communicate with parts who appear to be destructive, or who are overtly hostile, but it is what you must do. It is important to recognise that these insiders do their jobs in order to protect the system as a whole, and sometimes also to protect people you love who have been threatened. They persecute you in the service of protecting.

If you (the front person) are a polite person who does not swear or say things bluntly, you might not want to deal with parts whose words you consider rude, and whose manner reminds you of people you had to deal with in your childhood. But censoring them will get you nowhere. Ignore their manner and concentrate on learning why they are behaving that way. And if you have a good therapist, let them come out in therapy even if they are rude and crude. Therapists can take it (or, if they cannot, they are not the right therapists for you).

You might find that you need to talk with other inside protectors who believe the "persecutor" parts are "bad" and want to keep you from them. You need to explain to these ones that the persecutors are actually protectors like them, and are trying to keep everyone safe by doing their jobs: containing overwhelming memories, controlling rage, preventing abandonment, and avoiding external punishment by the abusers.

The persecutor/protector parts are actually lonely because they are internally isolated (because all the other parts are afraid of them), and they long to be accepted into the internal and external community, so just talking and listening to them make a great deal of difference.

When you are first talking with persecutor/protector parts, it is important to express appreciation for their strength and self-sufficiency. If you fight them or try to weaken them, they will demonstrate their strength by attacking. Do not mention their needs for comfort or help at first. This comes later. They think other parts are "wimpy", and they can often tolerate large amounts of physical pain, but not very much emotional pain. They see the expression of vulnerable emotions as a sign of weakness. They simply do not feel emotional pain; it is diverted to other parts—though they might feel anger. In some personality systems, each "tough" part has its own "inner child" to hold the vulnerable feelings.

Some of these parts might be trained to cut your arms (or make another part do it) as a punishment, to flood your entire personality system with despair, to prevent a memory from being completely processed and put together, or to stop you from talking by making you mute and terrified. These abuser-trained parts are the key to stopping your symptoms (many of which they create by doing their jobs) and to unlocking your mind-controlled personality system.

So, you need to find out why the persecutor/protector parts do and say what they do and say. At least some of these parts will be doing jobs that they were required to do by their abusers as an alternative to death or serious bodily harm. They might not understand the effect of doing these jobs on the body or the rest of the personality system. Persecutor/protector parts believed the aggressors' verbally abusive statements and threats, so they believe they have to keep the system in line to prevent bad, or worse, things from happening. This is not always a false belief.

You can ask these insiders about the content of the threats they have been given. Disclosing the nature of the threat is less likely to stimulate harmful behaviour than disclosing the abuse memories. Ask them what they believe will happen if they do not do their jobs, or if the system disobeys the abusers. Then you can give them a reality check on whether or not those things can really happen in the present.

It is, of course, important to first ask inside whether there is any current contact with abusers, because, in that case, certain actions might be protective in a concrete and real way. Some survivors have contact and do not know it; in other cases, they may have had no contact, but the protective parts might believe they have. This will be discussed further in Chapter Nine.

You might have heard about soldiers from the Vietnam or Korean wars who are found in the jungle somewhere, believing the war is still continuing long after it is over. Many of your parts are like them, still living in the past, doing what they had to do when the abusers could hurt or kill you at any minute. If you reach out to them, and help them know the present situation, they might respond by changing their jobs to things which are helpful in the current situation.

The most effective approach with persecutor/protector parts is to engage them as your allies in healing. As with any insider, you need to become aware of their ages, and of how much they know or do not know about life in the present. Empathise with the dilemmas they have faced and agree with them that their protector roles have been very important for your safety. Then you can help them to protect in more effective ways for the present circumstances.

Voices and faces

If, in everyday life, you had a very angry, critical, and punishing mother, you might hear your mother's voice telling you not to do something, or reprimanding you harshly if you do something your mother never permitted you to do. This happens to people who are not mind-controlled. By influencing your behaviour, the voice who reminds you of what your mother would say is trying to protect you from very real abuse from your mother. In ordinary life, people know their punishing mother is dead or far away, but still respond as if she were alive and lived with them. However, if your mother was an abuser, the situation becomes more serious.

Some persecutor/protector parts might actually believe themselves to be your real-life abusers. There could be more than one internal copy, for example, of a parent. This happens spontaneously, and its tendency to happen is exploited by mind controllers. One survivor I know has a whole hierarchy of abusive mother parts inside her, and they are all actually children who are terrified of her mother, who tortured them to the point that they only wanted to die. They were told they look like the mother, and to the other insiders, they do indeed look like that mother, which is enough to frighten all the insiders into submission. The girl at the top of the "mother" hierarchy was given control over all the "home kids", and, of course, is in charge of making sure they do not disclose anything about the mother's abuse.

As I mentioned in Chapter Four, in ritually abusing and mind-controlling groups, the main abuser will rape a child while saying he is "putting himself inside her". A new part is split off through the pain, and the abuser says that he has created it, and it is him or his child. It has to act like him in the person's inner world, replaying his words to the other insiders to keep them in line, and administering the pain from his rape if they are disobedient. This kind of insider has usually been severely hurt, believes the abuser knows everything, and is terrified of the abuser. It takes patience, compassion, and persistence to help such parts learn that they are now safe and no longer have to "be" their abusers.

Christian survivors and therapists, take note: ritual abusers frequently give parts demonic names in order to make them and the other insiders believe they are demons or evil spirits. They even teach these parts how to behave like demons, growling and making frightening noises. But this does not mean that the parts are actual demons. They are child insiders who have been given those jobs. Some parts have been deceived into believing they are demons, devils, Satan, or animals. They are usually very young (around age three) and imitate "demons" or animals they were shown to frighten them. The way they are made was described in Chapter Five.

There is a school of thought among some Christian therapists that suggests that actual demons are "attached" to the insiders who go through this. That is not my experience with the survivors I have seen, even if as children they were coerced into "inviting" demons to enter them. Rather, what happened is that a new part split off in terror and was then told it was a demon. For example, my client Tony had a little three-year old "demon" named Trevor, who was supposed to be the spirit of his dead grandfather.

Those insiders who imitate cult leaders or mind-controlling doctors, or "devils", or "demons" are really no different from the internal "imitation mother". They are trying to protect you from those persons or creatures. You might be many years and many miles away from those abusers, but these insiders do not know it. Or you might still be in danger, so the protection of these insiders is still needed, though in a different form now if you are an adult and have the capacity to make your own life choices.

The internal hierarchy

In most mind-controlled personality systems, the parts are arranged hierarchically. The first parts you meet who threaten you or object to your pursuing recovery are likely to be low down in the hierarchy, obeying orders from above. Even if they push internal buttons or flick switches to administer punishments, they are not in charge of this; they are just following orders from those above them.

As you or your therapist, if you have one, begin to dialogue with the "lower-down" parts, the higher-ups will make their presence known, either by coming out and objecting to what is being said or by creating symptoms or by threatening voices in your head. *If you get a flashback or a sudden pain, that is your chance to ask to speak with whoever is causing it.*

Although I am a therapist, not a survivor, perhaps you can learn from what I do. When I meet a new mind-controlled client, if possible I begin working my way up the hierarchy almost immediately. Whenever a new part surfaces doing its job, I ask it about that job, update the part who appeared on the front person's current life, introduce it to other insiders, and encourage it to take part in present-day activities suitable for a child of its age, such as going to the beach, or making models, or colouring pictures, or playing sports. As each new part comes up to protect the secrets, I invite that part to work with the others towards healing the whole person from the abuse. I offer it an opportunity to have a new job, a purpose other than the one it was originally given. I let it know that the abusers did not "create" the parts, but simply split them through torture. I help the members of the hierarchy develop respect for the hurt parts who resisted doing the jobs and were discarded by the abusers.

In getting to know a hierarchical system, I frequently ask each part if someone else is threatening him or her or giving orders, and then ask to talk to the one who is doing this. When I meet an insider called Satan, for example, I do not assume he is the only Satan. He could just be Satan 1, and there might also be, for example, Satans 2 to 9, and Immortal Satan, or Big High Satan. If I am talking to Satan 1, and he begins to respond to my suggestions about changing his job, he will hear threats from someone who might be Satan 2, or might be someone different whose job is to keep him in line. So, then I talk to the one who is threatening him, and so on until I reach the top of that hierarchy. I shall illustrate this in the next chapter.

The higher-ups

The higher-ups in the hierarchy, who issue threats and punishments to those who disobey, and order other parts to punish those below them, are generally aware of whether you are making disclosures or disobeying the abusers' rules. They have to watch that you do not become disloyal and begin to tell—or even remember—things you are not supposed to talk about. However, although they are listening for disclosures, they are often not aware of what else is going on in your everyday life—for example, that you have not seen the abusers for twenty years, or that the abusers are dead.

Although these insiders have observed the "real" world, they have rarely been out in it, and have very limited experience of anything in life other than perpetrator group events and training. Their rewards have been sex, drugs, and power; they know nothing of love, or caring, or pets, or anything else positive in life. Other parts can share these positive experiences with them to help them see what they have been missing.

These parts' experience of human beings is only of abusers, who would switch into other states of being, and torture and punish. For a long time they might think your therapist (or your best friend) is one of the abusers testing their loyalty, since this kind of trick has been played on them. In most cases, they have been conditioned against therapists, and warned against people who try to find out the secrets and express caring or empathy for them. They will be very cautious—as they should be. There are some therapists with cult connections (see Chapter Nineteen).

The higher-ups were taught in your childhood to believe that the abusers always know what is going on with you, and that if they do not punish the other parts, the abusers will punish them. This is what I call the BIG LIE, and I shall discuss it in more detail in Chapter Nine. For now, I shall just say it is a lie, even though it might have been true when you were a child.

It is important to gradually help the higher-ups realise that they have been deceived by their trainers. Higher-ups may believe they have never been hurt. They do not realise how many other insiders were hurt badly in order to create them, and they often do not realise that they were split from those pain-holder parts. They need you both to listen to them and to give them information they do not have.

By gently exposing their false beliefs, as you work up the hierarchy and talk to parts that have increasing authority, you will gradually build trust and help these parts see what has really happened to them. *You can only succeed in healing from organised abuse if the inside parts in charge of the hierarchy at first allow you to proceed, and later actively co-operate with you.*

Higher-ups have strong loyalty programming, including training to die an honourable death rather than betray the group. It is very important to be aware of this programming. Reason with the higher ranked members, and be sure to respect the loyalty, bravery, and sense of honour involved in their misguided allegiance to a perpetrator group that deceived them about its purposes. If they change their allegiance, they can be excellent protectors in the present from outside perpetrators.

Each internal personality in a mind-controlled system both takes pride in the job he or she has been forced to do, and is terrified of punishment for failing in that job. For parts low in the hierarchy, the punishment comes from parts higher up (through, for example, body memories of severe pain). Parts higher up fear being punished by the actual adults who abused them, who might or might not be still involved in their lives. They believe these people will hunt them down, torture them, and possibly kill them if they disclose the abuse. They often believe that the abusers have supernatural powers with which to find them. In addition, hidden parts of the personality system who believe they are demons or ghosts or spirits or aliens have the jobs of frightening and threatening and punishing higher-ups to keep them obedient and make them believe the abusers can always find them and hurt them, sometimes even after the abusers are dead.

The higher-ups' loyalty training

Higher-up parts have received some of the most horrendous spiritual abuse, in that they have been forced to perpetrate against other people to make them identify with the abuser group and believe that no one else will want them. When a survivor is re-contacted by the abuser group, there are reminders of these awful trainings. Often the higher-ups are forced to perpetrate sexual abuse or torture or even (apparent) murder on another person, and then told they will always be part of the evil group and if they disobey the group will kill someone they love. They have to repeat their loyalty vows, or sign them in blood.

Insiders who have been through experiences as heinous as these might be very ashamed, and they generally believe they are evil. They will be afraid to disclose these experiences to a therapist—or to you. They are often afraid of their own memories, and afraid you will reject them if you know what they have done. You need to be ready to accept them, no matter what they have been forced to do. You will need to explain to them, in ways they can hear, the coercion which was involved in their past behaviour. You must be patient. These parts can come to understand that their (and your) guilt is what distinguishes you from people who really are evil. If you were truly evil, you would not be feeling this way. Evil people do not feel guilt for what they do. This is true of not only the front person, but also the parts who were forced to do evil things.

Rewards given to the higher-ups

The parts in charge of the personality system, who hold the power over the others, have also been given rewards. Rewards include pleasurable sex, pleasurable drugs, and getting to do the hurting instead of being hurt. Those who are chosen for internal high office may be offered money, good jobs in the outside life, good homes, and prestige in the non-cult world. If they are supposedly demonic, they might have been taken to a simulated hell, and given the choice of being tortured there or being in charge of the torture of other children. Since they believed they were going to hell for eternity anyway as a result of the crimes they had committed, they might have naturally chosen to be the ones doing the hurting rather than the ones receiving it.

You have to remember that these parts had been split off from other discarded parts (garbage kids) who refused to co-operate with the abusers. When the higher-ups confess their guilt to me, I ask how many different parts refused to do the heinous act before these ones finally agreed to do it. In many cases, the perpetrators would not actually kill the child even if he or she chose to be killed rather than do what was required. They would simply continue with the torture and threats until a part was split off who would do the required job.

You need to have compassion for those who had to do the things that no one else inside would do.

Backups

If you manage to gain the co-operation of the higher-ups, you can expect some trouble for a little while. All insiders with jobs, including those in charge of the system, have "backups", parts who have received the same training and are supposed to take over the roles of any part who becomes disloyal. Do not be discouraged. This will be manageable. Backups are pretty easy to persuade to change sides, if the primary higher-ups have already decided to work for healing. Backups do not have much real life experience and are hollow compared to the parts they are backing up. Backups are often an earlier (younger) version of the part with the job—for example, Priestess 8 (aged ten) might be the backup for Priestess 9 (aged eleven).

Important principles

Delay memory work

As you pursue your healing process, it is wise to take your time about getting to the traumatic memories, and in particular about telling them to anyone, even your therapist. If disclosures are made prematurely, you can expect to have flashbacks and have insiders engage in self-harm and even suicide attempts; plus there is the risk that parts will report to the abusers that you are disclosing, and they will make moves to stop you. (I shall discuss this further in Chapter Nine.) Only after you have good co-operation from the leaders of the personality system can you begin your work with traumatic memories.

Get permission for any interventions

If you or your therapist are thinking of making any intervention, from self-soothing to more fancy hypnotic interventions, begin by saying that if anyone inside objects to this technique or intervention, they need to let us know and we will not do it unless we have their permission. If they deny permission, we can ask what they are concerned about, and if we cannot meet their concerns, we do not do the intervention. This approach is respectful and shows that we value their input and want to address their concerns.

Kindness and acceptance

When you talk with your higher-ups, their emotional response can quickly escalate to put you into a "booby trap" of suicidality or at least self-harm. Higher-ups (and other insiders too) have usually been led to believe they are evil, and have committed unforgiveable sins and crimes. Be careful, therefore, to accept these parts as they tell about their guilt and shame, even if they appear to be proud of what they did. It is important to emphasise that they were children when they did these things (if this is the case), or at least when they were trained to do these things, and they were deceived and victimised, and did not really have a choice. When they did choose, it was usually the "lesser of two evils", as the alternative that was threatened was worse. They deserve compassion rather than punishment.

Updating the insiders

The higher up a part is in the hierarchy, the less they are likely to know about the present world. The ones who enforce the orders of the perpetrators (primarily the "don't talk" rule) often have no idea what year it is, how old the body is, and how much things have changed since the abuse took place. It is very important to update them about these things. You can keep a calendar and a world map handy for this purpose, or know how to find them on your computer.

Helping higher-ups discover deceptions

Organised groups of abusers are very careful to isolate the higher-ups from the experiences of other insiders, in order to deceive them. One question you can ask the system while your higher-ups are listening is: are there any insiders who have to contact someone and report any rule-breaking? Before you ask this question, get your higher-ups to agree not to punish anyone inside who gives an honest answer. The answer is almost certain to be "yes". And the higher-ups did not know about it; they were not supposed to know.

Now that they are aware that they were deceived with this important lie, the higher-ups, who have thought themselves in control, will be more curious about what other deceptions might have occurred. You can ask them to access knowledge from the other "lesser" insiders. After a while, the system can be arranged so that newly emerging parts are instantly updated by insiders, and do not have to go through the painstaking process of learning from the front person.

Now I am writing for the internal leaders and enforcers: I hope I have described you adequately when I tried to help your front person understand what you are going through. It is up to you whether you take the risk of working for healing instead of continuing the protective job you have been doing until now. A job that was helpful in the past but might need to be changed to reflect the realities of the present.

If your personality system is to heal, you all need to become co-operative. This means that the persecutors, the front personalities, and other parts must negotiate your differences, resolve long-standing conflicts, and overcome past hurts, both real and imagined. This is often difficult, as other parts are terrified of the persecutors and will not go near them. It takes time to change this situation. Ask what each part needs, and listen to one another. In encouraging internal communication, sometimes "deals" can be made—for example, a persecutor will not create flashbacks if the little ones do not talk about their abuse. Agreements are very helpful, as is homework, but make sure you dot every "i" and cross every "t" in an agreement, as young parts can be very concrete.

Exercise 8. Internal conversation

What would you (the everyday person) ask your higher-ups about? Write down some questions you might ask. (Be sure to ask, not interrogate or accuse).

What would you like your higher-ups to know about your present life? Write down a few important points.

What would the higher-ups like to ask the rest of the system about? Write down some questions you might ask, and try to use gentle language, even if you are not used to doing that. Before you ask, assure those who respond that you will not punish them for their answers (and, of course, keep your word).

CHAPTER EIGHT

Talking with the higher-ups

In Chapter Six, I introduced you to Sally and her insiders, including the kids and the higher-ups. I have spent a lot of time talking with her higher-ups, and I decided to do some of this discussion by email. She has given me permission to share some of what we have talked about, to help you understand what happens when the higher-ups face the real facts and compare those facts to what they were taught in childhood.

By email, I asked the questions to Sally's higher-ups. My aim was to encourage them to think for themselves rather than just parrot the abusers' words. Their abusers had said, "You don't need to think, for we think for you and for your safety and your power." In fact, "Don't think, just do!" was frequently repeated when these parts were being trained. The abusers prevented logical reasoning as much as possible, because it might undermine the mind control programming. I find that asking higher-up insiders questions that get them to think and reason is very helpful for healing.

Now, when I asked these questions, Sally and all her insiders knew the questions were coming from me, an outsider and a therapist. But you do not need a therapist to ask questions to your own inside higher-ups. You can ask them yourself.

When you first try to talk with your own higher-ups, they might be angry and hostile to you, especially if you have ignored them and the child parts they control for a long time. You might need to apologise to them for this neglect. And when you ask them questions, be sure to ask with gentle curiosity, because they have probably been interrogated, and questions to which there is a "right answer", or even a desired answer, can be terrifying to them. I hope that you can sound encouraging and optimistic, as I have been told that I sound that way when I ask this kind of question. I sound that way because I truly believe that there is a way out of mind control, and this is the way.

Besides asking questions to your own higher-ups, you can encourage them to ask you questions. Most insiders, including higher-ups, often lack information about the present-day world.

They might believe things that are no longer true (such as that certain abusers are alive and nearby), and they might not know how the world has changed since they were last out in the body. They might also believe things the group told them which were never true.

Your higher-ups can ask questions to other insiders in your personality system. Members of abuser groups keep secrets from the higher-ups, and your higher-ups have a right to know what has been hidden from them. Nobody likes to be lied to, and I am sure that includes you and all your parts, especially the higher-ups. Mind control programming works through lies and tricks perpetrated on children by sophisticated adults. I know that some of your insiders do not want to believe that their "family" lied to them, but if this is the case, they deserve to know it.

Through respectful inner dialogue, you can help the higher-ups discover the lies and the tricks used by the abusers. This will undermine and eventually dissolve the programming.

Below you will see my questions or statements I emailed to Sally (in normal type), and her insiders' comments on the internal effect of each such question (indented and in smaller type). Several of the questions come from what her higher-ups said they were taught, which I quoted for you in Chapter Six. You may notice that her responses to any given question or statement sometimes come from several different insiders. My comments to you as the reader will be in the normal type size with italic formatting.

I need to warn you at this point that the dialogue in this chapter can be triggering. When Sally reread the dialogue for the purpose of this book, new parts of her emerged who were not aware that she was currently safe and would not be punished for having said these things. Fortunately, she had healed enough that her system head (whose words you will read later in this chapter) was able to speak with each part who reacted and tell them about her current situation and why he had chosen to take part in this dialogue and allow it to be in this book. He was also able to tell them to turn off any programmes that were triggered. If you are reading this, I suggest that your system head might want to read it first, and then decide whether other parts of you can read it.

Note that the perpetrator group who abused Sally and trained her insiders seems to have included people who identified themselves to her as SS (the secret police of the Nazis), KKK (Ku Klux Klan, including white knights), GIs (US army), and Luciferians (occult religion), and they all told her they were her Family.

Questioning the perpetrator group's ownership of the person

The group told you that you were theirs, you were property, to be owned only by them and for their use and no other. Did you know that slavery, that is, owning another human being, has been abolished and is illegal in all civilised countries? People are never to be property. Your group might have used people as slaves, but they would be in big trouble if outsiders found out.

A protective reaction

> Your question sets off an Alert alarm: "Alert, alert, someone is trying to penetrate our system." Those who were hurt are made to think of a penis penetrating us because the people in the group

did this a lot to us, and when it happens it makes the body become alert, as if it's under attack and needs to get into survival mode.

The lower ranking soldiers in the inside control room sense fear within the system and a switch is turned on, to let us know that we are being interrogated by the enemy just like the SS, KKK, GI, and Luciferian commanders and elders said would happen. "They were right; we must protect our Family at all costs" is the message we get throughout our system. You are the enemy. We are programmed to see you as nothing, less than, a thing to be destroyed. We must show you who is in control here, that we are loyal to our Family (that is, the group). Our note takers get ready to record your questions and our answers too, in case they have to report back to the Family. We were also taught to lie if we were interrogated so we don't give up the group's secrets. The soldiers in the control room will continue to monitor what is happening, waiting for the higher-ups to signal them to turn on or off switches, programmes, pain, to induce the body to become catatonic, just stare and not answer, show no emotion, or be hard and stoic, so that our system stays secure and no secrets leak out.

The soldier mode has been triggered. Consequently, Sergeant Major comes forward to speak. We wouldn't tell you or show you how scared we are because we have to give the appearance of being tough and impenetrable. We try to sense whether you are intimidated, scared, angry, unstable, or defensive. If you are, that is good, it shows that we are in control and so we can weaken and destroy you, psychologically and emotionally.

"Nein, nein" says a little German insider; "Don't answer, we'll get in trouble, we don't want to get hurt, please don't tell her." "It's okay," says another insider who knows you are trying to help us. "No it's not," says the little German insider, "someone, a higher up, will hurt me if we say anything."

Now a higher-up speaks.

It is me whose job is to hurt him, you don't know me. If I was hurting him in your office, this is when you could say "Whoever is hurting this little one, could you please stop or turn off the programme. This is a safe place, remember our rules, no one hurts anyone in this room, that includes me. Please come and talk to me, the one who is hurting the little one, I would love to speak with you."

If we were sitting in your office, you might see our body showing signs of sadness, punching our hand with our fist, clenching our fist, moving our face away from you in shame, or holding our head as we experience intense feelings. Or if we are feeling confused, the blue pile will start to come forward and show you via a body memory that some of us weren't protected.

Or another higher-up (a white knight, an immortal Luciferian, or a soldier who is trained to kill) may come forward and say "You do not question the group, it is forbidden. It is a privilege and an honour to be part of the group; they do what they must to ensure that the group's mission succeeds, that the Aryan race dominates this world, for they are the superior race." The higher-up would show no emotion; his eyes would try to penetrate through you and his posture would be upright, to show how strong and indestructible he is.

Note: Since it is you who are asking the questions to your own insiders, perhaps there will not be such alarm at being questioned. But often insiders cannot tell the difference between inside and outside people. And often higher-ups are trained to reveal nothing to the front parts who are supposed to live in the ordinary outside world.

You may notice that pain was mentioned as one way the higher-ups might communicate. If you get a sudden pain, speak internally and say something like "Please use your words to tell us what the pain message means. We would like to honour your message but if it is just pain, we do not understand what you want to have happen. Please use your words, and if anyone is in charge of you and using your words would get you in trouble, please let me ask whoever is in charge to let us know what message is being sent by sending pain."

An inner response to the question

Because you talked about slavery being illegal, connections will be made with the part (Sally) that is usually out in the body and is engaging with the outside world. Her interaction with the real world will at some point help us to be informed about what is legal or not legal in the country where we live now, and about the history of slavery, and so the part speaking with you will begin to know from within that you are speaking the truth. Our Old Lady, Sally, just watched a movie called *Amazing Grace* about the abolishment of slavery. We are seeing the chains and children being burned on ships that were used in the slave trade.

How can people be free when they have to obey someone else, and when they are someone else's property?

The higher-ups are saying "She is asking us to do the forbidden, to think, we can't think, we must be loyal to our Family. The Family tells us we don't know what "free" means. We just accept what they say because they were the adults, plus they have control over what we do, say, and think, so if they say we're free then we're free. Understand? All we know is what they teach us and let us do. We are free because we are allowed to live, we aren't killed like the others, and all soldiers or KKK or Luciferians and Freemasons who belong to our family are living in a place of privilege."

Note: In the next paragraph, a different insider is now responding to the question. With most questions, the first response comes from a higher-up who is trying to be loyal to the group, and the next response comes from an insider who has been thinking and learning that they can become free.

We didn't know what freedom meant until now. Now we are learning that it means not being programmed or living in fear, having fun and not having to worry that the bad people are going to get us, not being trapped in the memories, eating foods we like and not getting into trouble or hurt for it. We now know we are not property. Some of us still don't know but we'll help them know, we'll update them.

Questioning the military obedience training

The group told you that they were your fathers, mothers, military trainers, and family. They may have trained you as soldiers, but it is illegal to make children soldiers. It is also illegal and wrong for parents to abuse their children. If the authorities find out adults are doing this, they arrest the adults.

A higher SS is saying this inside as we're writing this answer. "Stop saying 'abuse.' We weren't abused, we were trained to be soldiers. There are soldiers in many countries fighting for what's right. All military operations involve intense training, and that is what we went through. We were selected to accomplish a secret mission so that the Aryan race will dominate this world—the superior, right race. Hitler would be proud of us—he is our leader, the father of all nations, to him we owe our lives. He said that we would face many people like you who will mess with our heads to make us give up our mission. I don't have any parents, I was trained by the SS, they do not abuse, they train us to be tough soldiers. Haven't you heard of tough love? There is no place for love in the military, only discipline, obeying orders and accomplishing the SS mission."

But I am hearing from others inside that we no longer belong to the group, that the body left the group a long time ago and is living far away now, that it's 2012, a long long time since I was with the SS; I'm twelve. I am being shown what it's like for children living in Africa being trained as soldiers—their parents, children, women and men of opposing tribes being slaughtered in the name of another tribe's beliefs—that this is wrong. So what I was trained to do was abuse? I am a child, not a soldier or tool for the Nazis? I am not nothing, but I have a right like all kids and people to live free without harm, and to be encouraged not to hurt others but to respect all people the same? This is too much information, I can't compute it all.

Does obedience actually make you stronger, or does it just allow people to use you for things you don't really want to do?

This is what the twelve-year-old SS was told: "Yes, obedience makes you stronger. You do what you're told to do and do it well, or else. Obedience produces respect, shows character, and makes you tough and able to take pain. It shows loyalty and respect for your elders and the father of all nations, Hitler. It is not your job to think, we think for you because we know what's best for you and have your best interests in mind. You were selected to fulfil a sacred mission that will make this world a better place to live, free of weak and useless degenerates. It will set an order that is unrefutable and indestructibly productive, and one that will be economically sound."

This is what they told us and I believed them and now you are asking me to do the forbidden, to think for myself and question my kommandants and the father of all nations. This is not allowed. Whatever they do is for my best interest, and so that our mission can be achieved without error.

So, I guess if I stop and turn off the soldier mode and allow the others to speak and share what they know: you are helping to free our minds so that we can question for ourselves if what we learned and were trained to do by our commandants is right, lawful or humane, and I guess it isn't. I never thought of it that way, never thought about it until now.

Did you like having to kill people and animals for them? Did you have a choice about it?

I am getting mad and scared and sick. No, I didn't like killing but I didn't have a choice about it. You weren't allowed to think for yourself, you just had to do it. If you do think and hesitate in killing then you could get killed or tortured, or they kill someone you know or hurt or rape someone like your sister. And the victim would get killed anyway because they're in control of everything, they have the ultimate power, not us. Our essence and some of the little ones didn't want to kill and neither did I, but they would take our hand and make us do it. Now there is conflict because you are making me think—yes, they were using me for things that I, or more correctly, the ones below me who took the pain, didn't want to do. I didn't have a say in what I wanted to do or not do. I just did it.

Do you have insiders who refused to obey? What happened to them? Were they as strong as you?

Yes. I am finding out that there are more of us, more than I knew existed. I was in charge of killing and giving orders to kill and induce pain to lower ranking soldiers, but I wasn't aware that we all live in the same body. That's weird. I see myself as one person and not attached to anyone, but a commander of lower ranking soldiers. I see these soldiers like a film that I watched and heard. Everyone has their job to do and must never step or do things out of line or without an order. I see the lower ones as a platoon, not as other insiders who are all part of this body.

Yes, those in the blue pile *[called that because they are black and blue with bruises]* disobeyed. They were tortured and raped . . . and so, perhaps they are stronger than me because they didn't kill or try to hurt other kids, babies, animals and adults.

This is stirring up something inside of me, a feeling of sadness and shame and pain like an aching heart and soul. I do not deserve to live, I must die, I have disgraced my family by talking to you, sharing their secret information, and disgraced myself and hurt and killed others.

Others are telling me "No, nein, it wasn't your fault, you're just a kid like us, it was the bad people who made you and others of us kill and do bad things to people and animals. If you were given a choice and not created as a robot to not feel or show emotion, what do you think you would do?" I don't know . . . I don't think I would kill or want to kill. I'm getting confused, I'm not used to thinking and it's hard to do. No, I wouldn't kill, unless someone is trying to kill me and I have to defend myself, I might. But to just kill someone, no, I wouldn't.

These questions make us really think, and they get some of the insiders mad, which is good, because they start to respect the ones who got hurt, and know that these ones are really the strong ones. They are actually starting to feel sorry for those of us who got hurt, because they now know what we went through before they were made. It makes them start to feel and really know the truth, the extent of what was done to us to try and make us like them—and that we are not like them, we were controlled for their sick purposes, but now we can become much stronger and healthier when we start respecting each other and working together as a team or an inside family.

Questioning the perpetrator group's teachings

The group told you that you didn't need to think, because they thought for you to keep you safe and make you powerful. How do you know those people told you the truth when they said that?

Why would they lie? You don't expect adults to lie, especially those in uniform. I wasn't allowed to question what they said to me. You're just supposed to listen, obey and that's it—simple—"Do what you're told, don't talk to anyone outside the Family, or anyone inside the Family unless we tell you to. You are here because we chose you, you have no rights here, you are nothing. We are making your life worth something special, it is a privilege to be a member of this family, you owe your life to us and will help us fulfil our mission to perpetuate the Aryan race at all costs. Do you understand?" "Yawohl, Kommandant" is what I said because that's what is expected of you. All day and night you watch movies of Hitler being saluted, hearing a crowd of people yell with honour for him, for all that he is doing for Germany and the rest of the world. All you know is

> what is being told to you or engrained in your head with electricity, or being yelled at you like a commander yells at his soldier to make the soldier feel like he's part of a special unit, a strong unwavering unit prepared to die for his Fuhrer.

The group told you that they worked for Hitler and for the Aryan race, who had the truth. Did you know that Hitler is dead, and the Nazis lost the war? Did you know that Hitler killed himself? Your trainers would call that a coward's death.

Note: This provoked an internal argument, and several insiders took part.

> You're making some of our higher-ups mad. He's not dead, I just saw him. He has black hair, a moustache, brown eyes, and wears a SS military uniform. Other twelve-year-olds and younger parts were raped by him too—that was to keep us afraid and make us know that he was our real father whom we had to obey and trust and follow and be loyal to. And he made little Hitlers inside to carry on his seed so that he would never die and always have power over us and the world.
>
> No, he's dead, he died before you were born. He did kill himself too, he drank poison so that the traitor Nazis and English wouldn't catch him because Germany was losing the war. You can check this on the Internet, and you will see that he is dead. You saw either a picture of him, a film of him, or a man dressed up like him.
>
> What? I saw Hitler himself, but if the real Hitler is dead, he must have been someone else dressed up as Hitler. I am being told that Mr Jones, a neighbour, was dressed up like Hitler. And I saw films of Hitler and admired his power and tried to be as tough as him, so that he would be proud of me.
>
> Hey, don't say "coward's death". Hitler is not a coward, you are, you are a woman, inferior, the enemy.
>
> No, she's not, she is a really good person and really brave too, she's not afraid of the people who trained us like all of us and you.
>
> Hey, watch what you are saying to me, I am a higher ranking officer, a commandant, you have no right to talk to me that way, I can send orders to have you punished.
>
> No you can't. You have lost your power over us, and the group has no power over you any more because the body grew up, it's 2012 now. The Germans lost the war in 1945 to Britain and the US.
>
> Arrrrrg, this makes me angry!

How did he make the little Hitlers? How old are they? Do they believe they are actually Hitlers? Do they like having that name?

Note: Several insiders responded to this, and argued about it.

> He made us with his thing (penis). It was a special ceremony. We are being told that our body when it was a girl was on a table, and Hitler put his thing in her, and it made us. Yes, we are Hitler but not the real Hitler, he's our father, we're his kids. He wanted to make sure that the world had lots of Hitlers in it so that no one could ever stop him from ruling Germany and the world.
>
> He wanted to make sure that only the people who he picks out will live in the world because they're the best, and the other stupid people aren't really people, they're degenerates, and don't deserve to live, they have to be exterminated.

> We're supposed to be Hitler, that's the best name anyone can have. It means you're special and that people have to respect you or else. It means power and privilege so we think we will keep our names.
>
> I don't want it . . . me either . . . me too, I want another name, like Shawn or Philip.
>
> I am the Hitler in charge of this whole system. When I first found out that I wasn't Hitler, it made me mad and confused because I had been told and shown how powerful Hitler was and how much everyone admired him and how tough he was, that he was like God himself and the father of all nations. But then after listening to the other insiders and checking for myself on the Internet I began to see what type of a man and coward he really was and that he is dead. I thought that I was given this name to recognise how much like the real Hitler I was, and I was honoured to have his name and felt as powerful and admired as him by the lower ranks in my system. We would never tell you this thought. It took a while before I was happy to not be him.

Dialogue about safety, protection and freedom

The group told you that they were your family, not the parents. Were your biological parents part of the perpetrator group?

> Some of us are really angry, because we know that our parents were part of the group. We keep getting flashbacks of seeing what our mother and father did to us, or did as part of the group, when the body was at different ages, and it is disturbing, makes us angry and sad. We know they never stopped it and we are afraid of them too, because you can't trust them, they are two different people or more. They act like good parents in public, and you never know who is going to be upset or what they will do when the body is at home with them, and then they act different again when they are part of the group. And your question is making us think of all these things, and have emotions, and some of us start to feel sick.

If your parents were part of the group, did they give you to the group?

> "So what if they did?" says the sergeant major inside. "The group is our Family and the body's parents are not high up in the ranks, and so, they are only in charge of the body when it is not around the group (when it is at home, being raised as a regular kid)." Some of the higher-ups feel proud because it was the leaders of the group who assigned us to be one of their Family members and it is an honour and a privilege to be part of the group; it shows us we are superior and special.
>
> The little ones in our system are sad, and the beasties are angry and enraged, because we really didn't like being with the Family. Those people really scared us and hurt us, but we little ones can't tell you that because we're not allowed to talk right now. And our little ones miss having a mum and dad that would save us and treat us well. The little ones are really mad because the parents made them go with the other Family. The blue pile (the bruised and discarded ones) are especially feeling sad and angry and betrayed by their parents and the group.

The group told you that they would always protect you if you obeyed them and were loyal. Did they really protect you? All of you? All the loyal ones?

> Hey, you can't ask us that. You're questioning the group's integrity. No one is allowed to ask questions about the group itself. This question is really disturbing because the blue pile, the babies, and those who were sexually abused know they weren't protected, and are sharing their memories with Sergeant Major and the other higher-ups. This makes some of the higher-ups mad because they either didn't know about this or they have to be loyal to the group no matter what.
>
> Some of the other insiders are getting flashbacks and memories and strong emotions, and faint thoughts of wanting to cut or worse, because they know they weren't protected, they were hurt and tortured, and were part of the killing. We are getting pictures of the group's leaders and priests and the commander of the soldiers, all showing us or reminding us to stay loyal and not talk, don't speak. We remember the group leaders saying "We always protected you, we are protecting you now." Some of the higher-ups are mimicking the group leaders' words and saying to us "It is you who is betraying us through the little ones who are speaking."

Were you really safe when you were with these people?

> No, I guess not, especially when I hear about what happened to those in the blue pile. They weren't safe. And if I think hard, I know that I was really living in fear, scared to get hurt or see someone else get hurt or having to hurt or kill another person. No one was safe with them, you never knew what was going to happen next or who was going to get hurt or worse.

Did you know that there are lots of people in the world who don't have those things done to them, who don't get tortured or raped? Only some people do such things to kids.

> This stirs up emotions in us and makes us sad. That's all we knew. It was normal, it was life, we thought it happened everywhere. I know now that we live far away from the group members and that it's 2012 now. The others are telling me. Some of the ones who spoke today thought it was 1975 or 1967, but they are being updated too.
>
> These questions are like swords penetrating our hearts and souls, going straight to the heart of the deception, and shining the true healing good light in the place that we call the tormentuous hell where we are eternally damned. We say this to show you how powerful your words are. They begin to speak to our essence and bring it closer to the front. Our essence is the part of us that knows the real truth, what is morally right and wrong, even if we can't articulate what is happening for us. Your words begin to shake the foundation of beliefs that we were told and made to accept as truth, and rock what we thought was hopeless to break down.
>
> The more questions you ask and the more we have to think, and/or the insiders start sharing information with one another, the more our head will start to hurt. We also begin to sense from a core part of us that what you are saying is true, and we know that you are asking us questions to help us, that you are being kind to us, and this is also confusing for us, especially the higher-ups, because we aren't used to people being kind or wanting to help us. We are used to being told what to do and when, from people who have no emotions or souls.

Effects of the dialogue

From Sally's insiders' responses, we can see that my questions and statements had the following effects:

1. Alerting the security system to turn on programmes.
2. Helping the insiders, including the higher-ups, begin to think for themselves and wonder about the answers to my questions and whether my statements are true.
3. Shaking the foundation of the beliefs indoctrinated into them.
4. Exposing the ways in which they were deceived.
5. Giving the insiders the opportunity to talk on an equal basis with someone who is kind and curious, as opposed to their abusers who gave orders and were cruel.
6. Reducing dissociation and ending the internal secrets by encouraging insiders to obtain information from one another and from the front personality.
7. Making the unemotional higher-ups aware of the emotional and physical pain which created them, which is still held in the discarded and lower-down insiders.
8. Making the loyal higher-ups begin to feel, or at least be aware of, the unmet needs, sadness and loss, and constant fear and anxiety experienced by other insiders.
9. Getting the head of the system (in this case, Hitler) to engage and begin to think.
10. Making memories of hurt insiders accessible to unhurt obedient ones who believed what they were told.
11. Helping insiders stuck in the past become aware of present-day reality and giving hope for freedom and recovery in the present and future.
12. Gradually dissolving the programming.
13. Connecting parts of the person to her own spiritual essence, and helping her regain control over her own life.

Sally told me that when the questions were written, more higher-up insiders responded to them than when such questions had been asked in person. As a result, there was more effective internal dialogue and updating.

If you have the time, you might try writing questions to your insiders.

What questions would you like to ask them? (See Exercise 8 in Chapter Seven.)

CHAPTER NINE

Keeping safe from the perpetrator group

How safe is it for you to work on your recovery? To put together your memories? To disclose them to a therapist or to friends?

Many survivors have ongoing contact with their abuser groups in one way or another. This occurs whether they are in therapy or not, and results in ongoing access and survivors' involvement in continuing activities throughout their lives, especially if they are living in the same vicinity where they grew up. However, this contact might not be consciously known by the survivor's front person.

Here is what is most important for you to know: it is not the group's magical powers, or omnipotence, or sophisticated technology that allows the group this ongoing control. If this is happening to you, it is likely that certain ones of your own insiders are contacting the group members and enabling the group to continue to access you. They report not only any physical relocation, but also whether you are in treatment, with whom, and what you are disclosing there, as well as (sometimes) any work you may be doing on your own towards healing. This is what allows the abuser group to take actions that trigger parts to behave in ways that sabotage your recovery.

Current contact

In general, the further a survivor is from where his or her childhood abuse occurred, the more likely it is that the abuse has stopped. But in some cases it continues via a different group, or a different branch of the original abuser group.

When a survivor begins addressing his or her mind control history, an insider (in that survivor) is likely to contact a designated person in the abusing group, who will then call out a reporting part for a recitation of all the survivor's behaviours.

Once a group discovers a current or previously abused person is telling secrets to outsiders, or is even beginning to remember what happened to him or her, various threatening things happen. If the survivor who has become a security risk is far away, the group will make certain long distance attempts to trigger parts into shutting down the leak. This will result in some disturbing symptoms, as internal punisher parts do their jobs. In some cases the person will be ordered to return home for further retraining. If the survivor is of particular importance to the perpetrating group, either because he or she was high up in the group's hierarchy or because he or she has knowledge of some important crimes, the abusing group might ask or pay another group in the survivor's area to harass the survivor.

However, if the survivor is far from the location where the abuse occurred, and the original perpetrator group does not have a branch there, harassment could be limited to phone calls, letters, emails, and cards which attempt to trigger parts into doing their jobs. If the perpetrators do not know the survivor's address or phone number, even this will not happen. (You can get an email address that does not have your name in it, and possibly a mobile phone that cannot be traced if you pay cash each month or put it in someone else's name.)

If a survivor still lives near the original abuser group, it might continue to pursue its goal of interfering with or destroying therapy and healing, by extreme tactics if necessary. When the group members contact the survivor, they will trigger parts into returning to them and into obeying their rules of silence and loyalty. When the survivor returns, the training experiences of his or her childhood will be repeated. He or she will again be tortured and forced to perpetrate against others. The therapist might be impersonated, and this "therapist clone" will abuse the survivor, and the survivor might be forced to abuse the supposed therapist.

Members of local groups will hang around the locales where the survivor spends his or her time and use signals to get young parts to come to them so that they can take the survivor for retraining. They will ask a cult-loyal insider to bring them a house key so they can make copies. If the survivor ignores the signals and does not come to the group, they will lie in wait and abduct him or her. If the survivor finds ways to prevent this, the perpetrator group will resort to more extreme measures, such as breaking into his or her home and lying in wait there, in order to torture and/or abduct the survivor.

Just as there is an escalation of these tactics, there is a gradual escalation of punishments for survivors who disobey, and in particular if they spill secrets to outsiders. For two of my clients, the original perpetrators travelled all the way across the continent to attempt reprogramming. If a survivor has become unmanageable and core secrets have been breached, true suicide training (as opposed to attempts designed to land the survivor in the hospital) could be triggered. If the survivor does not commit suicide, some groups might engage in murder attempts disguised as suicide or accidents. They broke into one survivor's apartment, found all the pills she had on hand, and stuffed them down her throat. Fortunately, she did not have a great deal of medication, and she did not die. Organised criminal groups protect their secrets at all costs.

How to identify whether you have current involvement

It might take time to find out whether or not you have any ongoing contact with dangerous people. In the worst-case scenario, you will find you have parts who are fully involved in a perpetrator group, attending rituals, participating in the training of other members, and carrying out other crimes.

There are, however, many survivors who have not had contact with their perpetrator groups for many years and appear to have been completely dropped by them. Errors in programming, a rebellious nature, or difficulty in keeping information nicely segregated in hidden pockets of memory or internal parts render many survivors useless to their programmers. After measures have been taken to "cap" their memories, "close them down", and encourage them to self-destruct through addictions and suicide attempts, they are turned loose to fend for themselves.

However, you do not need to be in constant contact with the group in order for them to establish contact under certain circumstances. When survivors begin to remember their abuse and seek out therapy, or work privately on their own recovery, the rule of secrecy still prevails. A survivor who has not had any contact with the group for many years might end up reporting to them and reactivating harassment by them without consciously knowing this is happening.

Other survivors move far away from their abusers to a location where the perpetrator group does not function. Sometimes the group itself has disbanded, or its original purpose (such as the Cold War between Russia and the USA, for some military/political groups) no longer exists (though often the actions of the abusers continue, with different rationales).

Even if there is minimal group involvement, survivors usually maintain contact with their families of origin. In most cases, family members, or generations of the person's entire family, were involved with the group when the survivor was a child. It is difficult to know whether you are reporting to family members about your therapy or healing work because you could be reporting in a dissociated identity state and have no memory of doing so. At the same time, you need to understand that failure to maintain contact with the family could arouse suspicion, and aside from the fact that you, and many of your parts, might genuinely care about your family members, it is probably best not to deviate from your usual contact patterns, unless you have some other urgent reason such as preventing the abuse of your own children, or being forced to abuse other people's children at cult events.

Indicators of recent or ongoing perpetrator contact, harassment, triggering and/or abuse

Early therapists working with ritual abuse survivors listed indicators that signified to a therapist that recent or current contact was occurring. This led to an inaccurate understanding of how things work, because, unfortunately, some of the indicators simply meant that programming was triggered and inside parts were doing their jobs. There is a vast difference between:

- internal punishment for disclosures by insiders doing their jobs (this is not "current contact");
- having family members or other cult members deliberately trigger programming;
- having parts who continue to contact (and possibly report on your recovery process to) family members whom you have been avoiding in your conscious life;
- being harassed by perpetrator group members and punished by them for disobedience;
- having insiders who continue to participate actively in perpetrator group activities.

If you "lose time", and do not know what has happened during the lost time, you might want to look for clues to indicate whether there has been some kind of current contact with the perpetrators, or whether it is just activity by insiders, such as a child part coming out to play, or a sad part sitting and crying, or a teenager enjoying driving the car. You can ask your insiders for an explanation. Be sure to reassure them that they will not be punished for whatever they did when you were not conscious of it, as it is common that they were punished severely early in life. If they give you a harmless explanation, you can perhaps arrange for times when they can come "out" into the body and do the things they want to do. If they do not give you an explanation, it might be because they fear punishment, or because they are doing something they do not want you to know about. That something may or may not be current perpetrator contact. And, of course, some survivors cannot hear their parts talk to them. If that is the case, you can write to them or think to them to draw what happened.

Arauna Morgan lists some signs of current contact in her article on Ellen Lacter's website: http://endritualabuse.org/healing/breaking-the-chains/. Some of the items in the checklist below come from that article.

Exercise 9. Tracing current contact

Do you have significant periods of amnesia, without reasonable explanations from your insiders about what may have gone on during those periods?

Do these periods of amnesia occur around cult holiday times (including your and family members' birthdays, Christian and pagan holidays)?

Do you find evidence that you have gone out at night without remembering it? Do not be too confident that an alarm system can protect you, as insiders or cult members might know how to disarm it.

Have you developed a fear of locking or closing your windows or doors?

Have you found yourself compelled to answer the telephone and then not remembered the conversation?

Have you received peculiar phone calls, particularly where the same thing is said over and over at each call, or calls that consistently hang up after a set number of rings?

Have you been approached by people in the street who say peculiar things, often with Satanic themes?

Have you found your car or home broken into and minor vandalism conducted, or objects put in a place other than where you left them? (If so, check with your insiders to see whether any of them did this as part of their job, to make you think perpetrators are around when they are not.)

Have you become afraid of your therapist or of the therapist's office?

Have you found bruises, pin-pricks, blisters, other pains or marks on your body, especially after lost time and with no plausible other explanation?

Have you suddenly become ill, with no clear explanation? (This could be a programme or a body memory rather than an indicator of current contact, or a result of poison left in your home or office.)

Have you discovered new parts who have no memory of childhood or adolescence?

Have you suddenly found you are unable to access your inside parts?

Have you suddenly felt "all better" so that you no feel you no longer need to work on your recovery?

Have you found known parts now split into two or more parts, with different knowledge, abilities, etc., and a fear of going back together?

Have you had a sudden onset of intense urges to engage in some complex, usually dangerous behaviour (e.g., suicide in a specified motel, go to a specific town, self-mutilate in a specific manner, etc.)?

(continued)

Have you had a sudden burning desire to return to alcohol or drug abuse?

If you have answered yes to several of these questions, you may suspect that you are being accessed by perpetrators. However, saying "no" to all does not necessarily indicate there has been no current contact. Current contact is designed to be hidden from the front person who lives your daily life, and from other inside parts, including the higher-ups, who are supposed to believe the group knows everything. Encourage all insiders to work towards permission to know whether there is contact.

Means of initiating current contact

It is extremely important to understand how the group is able to find out where you are and what you are saying. Not all current contact is a simple matter of access by the original perpetrator group or of insiders reporting to it. We must also be aware of the dangerous tentacles of the Internet for survivors. One of my clients told me that a man with whom she was in contact on an internet discussion forum was trying to figure out her personality system; the system subsequently turned upside-down, parts I had never met took control, and she left therapy. I do not believe this survivor had any current perpetrator contact prior to this; the man was actively searching survivor discussion forums for those whose personality systems he could disrupt. He told her he was going to come to meet her, and he might have done so.

Other dangers are seen in the recovery community. Another of my clients, one who had not been in contact with her perpetrator group (in another city) for almost forty years, met a fellow ritual abuse survivor in a sexual abuse survivors' group. This woman took her out to what turned out to be a cult meeting and reprogramming session. After that event, my client received regular telephone calls from local perpetrator group members, attempting to call out parts and get them to attend meetings. This is the kind of experience that would cause a survivor who is unaware of the function of inside parts believe that "They (the abusers) are everywhere, and know everything!"

I also had a meeting (arranged through a church minister) with a woman who had supposedly healed from ritual abuse and was now said to be healing survivors. She attended a number of churches in town. It was clear to me that what this person said about her programming and healing was pure hogwash. One of my clients recognised her as a cult high priestess who was going from church to church seeking out survivors and giving signals to trigger them to return, report, and punish disloyalty internally.

Several other survivors of whose safety I am fully assured have been constantly terrified that they were being followed and spied upon. That is because survivors who relocate and separate from these perpetrator groups still have parts inside who have been taught that they can never get away and that the offenders know everything. (The groups teach this to children precisely because it is not true, and they do not want the survivors to find out.) In most cases, you are safer if you have moved a great distance from the original perpetrator group. I shall discuss this at greater length later in this chapter.

Another possibility is contact that is minimal. A telephone call with a cult member (usually a family member), or a birthday card with a certain type of picture on it (e.g., a rose) can be enough to set off many of these symptoms. A survivor I have worked with for many years just recently revealed that this is a "recall year for her". The parts in charge of her system are supposed to organise the system to return to her place of origin, where they will report to her programmer (who by now is either dead or very old) about any parts who have broken the silence. These parts will then be "sacrificed", which could mean death, torture, or closedown. Her last recall year was sixteen years ago.

It cannot be stressed enough: current contact is a serious business, whether it is present all along, initiated by parts reporting to the perpetrators about therapy or other attempts at healing, or accomplished by contact with other survivors who are still involved and looking for disobedient survivors to trigger or recall.

The Big Lie

What makes survivors contact people who they know abused them in childhood? They do it because some of their insiders believe what I call the Big Lie, something they were taught to believe beginning very early in life,

Mind control groups know that the children they abuse and train will one day grow up and possibly move away, and possibly begin to remember what happened in childhood. So, they prepare these children with a great deal of training to make sure that the group's secrets do not leak out when the children grow up. They want and need their victims to believe they are all-powerful, all-seeing, all-knowing, and able to appear at any moment to punish disloyalty.

The most basic lie of mind controllers, which I call the Big Lie, is that the perpetrators always know where you are and what you do, say, or think.

First of all, they tell you that whomever they worship, God or Satan or Lucifer, is watching you. If you attended church or Sunday school, you may recall being taught that God is all-powerful, all-seeing, and everywhere. If some of your insiders were part of a Satanic or Luciferian group, they would be taught the same thing about Satan or Lucifer. There is nothing like an invisible, omnipotent watcher to make children behave in the desired manner when no one is really supervising them. This is especially effective if that deity has already been simulated by a costumed person who punished those children for disobedience with rape or torture, or by torturing someone else. And this is what they do. But even groups without a religious belief teach children that they, the abusers, have special powers or technology that enables them to know where you are and what you do and say and even think.

Punishment and trickery are used to convince each child of the truth of the Big Lie. The child is set up to hide, to talk to someone about the abuse, or to disobey. A hidden microphone or a one-way mirror permits the group to see or hear what the child is doing or saying. The group punishes the child for what he or she did or said when the child thought he or she was alone or hidden.

Often a child (and, therefore, a survivor) has a hidden floater part who observes the trickery and can tell you about it. If you have one, you can work on winning his or her trust so that part will tell you what he or she saw happen.

Abuser groups tell children many different versions of the Big Lie. They even tell different versions to different insiders of the same child. Here are some I have heard about.

What children are told

"The walls have ears." This is taught to a young child in a room with plastic "ears" glued to the walls. The abusers say the ears will always be there in any room but will not be visible.

"The all-seeing Eye always sees you even when you can't see it." This is taught with a plastic eyeball in a glass case, or even with an actual eyeball from a dead creature.

"Your stuffed animals [some given to the child by the perpetrators] report on you to us." When the child is little, there could be a tape recorder or "nanny camera" in a stuffed animal.

"We [the abusers] are always hiding in the shadows or in the walls." This is taught through an actual experience where people jump out from the shadows or from behind the walls—but of course, it would not be true in other places or at other times; this is a setup.

"Mothers have eyes in the back of their heads." This is taught to a child whose mother is an important part of the abuser group.

"Your mother can hear everything you tell anyone." When LisaBri was little, vinyl ears were put over both her ears and her mother's ears, and the child was told that everything she said was transmitted to her mother through the ears.

"The crows tell what you are doing or saying." The truth is that since crows eat dead things, they hang around abusers who kill animals, but they cannot really talk to them. Some groups may use other common creatures, such as spiders. They pick something that is always around so the survivor will always be afraid of that animal telling on them.

"Satan's eyes are always watching." This is simulated with flashlights covered with red crepe paper, in the dark.

"There is a microchip implanted in your body which tells us where you are and what you are thinking or saying." There are considerable technological difficulties with this. Even if a device could be implanted, it cannot both record speech and send radio signals over a long distance for a very long time.

"There is a device implanted inside your head which sees and hears everything, even your thoughts, and reports it to us." They perform fake surgeries to make children believe this.

"We have sophisticated state-of-the-art technology to listen to your phone conversations and read your emails and see where you are at all times." The truth is that it takes a lot of manpower and time to monitor someone's calls or emails, even if it could be done, and abusers cannot put that much time and energy into this. The important thing for the groups is that the child believes them and so keeps their secrets.

"We know things and do things by real magic." Every story I have heard about this turned out to be trickery. Stage magicians are very impressive, but their magic is not real.

"We always know if someone is lying, so you must always tell the truth to us." The truth is that this has been studied a lot, and no one can always tell if someone is lying.

"Everyone you know is linked to us and knows your every move, and will report back to us." This may have been true in childhood, but it is not true later. In some cases, it is not true in childhood either. Abuser groups can make a child believe his or her parents are present when they are not.

One of the abuser groups' favourite tricks is fake surgery, in which they make children believe they are putting things in their bodies. They dress the child up for surgery, put him or her on a stretcher, and tell the child they are going to implant such things as a device which records everything the child says or thinks and sends it to the abusers. The anaesthetic puts the child to sleep, and he or she wakes up with a bandage and the belief that this device is now inside his or her head, or tooth, or body. It is, of course, a trick.

Some of your insiders might be asking, "Then how do they know where we are and what we have said, if what they told us is a big fat lie?" The answer may shock you: it is you who tells them. You have reporter insiders who have the job of telling the abuser group where you are and what you have said and done, especially if any of your parts have been disloyal and disclosed secrets.

When you are a child, it is easy for your parents and other relatives to know where you are pretty well all the time. They also encourage siblings to spy and tell on one another, with threats of punishment if they do not. This is not magic or technology.

The main purpose of the Big Lie is to make sure that the group's secrets do not leak out to outsiders when the child's body has grown up and the person has left the area. In addition, some groups want to continue to use some survivors. For instance, ritualistic cults expect the children they abuse to become adult cult members who will transmit the group's values and practices to the next generation. Military/political groups continue to use some adult survivors of their training as spies, assassins, or couriers for drugs or political documents. While they "close down" the programming of some survivors, they keep others in active use. Child prostitution and pornography groups probably allow survivors to leave when they reach adulthood, unless they are also involved in the adult versions of the same things. (By the way, it is frequently only one section of a personality system who is involved in these criminal activities; if the child becomes too old for use in sexual services, other activities may continue.)

The group leaders realise that they will not have the time or resources to keep track of all their victimised children when they reach adulthood. Because of that, they get the (now grown) children to keep track for them, through internal reporters.

Fake surgery is also used to make children believe there is a bomb in their stomach that will explode if they talk about or remember the abuse. After the bomb is supposedly implanted, the abusers show the child an X-Ray that purports to show the bomb in his or her middle. Less sophisticated versions of this deception involve putting a small animal like a rat or a snake inside the child's orifices and telling the child it will devour him or her from inside if he or she talks.

There are many lies designed to keep the children and adults trained by the group involved. "Return" programmes are insiders' trainings based on lies that make survivors believe they have to return to the group at certain times or for specified events. "Access" programmes train insiders to respond to callbacks by abusers. "Report" programmes address the problem of members giving away secrets by forcing those who have done so to contact the group immediately. Particular groups of insiders (usually children) are given each of these types of training.

Note: The following material may be triggering or upsetting to some survivors. If you need help dealing with this, Chapter Ten is about dealing with triggering.

Training to return to the abusers

Most survivors of organised abuse have parts trained to return to their abusers, either at specific times or dates (e.g., for family birthdays, or important rituals, or full moons), or when they are called back. Young adults are usually allowed to go out and create an identity in the world, and then called back for use at a specific age or year. After their return, those people whose initial abuse was with an occult religious group are expected to continue to participate in the rituals that happen on the dates listed in the group's calendar. They will not incur any punishment for disloyalty—unless they begin disclosing secrets to outsiders. If they are parents, they are very probably programmed to take their children to the group's events, and their children are being abused on an ongoing basis within the group and possibly by some of the parents' parts at home. Those who have been trained by a military/political group might be sent on assignments for the group. A child, teenager, or young adult from either setting might continue to be involved in pornographic filming or prostitution. All of this happens in a life separate from the one they present to the world.

How are child parts trained to return to their abusers? Here are some specific types of training which survivors have disclosed to me:

"Return on Hallmark™ holidays"

This is the title one survivor client gave to me to describe the compulsion to contact family or go home at Christmas, Easter, her own or family birthdays, and other such times. It appears innocuous, but if there is a very strong compulsion to return, it could be a result of this programming. Important rituals are often conducted on these dates, and parts are trained not to miss them for fear of being severely punished (or someone else being punished because of their absence), or missing rewards if they do not attend.

"Return for rewards"

This is part of the training of insiders who have to take leadership in rituals or other significant events. Some of these parts might have experienced none of the abuse, and are rewarded with massage, drugs, pleasurable sex, promotions (with crowns or rings if it is a religious group, stripes if it is a military group, and various other symbols of authority) and power, such as the right to decide who gets hurt (which might be experienced as a punishment rather than a reward).

Abuser groups do, as they promise, give rewards to these insiders for coming on time. But they hurt other insiders quite badly if there has been disloyalty. Oh, they might give you a fake promotion if you go back, but it does not mean anything in the real world, and to earn it you might be forced to harm someone else.

Sometimes, the parts who have this training really want to go back to the group, and can only be completely stopped by other parts sharing with them the pain of what has happened to the body at cult events. Until the abuse memories have been shared with them, other parts with internal authority can keep them under control by making them forget the date they are to return, or getting them to go to sleep at that time.

External helpers, such as a friend or spouse, can also help. For example, someone safe can hide your shoes or block the driveway so that you cannot drive to a group event.

"Return at a specific date"

After making a lot of progress in her recovery, a survivor client of mine encountered callback programming for Easter of 2011. Just before Easter, certain parts that I had not known about "woke up". They were heavily drugged child parts who had been told that the world would end at Easter of 2011 and that they must return home by that time. (Other parts who woke up at the same time had the job of punishing the rest of the system if they did not comply.) I spent considerable time showing them current magazines and books with dates on them which showed that the date on which the world was supposed to end was already past.

Because the survivor had made so much progress in her recovery, the callback was unsuccessful. Her system was able to detect the new parts and update them on the changes in her life and her current safety. But if this were a survivor who had not worked hard on her healing, or whose system were not largely co-conscious and co-operative, she would probably just have booked a flight home and returned to whichever perpetrators were still around to reset her programming. Even if her original programmers were not still around, they would have had replacements (who had her records) ready to deal with her. Newly awakened parts are confused about present-day reality. Your system can help prepare for such events by having a method of updating any insider who wakes up after years of unawareness. Other insiders can act as helpers and share information with the newly awakened one about your present life, where you live, how many years have gone by, and what keeps you safe now.

"Return to avoid punishment"

This has several variations. For example, a cult child misses a ritual (usually for the full moon) and is punished with electroshock the next day. Or she is made to kill what she believes is a baby and is told that if she does not keep returning the police will be notified and she will be jailed. Parts who have this training are afraid not to return. These are young children, and their fear is based on their believing the Big Lie that the abusers know everything and will hunt them down. This probably actually happened to these insiders when the body was a child, but it is much more difficult for abusers to accomplish when the body is an adult. Those insiders who return to avoid punishment need to learn a simple truth: the abusers can only hurt them if they have access to the survivor's body. If the body is not where the abusers are, it cannot be hurt.

"Return to save someone"

This callback is used frequently with disloyal survivors. Insiders have been told that someone will be badly hurt or killed just because they do not show up for the event. They believe that they must return to save a younger sibling or friend from being killed. The parts who have this training feel a desperate need to return to the group, feeling that something awful will happen to someone if they do not.

In one setup, you (as a child) are made to be unable to attend an event on time. Then you are taken to the event and forced to watch someone else being punished and told it was because you were late. In another, you are told that you are the only person who can save another child from being hurt, but you are prevented from arriving in time to do so, and have to watch. Of course, these were tricks to make you believe that other people will be hurt because of you. But many years later, this will not happen. It only happened in your childhood because the abusers had planned for you to arrive and watch it. No one will actually be hurt because of you *unless* you are there to watch it or take part in it. So, do not be there!

These lies about what the survivor can expect to happen throughout their lives are all established through tricks that happen in the person's childhood. Because the child insiders remain children, and often do not know that years have passed, they still believe what the abusers told them when they were under their control.

I want you (the front person or the higher-ups) to remember that you can dialogue with the parts who believe they have to return for any or all of these reasons. They need to understand that contact with the group puts them in a *weaker* position and will lead to pain, while disconnection will protect them. For example, if a person returns to save someone else, he or she is often used to harm the person he or she was supposed to save, then accused of being a perpetrator, and told that disclosing what happened will result in the survivor being jailed. This is all a lie. *The truth is that the group is less likely to harm someone you love if you are not present.*

Sometimes, guilty parts think they should return to be punished for their crimes. The truth is that if they return they will be forced to commit more such crimes.

Training that ensures abuser access

Children (who later become child parts of survivors) are trained always to be available to their abusers—that is, they must respond to their abusers and come when called. This training results in programmed, immediate responses. I have frequently seen survivors with a panicky desire to call home, and an inability to turn off the phone ringer. This is based on the fact that when the body was a child, the abusers could get hold of that child and punish him or her for not responding immediately when told or signalled to come.

A survivor client of mine, who frequently denied the ritual abuse history that brought her to therapy, was trying to reduce her contact with her family (who might or might not have been involved with the ritual abuse). She told me that she just could not help answering the phone or returning phone calls when messages were left. Turning off the ringer did not work because she saw the flashing light that indicates a message. She had no knowledge of this specific programming, but clearly something was forcing her to respond to phone calls whether or not she wanted to.

Some of the beliefs that abusers instil in survivors are:

"You always have to answer the phone, or something bad will happen."
"Even on the phone, certain parts have to come out if they are asked for."
"You always have to answer the door and open it, even if you don't want to see the person who comes to the door."
"You have to go outside if you hear a certain sound."
"You have to go to anyone who makes a certain hand signal."
"If an abuser gets hold of you or signals you, you cannot run away or fight back."

Methods of indoctrination

When a survivor is no longer returning to the group or reporting to them, he or she might still be accessible to the perpetrators for some time because of parts trained to respond to cues from the perpetrators. Some of these trainings get the survivor out into the open where group members can get at them. Often there are specific auditory triggers, such as a certain number of rings on the phone, the honk of a car horn, or a beeping sound. Group members can use visual hand signals to call a person to come to them. Some triggers might make a survivor unable to move or speak, so that he or she will co-operate with an abduction.

Here are examples of some trainings I have discovered in survivors:

Answer the phone

A drugged child was painfully shocked until she answered a ringing telephone. Then "Satan" spoke on the phone and told her, "Always answer when Satan calls." In later life, the survivor always had to answer the phone. She had no conscious memory of the reason for this compulsion, until she uncovered the training memory.

Open the door

Abusers knocked on the child's bedroom door. If she did not open it, they kicked it down and then violently abused her.

Go outside

At about age nine or ten, a child was deliberately made addicted to narcotic drugs, and was conditioned to go outside at the sound of a car horn (for another child, it was a dog whistle) to get the drugs she needed. Many years later, feeling drug withdrawal symptoms and knowing she must go outside to get rid of those symptoms, this part responded to the sound cue. (Another insider used the memory to give her the feelings of withdrawal.)

Come to the handler

A young child was put in a back yard swimming pool, and called by a perpetrator, on the other side of the pool, to swim to him. A lid was put over the pool so that the only place she could get any air was where the man was. She swam across to him underwater in order not to drown. Later, the survivor felt the sensation of drowning until she went to the cult person who had called her.

Young children are also trained to recognise symbols that have special meanings to survivors. So, a card from a family member with a particular picture or particular words might be a message to come home. One survivor received a letter from her aunt, whom she believed was a safe person, mentioning the butter cookies the aunt would like to bake for her. Later, when the survivor discovered her internal programmer, he had a list of programmes including one called "Butter Cookies" which was a cue to return to the abusers.

Keep still and silent

A child was put in an enclosed space with some type of supposedly poisonous creature (bees, snakes, spiders). He was told not to speak or move or the creatures would bite or sting him to death. I have seen this training in several different survivors. In one case, the insects (bees) stung her and because she was allergic to bees she became unconscious. Then she was resuscitated. In later life, if a perpetrator group member approaches this person on the street and gives the signal for this programme, the survivor will be unable to move to run away. (This kind of training is also one reason that survivors so often have strong reactions to insects.)

No running away

A young child was encouraged to run away from the perpetrators, then punished by harm to her knees or feet when she was caught. An insider was trained to give her this pain if she considered running away from the group.

A client of mine recently arrived for her first session with a mysteriously broken foot. When she returned home, she sprained both ankles. These injuries were traced to an inside boy who had been trained to injure her feet.

Don't leave town

A child (and, later, teenager) was drugged and put through simulated car accidents, plane crashes, and other events designed to make her believe that these things would inevitably happen to her if she attempted to leave the town where the perpetrator group operated. (She has now successfully moved away, but she had to uncover these programmes first.)

Training to report any disclosures or relocations

We have already looked at the variety of deceptions that are used to make children believe that the abusers always know where they are and what they have said and done, and will hunt them down and punish them severely for disloyalty.

Abusers teach one or more insider parts that they must report to the abusers any time the child (or, later, the adult) disobeys or discloses secrets. These "Reporters" are also told to report any relocations, so that the abusers always know where they are living when they grow up. The paradox of this situation is that the parts who report to the abusers do so because they believe the abusers know everything and will punish them if they do not report.

If the abusers really knew everything, why would they need anyone to report to them?

Meanwhile, the rest of the personality system does not know about the secret reporting and its consequences, so it is easy for the abusers to "prove" that they know everything. Even the higher-ups are not supposed to know that there are insiders giving information about them to the abusers.

The survivor usually reports to the perpetrators through a phone call to a relative. The relative triggers reporter parts to come out, and the everyday front person is unaware this has happened. The one who makes the phone call might be unaware of the reporting. Generally, the reporting parts of the survivor, as well as those who make the phone call, believe (because of the Big Lie) that the group always knows where they are and what they are saying anyway, since that was often true in childhood. There is usually more than one insider with each of these tasks.

Child parts in an adult trauma survivor might not understand time or place, and might believe they are still in the places where the group had access to them in childhood. Here is how one survivor described it in a letter to me: "Most of the ones inside do not feel time the way you do. When you say it has been a long time or many, many years, it does not make the same kind of sense to the little ones as it does to you or to the older ones. Those little ones only know about time when they are out. So for them it isn't as long as you think it is since they were in that place. The older ones know better about time and how it works. The little ones kind of know about today, tomorrow and yesterday. They sort of only know where they are when they are out. They know the neighbor lady's house [where some abuse happened]. Some know the house with that mother and father and a few know the house we lived in later. Some of those same ones know different rooms where bad things happened like with the doctor and that other man. They only know all of those different moments. There is kind of nothing in between. A few of them have been lost in the town after your meeting. They just know they are lost. But they are not looking around and thinking this is a different place."

Because young child parts have so little understanding of the time that has gone by, or the distance they have travelled from the place where the abuse occurred, they often believe the perpetrators are still around even when they are not. It can help if you have a small object (like a little coloured stone, or a toy) from the present which you can hold to remind your inside children that you are far away from the abusers in space and time. It can also help to have a calendar on your wall, and a map, for your older insiders.

Methods of indoctrination

Here is how one child was trained to telephone her mother. At age eleven, she was heavily sedated so she believed she was asleep. Then, she was painfully abused by people in costumes, so that she thought she was having a nightmare. Her mother came in and soothed her, and told her that if she had nightmares she should call her. This event was repeated several times, and in different places, and in the later instances her mother was not present, but there was a telephone on which she could call her, and her mother responded by coming and soothing her. In later life, when this programme was triggered, the adult had nightmares (given by trained insiders) and the child part phoned her mother.

Usually the training of the reporters includes a horrendous experience designed to make the child terrified of the consequences of not telling the perpetrators what she has disclosed. For example, the child is told that another child has talked about the cult to an outsider. She watches this child being tortured until he or she discloses to the cult what has been told; then the punishment stops. The child being trained is then put in a position to receive the same kind of torture (e.g., put on the cross or the rack, or touched with a hot poker), and told *"You must always tell us if you have talked."*

Reporter parts are tested and trained; they have backups. It is important to the abusers that the rest of the survivor's personality system does not know about the reporters, so they will all continue to believe in the magic or technology which enables the perpetrators to know everything, so survivors can never escape or be free.

Let me repeat: the abusers do not know things through magic, or crows, or ears on the walls, or implants, or special technology. They know only because of reporter insiders. And if your reporters do not report, the abusers assume you are not remembering or telling things.

Dealing with reporting

As soon as you even suspect that you are a survivor of mind control or ritual abuse, you should (1) look for evidence to assess whether or not you could be currently involved with the perpetrating group, and (2) find a way to prevent parts from reporting to the perpetrators. Your parts, most of whom are child parts, have no idea that they have choices, and how much power they really hold simply by stopping the reporting and preventing the trained insiders from acting on their access programming.

Higher-ups, you need to know this information, which the people who gave you your positions withheld from you. So, begin by asking inside whether there is anyone trained to report to the abusers. Tell them they will not be in trouble for telling you about this, and that you will appreciate them for telling you. And make sure you mean it. I have several times sat with a client and asked them to just think the question to their insiders: "Do we have any parts who have the job of reporting on us to someone?" and if the answer is yes, "Are they still doing that job?" and "Whom do they report to?" and "How do they tell that person?" You need to know just where the danger is—in a phone call to a family member, in an email, or in a meeting.

If your reporters say that they are still doing their jobs, you might ask other insiders to arrange for the reporters to forget they told you about the reporting. Then they will not be able to report being discovered.

If you discover that you have reporting parts, I advise that you (the front person or the higher-ups) reason with those parts, or, if they are too young to understand, with the older parts who might be in charge of them. Ask them why the abusers would need parts to report to them where the person is, if they already know. Point out to them that the abusers knew that when the body became an adult, they would not be able to keep track of the person all the time as they could when he or she was a child. Explain that this is why they trained parts to keep track of those things for them, and if the reporters do not report, or do not tell the truth when they report, the perpetrators will not know that any disclosures have been made and you will all be safe.

If the reporters (or those in charge of them) decide not to report, you have the safety to proceed with healing and even with therapy. (You can still engage in therapy while you have insiders reporting, but it is much more difficult.) Reporter parts have generally been trained always to tell the truth. Be sure to look for "backups", however—parts who are supposed to take over the job of any part who stops doing his or her job. They will also need to be convinced.

Reporter parts are also observers, trained to watch and listen carefully to everything you do in the real world. Therefore, they observe therapy sessions and any other situations in which you might talk about the abuse. If the reporters are unwilling to stop doing their jobs, other insiders can be recruited to help. Here is one way that you can deal with this problem. There are usually some parts who have the job of putting other parts to sleep (the initial training is done with sleep-inducing drugs); they can put the reporters to sleep during most of the therapy session. You can arrange this with those in charge of the "sleep programme", then have those in charge of the "forgetting programme" make the reporters forget that you have made this arrangement. From then on, in therapy sessions, you talk about inconsequential topics for the first five or ten minutes for the benefit of the reporters, then, when the reporters have gone to sleep, do your real work. They can be woken up for the closing minutes of the session. All they will have to report is what happened in those first and last few minutes.

Another way of dealing with it is to satisfy the reporters' need to do their jobs by having them report internally to internal copies of the abusers (there usually are some). How do you find out if there are any? You just ask. Note, however, that some internal children cannot tell the difference between real present-day people and internal copies or memories, so older parts need to guide this process.

If you do not have sufficient rapport with your insiders to do these things, you need to proceed very slowly with finding your memories, so as to not accidentally trigger any reporting which will get the perpetrator group reinvolved with your younger parts.

What about relocation?

Recovering from ritual abuse is a serious business, and sometimes there are real dangers. Relocation to a place at a great distance from the original abuse is sometimes quite necessary if you are trying to leave the group and experiencing severe harassment to the point that you are unable to keep safe. However, relocation is most useful when the parts are no longer reporting to the abusers, and the abuser group does not have a branch in the new location. If there is no related group in the new location, it might reduce current abuse, but if there is a related group, the abuse could continue and you might not be able to recognise the group members in order to avoid them. Or a new group might be able to call out insiders using access triggers. It is imperative to continue your healing and disable triggers that allow you to be reaccessed. Failing to do so leaves you open to any predator who knows how to use triggers, and there are a lot of them, and some groups can be even worse than the home "cult" group.

One of my first ritually abused clients moved to a nearby town, where she believed she was safe. What actually happened, since she had reported, was that the persons who regularly abducted her were unknown to her, so it was more difficult to avoid them than it had been to avoid the people she recognised. She was actually less safe than she had been here.

A woman once came to me from a city some distance away. Her previous therapist had sent her to me because of severe harassment; she just knew too much and had breached security. She believed her life was in danger. About a week after she arrived, she disclosed with embarrassment that she had telephoned the perpetrator group and given them her location. A local group had already contacted and threatened her. This was now an emergency that would not allow time for inside work with reporters. I had to smuggle the woman out of town (while her apartment was being watched) and send her on to another location previously unknown to her. I sent her to the USA, hoping that the abusers (on the Canadian prairies) would have fewer links there. Still, I was aware that it was quite likely that the person I sent her to would have the same experience, unless he had the time to deal with her reporting training.

However, this probably only happened because of her high status in the group; if she had been a lower-level person, her original perpetrator group might have been content with phone calls and letters rather than paying a local group to harass her. It might still be safer to move a great distance from the place where you grew up, then disable the reporting in order to progress in your healing with minimal harassment.

In most cases, what I recommend if there is current contact is, first disable the reporting, and then carefully plan a move to a distant location, where the group is unlikely to have a branch, and, if you can afford it, where you can find a competent therapist (see Chapter Nineteen). I know that uprooting yourself can be very difficult and upsetting, but it is preferable to continuing to be abused.

What you can do

Most mind control survivors I have encountered, especially of cult abuse, have all of these kinds of trainings. You see how complicated they are for the survivor to deal with, and to unravel.

If you are a survivor who is being watched and/or harassed by perpetrators, it helps if you live with a safe spouse or roommate who can be informed of the situation and stay with you as much as possible. Although this frequently occurs, I do not recommend mind control or ritual abuse survivors living with one another; rather than keeping one another safe, they could expose one another to risk. For example, one roommate might have the strength to keep the door locked, but the other might open the door to abusers who then abuse both roommates.

One survivor found a creative solution. When she was being harassed by the cult that she had broken away from, the cult's van kept circling her neighbourhood, waiting for her to leave the house. So, she telephoned the police and said, "I keep seeing a van around here, and I think it may have something to do with those break-ins that keep happening in this area." After the police checked it out, they called her back. "It's funny," they said, "There weren't any burglary tools, but that van was full of illegal drugs and weapons and handcuffs."

If the perpetrator group is at a distance, you may only have to deal with telephone calls and letters or emails. If they harass you in this way, trying to trigger various trained behaviours, you can turn off the ringer on the phone (and place it where it is not visible), change your email address to something they do not know, and open any letters or parcels only in the presence of your therapist or another safe person with whom you can discuss their meaning and make sure that you will not act on any messages they carry.

In the end, however, the only solution is to work through the memories of the trainings so that your parts are no longer bound by the compulsion to act on their training. Programming such as this operates like post-hypnotic suggestions; it feels compulsory when the person is under its grip, even though the conscious adult does not understand it. Once the story of the programming becomes conscious, it loses that grip and the person becomes free. Some survivors find ways to make it conscious even when the memories have not yet been fully worked through. The exercise below gives some help with this. In the initial stages, before you have worked through your training memories, the important thing is to make sure that reporting does not occur so that you do not have to deal with perpetrators.

I have occasionally had marathon therapy sessions of a weekend at a time (all day long) with some current-contacting survivors, in which we went through all the access training memories to remove their effects. I also have a policy of working through all current abuse memories immediately after they occur, along with the memories of whatever programming was being retaught in the current contact. This is what enabled some of my current-contacting survivors to escape their group and become free.

Ongoing perpetrator contact is one of the most difficult issues for survivors of mind control and ritual abuse. It is my belief that most of the retractors of memories disclosed in therapy—the kind of survivors who were put forward as figureheads by the "false memory syndrome" advocates—were victims of ongoing abuse (and rewards) by perpetrator groups. Ellen Lacter has a very helpful page on her website with suggestions for survivors about safety: http://endritualabuse.org/activism/safety-tips-for-ritual-abuse-survivors/.

We do not want to know this is happening, but if it is, it is. If you are aware of this possibility, you can communicate with your parts before working on memories to prevent this kind of harassment.

Exercise 10. Recognising and defeating access programming

Do you, or do many of your parts, believe that the perpetrators always know where you are and whether you have talked about the abuse? If so, what do those parts and others (such as hidden observers) remember that made them believe this? Can the older parts detect the trickery in it?

Do you have insiders who do not know what year it is, and believe they still live with perpetrators when they do not? If you do, you can go about updating them.

Internal reporters

Do you have parts whose job is to describe everything you have done or said or thought when cued by a family member or another group member?

If you are in therapy, is there someone inside who is supposed to call a family member or other abuser after each therapy session? (If so, your higher-ups might want to make sure that those parts do not know who your therapist is, what goes on in therapy sessions, or even that you have been to therapy.)

Is there anyone who is supposed to call a family member or other abuser if you have a nightmare or a flashback or a memory about the abuse? Is there anyone who is supposed to give you the nightmares?

Do your reporter parts have backups?

If you have these reporter parts, it is important to help them realise that the person they report to does not actually know all these things. And to have your gatekeepers (those with the job of keeping parts inside or letting them out) make sure they stay inside (rather than responding to a cue to bring them out) if you are talking to someone they might be trained to report to.

Impulses to return

Do you have a very strong impulse to return to family on birthdays and cultural holiday dates and full moons? If so, try to discover whether you have any insiders who have to return for rituals or other events held on these dates.

Do you find that receiving cards or letters or emails from family members triggers a strong impulse to go home? If so, search for insiders who have recognised cues in those communications, and find out more about how they were trained.

(continued)

Do you have a fear of breaking off contact with family or other abusers, or not attending events, because insiders are afraid of being severely punished? Do those parts realise that punishment involves hurting the body, and that if the body is not present it cannot be hurt, and other people will not be hurt because of you if you are not there to watch or participate? (Note that it is not your fault if the abusers hurt other people, but you can perhaps prevent some being hurt by not being there to watch.)

Do you have insiders who believe that they will be rewarded for coming back to the abusers? What do they believe will happen? Are there other insiders who know that something different happens? Have these different kinds of parts talk with one another. Make sure they know they all share the same body, and those who experience rewards are in the same body that gets hurt if you return. Are those rewards what you really want?

Do you have insiders who are trained to return in a particular year or on a particular date? If you find these parts, you need to make sure they know enough about your present life that they will not act on their training.

Being accessible to abusers

Do you find that you feel compelled to answer the phone, and to respond to voice messages?

Do you find that you feel compelled to open the door if someone knocks or rings the doorbell?

Do you find that you are unable to block email senders or delete emails without responding to them?

Do you sometimes have an impulse to go outside, particularly at night?

Do you notice people on the street making hand signals or saying strange things, and find yourself responding with impulses to speak with them or to do something particular? Do you find yourself changing the direction from the way you meant to walk?

Are there times when you feel you are unable to move? Are there times when you feel a strong desire to run but are unable to do so?

Do you feel afraid to ever leave town, particularly if you live in the place where you grew up?

If any of the above are true, search for the insiders who have this training, find out how they were trained, and help them understand why they do not need to obey their training any more. You might need to rescue those trained insiders from their internal locations, which might be places based on their traumatic training memories, and take them to safer internal locations (see Chapter Eleven). If some of them are desperate to act on their programming, which would put you in danger, they might need to be kept deep inside or asleep until you have had a chance to thoroughly undo the programming by means of working through the memories.

So, what does it take to keep yourself safe? Counsellor Lynette C. Lins wrote the following to a professional discussion list (quoted by permission) with regard to how she and her ritually abused client worked on this problem:

> It takes a while to get the lie of the land to figure out whether external or internal safety is problematic.
>
> That said, some of the external things we worked on to increase safety: modeled and practiced safety while walking from a parking area to a building, and/or getting into a car; stressed physical safety in the home detailing what that means; encouraged changing phone numbers, using a cell number for work and keeping the house number private even from those inside; encouraged use of a post office box rather than home mail delivery; emphasized the importance of shutting off the phone at night; taught them what to do if followed; pushed for removal of dangerous items

> from the house (i.e., pills, syringes, ropes, cleaning supplies, razors, etc.); established boundary roads that they are not allowed to cross and stores they are not allowed to frequent (identified meet-up points); emphatically asserted that no one under the age of 16 is to be in control of the body when driving the car.
>
> And some of the internal things we worked on to increase safety: identified the patterns of lost time and circumstances under which they occur; explored lost time in detail so parts can see who it is that is hurt after they take the body to unsafe people; explored who inside projects the images that scare the others and convince them that they need to go back to the abusers; temporarily (and briefly) segregated dangerous parts inside until we are able to work with them; encouraged reporters to be truthful but vague in their reports; listened to and validated the goal of "complicit parts" (i.e., protector parts) to avoid far worse from abusers, sometimes coupled with asking "complicit parts" not to take the body to abusers; worked on empathy for child parts.

Lynette Lins noted that many of the external methods she worked on were very difficult for her ritually abused client at first. It was the internal work (on disabling the programming) that has helped the most. This is probably true for most survivors. The entire personality system has to work together in order to achieve safety. When your system is working together, then it is possible for you to use the ideas in the "external things" category to become safe and stay that way.

The power to become free is within you, the survivor. Freedom will make the difficult work of getting free worthwhile—in fact, nothing could be more worthwhile. If you have never experienced your life being your own, let me tell you that nothing compares to it. You will still have sadness about what happened, of course, but liberty is priceless.

CHAPTER TEN

Dealing with triggering

Post-traumatic vs. *programmed responses*

All survivors of trauma have post-traumatic responses, commonly called being "triggered". For example, you walk past a man in the street who wears the same aftershave as the stepfather who sexually abused you, and you have a flashback of your abuser. That is a post-traumatic response, but not a programmed one. However, if you walk across the street in response to a deliberate signal from a cult member, that is a programmed response. It is still post-traumatic, as it is based on trauma, since some insiders fear being severely punished if they do not go to the cult person, but it is also deliberately trained.

Post-trauma responses are not all deliberately programmed. As a survivor of mind control and/or ritual abuse, you will have both programmed and non-programmed post-traumatic responses. Non-programmed post-traumatic responses are usually triggered accidentally by situations that resemble the original trauma. Even programmed responses can be set off accidentally if something in the present situation happens to resemble the pre-set cues for those insiders to do their jobs. However, if a response is programmed, you need to negotiate with the insiders who are "doing their jobs" in setting off the response, to help them understand that it is safe to turn it off.

Kinds of programmed behaviours

If you have been to therapy, you probably know that most therapists put a lot of effort into training their clients to live in the present and avoid self-destructive behaviours such as self-harm and suicide attempts. But this effort is largely wasted when the child parts doing the cutting or taking the overdoses are doing their "jobs", in fear of death or torture to themselves or others if they disobey. The programming behind the behaviours needs to be recognised and addressed.

The first thing you need to know if you are a survivor is that parts of you have probably been trained to create a variety of symptoms and behaviours. Abusers actually train child parts to cut the body, to make other parts cut, to attempt suicide, to create flashbacks by releasing pieces of visual or auditory memories, to create body memories of pain or electroshock, and to create depression, terror, anxiety, and despair by releasing the emotional components of memories to the rest of the personality system. The front person and most of the rest of the system do not know that this is the source of these feelings and behaviours.

What kinds of symptoms or behaviours result from the insiders' training or programming? The most basic kind of training is for loyalty and obedience, and we looked at this in Chapter Five. We also looked at the different kinds of access programming in Chapter Nine.

Punishment symptoms

Many of the other types of programming produce psychiatric symptoms, usually administered as punishments by insiders who are trained to administer them, if the survivor has breached security or disobeyed the abusers' instructions in other ways.

These symptoms serve a variety of purposes, such as disrupting therapy, getting the survivor into hospital, or getting the survivor to return to the perpetrators to have the programming reinforced.

The following exercise lists symptoms that can (but do not always) result from programming. They are difficult to recognise as internal punishments, but each punishing symptom is

Exercise 11. Recognising programmed symptoms

Which of the following symptoms have you suffered from?

- Extreme depression
- Mood swings
- Insomnia
- Intermittent learning disabilities that get in the way of your academic or professional success
- Inability to concentrate on important issues, like saving money; it seems to inexplicably disappear as soon as you get it
- Physical pain without a current physical cause
- Flooding of unpleasant emotions (one emotion such as sadness or anger, or a whole series of emotions)
- Self-harm (cutting, burning, etc.)
- Suicide attempts
- Hearing frightening voices or hearing screaming
- Visual or other hallucinations (for example, seeing someone in the room who isn't really there, seeing someone as a demon, smelling or tasting something awful, feeling insects, snakes, or rodents on or under your skin)
- Seizures (which could be electroshock memories)
- Unexplained physical symptoms such as rashes
- "Disasters" (earthquakes, tidal waves, tornadoes, floods, fires) in your inner world

(continued)

- Rapid switching, causing mixed-up speech as different child parts come out and are pushed inside again
- Scrambling of sensory information so that you can't understand others or make sense of the world
- Bizarre delusions (these can be created with hallucinogenic drugs, films, and cartoons)
- Being told you behaved bizarrely or like an animal

The symptoms at the start of the list are less likely to be programmed than the more rare ones at the end of the list. However, any of these symptoms can be the result of trained parts doing their jobs.

For each listed symptom you have experienced, ask inside to see whether an insider turned on a programme to create this symptom. If you get no answer or just a "no", respect that. If you hear a "yes", ask why. Keep talking gently with the part who answered (or whoever gave the order to turn on the programme), trying to understand his or her reasons. After you have listened thoroughly, try to help that part understand why you believe it might no longer be necessary for that job to be done.

If the part feels he or she has to continue to do this job, find out what behaviour you need to avoid in order not to trigger the programme. For example, you may be talking about memories to an outsider while there are still parts who believe they have to report this violation of secrecy to abusers. The part who is punishing you with pain knows that it is not safe to make such disclosures until your reporters have stopped doing their jobs.

created when a trained insider uses parts of stored traumatic memories to retraumatise the front person or other insiders.

Perpetrator group members can give cues (apparently innocent words, touches, or hand signals) to parts to set off these programmes and have the spinner parts spin them out to the rest of the personality system.

This does not mean that real mental illnesses involving many of the above symptoms do not exist, or cannot exist in survivors of mind control and ritual abuse. They can. But they can also be simulated through programming. I always wondered, for example, why so many supposed paranoid schizophrenics had delusions about God and the devil, or about the CIA. Now I suspect that such people might be mind control victims. Sally's story in Chapter Six gives examples of the programmes that her higher-ups were trained to use to keep her under the abusers' control.

The most dangerous punishment programmes include self-harm, unsuccessful suicide attempts, and suicide attempts designed to be successful (if central secrets have been disclosed).

Self-harm

Certain insiders are specifically trained to do things to harm the body, such as cutting or burning when the person is disloyal or discloses secrets. Perpetrators can also give words or signals to trigger this behaviour. Sometimes, the cuts will form a pattern that serves as a visible sign of abuse by a cult group: this may make other cult members aware of the survivor's history so that, for instance, other patients in a psychiatric hospital can approach the survivor to bring him or her into the local group.

Here is an example of such a training: using a hot branding iron, abusers brand a child with the mark of a pentagram. She is told she is being marked because she is a servant of Satan. If she is disloyal, a particular insider has to make this mark on her own body to prove her loyalty. She does this because she has been made to believe that the perpetrators know she has been disloyal and will punish her unless she self-mutilates in this way. (Of course, if they know, it is because some part of her reported to them.)

Parts who are "introjects" (internal copies) of the perpetrators are told they actually are replicas of the persons who "created" them. Their jobs are often to speak their creators' words, and to harm the body in the exact same ways as those persons did if any of the parts become disloyal.

Unsuccessful suicide attempts

Although mind control and ritual abuse survivors attempt suicide more frequently than other extreme abuse survivors, their rate of successful suicide is no different, according to the Extreme Abuse Survey (Rutz, Becker, Overkamp, & Karriker, 2008). Organised criminal groups expend large amounts of resources on training children, and in many cases they expect to be able to use them for life. Also, successful suicides might prompt investigations, and these groups do not want to draw attention to their existence by actually having someone die. A suicide attempt, however, is likely to get a survivor hospitalised, and cults and other criminal groups monitor many psychiatric facilities to find and retrain survivors while they are there.

Because these groups want to avoid investigation but often do want survivors hospitalised, they teach children to take overdoses but to stop short of actually killing the body, for example by taking just a few less pills than a lethal amount. Children and adults are generally taught several specific ways of harming and attempting to kill themselves, down to the details of how many of each kind of pill to take.

There is also training not to die. For example, a child is drugged and assaulted by persons costumed as "demons" in a simulated hell; he or she is told that if the body dies this is what will happen because she is evil and deserves to go to hell. This child insider will work hard to be sure not to let the body die if other parts attempt suicide.

Serious suicide attempts

This is not to say that no one is trained for "successful" suicide. They are.

Training for successful suicide is not activated until either the perpetrators instruct the survivor to do it, or the security of the most important secrets is prematurely breached. It usually involves a group or sequence of parts. That is, triggers are given to bring out several parts in succession, and the one who is to kill the body can only come out if a particular other insider is already out. This is to protect against accidental suicide.

Suicide trainings are often really trainings for internal homicide—that is, one part killing the body with the goal of getting rid of the other parts. The parts who do this are usually trained to believe they do not belong to the body and will not die if the body dies. For example, an insider who believes he is a demon is taken to "hell" where others parts in the body are tortured, and this part gets to torture other (outside) people. He is told he will not die if the body dies, and that he will have a higher place in hell if he kills the body on command. He may be given an injection which makes him unable to feel anything, then invited to watch something painful being done to the body, without feeling it. There are different variations on this trick, but they all rely on trickery: the truth is that if your body dies, everyone inside it will die too, regardless of what kind of being they believe they are. Even the parts who believe they are outside people are really inside, and they share the same body.

Try writing on the hand of a part who is meant to die, then have someone who believes they are not part of the body come out and look to see whether the writing is on their hand. It will be! With several clients, I have written my initial on the hand of one part, and then asked another part to come out and look at his or her hand. They are always surprised and shocked. It is the beginning of realising how much the abusers lied to them. The lie that you will not die if the body dies is a particularly horrible lie, and I wonder how many mind control victims have discovered this too late.

The dangers of traditional mental health treatment

Psychiatric medications

Some of the symptoms that our psychiatrist colleagues see as amenable to medication are not, because they could be caused by abuse and trauma rather than a disease of the brain. However, while medications might not be appropriate for some of the symptoms that survivors have, they may be effective in managing other symptoms. I strongly recommend that survivors work with psychiatrists who have experience in treating mind control and ritual abuse survivors, if they feel that they need medication. (Unfortunately, such doctors are rare.) The training experiences that survivors have been subjected to have included psychoactive medications since infancy.

Antipsychotic medications can reduce the outside person's ability to communicate with the rest of the personality system, thus suppressing the survivor's ability to effect the necessary recovery. One of my clients was hospitalised when she unearthed a memory of a "bug" being placed in her ear to supposedly let the abusers know whatever she disclosed to any outsider. She became understandably alarmed. She and I scheduled the memory work to deal with this issue, but before we could meet to do it, the hospital psychiatrist discovered she was "paranoid" (since she believed the "bug" was there) and put her on antipsychotic medication. As a result, she was no longer able to contact the parts involved in the memory and could not do the work. My attempt to explain all this to the hospital psychiatrist failed. In his view, she was paranoid, this was psychosis, and so she needed the medication. This client had to pretend she was fine for two weeks, so that she could be discharged and stop the medication. The memory work was successful once the medication was out of her system.

Most psychiatric medications have serious side effects, especially if they are taken over a long period. Some are addictive, and you can have a lot of difficulty withdrawing from them. If you are already on such medication, you may have learnt to rely on it to suppress some of your insiders. This might be a short-term solution, but it does not heal you. To heal, you need all of your insiders to work together with the goal of healing, which means you cannot just knock some out with drugs. It is worth going through the drug withdrawal symptoms if drugs are impairing your capacity for internal communication.

Group treatment settings

I am very hesitant about all group settings and group interventions for survivors of organised criminal abuse, whether on an outpatient, self-help, or residential basis. Survivors who are currently involved with perpetrator groups are often trained to seek out other survivors in treatment settings, such as group therapy and hospitals, to get them reinvolved. When a colleague of mine facilitated a group therapy programme for dissociative people, the local cult conducted a similar group in the hospital basement at night, involving some of the same people (including one of my clients, who told me about it). Another of my clients, who had been abused by a group two thousand miles away, was taken back to a local abuser group by a survivor she met in a therapy group for sexual abuse survivors. Even those survivors who do not reinvolve others often have parts trained to give signals that will cause deterioration in those survivors' functioning.

Residential and inpatient settings

Hospitalisation can lead to a lot of serious problems for those with ritual abuse histories. Hospitals are medical facilities, and patients receive medical treatment. They are places where people with psychiatric emergencies are stabilised as quickly as possible, at the least cost. Most clinicians, particularly those entrenched in this "medical model", are uneducated about mind control and do not acknowledge it or know how to treat it. In fact, most are unable to properly identify or treat dissociative conditions of any kind (although, ironically, according to my clients who were hospitalised, some other patients may "look inside" the person to detect the presence of parts). In most hospitals, mind controlled patients are simply diagnosed with mental illnesses, and subjected to heavy use of psychiatric drugs and other inappropriate treatment, such as ECT (electroshock therapy), which resembles the original programming.

The abusers tell you that if you disclose the secrets, you will be locked up, drugged, and given shock therapy. Unfortunately, this is still sometimes true, and the medical staff who administer these treatments will genuinely believe they are helping you.

Another risk is exposure to the other patients. Before I saw her, one of my ritual abuse survivor clients had been hospitalised. For a long time, she would not discuss what happened, but made me promise not to hospitalise her. Eventually, she revealed that another woman in the hospital had handed her a note that said, "I'm sorry I have to kill you." When she told me the name of the woman, I recognised her as a ritual abuse client of another therapist I knew.

In some communities, perpetrator groups actually want their survivors put into outpatient day programmes, or hospitalised. When I was treating my first few ritual abuse survivors, the cult they belonged to had a regular pick-up system for hospitalised survivors at the dinner hour. The survivors would go out to the front door for a smoke, and the cult van would appear, pick them up, take them to be tortured and for their training to be reinforced, then drop them off at the time they were supposed to be back indoors. I have heard of organised perpetrator groups in other locations doing the same thing.

Although the hospital did keep patients from committing suicide during their stay, it did not keep them safe, because it enabled the perpetrator group's access to them. According to researcher Margo Rivera, it is a fact that during or immediately after a psychiatric hospital stay is the time when most patients commit suicide. I learned to avoid the psychiatric hospital for my clients who experienced current contact with their perpetrator group. Even a safe psychiatric hospital, unless it is specialised for treating dissociative disorders, is little more than a holding tank to prevent patients from committing suicide. At best, such a hospitalisation just delays effective treatment.

I have heard that some mental hospitals have members of the perpetrator groups on staff who are trained to recognize mind-control and ritual abuse survivors. The mother of one of my first ritually abused clients worked in our local mental hospital, and worked hard at making sure her adult child was thoroughly discredited in the view of other staff. That is not to condemn all such workers; most of the people who run mental hospitals are sincere professionals who really want to help those whom they believe suffer from a "mental illness". But mind-control-created dissociative conditions are mental injury rather than mental illness, and so require different treatment, especially when the abuser group is local and has an interest in preventing disclosures.

Hospitals specialising in dissociative disorders, when not infiltrated by members of organised perpetrator groups, can be quite helpful to survivors of organised abuse. The challenge is determining which ones are safe.

Many survivors, when hospitalised, almost immediately switch into a part who appears normal. E. Sue Blume (author of *Secret Survivors*) told me that before she understood ritual abuse, she had several dissociative clients who were admitted to hospitals in crises—including suicidal emergencies—who immediately became "all right". Neither she nor the hospital staff understood the nature of what they were witnessing. The psychiatrist was sure his medication had cured his patients, and released them. In one case, however, the nurses confided in E. Sue that something seemed "odd" about her client's transformation.

Exercise 12. Dealing with dangerous programming

Have you harmed your body in any way? If so, in what ways have you harmed it?

If so, did it feel as if you did it consciously, or as if you watched it happening, or did you find out it had happened after you "lost some time"?

If it was conscious, what do you think was the purpose? Is there another way you could achieve the same end?

If it was not conscious, enquire of your insiders who did it, and who made it happen (these might be different). Then ask them why they made it happen. Again, see whether there is another way they could achieve the same end. Do you want to achieve that end?

Did you make any kind of pattern on your skin with your self-harm? If so, what does that pattern mean? Enquire of your insiders.

Have you attempted suicide? In what manner? Did you do it consciously, or did it seem that you watched it happen, or did you discover afterwards that it had happened?

If it was conscious, why did you do it? Ask inside whether it was influenced by any other parts, and what they were trying to achieve. See whether there is another, less risky way they could achieve the same end.

Dialogue with the parts who were responsible for the suicide attempt. Ask whether it was serious, or whether it was a warning, not designed to kill you.

If it was a warning, ask them what they were warning you about, and see whether you can avoid this behaviour or you can persuade them not to repeat the attempt.

(continued)

If it was a serious attempt, ask the parts responsible whether they believe they would die if they killed your body. If the answer is "No", you or other parts need to inform them of the true situation—that all of you would die.

Are you taking psychiatric medications? If so, ask your insiders how these medications affect them? Do they reduce internal communication, which you need for your recovery? Do they help some of the traumatised parts feel better? Try to make an informed decision about whether these medications help you.

Have you participated in a group therapy programme, or been a patient in a psychiatric hospital? If so, did you or your internal parts experience any triggering of programmed responses while you were there? What were they? Who set off these programmes? Was the programme safe for you? Did it affect your credibility? Was it helpful?

How to deal with your symptoms

The above exercise helps you make the most important internal intervention: talk inside! Communicate with your parts. If you develop a symptom, speak inside to whoever might be causing it. Ask why it happened. Negotiate with them. If they are acting on orders from above, negotiate with their bosses. Try to avoid the behaviours which get you "into trouble" with the parts in charge until they are ready to co-operate with your attempt at healing. This often means slowing down your attempts to recover memories and focusing instead on developing co-operation with your insiders. If you have survived the abuse, you have the strength to find ways to communicate internally, and this can be a major factor in your healing. This is difficult, but it is crucial.

Of course, it is possible that some of these symptoms are genuine and exist for other reasons than programming (that is, no parts are trained to produce them). When one of my clients had two different gastro-intestinal symptoms, one of the symptoms turned out to be a medical illness, and the other was an intrusive memory of extreme pain being inflicted on one of her parts. We had the system put away the memory until they were ready to work on it, then worked through it so the part was out of his pain. But we could not do anything (except get medical help) about the symptom which was an actual physical ailment.

Sometimes internal children kick up symptoms because they are unhappy or their needs are not being met. This might not be programming. You deal with this the same way you deal with programming: negotiate with the kids. One survivor promised pizza to the children in return for them not performing a particularly problematic behaviour. Often the children need something—a new place to live inside, a guarantee that they get some time in your day to play, or read, or colour, a chance to exercise, some good food. Their needs were not met in your (and their) actual childhood, but many of those needs can be met now, thanks to you. This begins with your listening to them. Sometimes internal parts give the front person symptoms to prod him or her into taking action about an unsafe situation.

Learning from and putting away what is triggered

Some programmes reveal themselves early, as they are part of the abusers' plan to sabotage healing. If your attempts to heal or to get help immediately result in symptoms, this can alert you to the fact that your background might include mind control. Once that fact has been established, you know you must consider that any particular issue might be due to the activity of trained internal parts. Instead of just wasting time taking soothing baths to promote sleep (though perhaps this can help a little), you can search for the parts who are responsible for the insomnia. If you find yourself unable to stop cutting your arms, you can find the parts involved, ask how they were trained to cut and why they do it, and eventually work through these training memories. You can use whatever has been triggered to search for the trainings involved. Then you can gently negotiate with the parts responsible, and eliminate, arrest, or reduce the intensity of the problem behaviour.

As soon as you become aware of something coming from your inside parts, try to stop what you are doing and communicate with those parts. The something might be a pain, a body motion, a voice you hear, an emotion, or an impulse.

There are a number of steps that you, the survivor, can take to address programming and other post-traumatic responses without depending on a therapist. Here are some options you might choose. Only you can decide what feels comfortable and safe. The basic principle behind all these interventions is communicating with the parts who act on their training and with those in charge of them, rather than simply letting the symptoms overwhelm you. And with non-programmed post-traumatic responses, the most effective approach is also to communicate with the parts who have been accidentally triggered.

One of my clients once was triggered by an incident in which her cat caught a fly, which made a loud buzzing sound. All her parts went deep inside and hid for a week, until her next therapy session. Two different things were going on. In one, child parts who had been put in a pit with rotting meat and dead things and flies now began to think they were back in the pit. I had to give them a little biology lecture about flies, telling them that flies do eat rotten things like fruit, but have no interest in eating people. I made sure they knew they were safe in my client's apartment.

The buzzing of the fly also brought out a male part who had been trained with electroshock administered (with a buzzing sound) through a helmet. That part's job was to make a similar buzzing sound inside the head, which frightened all the other parts who had worn the helmet. I had to bring him out and show him that there was no helmet on his head, and he was in a safe place; he could let the others know that. I then had the part in charge of the memory storage put the memories of the pit and of the helmet safely away, so those affected would no longer have flashbacks. Although this client was a ritual abuse survivor, and had trained parts (yes, trained in the pit and with the helmet), this triggering was not programming; it was just post-traumatic. So, all that needed to happen was for the triggered insiders to recognise that the present situation was not the same as their original trauma. No programme needed to be turned off, since a programme was not turned on. The survivor did not need to work through all the memories of the "pit" or the helmet when we found what was triggered by the fly's buzzing, she just had to put them away. But she made a note of them, to return to these memories at a later stage of her recovery.

You will make your decision as to how to address a triggered programme based on your healing agenda. With mind control, it is wise to be systematic in your approach to recovery. Generally speaking, memory work comes only after a good deal of groundwork has been laid. (Memory work will be discussed further in Chapters Fourteen and Fifteen.) In this example, it was not time to work on these particular memories. This is an important point for you to understand: sometimes it is preferable to just turn off and put away what is triggered, and continue to work with whatever you have made your priority.

Negotiating with trained insiders

Often, a symptom is caused by a trained insider doing his or her job. When you search for parts who are creating programmed behaviours, keep in mind that their training probably included threats of punishment if they did not comply with the abusers' instructions. Usually, there are other parts who are supposed to punish them, and backups who will do their jobs if they become disloyal. You can search for the punishers and the backups and dialogue with them until they agree to turn it off. You will need to update any parts you speak with, explaining what you now understand about how the perpetrators can no longer hurt them (because of time and/or distance), or if the group is local and still harassing the person, the group can only hurt them if it gains access to the body.

Generally, however, as long as the trained behaviour has been performed, it might be all right to turn it off, though it could be turned on again in response to a cue or to other parts' disobedience to their instructions.

With programmes such as flooding of emotions, the parts involved might not feel safe in turning the programme off. But you might be able to negotiate that they turn it down so it is barely noticeable. Or you could ask the spinner parts to spin in the opposite direction, so that they spin the effects back into the part who originally held those feelings rather than out to the rest of the system. Or you could insert a hidden drain and start draining out some of the feelings. Or you could find a way for the parts doing their jobs to implement the programme without doing harm. One client of mine used to come into therapy sessions with instructions to harm me. So, she came up with the idea of taking a thumbtack from the notice board and pricking me lightly with it once. Then she would say, "OK, I've done my job," and we would have no further problems. Similarly, you can have the child parts draw on their arm in red ink rather than cutting it to draw blood.

Jean Riseman has been active in the survivor community for many years. Her website, www.ra-info.org was the very first one on ritual abuse. She also has a blog, www.ritualabuse.wordpress.com, which contains short essays, poems, and artwork, as well as information on ritual dates and news items. Here, she offers her own expertise about how to deal with programming. Like this courageous thinker, you can use the power of your own creativity, experience, and humour, to be an active participant in identifying and changing your own programming.

One of the things you will notice about Jean's approach is that she, the front person, does not have to identify or be consciously aware of the identities of her inside parts in order to communicate with them and make a difference.

Jean Riseman: "Programming: taking the wind out of its sails"

I am a Satanic ritual abuse survivor and was used as a government/academic mind-control experimentation subject from 1943, when I was six, to 1949, when I was twelve. The point of the experiments was to see how easy different programming systems were to install, how easy they were to use, and how useful they were. Some aspects of the systems studied were used in later mind control programming, but nothing was used in its entirety.

Since I don't have discrete alters, increasing internal communication, as it is usually understood, is not possible. I had, therefore, to try out different techniques and see what worked for me.

The first theory I tested was that my child-rearing experience could be applied to dealing with my programming. What worked with my kids was giving simple directions, using words that were easy to understand given their age level, and expressing myself non-abusively and non-coercively. Basically, I explained what was going to happen and described how I wanted them to behave. If my kids did a good job (assuming they remembered what I said!), they got a big smile and some praise. If their behaviour was less than stellar, all I had to do was remind them of what was expected. There was no need for punishment and drama was kept to a minimum.

So, how could I educate the discrete alters which I didn't have? I knew that there had been a real flesh and blood little girl present for the programming and that the experiences and beliefs lingered somewhere in my mind, just as learning maths and spelling had made an impression. So, if I could pretend I had alters and "talk through" to those parts of me, whatever they were, I might be able to make some intellectual and emotional changes. I would speak to them just as I spoke to my children, simply and respectfully.

I start by giving permission to my pretend-alters to learn new things, without telling them what to do. "Anybody who wants to listen can. Nobody has to. Anybody who isn't listening can ask others inside about what I said. And I will explain again, too, in case you want to listen later on. Anybody who objects to, or doesn't like, what I am saying can let me know if they want to. Anybody who wants to give me information may, as long as it's OK inside."

Then I educate and explain in simple language. I say, "We were raised by people who liked kids to obey and liked to hurt kids. But those people aren't around any more. We don't have to follow their rules. We don't have to agree with them any more. We can make up our own rules. We can change our rules any time we want."

I steer away from words that have a weird connotation to me. "Safe" for example, means to many of my parts that I am locked up, and that therefore I cannot hurt anybody or anything. I am "safe" because I am imprisoned. This is not a message that I am trying to convey inside, so I avoid the word and find words that were not used back then. "OK" is a fine substitute, as the members of my cult were too prim and proper to use that word. If I find that I'm getting anxious or panicky, I take a look at the words I have just used and apologise inside, and ask if I need to add to my list of double-meaning words.

I describe my present life. "This is my bed. I sleep alone in my bed. Nobody comes to my bed to bother me. Never! Those days are all in the past. I can go to sleep whenever I want. I can eat any time I want. I can eat anything I want. I don't have to ask anybody's permission."

I explain all the psychological things I have learned about PTSD and dissociation. I explain amnesia, alters/parts, and flashbacks. Again, I keep it simple so that the young parts can understand.

"This is a flashback. It feels yucky. It's something we are remembering. Once long ago we forgot it, and now we are remembering. It isn't happening now. It just feels like it is because the memory is so strong. But that's OK. It's like the mind is burping up a memory. Feels better after you burp."

I do this at random times during the day when I'm relatively calm, as well as in an emergency. Years ago, when all this was new to me and I was flooded, I held a stuffed rabbit and patted it, saying, "Of course you're afraid. You would have to have rocks in your head not to be afraid. It's OK to be afraid now." Day after day I repeated the same message. In time, with repetition, it got through. My feelings had been normal, there was nothing wrong with me, and I was in a different situation now, one where I could feel my feelings.

Without trying to change anything inside, I offer opportunities. "You never got to choose what kind of ice cream you wanted to eat. How would you like to choose what kind we're going to buy today?" I think what I am doing is introducing the idea of freedom of choice and expanding the number of jobs and skills each alter/part/fragment has, without challenging their fundamental sense of self.

This has turned out to be incredibly useful. I am usually a terrible driver, but I drive much more safely if I coach myself beforehand. "We are going to the supermarket. We are going to drive carefully and cautiously. We are going to pay attention to all the traffic lights, all the cars and bicycles and pedestrians and animals. It's going to be just fine." And when I get there I congratulate myself for doing a great job. Coaching myself like this works in all sorts of situations, like staying more present to cut down on the number of times I fall or bruise myself by walking into a wall or a piece of furniture.

I also adapted a technique I use when my mind wanders during meditation. If a thought, emotion, or sensation appears during meditation, I name it, refuse to act on it, and turn my mind back to my mantra.

To name a thing is to take away some of its power; a name is like an anchor in my mind. Labelling a thought "programming" clearly brackets the thought that I find undesirable and separates it from the "me" that I value. It is now something that was taught me without my permission; it is not my own thinking.

Not acting on the thought or impulse and turning my mind away are weakening the programming by not reinforcing it. Refusing to act on it is avoiding reinforcement and avoiding buying into the cult's value system. Refusing to brood on it, to beat myself up over it, is equally an avoidance of reinforcement. If I spend three days agonising over having had a suicidal thought, that is three days of driving that thought deeper into the grooves of my mind.

This is not the same as denial; I am not shoving anything under the rug. I acknowledge it, deal with it, and move on. If I slip, I just apologise to myself. I don't solidify the programming by feeling guilty about the intrusive thought all day and all night.

Here's how I handled a cult-implanted "don't talk" programme which was triggered by telling my therapist something I was never supposed to remember, let alone talk about. The internal backlash was something fierce. I was haunted by strong urges to suicide, usually in particularly revolting ways. So I started thinking "programming" every time I spotted a self-destructive thought. Note that I did not try to not think of suiciding, because trying not to think something is a losing battle, and consumes a vast amount of energy, besides.

I then gave my kitchen knives to my best friend to hold and recommitted myself to not acting on suicidal urges. Just let them be. If I act on them, I will never get a chance to understand where they came from and what they mean. I'm sure I would have experienced temporary relief if I had cut, but I chose to stay with the thoughts and feelings and see what happened.

Every time I had a suicidal thought I labelled it "programming" and then turned my attention back to everyday activities. After about three days the programme ran its course and faded. I emerged from the situation feeling more empowered. There was more of "me" and less of the programming. The next time a suicide programme kicked in, it was less intense and lasted a shorter time.

I would like to end with a couple of tips. The first one is to phrase things positively, not negatively. The unconscious doesn't hear the "nots" and don'ts", so that "don't crash into another car" comes across as "crash into another car". The other tip is not to give up if you don't get immediate results. You would not expect a three-year-old to remember to say "please" after telling them once. When you were programmed, the instructions were repeated many times and it will take many repetitions to counter them. You are not doing anything wrong—it just takes patience.

* * *

Jean has so many good points here, all based on her own personal experience. You may notice that she has a strong front person, who was able to take charge and talk to the inside parts like a mother to children. Even if you do not have a strong front person like hers, you may have some insiders who have taken leadership in the system, and they will be able to do this. One thing I really like about her approach is that she is not dazzled by "programmes" but can see them all as the results of training of younger parts of her mind. These parts were just trying to keep the whole system safe when the body was not safe, and they were happy when those in charge internally gave them permission to have their own life and choices instead of acting on the programming. Her inner dialogue went two ways: the outer part expressing curiosity about the training and educating about the safety of her present life, and the inner parts telling their stories and expressing their present-day needs.

She cautions survivors about watching the words they use in internal conversations, as perpetrator groups have taken ordinary words like "safe" or "love" and given them bad meanings. So, when you talk to your inner parts, ask them what the words you use mean to them. Some words can be cues to close doors so that information will not be available, but if you ask about those words you can discover the programming that is behind these doors closing. One survivor discovered that the word "really" did this—see Chapter Nineteen.

If your system is closed down and seems inaccessible, you might try the exercise she suggested at the start: "Let's pretend." Pretend that you are multiple and draw your system. Or pretend you were molested and write or draw what happened. Or pretend that the image you see is a memory and describe it.

Exercise 13. Dealing with a triggered response

Think of a recent time when you seem to have been "triggered", either with a strong thought or urge, or with an emotional reaction. What happened to you?

(continued)

What were the events in your present-day life that triggered this reaction?

Thinking of the same event, how did you handle it? If it was an urge, did you act on it?

Did you try to communicate with the parts responsible? If not, try to talk with them now. Find out how old they are and why felt they had to perform this behaviour or create this feeling. Be gentle with them; they might easily feel interrogated because of past experiences.

Enquire inside about whether this response was programmed (that is, the result of a trained part doing his or her job), or just the result of an accidental similarity between something in the present and something in a traumatic experience in your childhood?

If this was purely a post-trauma response, not a programmed one, what could you do to make these inner parts of you feel safer in the present? How could you reassure them that what they fear is not happening now (assuming this is true)?

If the triggering was caused by some insiders doing their jobs, making it a programmed response, find out why they did these jobs at this particular time. What signal did they think they received? Was that signal actually given to them by someone, or were they misunderstanding an ordinary event?

What needs to happen to get them to turn the programme off? Do you need to talk to their internal bosses? If so, do that. Negotiate with insiders until you can get an agreement to turn the programme off, or at least down.

Is there a memory that needs to be put away internally so that young parts will not be triggered? If so, ask your insiders to put the memory away.

Jean Riseman suggests that you now take your mind away from the programmed behaviour, thought, or emotion, and refuse to believe that lie, or dwell on it. Any time it comes into your mind, refuse to act on it or brood about it. As Jean said, "Labelling a thought 'programming' clearly brackets the thought that I find undesirable and separates it from the 'me' that I value. It is now something that was taught me without my permission, not my own thinking."

Using perpetrator-created programmes and triggers for your own purposes

The techniques in this section are somewhat specialised, but are ones which survivors I know have found effective in closing down programmes which are giving them disturbing symptoms. You can use some of the programmes the abusers created for helpful purposes. For example, a part trained not to feel pain can reduce the pain resulting from a re-abusive group contact. A part trained to put other insiders to sleep can put to sleep parts who are programmed to go to group meetings or to harm the body. A part trained to make the others forget events can make the parts who are supposed to report to the perpetrator group forget having talked about the memories.

Most programmes, if they have "on" triggers (cues which trigger trained parts to do their jobs), also have "off" triggers. Some programmes are triggered by particular hand gestures or touches on the body. I have often observed survivors performing such gestures or such touches on their own bodies. One client does a hand signal that tells all her insiders to be calm; another does a touch on her face that enables insiders to forget a memory that was giving flashbacks. There is a touch trigger for sleep, and a part who knows how could use it on your own body. You can ask your insiders to use triggers in this way. However, be sure that the triggers that have the desired effect do not create pain for other insiders, because sometimes they do.

Some survivors do not respond to hand signals or touch triggers unless they are performed by someone else outside the body. If your system works like this, you can ask insiders to show you the "off" triggers and, with their permission, you can ask someone else, such as your therapist or good friend, to use the triggers when you need them performed. Note that if it is necessary for someone to use touch triggers to turn off dangerous behaviours, a part should first be out in the body who does not mind being touched, and who understands that the person doing it is not an abuser just because he or she knows about triggers. One of my clients asks me to do a "sleep" touch trigger on her face to put young ritually abused parts to sleep between sessions, and then a "forget" trigger to make parts temporarily forget any memories we have worked on, so those memories will not "leak" and traumatise her when she is at home.

It must be remembered, however, that this use of perpetrator-installed triggers may be experienced as coercive if the parts being triggered do not consent. *Co-operation is always to be preferred to coercion*, and can often be achieved. For example, a part who is trained to harm or kill the body might agree to be put to sleep or internally isolated until the next therapy session, when the self-harm programme may be undone. It is preferable to convince the internal parts to do these things rather than having an outside person do it via triggers.

Using programme codes

Another way that parts can be helped to change their jobs is through their programme codes, which are sequences of letters and numbers which, when spoken or written by the correct person or in the correct manner, will turn programmes on or off, or even destroy them. These are spoken signals which are taught to parts, and which parts are expected to obey. Your insiders would have to tell you the codes or write them down for you.

For instance, one mind control survivor had assassin programming, the codes for which were songs on a particular record album. Certain insiders sang the songs in his head. Each song brought out a particular part, in sequence, the second to last being the assassin, and the last being one who was supposed to stand around to await getting caught, appearing crazy. The "off" code for the programme was all the lengths of the songs on the album (for example, 4:16, which meant four minutes and sixteen seconds). The survivor could not at that point just say these codes to himself; I had to read them off to him. Now, years later, those in charge of his system are sufficiently co-operative that the programme no longer is turned on at all.

Knowing codes and saying the "off" codes can help in undoing programming. Since it does not remove the trauma that created the programmes in the first place, it simply means that the parts involved no longer have to do their jobs. I believe that if you use such codes, it is wisest to obtain them from inside your own head rather than from elsewhere. Be very aware that if you use codes which you have heard from someone else, they might have unexpected effects, and they might alienate parts in charge of the personality system.

Using programme codes to disarm programmes can be a useful shortcut, but it does not resolve the trauma, which still must be worked through for complete recovery to occur. Neutralising the programmes can be helpful, as they will then not get in the way of the healing. The time period during which a programme is turned off can allow you to work through the memories of the abuses that these programmes represent. Be aware that programmes which have been turned off via codes sometimes get turned on again, perhaps after a time lapse, or because an internal programmer part has discovered they are turned off and turns them on again, or as a result of an internal reactivation schedule.

Asking internal programmers for programme charts

You may have heard of survivors having "internal programmer" parts. Do not be intimidated. These are parts who have been trained to turn programmes on and off in response to environmental cues. When someone speaks a programme code or uses a touch or sight trigger, it alerts an internal programmer to turn a programme on or off, usually through flipping a switch. The programmers usually do not know what effect their switches have, but are heavily trained in obedience and in memorising signals. In most such systems, the switches are located on internal control boards, such as would be found in an electrical circuit-breaker box. Every switch is labelled, usually with some kind of shorthand representing what the training was, when and where it was done, and how many times it was repeated at what ages.

Most deliberately structured personality systems have some kind of control system for the programmes. When you have reached the point where your insiders are working together effectively, you may ask the internal programmers to put together a chart of all the programmes existing within your system, based on the labels on the switches. Once that is done, it is possible to work through the programming memories systematically to permanently disable the programmes and rescue the parts that hold these programmes from their traumas.

As an example, here is how one survivor's internal programmer described his instructions:

> To turn on a programme hit the black button, speak the programme, and then press in the two-numbered code.
>
> To close the programme hit the red button, speak the programme, then press in the reversed two-numbered code.

The first number or numbers followed by a comma is the Programmer level that can activate that code. [There was a programmer part on every level of the system: levels 1 to 9 reflected ages five to thirteen, and level 0 meant every level.]

> The numbers after the comma are the numbers in the alphabet of the first letter of words except the last, and the last letter of the last word of the programme title.

So, for example, the code for the programme "Watching You" was 0, 23, 21. The number "0" meant that internal programmers at all nine levels held this programme, as the training was repeated every year. The numbers 23 and 21 after that were for the W in Watching and the U in You. If this survivor wanted to dismantle the programme by going through the memories, she would have to make sure to deal with all nine instances in which the training was given.

There were around 200 programmes listed. Each programme also had a spoken code, which would turn the programme on or off if spoken. For example, one programme to make the person go home was triggered by the words "butter cookies", which were innocuously inserted into a letter from her aunt. To turn this programme off, someone would have to say "Butter cookies 19, 2." The programme to make her go with someone was triggered by the word "cigarette".

With a list and chart like the one this internal programmer gave me, it is possible both to turn off programmes that have been triggered, and to identify the programmes for working through the memories. It should be noted that another inside part (hidden as a sub-part of a part with a different job) controlled a different set of programmes.

Creating programme "wiring diagrams"

Perpetrator groups sometimes arrange things so that if one programme is interfered with, another programme will be set off. I shall say more about how to deal with this in Chapter Fifteen, "Putting together the traumatic memories".

Here is an example of such a setup: the front person of a survivor kept alternating between flooding of horrible emotions to flooding of offender memories to having suicidal thoughts. All this started when this survivor began to remember and work on memories of some core programming. When questions were asked internally, she discovered that the insider named "8" (for his age) had been instructed that if the person began to make disclosures about, or to remember, a certain core programme, he was to do his job of turning on the "flood feelings" programme, in which all kinds of unpleasant feelings flooded the front person and everyone inside. This survivor had internal leaders who knew how to turn off programmes and did so when it was needed. However, the insider named "6" had been told that if the "flood feelings" programme was turned off somehow, he was to flood the person with memories of that person being an offender. The insider named "7" had been told that if this memory flooding was turned off, she was to turn on a "suicide" programme. A chain of programmes like this can be quite long. It can also be quite complex. In this case, the parts with the various jobs were from different sectors of the system, and did not know one another.

So, what can you do about it? You can ask questions internally to find out about the programme chain: "What happens if . . . [this programme] is interfered with? Who is supposed to do something? What is their job?" Then, as this survivor did, you can have the internal leaders gather all the insiders with the jobs of turning these programmes on, update them on their present-day life and why they (the leaders) have chosen to stop doing their old jobs. Invite all those insiders to take on new jobs, such as detecting when the programmes they were supposed to turn on come on for some other reason, turning them off and alerting the internal leaders. If you do this, be sure to invite the "backups" to help with this, too, rather than taking over the original jobs of the insiders whom they believe have now become "traitors". Now you will have a more co-operative personality system and your emotional life should stabilise.

Effective and ineffective shortcuts

The use of codes, triggers, and wiring diagrams can be considered shortcuts that temporarily shut things down and make you more functional. However, you should know that the key to dismantling or neutralising programming is in your long-term work with the personality system. There are a lot of desperate survivors, and many therapists who promise them that various shortcuts will heal them quickly without their having to go through any of the pain that they endured over their childhood years. It seems to me to trivialise your pain when someone tells you that your prolonged suffering over twenty or more years can be easily fixed by some simple technique.

Shortcuts can, however, help on a temporary basis, to settle down insiders temporarily while the long-term recovery work is going on. Some people have devised their own effective shortcuts. For instance, one of my mind control survivor clients told his inner children "Whatever they told you to do, do the opposite." He had spent several years actively psychotic while many bizarre programmes were set off. Once he got his inner children to "do the opposite", his system settled down, he began to access the significant abuse memories, and he is now much more functional.

The key to either using a pre-existing shortcut (e.g., finding out programme codes) or developing a new shortcut, like this man did, is for the whole personality system to work together in the service of healing. The parts in charge need to decide to do this. If they do, many things are possible.

The key to all effective shortcuts is really wanting things to be different, no matter what. As survivor therapist Arauna Morgan wrote to the Ritual Abuse and Mind Control (ISST-D special interest group) discussion list (reprinted by permission), "Of the survivors I know, one common thread seems to be that they finally decided that they have had enough. Some of the most impressive deprogramming I have seen was various ways of stating just that, 'I have had enough and I no longer accept . . .' (fill in the blank)".

Is "deprogramming" effective?

The term "deprogramming" is used in various ways. Self labelled "deprogrammers", such as Steve Oglevie, who work specifically with mind control and ritual abuse survivors, appear to know a great deal about the specific illusions implanted in the minds of survivors programmed by different groups, and the programme codes which have been implanted by these groups. They attempt to discover the type of structured personality system, speak the codes, and rescue the parts from the perceived abuses or internal situations in which they are trapped. The deprogramming is conducted over a period of several days.

However, therapists who have taken their clients to such deprogrammers report mixed results. It appears that the survivor's stage of recovery, along with his or her trust in the therapist, has an effect on whether or not such deprogramming is effective. Psychologist Randy Noblitt has done some of this work, and he sees this strategy as the equivalent of using temporary shutdown codes. In a post (reprinted by permission) to the Ritual Abuse and Mind Control Discussion List, he said that he does not "deprogram" because ". . . people are not computers even though they may be abused and under traumatic circumstances they may come to believe that they have computers installed inside them . . . I do not believe any of us can "deprogram"—the brain is not a programmable/nonprogrammable computer".

Noblitt is also critical of the process because, in his experience, it leads to complications: ". . . it only [gives] a temporary but false sense of recovery to clients (comparable to premature integration)". After applying a method he had learnt to "deprogram" robot parts, he found that

> . . . the method worked but it kept me and the client in an interminable loop of deprogramming rather than attending to the necessary therapy. For example . . . It took about 20 minutes for each

> robot and I could "remove" the robot parts one at a time. However, my client had 1,000 robot parts. Had we continued with that goal in mind we would have been sidetracked and missed the important therapy that she needed.

In fact, Noblitt found that, for his client, deprogramming was not even a shortcut. He developed a way to integrate these "robots" in less than fifteen minutes, without codes or passwords. In the end, he cautions, "Many of the tunnels, mazes, computers, files, etc. [found in these clients] can keep a therapist and client distracted from the work of therapy for a long time". The real work is developing communication and trust between the inside parts and, when they agree, processing the trauma which led to the programmes.

Exercise 14. Triggers, codes, charts, and diagrams for avoiding programmed responses

Are there any triggers your parts know which you can use to turn off programmes or stop programmed responses from being spun around in your personality system? What are they? Do you know what they will do? Can you use them on yourself, or do they require another person (your therapist, or a trusted friend) to use them?

Are there any spoken words or codes that can turn programmes off? What are they? Do you know what they will do? Can you use them on yourself, or do they require another person (your therapist, or a trusted friend) to use them?

Are you in communication with any internal programmers who could provide you with lists or charts of the programmes and the codes that can turn them on or off? (This generally happens at a late stage of recovery.) If so, ask them for a list to guide your recovery work. If you have a good therapist, give him or her a copy of the list.

Have you found that interfering with any programme (for example, attempting to remember the training) turns on another programme? If so, what has happened? Ask your insiders for a "wiring diagram" of which programmes are triggered by interfering with which other programmes. If you have a good therapist, give him or her a copy of the list.

Have you tried formal "deprogramming"? Has it been helpful? What do your insiders think of it? Do you know anyone else it has helped? Do you know anyone who tried it and found it was not helpful, or was harmful?

Do you have any shortcuts you have developed yourself to turn off and put away post-trauma triggering or programmed responses? If so, what are they? Do you use them consistently? Could they be shared with other survivors?

Are the leaders of your personality system at the point where they are willing to take some risks in order to become free of the ongoing effects of their abusers, know the truth, and know who you really are apart from the interference provided by the abusers?

Give the young part or parts of you that learnt this permission to learn, without being coercive. As Jean Riseman said, "Anybody who wants to listen can. Nobody has to. Anybody who isn't listening can ask others inside about what I said. And I will explain again, too, in case you want to listen later on." Then educate and explain to them in simple language. You might follow Jean's example here: "I explain that we were raised by people who liked kids to obey and liked to hurt kids. But those people aren't around any more. We don't have to follow their rules. We don't have to agree with them any more. We can make up our own rules. We can change our rules any time we want." Offer those young parts of you opportunities to change their beliefs and behaviour, without bossing them around. Answer any questions they might have.

CHAPTER ELEVEN

Building inner community

At the start of recovery, most multiples have internal battles for control. The front person usually has little or no control over switching. The parts might fight to be out, or might push others out in order to stay inside. It is important to work on improving internal communication, negotiation, and co-operation. Democratic decision-making is not usually learned in the childhood of a multiple, and can be incredibly difficult. "Eww, Jane got us dressed this morning", or "I don't like her having sex with *my* body", or "Why's she making us eat vegetables?" are typical comments that one part will make about another, if the system is a DID one in which the parts actually come out into the body. Parts will often express anger and even hatred for one another, including for the adult whose head or body they inhabit. And the adult front person often hates or resents the insiders, hearing them as threatening or frightening voices. It is hard for all parts, including the front person, to realise that they are all legitimate parts of a greater whole, and to respect the way in which each of them helped that person survive the extreme situation in which you all grew up. It takes a long time.

Survivor Svali puts it this way:

> Sometimes, a system that has broken free from the cult, and has no external hierarchy that they are accountable to, will go through a short period of chaos as word gets out: we're free, and don't have to do what the cult tells us to do any more! Hundreds of internal arguments may break out as to: what do we do for a living? Where do we live? What do we eat/what hobbies will we have? Everybody wants to come out, see the daytime, and live this new, free life. But the freedom may cause imbalance with all of the switching going on inside.

New forms of internal leadership and governance

So, who is to run the show? It makes sense that those who are used to being in charge continue to do it, at least at the start. If these higher-up insiders lose their authority, they might be upset and make trouble for your whole system. They are not intentionally unkind to others; they are just following the orders they were given and the rest of the system is used to obeying them.

However, they might need to learn new methods of governing, and of parenting the little ones, since they tend to do what they originally learnt, which is to threaten and punish. Internal leaders can be quite lonely because, although they are respected and feared, they are generally not liked by those they rule. They can gradually come to be liked as well as respected by maintaining order through kindness rather than cruelty.

And your system's governing council can move gradually from having leaders selected by the abusers to a democracy in which the leaders are selected internally to represent the needs and wishes of each group of parts. Insiders do not have to vie for control, but can learn to co-operate and to meet everyone's needs, though not all at the same time. The council can also guide your recovery work, selecting the memories to work through and avoiding or disabling traps. They can help you create a functional inner family to replace the one that the abusers made in their own dysfunctional image.

I use my stained glass lamp to explain the inner situation to my multiple clients. Each piece of glass is a different colour and shape, but if they all fit together harmoniously, they make a beautiful picture which the light can shine through.

Arauna Morgan's metaphor is a wisteria tree. She writes,

> Wisteria is a vine, so one alone will not stand up as a tree, but if you take each vine and wrap it around the others, then the vines will make a trunk that eventually all grows together and supports the beautiful flowers at the top and turns a flowering vine into a flowering tree with one, solid trunk. Any new vines can just be wrapped around the trunk just like the others were.

Using insiders' job skills to assist in recovery

Many parts define themselves by their jobs, and do not know who they will be when those jobs are gone. This can make them resistant to recovery. But they usually have special skills related to those jobs, and these skills, and even (in some cases) the jobs themselves, can continue to be useful long into the course of recovery. As you meet various insiders, ask them about their jobs, and show appreciation for their skills. Then help them find other ways to use those skills in the service of making the whole personality system healthier.

For example, file keepers have access to the training memories and can keep them contained until the right time, then bring them up when the system is ready to process and resolve them. Observers and recorders can watch your present-day life to make sure you are safe. Spinners can spin peaceful and calm feelings out into the system when other parts are anxious. Pain holders can assist with dental and medical appointments by keeping the pain deep inside, far from the front person. Soldier parts can get the body to exercise. Parts who hold "forget" programmes can make your reporting parts forget anything they might have been trained to report.

Changing names and appearances

Insiders who were named by the abusers sometimes have names that reflect their roles in the abuse. When these parts begin to help with recovery, they often like to give themselves new names. Other insiders might prefer, for example, to communicate with "Alicias" instead of "Satanic Legions", or "Simons" instead of "Satans".

One of my first ritually abused clients had a part who announced he was "Almighty God" (trained, presumably, to make other insiders hear the voice of "God"). I told him I had difficulty calling him that, so was there another name he would be comfortable with? "Well, I always liked Geoffrey," he replied. So he became Geoffrey. In another survivor, I met another "God" recently, whose job was to condemn the other parts and tell them they were going to hell. He was an internal copy of a frightening man standing up high on a pulpit in a church. When he noticed my little dog right in front of him, he softened and became the sweet child that he actually was. This part (and his backups) decided to become the "Dawgs". I sent him an MP3 of a very funny song by Bob Snider entitled "Dog".

You can encourage insiders who were made to believe they looked like fearsome creatures to take off their costumes in the inner world, so that they can look like the children and teenagers that they really were when they were deceived. Abuser groups dress drugged children up in costumes, then they wake up to believing they have claws and fur. They show children "mirrors" which actually have pictures on them, and tell the children this is what they look like. Steve Frankel suggests to survivors that they have "mirrors of truth" which are hidden and do not appear until it is safe for a particular part to see who he/she/it really is under the "suit" that he/she/it wears. *All your insiders are parts of you; none of them is actually an external person.* Those parts who look like abusers can also change their appearance. If they need to maintain authority internally, they can choose to look like someone they admire rather than like the people who hurt you.

Exercise 15. Developing inner democracy

Do you have conflict between some of your insiders, or groups of insiders? Describe it from the viewpoint of one side of the conflict, then from the other side. If this is hard for you, try sitting in a different chair for each side, as though each insider or group of insiders had their own chair. What can be done to resolve it?

Who is in charge of your personality system? How do they run things? What do they need to learn to make things better for all parts?

If you have a governing council inside, do they represent the needs of all parts? Who could be added to the council to make it more representative?

Do internal parts of you continue to do jobs assigned by your abusers? Is this necessary? Which jobs are still needed? Are there parts who have useful skills which could be used in the service of recovery instead of in the service of your abusers?

Do you have parts who would like to change their names or their appearances in the inner world? Who can give them permission? Can your system make this happen?

Exploring and changing your inner world

As we discussed in Chapter Four, most, if not all, survivors of mind control and ritual abuse have some kind of inner world where their insiders live. People's inner worlds differ. Some have magic castles and woodlands, others have prisons and fortresses and control rooms and military installations, still others have cellars and pits and dungeons. Some have what appear to be different worlds and other planets. Most have hidden sections with guards. It pays to explore your inner world, and to make changes in it that will assist your parts to heal.

Since your inner world was probably created by the abuser group, your first explorations of it need to be cautious, looking for traps, conversing with guards if you find them, and learning from them what their jobs are and seeing whether they can assist you in disarming the traps.

If your personality system is one in which the front person is not permitted into the inner world, your internal leaders can select an insider to take charge of the exploration. Regardless of whether you are the front person or a higher-up insider, you will learn a lot from your explorations. Some survivors can walk around their inner worlds and discover their layout and scenery; others only discover it by asking insiders where they are housed.

One good thing about an inner world is that it can be redesigned to give all insiders whatever they need.

Ask each of your groups of insiders where they are housed in the inner world. Often, some are in dungeons, cages, and other horrific places where their real-life body was placed during the abuse. Sometimes their memory was cut off at the point of the abuse, and as far as they are concerned, the abuse is still happening. They not only need to be introduced to the present world, they need to be removed from the abuse scenario and given safe bedrooms, playrooms, or hiding places. If they are naked, give them clothes. If they are cold, give them blankets or heaters. If they are lonely, give them company. If they are overwhelmed by people, give them solitude. If they are dirty, give them a safe way to get clean (I favour a warm, breathable waterfall). If they are injured, give them medicine, salve, and helpful settings such as a healing internal hot tub (this was Trish Fotheringham's idea).

You might wonder why there are structures in your inner world. This is because abuser groups like to know where to find everyone inside. Every part has been assigned his or her place in the structure. This is actually a good reason for you to change things! However, some parts of you might be understandably afraid to mess with what the abuser group has created.

One thing you need to understand is that the abusers cannot actually see into your inner world and discover how it has been altered. They only know what your reporters tell them. However, if you have some parts who are afraid of making changes, you need to get internal agreement first, and make sure no one will suffer punishment, or tell the abusers about the changes you are making.

Then, what do you do with the abuser-created structures? I have found that many survivors like to destroy them, after building better living quarters for the insiders. The soldiers or boy parts who like guns and bombs enjoy using their skills to blow up bad places. They appreciate the chance to use their training for good. However, be sure to get everyone out of structures before destroying them, and look everywhere, even in the walls.

Many survivors have parts trained to set off internal world disasters, which are actually memories of things that were done in childhood. Inner world earthquakes are originally created by abusers shaking up both the child and the model that child has created of his or her inner world. (See Chapter Four for the way inner worlds are constructed.) Inner world tidal waves are created by flooding the world model and almost drowning the child. Tornadoes are created with a leaf blower or wind tunnel, and fires by setting fire to the world model as well as burning the child. An insider is instructed to activate these memories in response to certain triggers, and the rest of the system then experiences the destruction of the inner world. Often, it seems that some parts are "killed" internally. If this happens to you, it helps to recognise that it is a programme, a memory rather than a present-day reality. You can create a healing stream in your inner world in which the "dead" parts can be placed to revive them. And do not forget to find the insiders who set off the programme, negotiate with them about not doing it again, and help them find more suitable jobs.

Exercise 16. Improving your inner world

Are you able to see where your parts live in the inner world? Take as much space as you need to describe all the different places they have let you know about. It might help to draw that world or the structure in which the parts are located.

Are there places in your inner world that are frightening or unpleasant for the parts who live there? Can you get those parts out of there?

Can you find an insider or a group of insiders who know how to build new places for the others to live in? What would you like them to build? It might help to draw what you would like.

Now, ask the builders, or those in charge of your inner world, to create new living spaces for the parts who need them.

Meeting insiders' needs

When you meet your inner parts, they bring with them many of your unmet needs from earlier years. When an insider's life experience gets cut off at a particular age because of trauma, he or she remains at that stage of development, and experiences the needs of a child of that age. One survivor I know (in her late thirties) tells me that she does not think there is any genuine adult in her, only kids who pretend to be adults. Many survivors feel this way. Most survivors of mind control and/or ritual abuse have many unmet childhood needs, such as safety, connection, nurturance, friendships, intellectual stimulation, physical activity, creativity, and play. In order for your parts to grow up, you need to meet those needs, at least in part, for each stage of development.

You can meet your younger parts' needs to some extent both within the inner world, and outside in the body. You can give the babies safe places to sleep, warm and comforting clothes, blankets, stuffed animals and imaginary pets. Older insiders can look after them, or you can make them new imaginary companions and care-givers based on good people you have known, or have read about in books, or seen in films and television shows.

Adults and older insiders can read children's stories to the younger child parts. When you borrow a children's book from the library, the librarian will assume it is for your front person's real children, or your niece or nephew. Recorder parts can store these books in the internal library for inside reading. Child parts can colour in colouring books, or do their own artwork. They can play at the park, climb trees, walk along the beach and throw stones into the water. They can look after a pet. Older children can construct models or play video games. All these things can happen either out in the real world, or internally, or both. The front person does not have to be present.

As you improve your life and the life of your inner parts, you need to strike a balance between adult activities (such as work, shopping, parenting, adult friendships, and relating to your partner if you have one) and child activities. If you are fortunate enough to have friends who understand your multiplicity, your child parts can even have real-world friends. Or they can sneak out or come close to the surface when you are playing with a real-world child, as long as an inner adult is watching to make sure they do not do anything inappropriate.

Sources of healing can also be both internal and external. If the insiders can let the front person know when they feel pain or discomfort, you can make sure you get proper medical attention. (Pain and discomfort are often held in child parts rather than experienced by the adult front person.) You might benefit from massage or acupressure, as long as everyone inside knows you will not be abused. Physical activity, too, is essential for health, and is something that many of your child parts may enjoy, especially if you choose activities that they like.

Sometimes, when parts connect internally, negative emotions and bodily pain "leak" from one part into another. In some personality systems, it is difficult for older parts to look after little ones because they begin to feel the little ones' pain. You can try various things to deal with that. LisaBri has her little ones inside bouncing around in "space suits" that prevent emotions and bodily pain from leaking from one part into another. Another survivor imported the whole cast of the television show MASH (doctors and nurses) into her inner world to look after the insiders. She also created nannies based on Mary Poppins.

Until the traumatic memories are worked through, you will have children inside who are in physical and emotional pain from those memories. Insulating the system by such things as space suits has to be only a temporary measure, until the memories can be addressed. Meanwhile, the children can be removed from internal places which are copies of the settings where they were abused, given better internal places to live, and taught that they are now safe and will not be abused any more.

Often the same child parts who took the original pain take new current pain from injuries or illnesses. They need to be encouraged to speak up rather than suffer in silence, as when they suffer, the whole system suffers. Tell them that their pain and unhappiness affects everyone, and if they can let the older ones know, something might be done to reduce that pain. It is often difficult for inside children to speak up when they are afraid, sad, anxious, or in pain, since they might have been brought up with the refrain "Don't bother the adults. Children should not be seen or heard."

You can give parts who are not yet ready to emerge into the external world viewing screens or windows so they can watch your present-day life, and discover how different it is from the years that they remember. Arauna Morgan gives such parts their own consoles, with big screens that they can sit in front of, with headphones and controls to turn the sound up, down, or off, adjust the brightness and colour of the picture (or turn it off), and turn the emotions up, down, or off. This way they can safely see and experience what is happening on the outside without having to come out or interfere with what the front person is doing.

Exercise 17. Meeting everyone's needs

Describe each of the insiders you know within your personality system. If it is a very complex system, describe the groups of insiders. For each insider or group:

How old are they?
What do they like doing?
What do they need?
How could you provide for those needs in the external world?
How could you provide for those needs in the inner world?

In the following section, survivor Jen Callow recounts her experience of making her personality system a happy and co-operative one. It has many inspiring suggestions for other survivors. (This article is also in my book for therapists (Miller, 2012).)

Jen Callow: "How I created my inner community: living happily without integration"

When I first discovered I was multiple, I had well over 700 inner parts and very little communication between them. Most of my parts didn't know the others existed. They were still very afraid and alone. After years of healing, I now have a loving community inside. We support each other and have inner cities and towns where we live and play together. Now, when we find new parts, we can help them leave their programme lines and become a larger part of our inner world (my abusers set up my inner system as a spider-web of interconnected lines holding programmes and parts). Throughout this process, we do our best to make sure everyone has a voice and is heard. We meet competing needs, and organise, plan, and develop a growing inner world that in turn helps us to increase a sense of belonging and connectedness, supporting and caring for each other.

When we finally started therapy with a therapist who understood dissociation, many of us were isolated and living in terror. We were shut away in our inner world—in boxes, cold basement rooms, and in any other number of locations depending upon our memories. We were locked in our programmes, often starving or in pain. Our inner system had torture and abuse going on similar to what our abusers had inflicted upon us. We didn't trust each other, and only a very few of us knew and trusted our therapist. We were afraid that we, someone we cared about, or the world would be destroyed if we started working with our inner system.

Over time, we came to trust our therapist and then slowly learnt to trust each other. After we learned how to be co-conscious and to create inner TV screens so parts could safely view the outer world, we created an inner movie of our life that we could show newly discovered parts, to bring them up to date and show them that we were safe now. (This movie's content was huge and growing, but it only took a few minutes for parts to see and absorb it, and now we can share it in seconds.) Eventually, we got so we could talk to each other clearly in our minds and didn't need the therapist as much for communication.

Our inner world's physical environment evolved, as well. At the end of each session, our therapist would make sure any new parts had a comfortable place to live with their immediate needs met. We built a welcoming mansion filled with many bedrooms, a large common area, full bathrooms with large tubs for bubble baths, a large kitchen and eating area with long benches and tables, and several playrooms. Each bedroom could be decorated and furnished however its resident(s) wanted, and had doors that could lock, and a window, if one was wanted. Stuffed animals were an important comfort item, as were pets. We made sure that none of the pets would harm any of the other pets (e.g., cats would leave hamsters and fish alone) and that they were friendly. When we later discovered infant parts, we added comfortable nurseries with care-givers, and created items such as slings to carry the babies in, bottles, rattles, and changing stations. Now, there was a more harmonious feeling inside.

Eventually, we developed many more buildings. We now had a healing area full of herbals, liniments, and soothing sights and sounds: beautiful gardens and grounds, an ocean and beaches, forests, and opportunities for expression and recreation. We created spaces for soccer games, a dance hall, music and art rooms, safe rooms for yelling in and letting out anger, even a skateboard park. Every addition encouraged us to work together, to interact more, and to have more relaxation and fun. As we played soccer, ate, and lived together, we began to feel more and more like the family we had missed out on. This was every bit as important in our healing as the actual memory work.

Some of our parts needed a lot of time on their own, so it was important to create and give them some quiet space. Some parts preferred to live in tree houses, or in cottages in the woods. Sometimes our inner towns didn't work at all for certain parts. Rather than force these parts to assimilate, we created other inner worlds for them. There was a group of teenagers that loved the Dragonriders of Pern series when they were growing up. We created a version of Pern with them, where they could live together with their dragons and fly through the skies each day. Several children were very attached to an animated adventure show they had watched when they were out in the body, and created a world like this for themselves to live in, complete with all the good guys. The bad guys were created as a vague danger the children were in complete control of; the bad guys would take whatever form and strength the children wanted and the children, who were the heroes, always won. Parts could travel between worlds whenever they wanted, so no one was truly alone and we could still access these worlds and parts when processing memories.

Running the programmes and keeping constant vigilance over our system had been the only way for many of our parts to feel powerful and to avoid feeling physical or emotional pain. After we'd processed a memory, our therapist made sure to help each part find a new job and purpose. This included the children, if they wanted a smaller job. For example, the soldiers who had terrorised our system were put in charge of security, record keeping, and maintaining the soccer field.

Some responsibilities in our inner world are large and time consuming, such as cooking, cleaning, and looking after the infants. Another task we struggled to fill consistently was taking the children on field trips to places inside, such as a fun version of school where we could teach them about the outer world. It was hard for the few parts doing this to come up with enough ideas. At the suggestion of a friend who was multiple, we set up a rotation of chores and responsibilities. Now, older parts that take on a larger role can take regular vacations and we have parts who have been taught how to fill in. Over the years, we have also created inner people (different from the parts already in our system) to help with various tasks, such as a healer, gardener, cook, and care-givers for the infants. We find it works best to still have our parts help with chores, as it builds a sense of pride in our community and shared responsibility, but this way the risk of parts burning out from overwork is reduced.

Many of our parts lived in suffering and deprivation. One aspect of their healing is recognising that they matter and that their needs can be easily filled, provided no one will be harmed in the process. If a part wants a specific toy or needs an extra blanket, those items can appear for them right away. However, sometimes more work is required to ensure a need is met. Although we can have food items available immediately, for reasons unknown to us we still need to cook and prepare these items for a proper meal, so outside of meal times we try to have pre-made snacks readily available. In addition to inner people to help with chores, we've added many other helpers to our inner world, from a therapist for the children to care-givers who give us back rubs before bed. The care-givers also help the younger parts with baths, getting changed, and getting tucked into bed. Many of our parts enjoy tending large flower and vegetable gardens, and we created several gardeners who help with bigger jobs. Female vocalists (we don't trust men easily) sing lullabies to parts who enjoy this, and can soothe crying infants.

After much debate, we also recently added loving, sexual partners for those parts who needed this inside. Many of these parts were children, but their sex needs were huge as a direct result of the abuse. In the end, we felt it was better to create people who could provide loving sexual contact, respecting the children's wishes and needs, rather than have these parts feel ashamed and suffer from their overwhelming urges. It has worked well for us, as several months later, many of these children are now asking more often for non-sexual, loving touch, with these inner people taking on more of a nurturing friend or care-giver role.

In addition to caring for each other inside, we take care of our inner environment. At one time, we were concerned that all the emotions we were releasing would have a negative effect on our inner world. We are very sensitive to energy and were taught that our feelings were toxic to others when we were growing up. So, we created some areas that transformed the energy from our feelings into the good feeling energy of our waterfalls, trees, and other natural spaces. In keeping with our own beliefs, we think of this transformative power as "earth energy", the earth changing the energy and helping good things to grow. This helps us in the outer world, too, as nature has always been grounding and nurturing for us. We envision our outer environment and the earth transforming our feelings, so it now feels safer for us to express emotions. In the interest of environmental sustainability, we also have inner areas where we bury our garbage, recycling it so the earth can transform it into electricity, food for plants, and other new kinds of energy for our inner world.

Our outer and inner worlds are deeply interconnected. In caring for each other and our inner world, we learn how to take care of ourselves in the outer world, and also how to care for the earth and other people. As we experience caring from others in the outer world, we learn that we matter and discover how we like to be treated, which we can then mirror inside.

Without the care and attention spent both on our parts and our inner world, we would never have made it this far. Even today, when things feel chaotic in our outer world, as is the case for us now during some major life transitions, we can look inside and help calm ourselves through creating more stability in our inner world and attending to parts' fears and needs. Lately, we have been holding regular inside meetings for any parts who want to attend. In our inner world, we sit out in nature; we sing, talk, play music, and release feelings and outdated beliefs (e.g., often we'll write these on pieces of paper and throw them into a small bonfire, over which we later roast marshmallows, which makes it feel less like a ritual and more like fun). The buildings, recreational areas, nature, and living spaces play a huge part in our sense of inner peace and security.

How we built our inner world is specific to our preferences and to the way our inner system was initially set up during the abuse. Every survivor's system is unique and offers many ways to build a community or create objects inside. It's important to work with what's already in the inner system, as opposed to fighting it and trying to shut it all down. Although areas can be transformed, in our experience the building blocks of the inner world remain the same. Through creativity and patience, it is possible to have co-operation and harmony between any number of parts, and a thriving inner community. With an increasing sense of inner peace and community, it is not only possible for survivors to create happier lives for themselves in the outer world, it is possible for them to truly heal.

* * *

Now, you do not have to do things the way Jen did. She is a very creative person who devoted a tremendous amount of energy and creativity to her inner world, creating and improving it as someone might do if they were writing a complex series of novels. The important thing is that she found ways to modify her inner world to create harmony and meet the needs of all her insiders—and so can you.

It might be helpful for you to go through Jen's article and write down any ideas that you would like to implement in your own healing.

Some inner worlds provide a particular challenge because they are designed with programmed traps so that parts cannot get free. Here is one survivor's highly detailed description of an unpleasant inner world, how she worked with it, and how she managed to dismantle it. But Arauna did more than that: as she discovered her inner parts, hidden inside the structures, she found out what had happened to these parts to imprison them there, and in getting their stories she dismantled all the programming and freed herself from the mind control that the abusers designed!

Arauna Morgan: "Dismantling my inner structures"

One of the purposes of my programming was to create inside parts who were trapped or imprisoned in an internal structure (that could be seen by the system internally, if they knew where to look) that the cult had created, so they could be called out for specific duties. Parts were only released long enough to perform a prearranged function, then they returned to the structure. In my inner world, every part of the structure, even the booby traps, was an inside part of me, programmed to be something else.

Deep inside, there were walls containing the only parts that had not been programmed. If I talked to them, the wall would dampen not only what they said, but also the emotions they projected. I learned to thin the wall in order to communicate with them. The cult had discovered these parts, sometimes years after their programming was done, and just neutralised them by enclosing them in walls. There was gold in those walls! Those were the parts that would later help rescue programmed parts and dismantle the programme structures.

In my system there were entities that would attack if not appeased in a prescribed way. After all of the entities were pleased and calm, no traps would be tripped. At one time, I thought the entities were not part of my system, so I tried to send them away. I found that they kept coming back; they no longer attacked, but were still there. I learnt that when something does not go away, there is an inside person in it somewhere. There were often shells that contain parts of me. The shell could look or act like anything that can be imagined, even a real person, but they were not themselves people. There were layers of shells.

I noticed that all shells would start to lose definition and turn into blobs when separated from their original placement by the programmer. I had an internal safe place where I put all rescued inside parts. There was one part that I pulled out of a cement floor. The part looked like a foetus. It did not move, but I knew it was alive. I could not help that part right away, so I left it in the safe place, while I tried to figure out what to do. A week later it had degraded into a blob. I thought it did not belong and tried to send it away, but it would not leave. I finally opened it, as one would unwrap a present, and there was a part of me inside.

My programming would be "unlocked" by a programmer to improve upon the training of an obedient inside part, then would be "locked" by the programmer to trap parts within the structure if they were no longer useful to the cult. In one spot, parts who were designed as mythical creatures were created at the top and bottom of the Tree of Life. Then a part was created with the sole purpose of antagonising the two creatures at the top and bottom of the Tree and turning them against each other. In my system there were several such scenarios where I had to convince antagonistic parts that the true enemy was outside and we needed to co-operate to be able to better our lives.

I took apart one structure by myself, using my primary parts as care-givers for the rescued ones. Then I was ready to take a break before diving into the next structure, but my primary parts did not wait; that night and every night thereafter, they worked at dismantling structures and rescuing the parts that were trapped inside. Daytime was reserved for me to remember exactly what the programmer said while I was being programmed for a particular piece of the structure we were working on, to be able to finish dissolving the structure and freeing the parts inside.

I am now integrated/co-concious with only one other part, but back then my primary inside parts were very helpful and often worked on problems on their own. Most of the time I was aware of what they are working on, because I asked them for help and I felt slightly dissociated while they worked. They would dismantle the programming structures at night, so I did not get a very good night of sleep when this happened.

The last and very necessary step of dismantling the structure, for me, was to remember exactly what the programmer told me and the imagery that I created from this; once I realised that the structure was that way because of what someone told me, I was able to dissolve it permanently. Strangely, just knowing that the programmer told me did not work; I had to remember *exactly* what he said, and what *I* did in response. What I did in response to what they said was just as important as what they said for me to get rid of the structure.

* * *

Arauna's approach was effective in removing her programming and freeing her inner parts, as well as in remembering what had happened to her. She is now a free, competent human being who is able to help other survivors. One thing I admire about her approach is that she was unafraid to discover what had happened to her, or to the child parts of her. Essentially she

- explored the inner world and structures created by the perpetrator group;
- found the children imprisoned there by their programming;
- discovered what had been said and done by both them and the perpetrators to imprison them there, thus dissolving the structures in which they were held;
- helped these parts escape and move to safe inner places where their needs could be met.

If you take this approach, you will not have to spend so much of your life resisting programmed urges and emotions, but will be truly freed from them. Jeannie's approach of identifying what had been programmed, resisting it, and giving inner children permission to be free in their present-day lives is a first step. Arauna's approach of discovering how the programmes were made is a wonderful second step which actually undoes the programming!

And now, for the next step towards complete healing, follow Arauna's approach: while not acting on the programmed urge, set aside some time to explore internally and find out who inside holds the programming and what happened to create this programme. Assist these parts to share their stories with one another and with the important insiders, so that you can discover how you were trained and deceived. Important to this process is remembering what the perpetrators said, and what you did in response. Chapters Fourteen and Fifteen will go into detail about working with the traumatic memories which created the programmes, because it is important to share not only the stories but also the emotions and bodily feelings involved in these traumatic memories.

CHAPTER TWELVE

Coping with daily life

Many survivors of ongoing childhood trauma often have difficulty managing daily life as adults. They are usually out of touch with their bodies, and so they do not know when they need food, or rest, or exercise. They are out of touch with their emotions, and so they do not know what they like or dislike. And their emotions are not accurate gauges of what is going on in their lives in the present, because they are so often a response to post-traumatic triggers. Survivors often do not have personal boundaries, as theirs were perpetually violated in childhood. They lacked an intimate, nurturing connection with their parents, and so they do not know how to build one with their friends, spouses, and children. Their sleep is disturbed, because it was disturbed by abusers in childhood. They have difficulty with many areas of everyday life, often because of post-traumatic reactions in which they react to something in the present as though it were the past when the abuse was still happening.

There are many self-help resources for childhood trauma survivors to help them deal with living, and I shall not try to duplicate what those resources offer. Instead, I shall share the problems—and solutions—that are unique to survivors of mind control and ritual abuse. In Chapter Ten, we looked at how self-harm, suicide attempts, flashbacks, panic, and despairing states are often the result of trained insiders doing their jobs, and we shall look at this topic in more depth, as well as looking at the post-traumatic responses which survivors often experience, such as difficulties with cult ritual dates and birthdays. Programmed reactions are usually post-traumatic reactions that are, to some extent, under the control of trained insiders. But post-traumatic reactions that are not programmed are also common in survivors, especially if they have also experienced abuse that did not involve deliberate mind control.

A theme you may notice in this and subsequent chapters is that often the best solutions to the problems of everyday living are the interventions we already discussed in the earlier chapters: getting to know the leaders of your personality system, building a co-operative inner community, and having the parts who have been doing abuser-assigned jobs find new jobs which are actually helpful to the system as a whole.

In my experience, there are particular areas of daily living that are common to survivors. In addition to giving my own suggestions, I asked LisaBri to comment on some of these topics, to add a survivor's perspective.

Improving your sleep

Almost all child abuse survivors that I know have difficulties with sleep. The most common problems are insomnia and nightmares. Insomnia often stems from the fact that much childhood sexual abuse occurs at night, most rituals happen at night, and inside parts prepare for rituals by abstaining from sleep for days. LisaBri writes,

> Sleep patterns need to be rebuilt—a continuous life filled with interrupted sleep can leave you angry, scared, tired, and unable to cope with daily life. Uninterrupted, continuous sleep every night will help heal your mind and body.
>
> If you have a cell phone or other battery-operated device, you know how important it is to plug it in and recharge it. Well, we too have to be recharged, and sleep is the time when we recharge our batteries. So anything you can do to make it easier to get plenty of sleep will help in your recovery process.
>
> It helps to have a night light. If it's too bright to have one in the bedroom, you can leave it in the hall just outside the bedroom door. Make sure that nothing in your bedroom is a particular reminder to your parts of events that happened to them—although the fact that it is a bedroom may be part of the problem for some parts. It also helps to have a lock on the bedroom door, and make sure the lock is closed (as well as all outside doors and windows) when you go to bed each night. If you can't do this because you sleep with someone else, or because you have children who may need you, you may find that some parts of you stay awake and "stand guard" when you are sleeping. This may not be harmful as long as they take turns and all parts get some sleep. A dog who will bark at intruders can also help.

People who are dissociative, and especially those who have experienced mind control and/or ritual abuse, might have inner parts who only came out at night in childhood, and are now awake primarily at night. These parts have a kind of reversed "biological clock", and become active when it goes dark. One thing you can do is give them some time during the day or the evening to be around and do things they want to do, such as using the computer, or drawing, or house cleaning. Then they can make themselves tired and may learn to sleep when the body sleeps. It is a bit more difficult than recovering from jetlag (which happens when you have been in a country in a distant time zone), as it is the sight of darkness that wakes these insiders up. So, you need to educate them about your present life, that (if you are currently safe) nothing is going to happen at night now, and they do not have to be ready for things that will not happen.

Nightmares might happen as punishments for remembering or talking about your abuse. You know how to deal with this if you have read Chapter Ten. If you are experiencing nightmares as punishment, this might give you a clue about the existence of insiders who are still doing their jobs when those jobs are no longer necessary. One of my survivor clients has recently been getting one particular nightmare and flashback, and it led me to discover some inside children who did not know they are currently safe and were giving these things as preparation for a ritual which they no longer have to attend. Finding these children, updating them, and asking their leader to join the inner council, resolved the problem.

Nightmares may also come up because some inner parts of you are remembering these bad events, and the barrier between conscious and unconscious is weaker at night. Nightmares and dreams can be an important source of information about what happened to you, and about the important issues to be resolved in your life. Try writing down your nightmares, and asking your parts about them during the day or taking them to your therapy session. Two of my ritually abused clients get the most information about what happened to them through their dreams and nightmares.

Nightmares and dreams also frequently represent the relationship between your parts, including conflict between them, and parts helping or rescuing other parts from bad internal places. These are worth recording, too, as they will give you clues about the insiders who need help and what you can do to help them. If you are going to have such dreams, you might as well make use of them in your healing process.

Making up for memory gaps

Some people who are multiple often have difficulty keeping track of their time, knowing what they have and have not done, and finishing tasks. This is especially true if they have DID. Parts might fight for time out in the body to do the things they want to do. You might find that you have begun an activity and then abandoned it when someone else came out into the body, and you might not remember things that another part did. You can have difficulty if child parts come out when you are driving, or even adult or teenage parts who do not know their way around town. Even if your front person never switches, you can suffer from poor organisation as the ones just behind the front shell change places and your memory for what you were doing or planning to do becomes confused.

One practical thing that may help is to keep a daytimer book in which you write your appointments and other plans, and make sure that whoever is out in the body looks in it frequently, and writes in it. It can also help if you keep a communication book in which all parts can write things they want the other parts to read, such as activities they want to do or food they want to eat.

The book *Coping with Trauma-Related Dissociation* by Boon, Steele, and van der Hart (2011) has an excellent chapter titled "Establishing a healthy daily structure", and I recommend it for detailed suggestions on this topic, and for many other topics relating to multiplicity rather than specifically to mind control or ritual abuse. The primary solution to organisational or memory problems is, of course, improving communication with your parts. If you do not remember a part of your day, ask your insiders what happened and let them tell or show you. If there is an important appointment that you must attend, or task you must do yourself, let your parts know that it is important they permit you to do this. If you have an inner governing council, they can make sure that child parts are kept inside when you have adult tasks to do.

Learning to relax and play

Many multiples had childhoods in which they were regarded as slaves, and had to work all the time. Mind control and ritual abuse survivors have many parts who believe they exist only to do the jobs assigned by their abusers. These parts are often young children. They have never experienced the joy of playing, moving their bodies, trying out new things, seeing what they like and dislike, and being creative. All these experiences are essential for children to grow up into their true selves. Play therapy is a recognised treatment for children, because through play they can tell the truth about what happened to them, express anger at their abusers, and work out their issues symbolically with dolls or action figures. You can allow your young parts to do this, too, at least when you are alone at home.

You can also go to the park or the beach, play with toys at home, borrow children's books from the library to read to the little ones, and sometimes find real children to play games with. When inner children get "air time" in the body in the real, present world, they begin to meet their developmental needs, and, as a consequence, they begin to grow up in a natural way. It is very important to give them this opportunity, dividing your time between the adults and the children in a way that works for all.

It is easy for people who were work slaves in childhood to remain work slaves in adulthood, when there is no external person to impose this on them. Take a look at your life and see whether you, or any inner parts of you, need more recreation, creativity, and play. Then try to find a way to build this into your weekly schedule. LisaBri's suggestion is,

> You have young insiders who want to play. Play is essential to their healing. If you as an adult are embarrassed to be seen in public doing childhood play things, e.g. swinging on swing sets with 4 year olds, or splashing in a wading pool, work up to it. Begin with play in your home in private, and when that feels all right invite a friend over who has a child and let your kids come out and play. Work towards venturing outside to public swing sets only when your inner kids are ready.
>
> You can pick a time when there are not many adults around, to reduce your front person's embarrassment.

Learning to enjoy your body

Believe it or not, bodies are designed to experience comfort and pleasure. They do experience pain, but the purpose of pain is actually a signalling system to help you avoid more pain and keep yourself safe. However, mind-controlling abusers actually use your body to exert their control over your mind by administering pain, sexual feelings, and drugs. So, many parts of you probably do not even want to have a body, because being in it means you might experience those sensations that you do not want.

Bodies have many senses: sight, hearing, taste, smell, and the various skin sensations. Each of these can bring pleasure rather than pain if you discover your body's ability to feel good in various ways. Sexual feelings are a special case, and will be discussed in Chapter Seventeen, because abusers have misused them so much. But discovering your body's senses can be a wonderful experience of coming alive. Survivors' bodies are often in a frozen state, feeling little or nothing.

In addition, some of your parts might have had their entire life experience in such places as dungeons, or control rooms, or cages, and have never experienced sunlight, or warmth, or comfort. It is very important that these parts discover the good that can come when their senses are exposed to positive things.

The following is Wendy Hoffman's account of how, even though she had been abused, she learned to live in her body and enjoy its sensory (non-sexual) pleasures.

Wendy Hoffman: "Defrosting"

I was fortunate that the teenage boy my handlers sent to love me before he was sacrificed was a very good person, saintly. I was three years old and had not yet been loved. On my mother's wing chair in the family living room, he let me sit on his lap, suck my left thumb, place my right ear on his heart, and match my breath to his. (There was nothing sexual about it.) And so I learned to commune with another person, feel part of the universe and a sensuous, comforting delight in being alive.

Few good things happened after that, but I enjoyed the sweetness of fruits, vanilla ice cream, the hills in my neighbourhood which gently rocked me to sleep and the breeze which caressed, especially right before it rained. I came to this enjoyment naturally.

I had a theatre-type mother and she took me to dance class in Manhattan three times a week. At that time, I hated the rigidity of ballet. It was not at all pleasurable and sometimes hurt. When I was fifteen, I discovered modern dance and became interested. I acquired a sense of sculpting space with my body, beginning and ending a sequence of movement on time and feeling underlying rhythms. I studied the transitions between one movement and another, which felt delicious to me. As an adult, I studied Kinetic Awareness with Elaine Summers in New York City. The goal of this body movement technique is to locate frozen tension in the body and release it. I noticed I held my breath, understandable because of all the traumas piling up, but not beneficial. Slowly, I started to exhale and consequently to feel. The frozen tension in my upper back was solid. By moving my limbs from my joints slowly and internally, I started to melt and feel as if I had bones, blood, organs, skin, and pores.

The more my body softened, the more I remembered breathing and sucking my thumb on that cherished boy's lap—that is, the boy they killed.

It had been difficult for me to communicate deeply with people. But when dancers move in a group, there is a deep wordless bond that forms between them.

I could not leave my body when I danced. In ordinary life, I orbited around my body. When I danced, I stayed in it, a new experience. In regular life, I slumped, hid my torso, and showed how beaten down I was. When I danced, I elongated my spine. Using my body as an instrument, as if it were a violin or vocal cords, I learnt it was more than an object for others to abuse.

If I were to stay alive, I had to have a little pleasure each day. It couldn't be all trauma. The front person did not know, or knew just a little, about the abuses, but the front person had the job of finding something pleasurable.

Soft ice cream, melons, walking in the wind, moving, sunshine—something to keep going and bring the body back to life, make it sentient, let it know there is more than just frozen tension.

Exercise 18. Exploring your bodily senses

Here are a few things you might try to take back your body and explore the pleasures of your senses.

- Notice your breath. Don't change it or judge it. Just observe it. Befriend and bless it. You are still alive.
- Scan your body for tension. Your whole body may be frozen in tension. Direct your breath to where your tension hurts you. When you exhale, exhale into those spots.
- Become aware of every inch of your body. Include your toenails, your eyelashes and the hair under your arms.
- Eat a piece of dark chocolate very slowly, letting each nibble melt in your mouth.
- Walk barefoot in warm sand or over a soft lawn.
- Stand outside in the sunshine and enjoy the sensation of the sun on your skin.
- Stand in the wind. If it's a little breeze, let yourself feel its gentleness on your skin. If it's a strong wind, lean your body on to it.
- Stand in the rain, and let it run over your face and into your mouth. Drink the rain the way the trees and flowers drink it.
- Run your fingers over the velvety petal of a flower. Put your face close to it and feel the texture of its fragrance.
- Walk through a flower garden and pause to smell each different kind of flower. Now, look at all the colours of the different flowers and their different shapes, and enjoy their beauty.
- Pet a furry animal. Rub your face in the fur. Hug it and enjoy the feel of the fur on your body.
- Move, run, dance through space. Feel the space as palpable.
- Dance, all by yourself, expressing your emotions in the way you move your body. Experiment with different emotions, allowing your inside parts to express these through movement.
- Sing, shout, scream as you move.
- Choose your favourite fruit and savour its flavour as you eat it slowly. Think of yourself as part of the bounty of nature, like that fruit.
- Listen to a bird singing. Watch a bird flying and imagine yourself flying, spreading your wings and riding on the wind.
- Run, jump, row, exercise, and feel the strength of your muscles.
- All the way through, say to yourself and to your inside parts "This is *our* body. We can enjoy it. No one else is in charge of it. It belongs to us alone."
- Resolve to give yourself a pleasurable experience each day. In the morning, or the night before, plan the next day's enjoyable experience.

If any of the items in this list are triggering for you, take time to put away any feelings that have been triggered and rescue any inside children you find.

Learning to eat normally

Survivors of mind control and ritual abuse often have difficulties with eating. Many find certain foods to be reminder triggers of various kinds of sexual abuses, especially oral sex, and sometimes the names of certain foodstuffs are code for various sexual actions that a survivor had to perform in childhood. In this case, it is important to avoid these foods at first, then gradually teach your child parts what these foods are and why they are not harmful. There are also programmes for bulimia, anorexia, and overeating (sometimes to hide pregnancies), and these can be triggered in a personality system that is at war with itself. If you have one of those problems, you want to enquire inside about whether it is a programme before you attempt to get help for it. If it is not a programme, you can benefit from eating disorders treatment. *Secret Survivors*, by E. Sue Blume (1991), has an excellent section on eating disorders.

Sleep deprivation and the withholding of nourishing food were ways to keep your body and mind weak and easy to manipulate into compliance by an abuser. This is why it always happened as preparation before rituals. Sometimes survivors find they have insiders who prepare for rituals by stopping eating (and sometimes sleeping) three or more days before the ritual date. If you find yourself hungry but unable to eat, check with your insiders to see whether anyone might be preparing for a ritual.

Good, healthy food and sleep rejuvenate your body, giving you the strength you need to heal. So it is important to work on helping your parts be at ease with eating. Give yourself permission to buy food that everybody likes, and learn about healthy foods so that you do not just live on sweet snacks, which some child parts might prefer.

Note: The next sections could trigger flashbacks, and strong emotional reactions, so be prepared to put the images away and comfort those with feelings. If your system leaders read it, they might be able to develop a plan to address these problems.

Becoming comfortable in the bathroom

Bodily fluids and excretions, as well as baths and drowning, are on the list of phobias in Chapter One associated with being a survivor of mind control and/or ritual abuse. This is because of horrendous childhood experiences. Washing after rituals is often a painful experience, drowning and waterboarding are common methods of torture, and bodily excretions are used both in rituals and as punishment. Many survivors have trouble allowing themselves to urinate or defecate, especially if child parts are out. This is because abused children are made to hold their urine for a long time, or are given enemas (which are a form of rape). One survivor was told as a child that every time she moved her bowels, the smell would tell everyone her role in the cult.

Bathroom privacy can help: a door that locks, and taking the time to let the inner child parts know that no one else can get into the room. With time and encouragement, they can overcome their fears. You might need to take time to explain the present situation to them: "We have our own bathroom now, no one is going to come and get us. It's OK to have no clothes on in the shower; no one will see us, and we can wash ourselves gently. It feels good to empty our bladder or our bowels and to be clean."

LisaBri says,

> As an adult it is okay to give yourself permission to let go and empty your bladder and you will not be punished. Wetting your pants in childhood was the result of your abusers not letting you pee. As a baby you soiled your diaper—that is what they are for!— and were punished. It is okay to be fresh, clean and empty of body wastes.

Learning to recognise illness and injury

Children being abused by organised perpetrator groups are taught to hide their pain and suffering so that no outsider will suspect the ongoing abuse, and also so that they will endure the abuse silently. When a child is being brutally sexually abused, for example in prostitution, he or she has to pretend to enjoy the experience. Stella Katz, a former cult trainer, says that the trainers deliberately link pain parts and sex parts, so that one part enjoys sexual experiences while the hidden pain-holder takes the pain. A cruder form of hiding pain occurs when a vicious parent is beating a child, and crying or screaming makes the beating worse, so the child learns to be silent. I have met several survivors with parts who scream constantly in the head, with the screams they could never let happen out loud.

People who have learnt in this manner to hide their pain and suffering tend to continue to do so even when they need to ask for help for such things as injuries and painful illnesses.

"Regular" childhood (including school attendance) for a ritually abused or otherwise tortured child is a time for pushing away physical pain, exhaustion, and drugged sensations in order to appear "normal" so that no one in the regular world will realise what is going on in that other world the child inhabits at home or elsewhere at night. Children are severely punished for showing pain, and usually their doctors are part of the abuser group. The "apparently normal personalities" who are out in everyday life, such as school, are not to show any sign that the body has been tortured, or sleep-deprived, or starved.

One of my ritually abused clients has a large number of very young parts, most of whom are visibly depressed and sad, but one part always smiles. Her face always used to light up when she saw me. I flattered myself that it was because she was glad to see me. Recently I asked the one who came out after her to tell me about the one who looked so happy. Scornfully, she replied, "It's called acting." This little child part was a superb actress! She was not happy at all. Children are taught to "act normal" and "act happy", for example, to answer the phone cheerfully.

In many cases, the parts who hold the physical and emotional pain are pushed deep down inside, and the ones who handle the present-day world have very few feelings, physical or emotional, and very little energy. When these children's bodies grow up, the adults they become do not know what is going on in their bodies. In some cases, they feel nothing. In other cases, they are in constant pain from flashbacks or from physical injuries that have left lasting damage to joints. Or they feel constantly nauseated because of flashbacks involving nausea. They might not be able to distinguish between these sensations and ones which might indicate an infection or a serious illness. They simply do not know when they are ill. In several cases, I have had to tell survivor clients of mine that they must go to the doctor because they might have something seriously wrong with their bodies.

It is important to learn to notice pain in your body. If your present-day pain is held by pain-holder parts deep underneath, you need to keep communicating with those parts, encouraging them to tell you if there is any unusual pain, nausea, or other physical sensations that might indicate illness or injury. You need to reassure them that they will not be in trouble for letting you know. Survivor therapist Arauna Morgan writes,

> When I discovered these parts, I thought, 'Great! I can give them all my pain and I won't have to feel it!' Then I talked with these parts and I felt ashamed that I was willing to add to the burden

> that they bore for me through all that abuse! Instead of adding to their pain, I started to gradually take it on to ease their burden and also to help them heal.

Learning to deal with doctors, dentists, and needles

All the survivors of mind control or ritual abuse I have known have been afraid to go to the doctor or the dentist. This is because their childhood experiences include abuse by doctors and dentists. Some of this abuse is in order to make them fear disclosing to such people; other abuse includes fake operations (for example, a dentist apparently cutting out the tongue, or drilling in a tooth and telling you they are placing a microphone or a camera there). Some abuse is from maltreatment by actual doctors who are cult members. Of course, survivors of "regular" abuse also have fear of internal examinations (reminders of sexual abuse) or being confined in a chair with something in the mouth (a reminder of oral abuse). And medical examinations and tests, as well as dentistry, are unpleasant experiences even for people who have not been through abuse.

Mind control and ritual abuse also involve drugs administered by needles, as well as torture with needles. As a result, the fear of needles, which occurs in many ordinary people, can be accentuated in survivors. It is important to find a doctor and a dentist whom you know you can trust, and to speak with the young parts before you go to appointments, explaining who the doctor is, what he or she will do, and helping the little ones who are afraid to stay deep inside and let the adult handle it.

About doctors, dentists, and needles, LisaBri says,

> These are all things that leave you in a vulnerable position in the hands of someone else. Think of a simple dentist chair reclining backwards and a yearly physical for women. A needle gives you medicine when you are sick or to prevent illness. (Notice a needle is not given between the toes to prevent the sight of track marks!) If you have concerns with your health professionals take the control back. Have a friend or the nurse in the room with you during your examination. Explain (you don't have to give your whole life history at once—except your doctor should know the basics) that you are uncomfortable and you will be amazed at what the doctor or dentist will do to make you feel safe. The difference between doctors and dentists in your childhood compared to in adulthood is that you have free choice now. Interview these doctors and dentists as you would a possible therapist.

One survivor I know finds that whenever she goes to the doctor she forgets all the symptoms she planned to talk with her about, and she has nothing to say. In her childhood it was not permissible to tell a doctor anything that was wrong with her body, so some of her insiders make sure the front person cannot remember the problem she went to see the doctor about. This situation is not uncommon. Reassure the parts who were traumatised by real or fake doctors in childhood that this doctor is different and will not hurt them. It also helps to make a list of what you want to talk about before you go to the doctor, and take it with you, so that if the programme to believe nothing is wrong kicks in automatically, you can refer to your list.

Be sure, too, that your current doctor and dentist are not cult members. Do not stay with the ones you had in childhood, and do not go to ones recommended by family members. Be careful with recommendations from other survivors, too.

Although it is important to be able to recognise and disclose symptoms of physical illness or injury, you need to be more careful about revealing psychiatric symptoms. Unless you know that your doctor understands trauma symptoms, including dissociation, you are wise not to reveal too much. Too many medical professionals, including psychiatrists, believe that hearing voices is a sign of schizophrenia, that mood swings mean bipolar disorder which has to be medicated, and that depression requires electro-convulsive therapy if medication does not relieve it sufficiently. The "medical model" simply does not work for dissociation, and many treatments can do more harm than good (see Chapter Ten). You do not have to tell someone everything just because he or she is a doctor. However, if you have a therapist, even a psychiatrist, who does understand, you need to encourage your parts to be honest with that person. Then you can get appropriate help.

Learning to recognise hunger and tiredness

Just as survivors do not recognise physical pain or other symptoms of illness, they often do not recognise the sensations of hunger and tiredness, which are messages from the body about what you need. When you are hungry, you need to eat; when you are tired, you need to rest or sleep. When you have been sitting or lying down for a long time, you get restless and need to exercise. People who underwent ongoing severe child abuse often spent much of their childhood in a state of being deprived of sleep and sometimes starved or imprisoned. As a result, they have learnt to tune out normal bodily sensations and to never speak of them. They do not know that a well looked after body can feel comfortable, well rested, energetic, and not hungry.

You need to teach yourself to pay attention to your body at regular intervals, asking yourself whether you might be hungry and whether you might be tired. Listen to its messages. It is trying to help you. Learn the pleasure of listening to your body say what food it wants to eat today and whether it needs an afternoon nap.

Learning to release emotions

According to Stella Katz, a former cult programmer, one of the first programmes installed in infants is the "Don't cry" training. Although it is done differently in different groups, the essence of this training is that crying is severely punished, either with suffocation or with physical abuse. A survivor starting to cry might immediately begin to feel as if she is suffocating, as the training takes effect.

Pretty well all the mind control and ritual abuse survivors I have seen have been unable to cry for a long time. The ability to cry is a positive sign of healing. Crying allows a release of emotions that should normally be released right after a painful experience, in the presence of someone who cares. If you see "normal" little children fall down and hurt themselves, you will see that, rather than crying immediately, they will run to a parent, and then begin to cry, when there is someone to comfort them.

The need to cry is an important reason that survivors can benefit from a relationship with a good, caring therapist—or at least a friend. Some (but not all) survivors have supportive partners with whom they can cry, and others have friends who can listen to them and encourage expression of their anguish. Unfortunately, many spouses and friends are so shocked by the realities of the abuse that it makes it difficult for them to listen. Much of society has the attitude that crying is weakness, and that people should "get over it". Many regular people cannot handle hearing about the horrors of abuse. So, you need to choose your friends with care. We shall talk about this more in Chapter Eighteen, and about emotions in Chapter Thirteen.

Avoiding drugs and alcohol

Ritual abusers, child brothel owners, and mind controllers use drugs extensively to control the children they hurt and train. As a result, those children are used to being in a drugged state much of the time. When they grow up, they still feel this is normal. It is easy for them to try to regulate their emotions or physical sensations by using alcohol, marijuana, nicotine, or various stronger illicit drugs, or misusing and overdosing on psychiatric medications. One of my early ritually abused clients had a war going on between his parts about drugs. One group would take "uppers" in order to gain the upper hand in his personality system; another group would take "downers" in order to suppress the first group. As a result he was a chaotic poly-drug user. Another client tends to take too many of her prescribed medications whenever something upsets her. Another uses alcohol to get to sleep, not realising it actually causes the insomnia for which she is using it.

It is very important not to give in to the impulse to medicate away your feelings. Instead, when something is upsetting, you need to:

- search within your personality system for the parts who are upset;
- ask your system to close down any programmes which might have been triggered;
- rescue the insiders who may be caught in a memory and take them to a safe place;
- ask your internal leaders to contain the memories and emotions until you are able to work on them safely.

You could print out this list and post it somewhere in your home, where you will see it when you need it.

Learning relaxation, deep breathing, yoga, or other techniques to help you relax can be much healthier than taking medication every time you are upset. Physical exercise is a wonderful drug, as it stimulates your body to produce natural painkillers (endorphins). However, these things mainly work for the front person, and if insiders are still upset you need to do the internal work that will help your insiders.

Survivor LisaBri, who was an active alcoholic for fifteen years, says,

> If drugs were a part of your childhood abuse, know today it is unacceptable to continue to hurt your body this way. You don't need drugs to live; in fact, health is shown by your refusal to continue childhood patterns of hurt. You also don't have to do it alone. Seek out AA or NA or friends or your therapist. Remember you are not only hurting yourself but also child parts who feel the abuse has not stopped as a result of your continued use.

AA is itself triggering for some survivors because of its talk about a higher power, and often having meetings in churches. But there are other support groups or programmes which do not have religious overtones, if AA is too triggering for you.

Another thing you need to do, which you could not do in childhood, is to face up to the present-day situation that is causing the problem. Once you have dealt with internal triggering, you need to see whether there is something in your present-day life which you need to deal with—for example, stand up to someone who is bullying you, or reduce your workload, or improve your living situation. When you were a child, you were helpless to change such things, so you might have learnt to feel helpless and do nothing but self-medicate, even though in your adult life you actually are not helpless and can do something about these situations. Chapter Thirteen will go into this in more detail.

Anticipating difficult dates

People can have "anniversary effects", times of year which remind them of traumas they have experienced, whether or not they have experienced ritual abuse. But survivors of ritual abuse often have worse anniversary effects than those who experience of mind control does not include ritual abuse. Evil cults are religions, and they hold their religious ceremonies, many of which involve torture and murder, on certain dates. Dates vary between groups, but the most commonly used ones are: Christmas and Easter (for Satanic or Luciferian religions which reverse Christian ceremonies), the summer and winter solstices, the spring and autumn equinoxes, and the pagan holidays of Candlemas (February 2), Beltane (May 1), Lammas (August 1), and Samhain (October 31). All these "ceremonies" last for three days and nights. Birthdays of cult members are also celebrated with painful rituals. (If your birthday was near a major cult holiday, your family might have adjusted the date, and your birth certificate, to fit the holiday.)

Survivors often have difficulty functioning around these dates, especially as they are supposed to prepare for rituals by fasting and abstaining from sleep. Eating and sleeping can be problematic for several days before cult ritual dates, because certain inside parts have been trained to prepare for rituals by not eating or sleeping. One survivor gorged on food for a whole month because she had insiders who believed they were going to be starved. It is important to speak with these parts and bring them into the present, letting them know they will not have to attend any rituals so they need not prepare. It can also help to change the meaning of the holidays, or change the date when you celebrate your birthday.

It goes without saying that those who continue to be involved in cults have the most difficulty. If your family of origin was involved in ritual abuse, they might well expect or invite you to go home at the ritual dates. Survivorship (http://www.survivorship.org/resources/articles/holidays.html) has some excuses you can give to relatives about why you will not come home at those times, as well as descriptions of the historic meaning of some of the holidays.

If you know that you will be expected to be present at rituals at any of these dates, make arrangements to be with a safe friend at those times. Have them sleep in the room with you or just outside your door, and hide your shoes and your car keys.

Here's survivor LisaBri's advice regarding dates:

> It's a day on the calendar reminding you that 30 or 40 or more years have passed since the true significance of the day rang true. Hallmark dates are on a piece of card stock, folded to form a card, and sold to people, innocent people, to help them celebrate a certain day. You were taught to act in a special way, to do something you didn't want to do on a particular day. Today you can choose how you will acknowledge that date. Take your birth date, (a day usually filled with fear and anxiety recalling past cult birthdates), and change it. Your son's birth month can be the month of your new birthday. Your dog's birth date can be added to create a meaningful and fun day. It works if you are creative and if DID's are anything, you are creative.

Dealing with church and religion

Much ritual abuse is conducted in churches, and it frequently involves "priests" in clerical garb, whether or not they are real priests. Ritual abuse can involve unorthodox Christian belief systems, or can reverse Christian rites for Satanic or Luciferian worship. It is no wonder, then, that being in a church can be frightening for young parts of survivors. Many survivors avoid churches for this reason, but, unfortunately, weddings and funerals are usually held in churches, so attendance cannot be entirely avoided. It is important to reassure the young parts that it is daytime (if that is the case), that you are with someone safe (make sure you are), and that no evil rituals will happen.

Survivors might hear voices that sound like demons and devils, especially in church. These voices, in my opinion, are either young parts doing their jobs, or the result of "playbacks" of abuse events involving costumed adults pretending they are demons or devils. Be careful whom you tell about such voices. Fundamentalist churches may attempt to exorcise (cast out) parts who say they are demons or devils, and this can really upset your personality system and lead to reprisals by the higher-ups. Often the "good" or "light" parts in a personality system want to get rid of the "dark" parts. But this does not work; it just intensifies the internal conflict, and leads to an increase in problems of daily living. If you attend a church, be discreet about what you say to church members, and try to choose a church that emphasises God's love and forgiveness rather than his judgement. Churches that preach about hell and damnation will help convince the "dark" parts of you that they can never experience kindness or be part of your recovery. As this is what the abusers also said to them, it will delay your healing.

Dealing with accidental triggering

Survivors sometimes have reactions to things that other people do not react to. One common example is sitting in a circle. Some survivors have difficulty with symbols like circles and triangles, or with certain numbers or number sequences, or combinations of numbers and letters, or certain words. Words with positive meanings (such as "light", or "care", or "love") might have been distorted by abusers to mean something terrifying. These everyday triggers can be activated accidentally, or as part of programmed reactions administered by trained insiders. If you find you have reactions like this, gently enquire inside about what your children were taught about these words or symbols, and help them learn that these things do not have those scary meanings in the real world. You learnt about this in Chapter Ten.

Punishment and discard programming

The following are excerpts from consultant, author, and mind control survivor Trish Fotheringham's contribution to my book for therapists, *Healing the Unimaginable* (Miller, 2012). Her full experience of the "Patterns in mind control" was published in *Ritual Abuse in the Twenty-first Century* (Noblitt & Perskin-Noblitt, 2008).

Trish Fotheringham: "My fail-safe and discard programming"

> From the start of my training, various self-destruct, booby-trap, and time-bomb programs were implanted, which I call "fail-safes". They became more detailed, involved and tailored to me and my alters, as time went by. My instructions were to never tell, to keep silent, to whisk knowledge or memories away, to keep the pieces separate, or to go crazy. Later, I was programmed to destroy my own credibility, sabotage myself, attempt suicide, or engage in addictions in order to cope or belong. The same instructions were imparted to the internal systems that reported infractions so that punishments or repairs could be done. These programs made me crash or become flooded with unbearable feelings, that locked away certain memories, or that made a memory or programmed belief impossible to escape from. Like a spider-web, they were linked, woven together to intersect, support, and back each other up. This was done by repeating such phrases as "too much trouble," over and over. The same instructions were woven into many different trainings, so that a particular trigger phrase could set a cascade of programs into effect. The effects of the programs were designed to spiral, and to operate as a paradox. Thus, for instance, affirmations that work well with the average person might actually trigger increased problems for me. It was confusing for me and those assisting in my recovery that I would be getting worse when I was using methods that should make me get better.
>
> One significant type of fail-safe programming involved "trip wires" which could trigger actual physical responses, such as an arm jerking or pain in the chest that felt like a heart attack. These began early. They were part of two separate aspects of my training: "flying" (for fairies, witch, and genie alters—done in a harness of the sort used in circus/gymnastics training), and being a "puppet on a string" (mostly to prove I was not in control of my own body). I was encased in wires and/or string (hidden from sight so the alters didn't know they were there) in a way that led me to believe my trainers controlled my movements from a distance through their magical powers. Over time, these wires were used to form a network of control points throughout my body, each of which had specific fail-safe body responses linked to it. Telling a secret produced the feeling of being choked. Ignoring an internal warning about a fall could make a knee buckle to make me actually fall, thereby enforcing the validity of the warning.

If a person has in the opinion of the perpetrator group become untrainable, or is no longer useable, programming is put in to do two things: (1) ensure that all trained insiders and their memories are permanently locked away and unknown to the person who lives everyday life, and (2) make the person so miserable that he or she will self-destruct and eventually die of suicide or an accidental drug overdose. Here is more of Trish Fotheringham's story, describing her discard programming. (Remember that when she uses the word "alter" she means "part" or "insider".)

> ... when I was eleven years old, I committed more major acts of rebellion, including putting poison in the ceremonial drink at a ritual. This, along with increasingly poor test results, proved that I was irrevocably uncontrollable. "Adjustments and fine-tuning" suddenly and drastically changed. Now, my lessons—drugged, brutally painful and confusing nightmares come to life-changed to what I call "shutdown" and "discard" programming. The plan was to severely and permanently cripple or destroy my credibility, my ability to function coherently and consistently, my sanity, and, if necessary, my physical body.
>
> White alters, who had previously been taught that they were the "voice and words of the gods" (the scholar/writer, oracle, and preacher) were now "outcast from the realm of the gods." Tests were deliberately engineered for them to fail. These were followed by terrifying and humiliating belittlement about their inability to fulfill their responsibility to the gods and the people. They were accused of putting their loved ones and others in danger through their stupid, careless, selfish choices and actions. My perception and sensation were distorted by drugs, and I was exposed to initial shutdown scenarios through a combination of hypnosis, holographic projections, movies and scenarios acted out by actors on a stage. I saw masses of people rioting and being injured or killed because of my failures. Strapped in the now familiar magic gateway chair, my white alters "rode the rainbow" to "the realm of the gods". There, they were told by the "gods" (and shown, using holographic projections in smoke-filled air) that they were "no longer of value and had become too much trouble." They were cast out, tossed into a simulated hell and told that this was where they belonged. These experiences transferred into the inner world. One alter was left trapped in "purgatory", on the "outskirts of heaven", in smoky clouds of grey fog, hiding from the gods to avoid being sent back to hell.
>
> My handlers used re-activation codes to open the seal. They individually called forth three of the original foundational virtues alters (red, green, and yellow). After receiving paralyzing drugs, these alters were "encased" in "webs" by my handlers, who systematically carved my whole body with fine spider-web-like lines which they painted red and/or black. When the paint dried and shriveled, the lines looked and felt like burning traps that had constricted. Then these alters were "thrown into the (inner) tunnels" (by throwing them into actual tunnels) and "left to rot." Thereafter, they were only allowed immobilizing, excruciatingly painful, restricted roles. This effectively silenced them. There were more shutdown and discard events, designed separately for the alters of each colour path.
>
> From the age of twelve on, each colour path was taught that their only avenue to feeling good or powerful was to be "bad." Being stupid, scary, tough, weak, crazy, a hippie, a rebel, a partier or dropout were now good, necessary, and desirable. Alters were trained to embrace "wild times" filled with sex, drugs, alcohol, criminal activities and/or weird, flaky practices.
>
> In order to give my personality system a new structure, a combination of four alters were to be simultaneously present in my consciousness at all times, though only one could actually be out at any given time. This would ensure two things: that I would always appear normal (not multiple) to the world, and that only the appropriate skills and knowledge base would be accessible in any given situation. A young alter called Pat memorized patterns for who should be out in each situation, and conveyed them to a Controller alter. The controller alter flipped the right combination

of switches to bring the correct alters to "just below the surface" where they could then take their turns out as the situation warranted. Songs and rhymes continued in my head as instructions to the alters who were out.

At fifteen, a "stage-of-life" was created for the alters who were allowed to take part in my real life from then on, and each stage-of-life alter was individually called forth and given a false "memory shell." Thereafter, if they ever told tales, shared secrets, or otherwise broke the silence, their initial statements would be either false or fragmented and confused. This would discredit any revelations of truth that might manage to surface. These memory shells provided a common but false background of life experiences that naturally progressed to my programmed lifestyle and beliefs—those of the shutdowns, outcasts, and later, disables and lockdowns—making everything feel, and appear to have been, the product of my choice or true nature. The memory shells were created by showing each alter bits and pieces of "memory" that had been photographed, filmed, or otherwise recorded on a "brain imaging screen", spliced together with new clips of staged scenes with characters alters were told were them.

Finally, when I was eighteen, my handlers stopped layering more programs into my failed system. A "brain wipe" was done to erase everything that had been installed, and my memories were "rebuilt" over a period of nine months. These events occurred in a mental health center where I believed I was attending therapy appointments with a psychiatrist. I lay drugged on a stretcher, watching a screen which displayed photographs and films which I was told belonged to each alter. All of my experiences that were known to the mind controllers were included to the degree necessary for each alter or group to believe it was real. All alters (even those who had previously been made to disappear) had to sign contracts agreeing to whatever they understood needed to be "locked away forever." They were all regressed to infancy, and the ones who were to live my life from that point on were "re-grown" to my current age with newly implanted false memories.

In this regression part of programming that erased and rewrote alters' life experiences, my trainers told me about both the "false life" that was being erased and the new "real life" which was being installed, thus informing my file-keeper alter of which file to pull for whatever was to be done. In my healing, this helped distinguish what had actually happened to me from the fake life that had been created in installments over the years. Examples include "You were never or never did . . .," and "You did not receive . . . training," which really meant I was, and did, and had, and was now supposed to forget it forever.

New alters were created to guard the hidden system, including a "rear guard" and a "captain." After sufficient time for my body to recover, the control mechanisms were drastically adjusted and the controller was given new instructions yet again. Then I was taken back to the mental health facility, where the "brain imaging screen" was used to update the "memory shells."

After the final lock and seal was done I never encountered my programmers again, although they continued to have me watched and triggered by others when they felt it was needed. Calculated caution, along with terror of being locked up or trapped back in their control, has helped me get where I am now, integrated and able to write this paper. When watchers would visit me during the years of my recovery, I made sure to appear as dysfunctional as I had been programmed to be, and they would go away satisfied that the shutdown programming had worked.

I believe that I am still watched and occasional attempts are made to trigger me. But I really am free to live my own life now, the life my heart and soul choose, not the one they designed for me. Patterns can crumble. I am proof.

Other survivors report similar shutdown and discard training. One client of mine had people dressed up as God, Jesus, and angels reject her, telling her she was too evil to be acceptable to them so she might as well kill herself. Others had training encouraging them to smoke, drink, and become addicted to dangerous drugs. Sally referred to "Snakes and Ladders" programming in which she was permitted to move towards success, then fail and become self-destructive. Some survivors have large numbers of insiders shut away, sometimes by cult-involved therapists. These persons can appear quite functional, but are missing out on their full potential.

If you have frequent feelings or beliefs that you are totally useless, unacceptable, or evil, and that you can get nowhere in life, or you hear words in your head telling you such things, chances are you have what I call "discard programming". You need to talk with the voices who say these words, as they are parts trained to tell you these things. Discard programming is like any other programming, and can be undone by communicating with the parts involved and eventually helping them put together the memories of the events that caused their beliefs or behaviours.

The following difficulties often result from discard programming.

Difficulty accomplishing things

Survivors with discard programming often have difficulty completing courses or study and working consistently at jobs. Their personality systems can be dominated by parts whose job is to make them fail at whatever they try. To overcome this, it is important to get to know these parts and convince them that they can do a better job of protecting if they allow the person to succeed.

Difficulty "having a life"

Discard programming also interferes with the survivor's ability to "have a life"—that is, engage in fulfilling activities such as exercise, being outdoors in nature, having pets, having friends, playing and singing and dancing and painting and doing things which feed the soul. The massive depression induced by the belief that you are nobody, nothing, and worthless, or that you are evil and will infect everyone around you—both lies told by the perpetrators—can cause survivors to just sit and do nothing for hours at a time, never doing any of those things which teach their systems that there is light, and hope, and joy, and fun, and many wonderful, positive things and activities which they might believe are not for them. I have heard some survivors report that they sit in a chair and do nothing all day, or just play solitaire. They do not even get the housework or the grocery shopping done. This can look like a regular depression (which doctors tend to treat with medication), but it is actually the result of the lies told to the parts in the discard programming. Other, stronger parts need to resist this programming and make you do the fulfilling things which will let you know that the good things in the world *are* for you, too, and that you do not bring evil and darkness into the world as you were told. This will be easier, of course, when you have uncovered the memories that make parts believe these lies.

Survivor therapist Arauna Morgan writes,

> In my own recovery, I found that it was very important to go back to the earliest memory of when I was told some self-defeating refrain, for instance, "You are worthless and will never have a family or be able to hold a job!" The first step was to be able to remember it being said to me, the next step was to remember who was saying this, then next, *what were they doing to me while they said this*. When I was able to remember the circumstances, I was able to see, as were all parts involved, that what was being said was being said by a deranged person who only wanted me to have as miserable a life as he had! After that, it was very easy to discard the self-defeating refrain from my life and when it slipped back, I had only to remember again to remind me why this no longer applied.

Understanding and overcoming programmed reactions

Many of the difficulties we have discussed in this chapter are actually related to programming, and many of the suggestions I have made are stop-gap measures. When you build a co-operative inner community, so that your insiders turn off programmes, it makes a huge difference. And when you actually work through the training memories, it makes your life much, much better. Sally's story in Chapters Six and Eight illustrates both the programmed difficulties, and the changes that can happen. She struggled through university with great difficulty because of programming to give her apparent learning disabilities. When her insiders decided not to do those jobs, she became much more competent, using her real abilities.

Exercise 19. Daily life problems and solutions

For each of the following areas of daily life, describe:

- what difficulties you have;
- what actions you are taking to deal with this problem;
- what else you plan to do about it.

Sleep
Memory and organisation
Relaxation and play
Bodily enjoyment, using your senses
Eating
The bathroom
Recognising illness and injury
Dealing with doctors, dentists, and needles
Recognising hunger and tiredness
Avoiding drugs and alcohol
Difficult (cult) dates
Church and religion
Other triggers

Which of your difficulties might be a result of punishment programming? Is there something for which you have always felt that you were being punished? Explore this with your inside parts and keep asking until you get an answer. "I don't know" is not an answer; keep asking until you get a real answer.

(continued)

Try to communicate with your insiders about what might have happened, or what you did that set this off. When you find out, dialogue with them some more about their concerns and yours.

Do you have indicators in your life that shutdown and discard programming might be operating? What indicators (such as difficulty "having a life" and difficulty accomplishing things or behaving appropriately) do you experience? If you have such indicators, try to communicate with the insiders who are causing these difficulties. It could also be interesting to know which behaviours of yours (that the perpetrators did not want) caused the perpetrators to put in these programmes.

CHAPTER THIRTEEN

Emotions

Every part of our being, including each of our bodily sensations and each of our emotions, is designed by nature to help us meet our needs and achieve wellbeing.

Just as physical pain tells us what is happening to our bodies, emotional feelings tell us what is happening to us in other respects. They let us know what we need. We might not like pain or negative emotions but they are a necessary part of life. Pain hurts and yet it actually protects us and helps us to live safely. Physical pain tells us when we need to attend to a part of our body. If our tooth hurts we can get it checked so that the tooth does not rot. If we experience painful emotions such as anger, fear, anxiety, loneliness, and sadness, we need to check what those messages are about in order to achieve and maintain emotional and psychological health and happiness.

When we lose touch with important emotions, we become vulnerable to violations from others (which is, of course, what abusers want). The sad thing is that we might not even know that we have been affected by these violations. In the disease leprosy (Hansen's disease), people lose their fingers and toes not from a disease process that eats up the hands and feet, but by the inability to feel these body parts. The pain that is meant to protect is not there, and the person develops an infection or injury which goes untreated. Emotional pain has just as important a purpose as physical pain, and we ignore it at our peril. Emotional pain, just like physical pain, serves the purpose of drawing attention to what we need to do to keep ourselves safe and healthy.

Emotions, abuse, and dissociation

Of course, if you suffered ongoing childhood abuse, with no source of comfort, you were unable to keep yourself safe and healthy during your childhood and possibly into your adulthood as well. For all those years it was not helpful for you to pay attention to your emotions because you were unable to act on the messages they gave to you. So, you probably learnt to dissociate those emotions into hidden inside parts whose main purpose was holding feelings for you, while the external you did what the abusers told you to do.

All survivors of childhood trauma—or even inadequate parenting—have difficulty with their emotions. If a child's early emotions are denied, shamed, and ridiculed, the child buries them, seeing them as pathetic and unsafe. Even when they have not experienced deliberate mind control, people with abusive and neglectful childhoods have usually not learned to understand their emotions and respond to them in helpful ways. They often either fear emotions or swing from one extreme feeling to another as different post-traumatic emotional states are triggered by relatively small current events.

Anyone who has undergone unresolved traumatic experiences, especially in childhood, has areas of sensitivity in which present-day triggers bring back the old reactions of childhood. When this happens, the person feels as if the childhood pain were happening all over again, even though he or she might not even remember the original situation that caused the emotions. That person might then believe the emotions belong to something in the present, when they actually arise from some accidental resemblance of something in the present to a past trauma. The intense feelings of rage, terror, or despair are totally disproportionate to what is actually happening now. In Chapter Ten we looked at triggering, sometimes when programmes are set off, but also when reactions from old trauma intrude into present life. It is because of over-reactions that many people do not want to deal with their feelings at all.

Denial of emotions

Denial of emotions is the process of pretending that emotions do not exist or pretending that they have been dealt with sufficiently—"*everything is fine*".

When someone asks survivor LisaBri how she is, she responds, "I am just fine. F=Fucked up, I=Insecure, N=neurotic, E=emotional."

Denial is actually lying to yourself and others about a truth that for some reason you just cannot face. Except, if you are dissociative, you are not consciously lying—you just do not know you have the emotions because they are hidden within insider parts.

Strong emotions do not just go away when they are ignored, because they are signals of unmet needs, danger, or harm. They might seem to have gone away, but they go "underground", and they continue to build up as new situations trigger more emotions. The "sack" in which we have stored the emotions gets more and more full, even if we are not aware that it is happening. When the sack finally bursts open, the emotions are out of proportion to the situation that triggers them.

In dissociative people, the "sack" is actually hidden child parts who specialise in particular emotions. The everyday life person may be unaware that emotions are even occurring, until these child parts' feelings become so strong that they burst forward and the person acts childishly.

Many experts now believe that unresolved emotions are stored in the body and that much bodily illness is a result of stress, unresolved emotions, and unmet needs.

Depression is often a result of unacknowledged experiences and their associated emotions. There is a deep sense of unhappiness without clear awareness of the cause. This often goes with considerable guilt and self-blame, sometimes about trivial things. Instead of the person feeling anger when taken advantage of, he or she turns the anger inward and becomes depressed. It might feel much safer to punish yourself rather than run the risk of "losing it" with others and losing your connection with them. And it could be unsafe to be mad at an abusive partner or relative. Depression can also result from unresolved grief over losses and unmet needs. Much depression is just the experience of "keeping the lid on" what the person really feels. This is different from appropriate sadness. Sometimes, the person feels that if the lid were taken off, he or she would never stop crying. This is actually not true. Grief and sadness have a natural process and come to an end, if they are felt.

Organised child abuser groups know that grief can be healing, and for this reason, they train children from birth not to release their distress through crying. So, it is important for your healing to learn to cry again, if necessary working through the memories of being taught not to cry. Abusers frequently tell children that being emotional or experiencing and expressing pain is weakness, but that is simply a lie.

Healthy grieving follows remembering. Child abuse survivors have a great deal to grieve. If the emotions from losses overwhelm you without the conscious memory of those losses, depression can disable you. This is one reason it is important to become conscious of your traumatic memories. How to do this will be discussed in Chapters Fourteen and Fifteen.

Emotional pain-killers

A person feeling a strong degree of discomfort is likely to turn to "emotional pain-killers" in order to feel better, even though the improvement in feeling is only temporary. Emotional painkillers are self-indulging habits that temporarily make a person feel better. Any of the following activities can be used as emotional painkillers: alcohol, prescription and non-prescription drugs, smoking, sex, pornography, work, gambling, shopping, saving money, spending money, sports, jogging, vomiting, chocolate, eating, the Internet, some kinds of religion, and television. You can probably think of others.

Most of these things are harmless in moderation, but harmful when they become addictions. They only work for a short while, so you have to return to them again and again, wasting time and money in order to improve your mood, and you need more and more of them to feel satisfied. Like any pain-killing drug, emotional pain-killers deal with the symptom rather than the cause of the pain. Unfortunately, most emotional painkillers are capable of ruining a person's life and relationships.

When a person becomes physically addicted to some chemicals, the chemical replaces certain substances in that person's nervous system. These substances are no longer manufactured by the body, so when a person withdraws from the chemical, he or she suffers symptoms caused by their absence. In psychological addictions, the substance or the activity makes the person feel temporarily better. Eating fills some kind of internal emotional hunger. Gambling, or shopping, or spending makes the person feel temporarily rich, and allows for the impulsive release of some desires. Work, or exercise, or saving money creates a sense of control, but eventually psychological withdrawal sets in, and the person needs another "fix" to take away the pain of the unpleasant emotions.

People who, as children, were not allowed to express and explore their emotions are especially prone to self-medicating with drugs or other addictions. If they can learn to deal with stress in a healthy way and develop these skills when they are young, they can avoid sliding into the trap of addiction.

Drugs and alcohol can easily present problems for survivors of mind control and ritual abuse, because these substances are used during the abuse. Different insiders might be addicted to different drugs, and may take over the body when these drugs are in the body. The abuser groups sometimes supply drugs to addicted survivors in order to keep them coming back to the group.

The meaning of moods

Many people get into good or bad moods without knowing why and then feel trapped in their mood. It is helpful to learn to identify our emotions, and use those emotions to detect both the situations that trigger you and the underlying causes of the moods. We can ask ourselves questions such as "Why am I feeling this way? What's going on?"

When we grow up learning to reject or ignore our emotions, we learn not to trust ourselves. We use the unspoken rules of the dysfunctional family, which are: "Don't feel. Don't acknowledge that anyone has hurt you. You have no right to feel hurt. It is your fault. Don't be a wimp. Don't be selfish. You should be grateful for all that has been done for you." When a person loses his or her conscious awareness of what has happened, a "bad mood" happens.

Every bad mood begins somewhere. You can learn (1) to notice a bad mood as soon as it begins, (2) to detect the trigger that got it started, (3) to identify the feelings produced by that trigger, and (4) to problem-solve the situation in order to prevent the same thing from happening again.

When a person has hidden inside parts who experience themselves as separate, the different emotions (which create the moods) are held within these parts. So, rather than just thinking about the problem, you need to communicate with the parts who are holding these emotions. Find out who inside has this feeling, how old he or she is, what in the present triggered this part to come up to the surface, and whether the feeling actually belongs to the present or belongs to some past event. Ask that part what he or she needs to feel safe and cared for. Let that part know about your present life, and how it differs from the years that part remembers.

Emotions in mind control survivors

A survivor's emotions are often tied up in insiders, sometimes very young ones, who are still stuck in the experiences of their abuse. Present-day reminders (post-traumatic triggers) of those experiences will bring those insiders close to the surface, and the person will be flooded with their overwhelming emotions.

Mind-controlling abusers manipulate this process of emotional dissociation, distorting your emotions to serve their purposes instead of your own. They deliberately create internal parts who hold specific emotions, such as anger, or despair, or sexual lust. Sometimes, their emotions are enhanced by drugs, such as amphetamines ("speed") for angry parts. The angry parts are designed to come up when they are called upon to engage in violent acts. Despairing parts are designed to come up for suicide attempts. These programmed acts are to be performed by parts who are in extreme emotional states and have very little awareness of everyday life and current events when they take over the body.

Many, if not most, of the inner parts of mind control survivors have characteristic emotions, or characteristic ways of handling emotions. Because many of their childhood experiences were emotionally overwhelming, they have developed personality systems in which certain parts contain only sadness and despair or shame, other parts contain only anger and rage, others are filled with anxiety and panic, and still other parts appear to have no emotions. Often the sad parts have been put through experiences that make them suicidal, and it is their emotions which are accessed when a suicide or self-harm programme is turned on. The rageful parts (who may believe themselves to be monsters) have been made angry and then forced to perpetrate crimes against others, then told they are evil and no one wants them (except the abuser group). These strong emotions are not supposed to appear in everyday life, so a survivor's front person often feels numb rather than experiencing a range of emotions.

You need to be aware of the existence of these extreme parts who are capable of engaging in desperate acts. Keep them inside while they are gradually educated by other parts about the realities of your present life. Eventually, they need to work through the memories of the events that caused them to experience such extreme emotions. This will free them to connect with other parts and experience a range of more normal emotions. It will enable the rest of you to be in touch with your own anger and sadness, which might not currently be available to you except as extreme rage or despair.

The following is survivor therapist Wendy Hoffman's description of the emotions she experienced as part of her recovery process:

Wendy Hoffman: "Feelings"

Usually, I can go to work, do my job, have conversations with friends. But when I have free mornings or on the weekends, when I have space before me, memories emerge followed by spurts of strong feeling. Then I stop functioning in the real world and begin functioning in my inner world. Anxiety, shame, grief and angry depression hold hands and dance in my brain. The feelings are too big for the child's body and too strong for the adult's heart. The feelings crush me as if I were a closed accordion, but then a source of comfort from the outside or inside or both rescues or appeases.

Terror obliterates all other feelings. It wraps around my body like a serpent and shakes me until I am breathless. When I think of the repeated break-ins or the torture and threats, terror erupts like a personal mini-earthquake. When it subsides, I can see what's underneath. And I feel shame, the kind of shame that turns my body crimson red. No cliché. For real. A therapist would say "You have survived the unthinkable and have made some right choices. You can't blame yourself for being tricked into making some wrong choices. You thought you were saving other people or warding off something worse." And the therapist would be right, but I am nonetheless filled with shame about not having had a normal life, not being part of a family, knowing close up what mankind is capable of. And I am ashamed of what this abuse has made me into and that I have to hide who I am. I am ashamed the abuse has gone on my whole life.

Grief is the other big feeling I live with. One life is not enough to fit in all the grief I feel. There have been instances of love. It doesn't matter that the relationship was scripted and staged, there was still a real friend who understood who I was and cared for me. Love can melt a frozen person and bring someone to life. The memory of his love has probably been the one factor that got me through my arduous life. I believe I would have been evil had if not been for his love.

When they killed him, the tempest of grief entered not to be killed. Love and grief are mixed for me now. I grieve the pets I lost and loved and a friend in the outside world who loved me and died from a heart attack after a gastric bypass.

And I grieve the family I had to leave behind and that I gave birth to children who were either stolen or killed as newborns or who were coerced into being a cult participant. I ask why with all this similar DNA and genes, why am I the only one in my family line who really wanted freedom? Perhaps because of the love of that one boy. So grief and I get up in the morning, go to work, have dinner, go to sleep. As I eat my breakfast cereal, grief can open its jaws around my heart. Yet, without the love that caused the grief, where would I be now?

To live without your family is to live without large parts of yourself. Family can be a pulse that insulates and protects but not for survivors of criminal groups. Family for them is what makes people not know who they are, give up their souls and fear for their lives.

I used to be mainly angry, reacting to life's injustices with rage. When younger, my anger was tinged with sexuality. My anger was justified. What was overwhelming were its tentacles that went back to my earliest trainings, which I was unaware of. I felt the feelings but didn't know why.

My anger has recently subsided considerably. The young parts still react angrily but I can locate them in my system and model for them an alternate way of expressing anger, such as putting it into words, exercising it off or understanding its genesis. Knowing who is reacting angrily and causing huge overreactions quiets the rage.

I think my getting older is helping reduce anger. My hormones are diminished, I expect less from life and people and am used to injustice and corruption. My being shocked less easily has also quelled anger.

When I have big memories and parts in me rush to my inner safe house, I feel gratitude and relief. Relief for me is as good as it gets. I would not choose to live my life again. But as I emerge into the other side, I feel my old friend relief but also proud of myself. I feel that I have protected my soul. Could there be anything in this world more important than that! And so I am walking through life with a soul somewhat intact though I have a way to go in my healing. When shame and terror grip me, I keep going anyway. When I think of my parents and grandparents who never tasted freedom, I feel sadness and pity. When I think of my family mind controlled to be what they never would have chosen to be and whom I am leaving behind, I feel my companion of grief but I keep moving forward toward freedom and belief in myself and gratitude for the few non-impostor people who have helped me, and the invisible power in the world that still cherishes us. Perhaps currents from the freedom I strive for will touch the dead and the unborn, travel generations backwards and forward and give them courage and hope.

From the time I was born, my handlers suffocated and tortured me whenever I cried. First they caused infants and children to cry, then they prevented it. Lately, in difficult and advanced therapy, I have understood their diligence in reinforcing the 'don't-cry' program throughout my life.

If I could allow my inside parts to cry, I could connect how I felt on the most visceral level to what happened to me. Not connecting these emotions leaves me still in a partially split-off state. The 'don't-cry' program is the glue of my mind control.

Crying is also a time of reaching out to God. The branch of the cult I was born into focused on preventing that communion.

* * *

Reclaiming your emotions

You need to reclaim your emotions, and you can do this, even if they are separated internally by being held by different insiders. If your personality system works together, you can regain the use of your emotions for your own health and safety.

The first stage in learning to handle your emotions is to acknowledge that you do have them and to become aware of what they are. Simply stated, all feelings are messages. Their purpose is to tell us what is going on inside us, psychologically.

Using your emotions effectively begins with accepting and paying attention to the emotions, and then expressing them, in order to "get their message". This process includes noticing the present triggers of those emotions, noticing any old connections which make the feelings more intense, and noticing the unmet needs that the emotions are telling you about. Then make plans for careful action to see that your needs are met and the situation does not recur in the same way again.

If you pay attention to your emotions when they happen, they will not overwhelm you later.

Finding and expressing your emotions

Emotions need to be discharged in order for healing to occur. It is important that the emotions be associated with the actual events that have caused these emotions, not only the present-day "triggers", but also the old traumas. You can relieve some tension by releasing emotions whose cause you do not know, but because their causes are not resolved, they will recur.

Certainly, while you are in the grip of an intense emotion, you cannot plan rationally. You first have to discharge the physiological arousal associated with the feelings by expressing the emotions. If the expression is allowed to take a natural course, through such acts as talking, crying, praying, writing, and/or drawing, it leads to new awareness. You will become aware of other emotions behind the original one, such as hurt covered up by anger, or hope replaced by disappointment. You will begin to see the unmet needs that the emotions are pointing to. Each emotion points to a specific kind of need.

Often, mind control survivors have been trained in childhood not to express their emotions in these ways. "Don't cry" is one of the first trainings given to infants, through smothering or beating them when they cry. This makes it very difficult for survivors to release their emotions, not only by crying, but by vomiting, shaking, screaming, or other visible or audible means of expression, all of which were violently suppressed by the abusers. Survivors often hear screaming or crying inside their heads, because parts are constantly crying or screaming on the inside. Those parts (who are often very young) need to learn that it is now safe to express their feelings.

However, there is a problem here. The feelings these insiders hold belong to many of the childhood traumas rather than to the present, and the extreme emotions from those childhood traumas can come up as a response to minor present events. The long-term solution is that these insiders need to be involved every time you work through a traumatic memory, releasing the emotions that belong to that particular memory. Some survivors try to access the content or story line of the memories without dealing with the emotions. This leaves the crying or screaming children stuck in their trauma, so it does not fully resolve the trauma. It is fine to access the narrative first, but then you have to go back and dig out the feelings.

Someone in your personality system knows which insiders hold the emotions belonging to each memory, and can guide these little ones to releasing those emotions when you do the memory work.

Feelings from the present and the past

To use your emotions intelligently, you have to be able to access the emotions that give you information about what is happening to you in your present everyday life. Our initial awareness of emotions is often only whether they are positive or negative—are we happy or unhappy? These general emotions, and others like them (joyful *vs.* depressed, satisfied *vs.* dissatisfied, comfortable *vs.* uncomfortable, hopeful *vs.* anxious, peaceful *vs.* fearful, optimistic *vs.* pessimistic) are the general indicators of how things are going for us and what we expect from the path we are on. The positive emotions are signs of health, of needs being met. The negative ones are warnings, signs that we need to look at more closely to find out what is wrong in our lives.

Negative emotions are present to tell us about problems, so that we can take action to remedy the situation. Emotions are not there to be medicated away! We can use these emotions to correct our behaviour or plans before it is too late. For example, a woman who was about to be married kept feeling a great deal of anxiety about the wedding. Upon closer examination, she discovered a lot of "danger signals" she had been ignoring about the character of her husband-to-be. The anxiety that she had thought was about the wedding day was really about the marriage. She was able to face the possibility of marriage more realistically when she realised this.

A mind control survivor was about to entertain weekend guests, and had recently discovered some insiders who had experienced abuse by a particular man. Unfortunately, the man who was going to visit her with his wife had a physical resemblance to the abuser, so some of her inside children had a strong reaction of fear and revulsion to him. They were afraid to look at the face of the guest in case he was the abuser. But the adult parts of the survivor knew that the abuser had been dead for many years, so they deliberately looked at the guest, to compare his face with that of the abuser. When they did this, the little ones still felt uncomfortable with the guest, but they knew he was not the person who had harmed them. The adult was able to push through the trigger, and relate to the guest as the person he really was, even though she could sense the little ones' emotional reactions within.

When you experience a strong emotion, one that seems out of place or too strong for the situation, you might need to look for insiders who are reacting to something in the present that resembles something in the past. Often, young inside parts are confused about time, and do not realise that years have gone by.

You might also experience emotions because particular insiders who hold those emotions just happen to be close to the surface. Inside children who have discovered they are safe in the present want as many opportunities as possible to meet their own unmet needs. So, they may come to the surface at school or work and get bored and want to play. I once treated a dissociative ten-year-old girl. Her three-year-old part would come out in the classroom, sit on her desk and sing, and get sent to the principal's office. The ten-year-old would not remember what happened.

Once parts from the past are around, even if they are just behind the front person, they might misinterpret what is going on in your adult life and have emotional reactions to things they do not understand. Children do not belong in adult situations, and your system may need to devise some way to make sure they do not come up when the adult needs to work. Another common problem is that abandoned parts who want closeness lead a survivor to hook up with an inappropriate partner.

In each situation in which you experience an emotion, you as a survivor need to find out who inside is experiencing that emotion, and whether or not it is a realistic response to the present.

Often, the situation is the reverse: you do not experience an emotion when the situation would normally provoke one. In this case, you can still search for whoever inside is having this emotion, and why it is being suppressed. Emotions that belong to the situation are helpful guides, and need to be experienced and expressed to receive their message. It is not uncommon for survivors to experience the emotions a day or two after the situation, when it is too late to act on the information they give.

The purpose of each emotion

The sections below indicate some of the major emotions we all experience and the present-day needs they are meant to tell us about.

Boredom and the need for challenge

The need for challenge, stimulation, and achievement is a basic need. We all need to be using our abilities, doing something worthwhile, learning and experiencing new things. When this is not happening our natural response is boredom. If this need goes unmet, we begin to feel rebellious and have thoughts of walking out of our home or driving past our workplace and heading south because we are bored with our job.

So, boredom, like a pain, is a signal that something is wrong and we need to pay attention to it.

Survivors of mind control and ritual abuse have plenty of inside parts who used to have "jobs" when they were children. Some of them might have been told that they are that job, and if they are not doing that job they are nothing. They might have been told that they were "created" for that work. And they might have gained some self-esteem and satisfaction (as well as praise or rewards from the abusers) for doing their jobs well. These insiders feel useless when they are away from the abuser group. They will get bored unless they have new jobs. So, put them to work. Think about what better job each part could claim. For example, soldiers can maintain your safety; programmers can make sure all the programmes are turned off unless you need them for some reason (e.g., to temporarily forget a memory you are working on and have not completed, or to reverse a programme); spinners can encourage and spin something positive, and spin away flashbacks.

Another kind of boredom can occur in survivors if they have been discarded by their abusers, and programmed to fail at life tasks. It might be difficult for such survivors to allow themselves to succeed or to take on new challenges. But it is possible, if the whole personality system works together co-operatively instead of some parts sabotaging other parts' attempts to succeed.

And then, there is just regular boredom, which everyone experiences from time to time, a signal that you need more challenge and stimulation in your life. Pay attention to this emotion and try to meet those needs. Sometimes what you need when you feel bored is physical exercise. Exercise is active, and everyone needs to move their body and use their muscles. But you may not be consciously aware that this is what you need. I notice this need in my dog, because he is very clear about when he needs exercise, and he shows his restlessness until I satisfy that need.

Confusion and the need for meaning and order

The need for meaning, sense, and order is a basic human need. It is easy to become cluttered in our minds or our surroundings. Often, too much is going on at once: too many activities, obligations, and commitments, too much stuff and not enough space. Whether the clutter is in our kitchens, our offices, or our minds, we need to take time to clear it out. If we do not, it can leave us feeling confused, perplexed, and overwhelmed.

At one point, I had a sense of confusion and clutter about my entire life. I had been very busy, and experiences, like house clutter, had piled in one upon another without my taking time to sort them and work out their meaning. Relationships were unexamined, even though they had generated all kinds of feelings that were clues about how I needed to handle certain people. I felt as though I was making my way through life without knowing where I was going. I felt that I had no priorities and was just dealing rather inadequately with whatever happened to capture my attention at the moment. I took a weekend to retreat alone to a little cabin. As I drove there, things crowded into my mind in almost random order—thoughts and feelings that seemed unrelated to one another. I spent the weekend alternately doing a huge jigsaw puzzle and working on the puzzle of my life, sorting the pieces by shape and colour until they fitted together into a meaningful pattern. Gradually, the confusion and feeling of being overwhelmed lifted, and I could make sense of my life. Some of the things which gave me bad feelings were still present, but I now knew what each problem was, and could prepare myself to deal with it. I realised that certain relationships were affecting the rest of my life, and they had to be either changed or ended. Sorting through it all was a very satisfying experience. I felt closer to myself, that I understood myself better.

Sorting like this can be particularly helpful for dissociative people, because they have so many parts operating almost independently. If you make the time to contact all the parts and let them communicate about their feelings and needs, it can be very helpful.

People who are multiple sometimes need special solutions to achieve continuity and order in their lives. Each part of you can write things down, leaving notes for other parts about your concern. Many multiples keep a book in which they can write to one another. Talk internally before making decisions, rather than acting impulsively just because you happen to be "out", fearing that you might be shut up inside again. Ask the other parts to let you know their needs and their concerns. Internal communication and co-operation can reduce confusion significantly.

Irritability, stress, and the need for self-care

When we are under stress, we all tend to become cranky and irritable. Stress, often caused by too many demands, failure to prioritise, and not enough self-care, is one of the major contributors to aggressive or impulsive behaviour. Stress can come on in response to sudden unexpected events such as the loss of a loved one, an illness, or accident, the loss of a job, or a marital conflict.

Sometimes, our basic needs (such as sleep or safety or attention or affection) just are not being met, and during those times it is hard to keep our cool. Sometimes, our irritability is a signal that we are doing and giving more than we can comfortably do or give, that we are not addressing an important emotional issue in our lives, or that too much of our self—our beliefs, values, desires, or ambitions, are being compromised in a relationship. If we do not pay attention to the stressed-out, cranky feeling we get, it can easily turn to anger at the people who make demands of us, including our dependent children.

When other people (for example, our partner or our children) appear to be stressed, and are becoming irritable, we can help by encouraging them to relax and take time for themselves. Not by saying "Relax, keep your cool", but by offering to take on some of their responsibilities or at least giving them room to do what they need to take care of themselves.

Survivors know that in their childhood they were expected to function "normally" no matter how much abuse, neglect, rejection, sleeplessness, and pain they had to endure. So they have learned to pretend things are all right when they are not. It is important to change this pattern, to listen to our stressed-out feelings and give ourselves permission to look after ourselves in a healthy way.

You might feel irritable when you are ignoring your insiders. They hold emotions, physical sensations, and needs of which you, the outside person, might be unaware. So, make a habit of listening to your insiders.

Tiredness and the need for recreation and rest

Many people, especially abused children, have been raised with the belief that rest and recreation are not real needs. This is particularly true for child abuse survivors. Even in general society, workaholism is often not only accepted, but held up as a sign of success. Physical exercise is really important for our health, and is also enjoyable, but many people have even gone so far as to make recreation hard work! Recreation means to re-create. How do you re-create yourself? Do you believe you can re-create yourself by playing or by having a nap? Are rest and play priorities for you, or are you influenced by expectations to perform and excel every waking hour?

We need rest: sleep, in which the body's muscles are inactive; dreams, in which the mind "digests" the experiences of the day and fits them in with its past experiences; play, in which we explore new ways of being; and humour, in which we gain perspective on ourselves and our human struggles and pretensions. When we do not get these things we "burn out". Our bodies and our minds become tired and exhausted. If we define this tiredness as laziness, and pay no attention to it, we break down.

Another type of feeling we get, and this feeling indicates the need for play, is the feeling of wanting to goof off, to get up to mischief, to do something "dumb", or silly, or useless. We should pay attention to this feeling. Perhaps this is just what we need! Watching a comedy, or playing video games or charades, or reading a comic book, really does meet an important need. In such situations, our mind renews itself and gains perspective and energy for the tasks ahead.

Survivor therapist Arauna Morgan writes,

> Since I have started to pay more attention to the needs of my entire system, I find that I need at least one day a week to do "insignificant" things, i.e., things that are not associated with studying, do not make money and no housework. About once a month I also need a "down day" where I can sleep in the living room all day, interspersed with watching movies or TV. I am a workaholic, by necessity, and this adjustment has been very hard for me. Alarms keep going off that there are things that need to be done! I have to keep reminding those alarmist parts that if I do not take these days off, I will get sick and have to take them off anyway; this way, I keep my health.

When a person has children inside, those children need activities appropriate to their developmental stages. Part of the reason inside parts stay very young is because the needs they had at this stage of development were not met. So find out how old your inner children are, and this will help you work out what they might need in order to mature and grow. If you are not familiar with normal developmental stages of children, consult a parenting manual.

Worry, fear, and the need for safety

Worry, like all emotions, serves a purpose. When anxiety works normally, it alerts us to possible future dangers so that we can take action to prevent these things from happening. We need to tune in to our anxiety enough to see whether there is any real danger. When we feel worried or anxious, it is important that we slow down and pay attention to what is worrying us. Sometimes, there is a problem we have not been paying attention to. Sometimes, we are worrying about the wrong thing, like the woman who fussed over the wedding plans and ignored the problems in her fiancé's character.

Unfortunately, worry can run away with us even when the possibility of danger is very low. This is particularly true for child abuse survivors. You probably have parts who live in a perpetual state of terror, because they were split off during a genuinely terrifying event. Survivors know (at least, their inside parts know) that some of the really awful things can and do happen, and have happened to them frequently. Some insiders still live in the memory of those traumas, and can easily think they are happening again when they are not. It is important to update your insiders, as they make themselves known to you, if you are currently safe, so that they know what year it is, how old you are, and how far you are from the people who hurt you.

At the same time, some survivors are oblivious to danger, in particular the danger of recontact and ongoing abuse by the perpetrator group. Personality systems are designed in such a way that the everyday adult part is unaware of such dangers. Your watcher parts can be given the new job of watching for actual dangers, and letting you know if there is such a danger.

Sometimes, survivors will experience extreme terror without knowing the cause. It can be a present-day situation that is actually dangerous, or it can be the fear from a memory. There are such things as emotional flashbacks, where the emotions from a traumatic memory flood the person without the content of the memory. These can, in perpetrator-designed personality systems, be punishment for disobedience or disclosures, or they can simply be flashbacks triggered by something in the present. You can only find out by talking with your insiders.

Our worries need to be examined and approached head-on. Chapter Nine addressed safety from the perpetrator group in more detail. But, of course, there are other dangers, some of them common to anyone, from crossing a busy street to hooking up with a dangerous or uncaring partner. The key is to make sure you have listened to all the concerns of your insiders.

Loneliness and the need for love

We feel lonely when we long to be near someone who loves us. This emotion leads many people into relationships that turn out to be destructive, whether it is one-night stands, affairs, or hasty marriages. It is important to recognise our loneliness, but not rush into something we might regret. The same goes for sexual feelings, which we shall discuss in Chapter Seventeen.

Loneliness can be an overwhelming emotion for survivors whose own families were child abusers. So can fear of getting close to anyone. Organised abuser groups exploit these emotional states to create bonds with the group rather than with healthy family members or friends. They deliberately prevent or break each child's natural bond with his or her mother, even if the mother is not part of the group and does not know what is going on. This lack of a safe secure attachment does huge damage not only to the person's ability to trust, but to every part of their being. The inside parts might include some who cannot trust anyone, and will sabotage any possible relationship, and others who will allow themselves to be exploited by any person who offers the faint possibility of caring. Because of this, you need to be very cautious in developing relationships. It is important to recognise and acknowledge lonely feelings and the needs behind them, see which of your insiders contain these feelings, and just remain aware of the needs without either rushing into lustful action or isolating yourself from those who could offer love and companionship. Sometimes, loneliness can create anger with people who are near but not emotionally available.

We shall look in more detail at the emotions and needs concerning love and belonging in Chapter Eighteen and concerning love and sex in Chapter Seventeen.

Sadness and the need to grieve

(Warning: This section may be very upsetting to some survivors, just because it is true.)

Because of our society's denial of emotions, many people are living with unresolved grief. The loss of a loved person or pet, whether through death, divorce, or relocation, can affect us deeply, and if we "get over it" too fast people will say we are coping well. But the grief might have gone underground and can cause irrational anxiety in new situations.

For mind control and ritual abuse survivors, grief is a huge need, and sadness may well up, seemingly out of nowhere. Most survivors have seen persons or animals they loved murdered, and have even been forced to participate in these atrocities, or at least to be blamed for them.

All losses need to be grieved. Grief can feel overwhelming, but it is a time-limited process that comes to an end if we allow ourselves to feel our sadness. If our grief is complicated by guilt and shame, there is also a need for some kind of acknowledgement and forgiveness. The process ends with acceptance of the losses and the beginning of a new enthusiasm for life as it is now.

It is important to grieve for what we never had, not only for what we had and lost. When my marriage ended, my primary grief was for the marriage I had wanted and did not have. Grieving for our ideals validates our needs, and says we were not wrong to want these things.

Survivors have a great deal to grieve about. They grieve not only for what they have lost, but for what they never had. Innocence. A happy, normal childhood. Friendships. Loving parents. Pets who survived and whom they were permitted to love. Pets who did not, whom they were forced to hurt or witness being tortured. Children whom they bonded with, and were then forced to rape or kill. Loving fathers and mothers who did not sexually abuse them, either selfishly or because they were forced. Emotional security and bonding. The ability to trust. Unmet needs throughout childhood. The gradual, healthy development of healthy sexuality in the context of loving relationships. A brain that could develop in a healthy way, with sufficient sleep for rejuvenation when needed. The opportunity for the cortisol released because of trauma to relax into a normal level and not be constantly in overdrive. An education which would develop their true abilities and fit their true interests. An opportunity to use their intelligence. The ability to make their own decisions. Potential achievements which an overwhelmed child or teenager, struggling with ongoing abuse, could not manage. Physical safety. Physical health and functioning. A feeling of being able to live in their own body. A sense of being a unified person with an ability to know and meet their own needs and develop their own purpose. And independent thought. If they come to these, it is generally at least twenty years later than other people. They must grieve for the person they could have been without the abuse, for not having the opportunity to become their real selves.

The more time I spend thinking about it, the longer the list grows.

Survivors whose families were involved in their abuse have permanently lost family. In fact, they have been cheated of the opportunity to even understand the concept, just as they have been tricked about the meaning of *love*, and *safety*, and *trust*. They have no parents who can safely mentor them through their own children's births and childhoods. They cannot trust siblings, aunts and uncles, grandparents. They have to attempt to create artificial families from unrelated friends. They are often excessively dependent on therapists because of the lack of supportive family or healthy childhood dependency. Some have supportive spouses or life companions, but many more have remained single or have unsupportive partners who cannot face or cope with the degree of injury that survivors undergo. Some choose partners who re-enact an aspect of their abuse. And when is it safe to confide the truth in friends? So, there is also social isolation, and broken relationships, and huge disappointments in people.

Much is now known about the stages of grief. They often occur simultaneously rather than in sequence. One stage is denial. As long as a survivor pretends the abuse did not happen, he or she is unable to grieve any of this. Yet, if all the abuse, and all of the losses become available to consciousness at once, they will be overwhelming. So, a survivor will have to reduce his or her dissociation very gradually, confronting one loss at a time.

Anger is another important part of grieving. As with other emotions, mind control survivors' relationship with anger has been distorted and manipulated by their abusers. Their anger and rage have been deliberately buried in internal parts who are brought out for violent rituals or killing, the rage being channelled on to a helpless victim rather than on to the abusers who set up the whole situation. The anger and rage need healthy expression, through art, through screaming, through writing, whatever means gives voice to these justified emotional responses to the horror of what happened.

Sadness is the core of grieving, and its natural expression is crying. I have found that recovering the ability to cry is one of the most difficult achievements for my mind-controlled and ritually abused clients, but also one of the most significant, as well as one of the latest. Crying, especially in the presence of someone who cares, is enormously healing. A client whom I have seen for many years has never been able to cry, and recently, in the company of a friend, had a big emotional outburst. She was ashamed about this because of all her "Be tough" training. When we investigated her inner world, we found a large number of "weak" crying parts, holding her true feelings, locked away in a dungeon.

In her book, *Safe Passage to Healing* (p. xxiv), survivor Chrystine Oksana writes of expressing her anger and sadness:

> My recovery has been a quest to reclaim all parts of myself and then connect that whole self with the good things of this world. My journey is ongoing. Today, most of my illnesses are gone. Now I know that they were symptoms of my repressed feelings—mostly rage and grief. My emotional pain is leaving more slowly, but it is leaving.
>
> Today I am able to cry freely. And in addition to deep grief, I also feel gratitude. It is my tears, not my smiles, that are healing me. Today, my tears speak *my* truth and reveal *their* secrets. It's through my tears that I am breaking free.

It is a paradox that re-experiencing the traumatic memories, including the emotions, in the presence of a safe person in the present, actually brings relief. Not immediately, but eventually, and sometimes sooner than later. One of my ritually abused clients goes through a gruelling piece of severely traumatic memory each week, leaving dazed and exhausted. She later emails me to tell me how much better she is feeling, how she has been able to do things like play basketball, which she was never able to do, and how well her recovery is going. It is the memory work, the experience of having a witness to her trauma, and the emotional release that enable her recovery to move forward in this way.

The ideal way of expressing the emotions connected with the traumatic memories is in a safe place, with a safe person who is tuned in to what you are feeling and accepts your process. This kind of connection (whether a therapist, a partner, or a friend) is hard to find. However, it is still healing to express those emotions alone, with the compassionate life force as your witness, along with the other parts of your full self. Inside every person is a connection to that life force, and you can still renew your connection to it, knowing that this compassionate life force will never reject you. Crying alone can give you this sense of connection. When you were a child, you might have been told to pray to a rescuing "god", who did not rescue you. But the compassionate life force is within you and within the universe, not a magical rescuing religious superhero but the essence of life.

Despair is the most extreme expression of sadness and hopelessness. When a survivor feels extreme despair, it may be a part of their normal grief. But it may also be the feelings of an inside, mind-controlled child part leaking through into the adult. The "booby traps" which abusers design to lead to suicide use the despair of an insider to flood the personality system. These insiders with extreme emotions are often deliberately isolated from the rest of the personality system, their emotions being used for the booby traps. They "live" inside in cages, or torture situations, or "hell", or a place where "God" is rejecting them, and that is all they know of life.

Many such insiders live in literal darkness and are unaware of daylight, especially those trained at night in secret programming sessions. When I met one recently, he asked me, "What's that bright?" as he pointed to a tree outside the window. I did not understand what he meant, until the adult told me it was the sunlight on the leaves of the tree. This part had never seen sunlight.

Let us look at what despair means to a mind-controlled structured system, on not just a physical level, but an emotional and spiritual level. Many of the inside parts have never experienced anything positive. They believe the entire world to be similar to the situations they experienced once, in which they have continued to be trapped, frozen in time.

When survivors feel that they do not want to live in this world, because the world is so dark and evil, the emotions and belief may well be coming from insiders who are still trapped in the memories of their traumas, with all the feelings that belong to that time. For them, it is as if the abuse is still happening, over and over again. Until their memories are worked through, they will continue to feel this way, and their emotions can infect the rest of the system, especially if there are programmes that cause this to happen.

The long-term solution is working with the memories—see Chapters Fourteen and Fifteen. In the short term, other insiders can share positive experiences with these insiders, to show them that their experience is only a very small part of all that is. And they can be rescued internally from their horrible situations, given new places to "live", and given positive experiences of safety and nurturing in the present. Pleasure comes from the simplest experiences. One survivor first discovered this when she found an insider who had never seen or felt snow. She had her spinners send the experience of playing in the snow through the system, making all the children happy.

Anger and the need for secure boundaries

Anger is what we all normally feel when our own or someone else's boundaries are violated. Like fear, anger is about safety, but fear warns us that a future situation might be unsafe, whereas anger tells us that a boundary violation has already occurred. Anger is also about justice: we tend to feel angry and outraged at injustices not only to ourselves but also to others.

Anger comes in milder forms: we often feel irritated or annoyed at small boundary violations or injustices. We feel frustrated when a person is unresponsive to our efforts to communicate. These feelings escalate to fury if the violations continue or if we deny our milder feelings and take no action. If we respond effectively to these minor feelings, we will not escalate to full-blown anger.

Anger is often viewed negatively, and for good reason. Often, anger leads to violence or hurtful actions. When we feel anger, adrenalin is pumped into our bodies. This prepares us for the "fight or flight" reaction by giving us energy to attack or run away. But the emotion of anger is not the same as an act of aggression. We can be angry with someone without calling him a name or punching him. Anger, the emotion, is important to our wellbeing. On the other hand, aggressive behaviour needs to be controlled and stopped.

Our upbringing plays a large part in determining when we experience anger. Survivors of mind control and ritual abuse sometimes have young insiders who see themselves as queens or princesses, or kings and princes, and believe everyone should obey them. It is hard for these parts to learn that this was a deception, and they are just human beings who need to balance their desires and needs with those of others.

We might become angry too easily if we had an unsafe childhood, and have learnt to perceive things as threatening which are not actually dangerous to us. If something in a situation triggers feelings related to a previous trauma, we can have an inappropriate reaction. Poor communication can play a part in this, and can lead to misperceptions such as believing someone is putting us down or criticising us when that was not their intention. Misunderstandings such as this happen frequently and it is best to refrain from retaliating with hurtful comments. It pays to hold ourselves in check before we lash out at others for what we think they intended. When you feel an initial hurt and begin to feel angry, do not react immediately; take time to examine what is really going on and communicate with the other person respectfully. Sometimes you need to take "time out" to make sure your angry parts do not get you into trouble by engaging in behaviour you will regret later.

There are, of course, special issues regarding anger for survivors of mind control and ritual abuse. Whether your angry parts were used to assassinate "enemies", or to ritually kill victims, your anger has probably been concentrated in a few insiders who have been made angry through cruelty to them, then trained to hold in this anger and release it as extreme rage only on the designated victims. Often, there is a rageful child part, which might believe it is a demon or beast, and above it a cold, emotionless killer part. It is likely that there are both these kinds of parts at each level of your personality system, since the training begins very early and is refined by splitting off a new set of parts each year. Some parts also might have sexualised rage, again trained into them by pairing sexual arousal and release with acts of violence. You may be shocked and horrified at what some of your thirteen-year-old parts were capable of doing and feeling, but you need to remember that they were split off each year from younger ones, to the point where the final part who did these things knew very little or nothing of the torture and mind control and ongoing training which made them capable of this.

Meanwhile, survivors often report either that they have no anger at all, or that they have intense rage that they want to release, and nothing feels adequate for that. Sally, who told part of her story in Chapter Six, tried to "let out" her rage with one of her early therapists. This was completely ineffective, but putting together the memories to which the rage belonged did dissipate it, and allowed the rageful parts of her to feel once more like parts of the human race, and recognise that they were children who were forced by adults through torture to feel this emotion and perform these acts; they did not choose this.

We shall address the issues of guilt and shame regarding such acts, and how these parts can recover, in the next chapter. Meanwhile, other insiders need gradually to educate the rageful parts about your present life so that they do not pop out at the wrong time and express their rage in the only way they know. Many survivors want to isolate or get rid of their angry and rageful insiders, believing them to be evil (which is what the perpetrator adults told them). You need to know that it is impossible to get rid of any part of you. You also need to know that these angry insiders are part of a larger whole, and contain an emotion which is not, in itself, evil. Your anger, and the parts containing it, were used for perverted and evil purposes by adults, but they can be reclaimed for self-protection and for achieving justice for others.

Guilt and the need for moral integrity

Guilt (sometimes called remorse) is another feeling with an important purpose. Guilt is meant to stimulate us to take action. Healthy guilt says, "The way I acted was wrong." We feel guilty when we violate our own integrity or moral standards, often by hurting someone else. It is a basic human need to have moral integrity and purity. Guilt is a signal that helps us take action to clear our slate and live according to our own moral values.

There are three different ways to react to a feeling of guilt. One is to go deep into shame. Guilt is not the same as shame and it is important not to confuse them.

Here is what Dr John Bradshaw (1988, pp. 2–3) says about guilt and shame:

GUILT	SHAME
I have *done* something wrong.	There *is* something wrong with me.
I've *made* a mistake.	I *am* a mistake.
What I *did* was no good.	I *am* no good.

Shame is an overall sense of dirtiness and no-goodness. It usually results from having been blamed and shamed by other people. It is usually harmful rather than helpful. Wallowing in shame makes us feel bad but does not change the situation. It is important to be able to feel guilt without getting into shame. Sometimes, people are afraid to allow feelings of guilt because they can lead to overwhelming shame.

People raised with a lot of punishment can easily get into shame and emotional self-punishment. This is not useful. The purpose of useful guilt is to get us to change the behaviour or habits that are harmful, not to make us feel as if we need to be punished.

Another way of dealing with guilt is to hide behind a defensive coat of armour. When feeling the guilt is too painful or difficult, we would rather blame someone else and make it that person's fault. People who do this usually associate guilt with shame and being "bad". Defensiveness enables us to push the feeling of guilt away. While this might help us feel better, the guilt will come back, and we might repeat the same violation of unfairly blaming others because we have not listened to our guilt. Some families get stuck in throwing blame around like a ball of fire. When each family member catches it, he throws it to someone else so he will not have to feel the shame that comes with the blame. In families like this, people feel worse and worse even as they deny their guilt.

The real purpose of guilt is to enable us to respond to it by becoming aware that we have hurt someone, apologising, and making restitution to that person. Once this is done, we can let go of the situation. Taking this kind of responsibility actually makes us and the other person feel better.

Sometimes, we feel guilty for things which are not serious violations, but merely things which may be disapproved of by society—or at least by our parents. In order to distinguish between useful and useless guilt, it helps to sort out our own beliefs about right and wrong, and not be influenced by social pressures.

A good example of this is the story of Huckleberry Finn, who felt guilty and assumed he would be going to hell because of his failure to turn in his friend Jim, a runaway slave. He followed his own conscience but was unaware that his conscience was right and his society's racist values were wrong.

Now, there are very special issues with regard to mind control and ritual abuse, because most, if not all, survivors have been forced to participate in crimes, including rape, murder, sacrifice of human beings and animals, and cannibalism. I have learnt from my survivor clients that even a little child knows these things to be very wrong, even if he or she is told he is being "good" in doing them. We all have "mirror neurons" which allow us to experience empathically what other people (and animals) are going through. This biologically based empathy is the source of our accurate conscience, no matter what adults tell us during our childhood about right and wrong.

So, when a child is forced to do these things, or when later (because of years of forcing and conditioning) he does them apparently on his own, he feels enormous remorse. This emotion is, of course, hidden in feeling-holder parts, so that the ones who had to perform these acts of evil were able to do their jobs in an unfeeling manner.

The matter is even more complicated, because after a child has committed such an act, the adult perpetrators point it out to him and tell him how evil he is, how even God would not want him, how only Satan and/or Lucifer will accept him now, that he is going to hell because of what he did, and he might as well kill himself because he only brings evil into the world. Most survivors of ritual abuse especially have a huge load of shame induced by this programming. Such memories, along with their associated guilt and shame, are designed to come up if survivors try to find out what happened to them, to give them the message that they are the evil ones, not the adults who trained and forced them to do acts of evil. We shall go into these issues in more depth in Chapter Twenty, "Overcoming spiritual abuse".

Meanwhile, we can learn to be more sensitive to our normal feelings of guilt and remorse for how we treat others in our present life. If we have hurt someone, it is normal to feel remorseful, and this emotion can stimulate us to apologise and to be more careful in the future. At the same time, it is important that we stop ourselves from moving into shame when we make a mistake or behave unkindly, and instead just apologise, change our behaviour, and move on.

Exercise 20. Tuning in to your emotions

Reflect back on your day. Use three "feeling words" to express your general mood.

What do those emotions, either negative or positive, tell you?

Did you have contradictory emotions at the same time?

If you were to sort through those emotions and associate needs with them, what needs would you record?

If you felt unpleasant emotions, when did those emotions get triggered?

How can you express those emotions?

What needs are those unpleasant emotions coming from?

Can you think of any strategies that would help get those needs met?

You can use this exercise daily, or even several times a day, to get in touch with your emotions and needs.

Using emotional awareness to get your needs met

The emotions discussed in this chapter are only a sample of some of the important emotions and the needs they point to. You may discover different ones in your own life, especially as you get to know those inside parts who hold emotions for you.

The first step in handling emotions with awareness is noticing and expressing your feelings, in private or with an understanding person. Through this, you become aware of your unmet needs. Next, you need to take careful action to see that your needs are met.

No one can know your needs as you yourself (including all your inside parts) can. Even if your spouse and close friends are aware of your feelings, they are not mind-readers, and they are unable to know what you need and automatically supply it. It is easy to become angry with someone else and think you are unloved, when it is really up to you to discover and express what you need. If you need peace and quiet, privacy, nurturing, or challenge, you need to make changes in your life to see that these needs are met. Sometimes, this involves asking someone else for what you need; sometimes it involves spending your time differently, changing your job, or your leisure activities, or your friendships.

By working with your feelings and your thoughts together, listening to all your parts, expressing your feelings, tuning into your needs, and planning action which meets your needs without harming others, you will ensure that your life and those of your loved ones are happier.

Taking action to have your own needs met is often very difficult for survivors to do. This is because in childhood it was generally forbidden not only to pay attention to your feelings, but also to do anything about your own needs. You were at the mercy of others. So, you may have developed learnt helplessness.

People who were made helpless during their childhood years frequently continue to believe they are helpless in adulthood, when things have changed. Thus, they will complain about situations, ruminating on their mistreatment and victimisation, but take no action.

Experiments with rats show that those who have been exposed to avoidable shock try to save themselves by swimming hard when put into deep water, but those who were exposed to unavoidable shock give up and start to drown. People are similar. Child abuse takes away your sense of your own power to change things, but in adulthood you do have that power, and you can use it. Your unhappy emotions will tell you what is wrong, and then you can do something about it.

Exercise 21. Interpersonal emotion log

Think of a situation in which you had an emotional reaction when dealing with another person and write down what you can identify about it, using the points below as a guide.

What emotion did I feel?

What triggered this emotion?

What other emotions were underlying?

What other causes did these emotions have?

What past situations triggered these emotions?

Which insiders felt them, and how old are they?

What did I do in response to this emotion?

What needs did I have in this situation?

Did my behaviour meet my own needs?

How did my behaviour affect the other person:

What emotions did the other person show?

What needs did the other person have?

How can I resolve the situation now?

CHAPTER FOURTEEN

What about the memories?

Pretty well all survivors of mind control and ritual abuse suffer from post traumatic stress disorder (PTSD), the same disorder that war veterans frequently have, although theirs has been caused by several years of war trauma whereas yours were caused by a lifetime of terror. The first diagnostic criterion for whether you have PTSD requires that you have been exposed to a traumatic event in which you experienced, witnessed, or were confronted with an event or events that involved actual or threatened death or serious injury, or a threat to the physical integrity of yourself or others. I cannot imagine a survivor of mind control or ritual abuse who has not had such an experience, whether or not they have a clear memory of it.

The second criterion for PTSD involves persistently re-experiencing the traumatic event or events through recurrent intrusive recollections of it, including images, thoughts, or perceptions, distressing dreams of it, and acting or feeling as if it is happening now. You are intensely upset, and your body reacts as if the trauma is still happening. In general you are hyper-aroused, which results in insomnia, irritability, difficulty concentrating, hyper-vigilance (being always on the alert for danger), and startling easily and strongly.

At the same time, if you have PTSD, you persistently avoid anything connected to the trauma. You do not want to think or talk about it; you avoid anything that might bring up memories. You do not remember important aspects of it. (Many of your memories are hidden away in inside parts of you who have been assigned their places by the abuser group.) You may lack interest in regular life, feel detached from others, have difficulty feeling positive, and may not expect to have a normal life.

Have I just described you? The memories haunt you, but you hate it when they emerge, and you do not want to deal with those memories. If there were any way to just get rid of them, you would welcome it. I guess by now, however, you have worked out that this is impossible, just as it is impossible to get rid of your inside parts. The parts were separated from one another and from the front person by the traumas they endured, and the only way to resolve all this is to find a way to resolve the memories of those traumas.

Your situation is more complicated than it would be if you had simple PTSD, because not only do you have many years of hidden traumas that start from the moment you were born or sooner, you have insiders who are trained to punish you by causing flashbacks and body memories. They administer physical pain, or the sensation of electroshock, or overwhelming despair, if you approach the memories to find out what happened to you. Abuser groups do not want their victims to remember or talk about what happened, so a considerable amount of the programming they perform is designed to make you afraid of remembering or talking. This is not to protect you, even if they said it is. It is to protect them, the abusers, because they were doing things that are both illegal and immoral, and they could get into big trouble if society in general found out.

So, you cannot approach your traumatic memories (at least, at first) without triggering punishment programming as well as programming designed to make you return to the group.

However, even if your personality system is now so co-operative that insiders hardly ever turn on programmes to hurt you, you probably still get spontaneous flashbacks, and these are unpleasant and often horrifying.

Do you need to process the memories?

Then, of course, there is the question of whether you want to deal with the memories at all. Some of your parts probably do; they are angry about being abused and they want to know just what happened and who was responsible. Other parts are fearful, and would prefer to leave the memories alone.

It is up to you to decide to what extent you want to put together your memories and your fragmented inner parts. The memories are painful and disgusting; that is one reason they are dissociated. They usually involve betrayal. It is probable that they involve forced perpetration—that is, the abusers made you participate in their acts of cruelty and then told you that you were evil like them. It can be very upsetting to re-experience such memories.

Many survivors can become significantly more functional without working through their memories. I have worked with some people who chose to know just enough of what happened to them to be able to continue to live in the present and not have to deal with their childhood trauma directly. If you are able to function well, without the memories or the associated emotions, bodily pains, or programmed urges intruding into your daily life, and you are now free of the perpetrator group, perhaps you do not need to process the memories.

However, if you choose to leave the memories alone, you are also leaving hidden parts inside who feel as if they are still suffering in the traumatic situations. Is it fair to leave them there? Survivor therapist Wendy Hoffman disagrees with the choice not to remember:

> The problem with wanting not to know is that you are leaving inside another person without a voice, witness or friend. That part then will be permanently disenfranchised. You are silencing that part the way the perpetrators silenced you. And that part may be able to open the door that releases the full soul.

These parts also hold pieces of the story. It is, therefore, likely that you will have to continually resist the programming rather than be assured that it has been dissolved. You will also be open to being accessed by other groups who look for programmed people and know how to spot and access them.

If programmes are constantly being triggered, or if you keep having flashbacks or nightmares of some aspects of the memories (for example, pictures, or voices, or physical pain, or sexual arousal, or overwhelming emotions), you will definitely benefit from putting the memories together. This is especially true of the training memories that are behind the mind control. Your parts were led to believe that their lives or the lives of others were dependent on their doing the jobs that they were programmed to do, and their emotions are all tied up with that belief. When you see how you were deceived, their overwhelming panic might lead them to continue to do those jobs.

Can you find out what happened and avoid the pain?

If you view memory work as detective work to find out "the facts", you will not be able to do this work effectively. A survivor's front person often presses to know what happened because there is an investigator part pushing from inside. It is natural to want to make sense of your life. However, with mind control or ritual abuse there are usually other parts inside whose job is to make sure the front person does not come to know things, and will punish if you do come to know. Punishments can include pain in various parts of the body, for example the places where the abusers told you recording devices were implanted. If you do not remember all the punishment programmes which Sally's insiders used when she was trying to discover her memories, you could review Chapter Six. Before your front person tries to get information about your traumatic past, the parts in charge of punishment must be willing to co-operate with your recovery plan.

Often, survivors believe they can access "the memories" without re-experiencing physical or emotional pain. They try to make recovery a fact-finding mission. Many therapists and some well-known survivors, such as Carol Rutz, whose book contains some excellent research, believe this is possible. They take a largely cognitive approach, believing that if survivors can look at "what happened" and identify the deception and coercion involved, they can become free from continued loyalty and obedience to the abusers. This appears to work for some people, especially if they have had many years of freedom from the perpetrator group. Many trauma survivors, even some who are multiple, have the luxury of saying, "That was in the past, and I do not need to re-experience all of that pain in order to live my life."

However, many survivors of mind control and ritual abuse find that even if they know what happened to them, they still experience panic attacks and strong urges to engage in programmed behaviours. The basis of the programming is the emotions involved in the memories. Abuser groups deliberately store the physical pain in one group of insiders, each different emotion in another group of insiders, the hidden words and instructions in others, and the visual record of what happened in others. Some abusers deliberately hide away the feeling-holders, and some hide away the soundtrack and words. In my opinion, you cannot really undo the programming unless you find all aspects of the memory, not just the story. You might be able to find the feeling-holder parts and relocate them in the inner world, but they will still be in pain (physical or emotional) until they are able to connect their feelings to the memories that caused them to split off. Even if the feeling-holder parts have conscious knowledge of how they were deceived, their emotions will easily be able to push them into programmed behaviours such as telephoning perpetrators or cutting themselves.

So, I believe that trying to discover what happened to you, without dealing with the feelings, is not very effective in freeing you from mind control, and can simply be an invitation to internal punishers to do their jobs, unless you have a very co-operative personality system. If you do decide to pursue the memories, you need to "go for broke", including all the emotions and body sensations, and involving every insider who has a part of each memory to take part in processing it.

Do not be discouraged, however. You can work through the memories thoroughly, and you can heal. Many survivors have already worked through their memories and are free of their programming; some of them are speaking out about their experiences. You can find their blogs and much more on www.ra-info.org.

Dealing with flashbacks

A flashback is a memory fragment that intrudes into your everyday consciousness. It may be visual (hallucinating something that happened), auditory (hearing a voice or a scream), emotional (such as a panic attack or a feeling of overwhelming despair), or physiological (a "body memory" that can be a pain in a part of the body that was injured during the unremembered event, or an unpleasant smell or taste). Until the trauma is resolved, these flashbacks might recur, often in unacceptable times and places.

Many flashbacks appear to be caused by some parts pushing their piece of a memory up to consciousness while others are resisting the knowledge. Memories usually first surface through flashbacks, and traumatic memories that have not been organised and catalogued by an abuser group can often only be found through flashbacks. In order to resolve the trauma, you need to put all the components of those memories together. I have worked with several survivors whose previous therapists spent untold hours assisting them in "chasing flashbacks": re-experiencing bodily sensations of abuse in the hope that this would resolve the trauma (this happened to Sally, see Chapter Six). Just as going through the story of a trauma without the emotions does not resolve that trauma, going through the emotions and pain without the storyline also does not work. In fact, it feels like re-abuse when you open up the pain without attaching it to its cause.

At the other extreme, many therapists and survivors who recognise that flashbacks generally do not resolve trauma have taken the stance that "stabilisation" involves preventing flashbacks from occurring, and that memory reconstitution is unnecessary. But survivors who are merely "stabilised" continue to be at risk of destabilisation if present events trigger aspects of their trauma. If they are survivors of organised abuse, they are also susceptible to deliberate triggers for programmed behaviours. As I said earlier, only working through the memories thoroughly will create long-term stability and destroy programming.

For survivors of mind control and ritual abuse, what appear to be spontaneous flashbacks are frequently internal punishments for disclosures of secrets. If you are having a lot of flashbacks, you will need to discover whether someone inside is punishing you for something. Slow down the disclosures and get to know the parts who are doing their jobs by giving or ordering those flashbacks. You can review Chapter Seven for more about this.

One of my clients kept having a particular flashback recently, and insisted we process the memory it came from. At the same time, many of her parts were terrified of going into this memory. When she investigated internally, she found a little boy inside doing his job of reminding her that a big ritual date was coming up and she should be ready. He did not realise that many years had gone by since she had attended any rituals, and that he did not need to do that job any more. She asked the leader in charge of that section of the personality system to release him from his job and to join the internal council. Problem solved, without going into the flashback memory.

Most trauma therapists recommend "grounding" in the present to help you deal with intrusive flashbacks—that is, bringing the front person and anyone else who is near the front clearly into the present. Here is a way to "ground" yourself if you are experiencing a flashback: open your eyes, which often spontaneously close during flashbacks. Listen to and name the sounds around you, such as birds, city noises, or traffic. Name the things in the room, including what you are touching (couch, pillow, etc.). Put your fingers on your clothing, and name each item, noting that you are clothed, which is important because child parts are frequently naked during their abuse. You can also use a signal, such as ringing a bell, to bring yourself back to the present, but make sure that any signal you use is not one that the perpetrators used.

Grounding, like other forms of containment, just prevents a flashback from occurring at any particular moment; the flashback is still likely to erupt later when you are alone, or as a nightmare. If it is caused by an insider doing his or her job, you can communicate internally to stop it. Internal negotiation is an important skill for the survivor in dealing with flashbacks. For example, a survivor client of mine was having horrible bodily symptoms of choking. He found the part responsible, and struck a deal with her: she (his insider) would remove his symptoms, if, in our next therapy session, she could tell me about the abuse that caused those symptoms. This allowed him to feel better until the therapy session, when he (the front person, who was a man) kept his part of the bargain and listened to this girl part's story.

When you negotiate with your parts regarding the flashbacks, it is important to talk with the parts *causing* the flashback rather than only the ones *experiencing* it; they are usually not the same.

If you have been mind-controlled or ritually abused, you are likely to have one or more gatekeeper or file keeper or librarian part in charge of keeping memories and feelings put away (or letting them out on command). You might be able to close down a flashback by asking one of these insiders to put away the memory until it is time to work on it. Sometimes, too, the spinner parts might be able to use their spinning abilities to spin something away.

After you have closed down the flashback, ask the parts inside whether any of them deliberately made you go through it, and negotiate with them to change the situation. Also, make sure you look after the parts who were having the flashback. They can be put in safe rooms in the inner world, go to sleep if they agree (through the internal use of the sleep programme), or be given care-takers, such as nannies or older girls to look after little children.

Storing the memories

Your abuser group has probably already created a storage system in your mind for the memories, and at first it is that system you will use when you ask your internal librarians or file keepers to put away the memories that are flashing back. Personally, I enjoy using things that abuser groups installed for purposes that are the opposite of the abusers' intentions!

However, in order to keep memories, and parts of memories, contained, you might want to make a new system of your own. In addition to the original storage for the memories which have not yet been worked on, you can have your internal builders (who built your inner structures in the first place) construct in your inner world a place where partially processed memories and feelings are to be kept in containers, and some containers in which to put them, such as a cave containing barrels, a bank with a vault with storage lockers, a well with buckets, or a storage room with jars on shelves, or anything you think will work. Both the containers and the place in which they will be kept should be able to be locked, but there should be a way to put things in the containers after they are locked. A spout or straw might work (if the memories and feelings are thought of as liquid), or a "doggie-door" which snaps shut may be created. Let your mind come up with the image best for you. As with all such creative solutions, it does not matter what the image is, as long as it works for you. It helps if you draw a picture of the storage place and containers. Some survivors discover that their insiders have already created such storage but their front people were not aware of it.

You probably need two types of storage:

1. Containers where the feelings (emotions and bodily sensations) of a memory in progress can be stored temporarily while your insiders watch the "video" of the memory (to be discussed in the next chapter) to get the story line.
2. Containers where unfinished memories can be stored between memory work sessions, or where flashbacks can be put.

Once you have these containers, try putting the emotions and bodily sensations from some easy memories, and eventually entire memories, into the containers. (Make sure you put only feelings into the containers, not inside feeling-holder people.) For example, the emotions from an argument you had yesterday with your partner can be put safely away first, or the taste of the milk that went bad, and then, the flashback of the hands of someone who abused you. It gets easier, and you get better at it, the more you do it.

When to begin memory work

Often, dissociated survivors are in a rush to get their memories back. When asked why, they say they "just want to get this recovery stuff over with". It certainly would be nice if all you had to do was recover the knowledge of what happened, but that is not the case. The process takes a long time. It takes that long because you need to take care of yourself, not push yourself too hard (as the abusers pushed you), and it is very hard work, and the memories you have to discover are traumatic and create strong emotional reactions.

You cannot rush into memory work such as this. You need to be at a stage in your life where this work will not disrupt important daily life tasks, such as raising children or full-time paid employment (although Stella Katz, who was a housewife, did her memory work when her children were at school—see Chapter Twenty-one). There are many healing tasks that must precede the memory work. In general, you are ready for memory work when your personality system is co-operative, and the parts in charge permit all those involved in the memory to participate in its processing. If your main higher-up parts are not aligned with the process, protector parts might punish those who access or disclose forbidden material prematurely. Delay is important when your personality system is not ready, but the process cannot be delayed forever, if you want full healing. If you have a disconnect between the parts who want to rush and those who do not know it is safe, your inner leaders need to get these parts to share information with one another so you can make a balanced decision.

What if you are still being accessed by the perpetrator group? Should you attempt to work with memories? If you have insiders who report all the recovery work you have done, you might be inviting the group to access you and re-split your child parts in order to reinforce the programming and even make new programmes. However, you can combat this by immediately working through the memories of the reprogramming as well as those of the original programmes on which this reprogramming was built, as well as the access programmes (described in Chapter Nine) that keep you in contact with the group. My first survivor clients were all involved in a Satanist group when I began seeing them, and they used this method to stay ahead of the group's interventions.

Finally, it really helps, though it is not essential, to have a safe person who can be with you when you process your most difficult memories. This person can make sure you are simultaneously in the present and the past when you work through a memory, and pull you back to the present if you get "lost" in the memory experience. They can also help you talk about it afterwards, to come to a better understanding of what was done to you and how it has affected you.

If you do not have such a person, you can still work through memories on your own. You can use a bell or other noise-maker to startle you into the present if you get lost in the memory, and you can write out both the content and the feelings, as well as your present reactions to it all, after you go through the memory. If you do not, you may lose the content, as memories, once consciously known, tend to have the details fade and become assimilated with the rest of your experiences quite quickly.

The front person's role

Should your front person or people be involved in the memory processing? It depends on how your personality system works. If you have a very strong front person, he or she might want to be involved or even to take the lead. But most survivors have front people who are primarily shells, and who can function in the world because they do not know about the abuse or experience feelings from it (though these might leak through sometimes.)

Insiders often make a strong case that the front person cannot handle the truth, and they are often right. This is because the "front person" has the job of managing the adult world, which is pretty complex in itself. Front personalities are created for this purpose, and in order to be an effective life manager and not be overwhelmed with symptoms, it is often best that they do not know the secrets or feel the emotions carried by the insiders. The piece of the personality that has to deal with work and the outside world is usually not big enough to also handle the other information; there either has to be integration of some other parts to make it "bigger" and have more energy, or some of the inside parts need to take over some of the tasks of this part to free some energy.

However, you can work through memories with internal parts without the front person coming to remember these events. If the front person agrees, you can embark on a course of working with memories without that part finding out the memory content. Sally (see Chapters Six and Eight) does her memory work this way. Her front person usually does not find out what the insiders are working on, but reports that she feels lighter and better able to function after they have done pieces of memory work. Whether this will be effective for you depends on the strength and the importance of the front person in your personality system. It also depends on your degree of co-consciousness. If there is a lot of co-consciousness between your front person and the rest of the parts, you might not be able to process memories without the front person coming to know the content. If your front person has developed strength over the years, you might want him or her to know what happened.

Some survivors have a series of front people who share the job and switch when the going gets too rough. Some front people are tougher than others, and whether or not you want to allow the tough front people to know the memories may depend on how much those ones share with the more vulnerable front people. Sometimes, front people are relatively separate from one another, and one can know things without the others coming to know them; in other cases, if one front person comes to remember something, the others do, too. Your decision about whether to let front people know what memories have been discovered should take into account whether they, and other parts they are connected to, can handle the knowledge.

Exercise 22. Assessing your readiness for memory work

Do you have a tendency to speculate on what might have happened to you, rather than allowing the parts to share their experiences? What effect does your speculation have on your certainty about your memories? (For some people it confuses them and makes them unsure of what they have remembered and what they have merely imagined.) Explore inside and find out whether there is a part who pushes you to do this, and explain to that part why it is not a good idea.

Do your parts want to see the tricks and lies that their abusers employed, in order to be freed from their overwhelming compulsion to do their "jobs"?

If you have a strong desire to know what happened to you, are you aware that the memories probably contain much pain, betrayal, horror, and shame? Are you prepared to undergo these experiences in order to reclaim your history, knowing that your identity will change as a result?

Are you now free of the perpetrator group's interfering in your life? How do you know this?

Are you now able to function well, without the memories or the associated emotions intruding more than minimally into your daily life?

(continued)

If so, do you want to put together the memories anyway, or would you prefer to leave them alone? Let your front person answer, and then ask your insiders the same question, perhaps one group at a time.

If you are having a lot of flashbacks, you need to discover whether someone inside is punishing you for something. If so, you will need to slow down the disclosures and get to know the hierarchy of parts who are doing their jobs by giving or ordering those flashbacks. You are not yet ready to work on the memories. You might decide to push through anyway, but, if so, be aware that you will get symptoms such as dizziness, dental pain, or other reminders by insiders that you are breaking the abusers' rules.

Do you have parts inside whose job it is to make sure the front person does not come to know things, and will create problems if the front person does gain access to memories? If so, those insiders in charge of your system need to talk with those parts and make an agreement with them that memory work will not involve the front person at this point.

Is your personality system sufficiently co-operative that the parts in charge will permit all those involved in a memory to participate in its processing, and permit all aspects of the memory to be included?

Do you have a safe person, such as a competent therapist or a good friend, who will not be overly shocked by or afraid of the content of your memories or the pain you experience in the process, who can understand why you need to put the memories together, and assist you with your memory processing? If not, do you feel solid enough to do the work without a support person?

Have you practised with an effective "grounding" technique to let you know that you are in the safe present when you have a flashback or are reliving a memory?

Depending on your answers to all these questions, you can become aware of whether or not you want to resolve your traumatic memories, and whether or not your personality system is ready to go ahead with it. Try not to underestimate yourself.

Choosing the memories to be put together

Here is the place where you need to proceed differently as a survivor of mind control and ritual abuse than you would if there were no organised abuse. For memories of abuse within the family, such as beatings and/or incest, you might have to wait for memories to emerge, and work with them. For some survivors, these memories come up first, because they are more "normal" than those of rituals or mind control experiments; for others, they come up last because they involve significant betrayal by people you love, which is hard to face.

With the mind control memories, it is most effective to choose memories strategically in order to dismantle the programming. It is possible to do this because of the storage systems for memories that the mind controllers deliberately installed. So, your first step is to find those insiders (file keepers, or librarians) in charge of the memory storage systems. They might have stored just the programme training memories, or they might have filed the other abuse memories, too. Those in charge of your system can work with these parts to find the memories you choose to work on.

Start with a relatively easy memory, a minor trauma that does not have too much shock, or horror, or physical pain, so that your parts can learn the process. One survivor, for instance, began with memories of her mother washing her hair and pulling it while combing it. Another chose to work on the memories of being teased at school, which caused splits between her school-going parts. In this example, there was no physical pain, and the emotional pain was bitter but not overwhelming. Ask the parts who have more difficult memories to observe what happens when you process the easy ones, so that they can see how to put memories together, and what happens as a result.

After those in charge of your personality system know how it is done, your inner leaders or council can select the memories to work through on a logical basis. The goal is safety. Do not focus on what is flashing back, as flashbacks can be a distraction from what is important, and are sometimes programmed. Instead, go for the most dangerous trainings of the insiders. The highest priority memories to process are the ones that make you unsafe (e.g., reporting or suicide programmes), or the ones that create symptoms which interfere with everyday life. You may already have made considerable progress with these issues (at least temporarily) by communicating with parts, but they are still important memories to deal with, to get rid of the urges that some parts might have to engage in unsafe behaviour.

Here is one survivor's account of how she puts her memories together.

Wendy Hoffman: "My memory process"

I am not fully aware of how my memory process works even as I can't feel how my blood manages to flow or breath passes through my lungs and the pores of my skin. They have their own inner mechanism, mysterious to me.

I imagine everyone's process is somewhat different and somewhat the same. Mine starts with a feeling that appears to come from nowhere but also from deep inside the person I am whom the rest of me doesn't know. The feeling is just about never pleasant. It is raw, spiky, and shakes me. After a while, it subsides. It can come in my sleep, while I'm walking my dog, when I'm cooking oatmeal, or at work. Next comes a body sensation. Two days ago, I had such severe pain in the left side of my lumbar spine that I gave myself a back treatment. I thought a vertebra had slipped and pressed on a nerve. Days later, I realised I was in a body memory of needles going into my spine in Montreal, Canada in 1961. Very slowly, the memory unfolded. I have learnt the theory that the parts of my mind holding different pieces come together and communicate their past with the outside part of me that is living our life, or at least going through the motions of living life. I have also learnt that the leaders of my sections decide what will be remembered when. I believe that that theory is true and accurate, a revolutionary piece of knowledge really, but I can't say I experience it step by step. I am not yet sufficiently self-aware to feel exactly what is going on internally.

All I know is that many mornings, when I am in a preconscious state, I wake up and a new or continuation memory unfurls. It is almost always connected to the body memory and emotion I have recently experienced. As I get closer to what happened, I am seized with chills. I imagine that's a personality shivering with fear. If I sense resistance to going further into the memory, I talk with the inside person who has the programme to stop me. Often, someone gets hungry and I tell that one to step aside into the internal kitchen and have a glass of milk and a cookie. After an hour or two, I need to take a break. For the pause, I don't do anything fancy, I just say we'll come back to it later. More usually starts pouring out that afternoon. I am jealous of these hours right after awakening and guard them the way a good mother protects her babies. If neighbours ask me to baby-sit, I tell them I am only available in the afternoon. Every morning I am not at my job I save for memory work. If I do memory work on a day I go to work, I find I am more tired than usual.

To help with the memory work, I get out a tiny machine that gently taps one hand, then the other. I hold each pulsar and the back and forth motion seems to loosen the memories and bring my inside parts out. I tap slowly and lightly because all my nerves are already agitated. It also helps if my dog is beside me. She and I have been through a lot together and we trust each other. Once the memories finish pouring out, they aren't so real any more. I used to write them down as they revealed themselves but that divided my mind further into processor and recorder. I found parts inside who could remember. Now after the memory or part of the memory finishes, I quickly record it in my journal. If I wait till that evening, I'll lose some of it. I want to hold it all.

I stumble cognitively. Did I really have such a gruesome life? Have people from the beginning of time gone through this? I can't believe all this happened to me and I didn't know it before. Was I made into an evil person? I must have asked myself these questions hundreds of times, but every time I ask it again. That's a lot of evil to exist in the world.

The other impossible part for me is the feelings. Emotions shredded my insides. I'm talking about the kind of emotional pain that folds the body in two. I can't store the feelings. They are always there. In my inner world, the parts with these intense emotions are housed in towers. Sometimes, it is impossible for me to be near people. I'm in too much pain to deal with their insensitivity. In my imagination, I have installed a pipe underneath my heart. The feelings from this abuse are constantly dripping out from me. It may take a lifetime to expel them. I have to excrete the feelings from the inside and I think for me an imaginative surgical intervention was needed. When the intense heart pain starts, I have to keep moving. Sometimes, I get chest pains so severe that I have to stop working for a while.

I help my memory process by letting my inside parts know that I love and respect them no matter what they did or who they had to become. I stand by all parts of myself. Without that attitude, I would not heal. Whichever parts talk to me from inside, I take their hands and let them lead me to where they need to go. Although I flinch, I follow. This journey can be isolating but they at least have me, for better or worse.

* * *

Different survivors have different kinds of memory storage, so you have to find the method of memory processing which works for your own personality system. There are many creative ways to achieve recovery. In the next chapter, I shall describe step by step a method which has worked well for most of my survivor clients.

I have found, however, that survivors whose mind control or ritual abuse experiences only happened very early in life, and ended by the age of about six, have difficulty approaching memory work this way. Their personality systems are not as clearly organised, and they do not have older insiders to guide the process, or, if they do, those are not from the mind control experiences but from spontaneous abuse and trauma in other settings, and are unable to understand and help the younger insiders.

If you are like this, you need to allow the memories to emerge at their own pace, and this can be much slower than the more efficient way that people can do it when they have well-organised internal hierarchies to direct the process. The key to finding your memories is finding your insiders, and helping them find one another, so that they can put together the memories which they share parts of. This is also the way any survivor needs to approach the traumatic memories that the abuser group did not deliberately structure.

Many therapists now use fractionated processing to help their clients work through traumatic memories. In his recent book for therapists, *Shelter from the Storm* (2013), Dr Richard Kluft says that he originally developed this (calling it "fractionated abreaction") in order to make memory resolution easier for his patients. The essence of the method is to process one part of a traumatic memory at a time. There are several ways to do this:

- by dividing the duration of the event into small chunks, and processing one chunk at a time;
- by letting one insider at a time share his or her portion;
- by processing feelings, thoughts, sounds, and sights separately.

If your personality system is not very logically developed, and if you have been able to retrieve only small parts of a memory, German psychotherapist Gaby Breitenbach has developed a memory work technique which might help you. (You may observe that this abuse is international and going on in Germany and other parts of Europe, as well as Africa and English-speaking countries.)

Exercise 23. Processing difficult experiences (Gaby Breitenbach)

You can do this exercise alone (taping or writing it all down) or with the help of a friend or a therapist, who will write the contents down and also help you keep things in perspective as you go through the memory.

This is an exercise in inner teamwork. Working with your inner people, you can co-operate in order to put together a complete segment of your life experience, attaching the emotions and bodily sensations and thoughts that belong to that experience to its story. This process helps you discover parts of your experience that are stored separately because the experience was traumatic. Ask your inner parts to sit beside each other, looking at an imaginary television that shows the story of the difficult experience.

Instructions, Part I

As you watch the difficult experience on your inner television, describe it in words. Make sure to tell it without any feelings, sensations, or thoughts about it. Just describe what happened, the events, and the sound track, as if you are watching a film on a screen. If things were said, please tell the actual words, and if noises could be heard, describe them as well. Describe everything any part of you could see or hear.

If you need a sense of more distance, you can talk about what the person of the past, for example the ten-year-old girl, or the five-year-old boy, saw and heard.

Please describe the beginning and the end of the scene first, so that you (and your helper, if you have one) are telling exactly what you have chosen to tell. You can control it.

Beginning:

End:

The whole scene:

(continued)

If you get stuck, go to the last part of the memory which was clear, and ask yourself or let your helper ask something like: "and in that moment when [whatever was just described], did she (or he) react? Say or do something?" If that does not work, widen the focus with questions like "What did you see close by? What did you hear?"

Part 2

Listen to your story (on the tape, or told by your helper) in the same way it was told, without emotions. Make no comments unless to correct a mistake.

After listening to the story, what are your *thoughts*, right now?

What are your inner *feelings* in response to the story?

How do you experience those inner feelings in your body right now? If there is one main feeling, where do you feel it in your body and what kind of feeling is it?

What kind of body sensation is it (burning, pushing, pulling, pressure . . .)?

If it had a texture, what kind of surface would it be (coarse, smooth, bumpy . . .)?

What kind of material would it be made of (wood, stone, iron, cloth . . .)?

What kind of weight would it have (heavy, light, featherlike . . .)?

What colour or colours would it have (dark, light, translucent . . .)?

What would its edges be like (sharp, jagged, irregular, rounded . . .)?

Try to find a symbol that stands for the feeling created by this experience, and draw that symbol or imagine it in front of you.

Watch the power of that symbol reduce as you find a way to bring it under your control. For example, if it is a balloon you can prick it with a needle. If it is a metal object you can melt it with heat . . .

Try to find a single word to describe the feeling. The symbol may help you find it. Now imagine that the whole film has been recorded with that word as its name. Take the tape or disc and put it safely away in an inner storage place, such as a safe.

Part 3 (optional)

If you wish, you can visualise these questions as a puzzle. The puzzle can be any shape you like, as long as it has separate but connected pieces for each aspect of your experience.

You can use the acronym NEST to help you identify the aspects of the experience. Each aspect

N (narrative),
E (emotions),
S (sensory experiences) and
T (thoughts and beliefs)

occupies a piece of the puzzle.

You can break these down further. For example, Emotions might have a section for Fear, another for Anger, another for Sadness, another for Guilt, and so on.

For each part of the experience, ask yourself: Is this complete? When I look at a particular sequence of the story, am I convinced that this is showing all the feelings that belong to it? If I ask my inner people of other age levels, can they add things to it? What might be missing? Ask about all your senses: smell, taste, sight, hearing, and about every bodily sensation.

(*continued*)

Part 4

When you have, for instance, a thousand experiences of pain or fear, it is also useful to discover where each one belongs in your life experiences. When you have put together one experience, ask your inner people what other similar experiences they have, at different ages. Imagine the puzzle being three-dimensional, with one level for each age at which a similar experience occurred: a puzzle behind a puzzle behind a puzzle. You can fill in the levels by asking your inner people about their experiences at each age.

Working with the puzzle, you and your inner people can learn to open just one experience at a time, and see how that experience has been fragmented into its components, split into inner narratives that belong to specific inner people, who have been trained to hold one or more components of the experience. At the same time, they can recognise the existence of other similar experiences and prepare to put those experiences together, too.

You may want to try these ideas as well as the one I shall describe in the next chapter, and find which method is most suitable for you when you approach your traumatic memories. Gaby's method provides a way for your front person to find the aspects of a memory, or series of related memories, which you might not have put together. This is particularly helpful for dealing with less well-organised abuse, when your inner leaders have not stored the memories deliberately in places designated by the perpetrator group. The next chapter describes a method I use, assisting internal leaders to find all the insiders who have pieces of a memory, and using the structured internal storage created by the abuser group.

CHAPTER FIFTEEN

Putting together the traumatic memories

To be fully healed, survivors of mind control and ritual abuse need to put together all components of the traumatic memories that caused the splits between their parts. This is what dissolves the programmes and frees insiders from the internal memory landscapes where they are stuck and the compulsions to do what the abusers trained them to do. It is, in many ways, the core of the recovery process.

Let me clarify what I mean by "memories". What most people mean when they use this term is "the story", or the narrative—who did what, where, and when. But each of your traumatic memories includes not just the facts, but also, and perhaps most importantly, the physical and emotional pain. Different separated, insulated parts of your brain hold fragments of the memory. The narrative is only one aspect of the whole memory, and is stored in a different part or circuit of the brain from the rest of the experience.

In your personality system, this means that different aspects of the same memory are held by different parts of you. You have parts who know what happened, parts who saw things, parts who heard sounds and words (including programming commands), parts who hold various different emotions (such as fear, sadness, and anger), and parts who hold bodily sensations (such as pain, sexual feelings, or electroshock). A single traumatic memory may be divided among ten or more insiders. The abuser groups create these divisions deliberately to reinforce your dissociation and prevent you from putting the memories together.

Even if you think you "remember" a trauma, you can still be affected by it, flooded with post trauma feelings, and parts involved in that trauma can still feel compelled to act on the instructions their controllers gave them. This happens when you have not put together the entire memory, including the emotions, physical sensations, and instructions, as well as the story of what happened.

Organised abuser groups worked out long ago that the only way to fully resolve a trauma is to put together all aspects of it. They deliberately create "recycler" insiders whose job is to withhold some part of each memory so that the survivor cannot put that memory together and, thus, destroy the programming anchored in that memory. The piece of memory held by a recycler part can be anything—some pain, certain words, an emotion—but as long as it is withheld, the memory cannot be fully reconstituted and the programming dissolved.

In order to resolve the trauma and the programming from a memory, every part of you who holds a piece of that particular memory needs to share the part they hold with every other insider who was involved with that particular experience. I do not mean just a piece of the story. All aspects—the different emotions, the physical pain and other sensations, the narrative, the drugged feelings, the instructions, etc.—must be included. You must take that memory from an ordinary life experience such as driving in the car to a ritual site, on until you return to ordinary life again, such as waking up in your own bed. When *all* the parts who were present share their parts of the memory with one another, the trauma will be resolved and the programming dissolved. You do not have to do it all at once, as that can be overwhelming, but it is important to do it all.

Reintegrating memories with all their components to remove rather than merely resisting programming is a lengthy and painful process. However, those who have done it say it is more than worth it. They get their lives back. They get to own whatever happened to them, and recognise what caused the emotions they have experienced all their lives. They release trapped energy and emotions, and, as a consequence, feel lighter and freer. Each time I assist a survivor client in working through a traumatic memory, that survivor reports that although he or she is tired afterwards, a huge burden has lifted and its removal has made room for a new joy in life. Even more important than getting your life back is becoming yourself again or, more likely, for the first time.

Principles to make memory work effective

In my experience, a few key principles can make memory work efficient, minimally traumatising, and permanently healing. These principles are derived from what I have learned from survivors' minds and experiences about how the mind-controlling abuser groups work when they create and train insiders. The abuser groups, including scientists among them, have extensively researched the way that traumatic memory and dissociation work. Unlike those scientists working on the visible side of our society's dissociative barrier, they do not have an ethics committee, and they have experimented considerably with children to learn how to create programmed dissociative inside parts, how to keep memories (including physical and emotional pain) stored efficiently, and how to keep trauma from being resolved. The method I recommend here is based on what they have done as well as on the visible research of genuine ethical scientists, and on my own experience as a clinical psychologist.

The keys that make this method of memory processing effective are:

1. Make sure that all bodily sensations and emotions, and all words and pictures, are included in the memory processing.
2. Make sure that all insiders who have any aspect of the memory participate, including "recycler" parts.

3. Utilise the memory storage already built in by the abusers.
4. Utilise the internal recorders' knowledge of how to find memories and insiders who hold pieces of each memory;
5. Work through each memory in stages, usually beginning with the storyline while the other aspects are stored.

I do not claim that the method I am about to describe to you is the only technique, or even the best technique you can use; I can only claim that it is very effective for most of my survivor clients. It takes advantage of the way the organised abusers have stored the memories and the personality parts inside their victims. It has been carefully honed for a number of years, during which time I have worked the "bugs" out of it, correcting the most common errors that I used to make.

If you are a working with a therapist, or are a therapist yourself, you can enhance this memory work by any one of a number of existing trauma techniques, such as EMDR, energy therapies, and hypnosis.

Finding and selecting memories

I first described recorder parts in Chapter Four. Recorder parts know everything about the system and the history, and observe it with apparent disinterest. They are trained to do nothing but store information, which they tell to their handlers or others when required. In preparing to process a particular memory or programme, I ask the internal recorders to find both the contents of the event and all the parts of the person who are holding any part of that memory. Although they are not usually allowed to deliberately intervene on their own initiative to help the person, they are glad to assist when asked. Recorders I have met often believe they are not human (for example, are aliens or whales) and, therefore, cannot act in this world.

Thanks to the recorders, it is actually easier to access and reconstitute memories held within mind-controlled or ritually abused survivors than those within other kinds of trauma survivors. You do not need to chase flashbacks. You do not need to spend weeks retrieving the content of the memory. You can do what you need to do in an organised rather than haphazard way. For example, you could simply ask your parts for "the suicide programme", "the memory that gives me the stomach ache", "the programme that makes me bulimic", "the memory that I see part of in the nightmare", "the memory that gives me that awful feeling of sadness", or "the memory that makes me get up and go outside at night". You have insiders who know how to find the right one, even if several different memories are causing a particular symptom and need to be processed one at a time.

It can also be helpful, especially in the later stages of recovery, to have your internal programmers create charts or lists of the programmes, and then work through them systematically (as I described in Chapter Ten).

Before processing a memory, all you need to know is that it is the one causing the symptoms or behaviours that need to end, and that you will have enough time to get through it from start to finish (or can contain it well if it is unfinished). If you are processing it with a therapist, please note that I, as a therapist, prefer *not* to be told ahead of time what the content of the memory is. And it is wisest that you not know ahead of time either. Speculation by the front person and other parts about what a memory might contain can contaminate the process and make it more difficult to get at the actual memory. Also, in these days when therapists are being accused of creating "false memories" in their clients, I want to avoid all possibility of suspicion. And since abuser groups tell clients they have made it all up, you are more likely to believe your own memories if you have not tried to figure them out ahead of time.

How much memory to process at once

Now, when organised abusive groups decide to traumatise children, they do not do it neatly in little pieces that are just the right size for an hour or two of memory processing. Sometimes, they take a child or a group of children to "cult camp", or "military cadet camp" for a week, while other children are going to regular camp. Some major rituals or pornographic film shoots go on for days. Programme creation, however, usually involves a deliberate trauma in which a new part is split off and given instructions; each programme is repeated at different ages, and this repetition is documented both externally and internally within the records of the internal programmers. A programme creation training event might be embedded within a longer event, but it does have a beginning and an end.

When you select a memory for processing, your internal leaders need to select an event, or a piece of an event, which has a beginning and an end (even if other bad things happened both before and after this piece), and ideally can be processed in a single sitting. If this cannot be done with a particular memory, more care must be taken to put away the remainder of the memory temporarily so that you can manage your daily life before you do memory work again.

When you work through a traumatic memory, always begin the story in "normal life" (e.g., getting into the car to go to an event, or being awakened in the middle of the night and told to get up) and follow it through until you are in "normal life" again, with the traumatic event having happened in between. The parts of you who hold the beginning and end of a memory are usually different from the ones in the middle, but selecting a complete memory, normal life-to-normal life, in this way helps you understand how the traumatic events fit in with your everyday life.

Often, for a survivor, the memories of bizarre and horrible events seem unreal because they seem unconnected to the daily life remembered by the front person. When your memory work includes the connection between "regular life" and your hidden life, it all begins to make sense, and you begin to realise that these events not only occurred, but were arranged and conducted by actual people, many of whom also existed in more benign positions in your "regular" daily life. This helps you gain perspective on what was actually going on.

Getting internal agreement to do the work

Often, the insiders who have only the awareness of what occurred do not want to experience the pain, and the ones who just have the feelings do not want to know what happened to them; in that case, you have to talk with them about the advantages of memory processing.

In speaking with the parts who do not want the pain, emphasise that everyone inside shares the same body, and while *they* may feel fine, someone else inside is in pain. Some parts might scoff at the pain holders as "garbage kids", and weak, but it is fairly easy to help them see that those pain holders have done a very helpful job so that the "tough" parts can do their jobs without feeling the pain, and that the pain-holder parts will remain in pain until the memory is put together, which is unfair to them.

In speaking with the parts who have the feelings but do not want the knowledge, emphasise that the abuse is now over (if you know it is actually over), and that the awful feelings they have belong to the time of the abuse, not to the present. Tell them that if they participate in putting the memories together, they will be truly aware and even feel that the events are over, and that their feelings from the time of the abuse will be discharged and will no longer plague them. If the abuse is not over, but is ongoing, then their shared awareness will help end it and keep them safe in the future. It is very important to understand that the parts you do not want to know about are still you, and that they are not freaks, but have your good qualities also.

Preparation for memory work

You do not just dive into a traumatic memory and hope it comes out all right, any more than you would start on a road trip without a map or GPS, and enough fuel and money to get to your destination. You need to prepare carefully. All of the following steps ensure that the memory work will be effective. Once you have chosen an actual memory to be processed, and you have developed the internal containers for feelings and incomplete memories (discussed in the previous chapter), you are ready to begin.

Gather the parts

As much as you can, make sure that all the insiders who contain pieces of the chosen memory participate. By "pieces of the memory", I mean not only the story but the sounds, tastes, smells, bodily sensations, thoughts, and emotions. This means speaking with these insiders ahead of time (or having other parts or your therapist speak with them) and getting their agreement. You do not have to know their names, as long as you know you have all those involved in the memory. Sometimes, it is hard to know whether you have everyone. If you do not, the memory processing might stall, and at that point you might have to look for whoever was left out. Someone inside will know who it is.

This is very important: if even one insider who holds a portion of the memory stays out of the memory processing, or withholds part of what he or she knows, that insider is likely to experience ongoing flashbacks of the traumatic event that might affect the whole system. In a way, this is helpful, because it signals that there is a missing piece you need to retrieve. Sometimes, it is impossible to gather all the insiders involved in a memory because some of them are still hidden. If this is the case, it will help to keep an indexed summary of the memories you have worked through, and, if they are memories of the abuser group's deliberate programming, their purpose. If you do not have time to write down all the details, just make sure that some insider has the (possibly new) job of keeping track of which memories were processed and how they relate to the programmes. One of the internal programmers or recorders might like this job.

It is sometimes helpful to invite parts to be present who were not there for the original event—for example, a care-taker for little children. Other parts might also want to watch from a distance, to acquire knowledge of how to process memories or of what happened to the body. Over time, you will be able to find one or two parts who will specialise in helping the others with memory processing. I have found that often the most effective ones are severely traumatised, empathic child parts. These parts, especially, remind us what a great gift a personality system can be. Many people who have not been traumatised have the luxury of going through life without much caring what is happening to other people whom they do not know personally. Trauma, like the fire that refines metal, can create good people who care, and are not indifferent to the suffering of others.

It is not necessary to have the front person present during memory work unless that personality was involved in the original experience. Memories that have been completely processed often gradually "leak" through to the main adult personality in the days following the memory work, but if this does not happen, do not require the adult to know their content. If you intend to work through until you are completely healed, a time will come when the front person will come to know. But for now, you can trust the wisdom of those in charge of your personality system. The adult needs to function in the present external world, hold a job, study, look after children, relate to other people, balance his or her chequebook, and cook without burning the food.

Insiders who do not have any part of the original memory do not need to participate. But do include those who have the transition from "regular life" to the special traumatic events, for example, those who rode in the car to the rituals. This way, you can clearly identify when and where the events occurred.

Other insiders might want to observe as you process a memory to see how it is done, so they can be ready when their turn comes.

Include the internal recyclers

Some parts, usually known as recyclers or reactivators, are trained to deliberately withhold and hide a small part of each training memory so that the effect of the training cannot be destroyed. The hidden bit may be some words that were spoken, something they saw, an emotion, or some physical pain. If this piece is not included in the memory, the perpetrator group will be able to re-create the programme from the missing piece. (I am not sure how this works in the brain.)

I remember my shock when all the programmes I had worked through with one of my first survivor clients suddenly began to activate once more. Her recycling programme, which I had not known about, was operating. If the perpetrator group accesses you, they will have the capacity to set off many programmes at once if they discover you have done memory work but not included the recycler's part. That is what happened with this survivor.

Prevent this disaster by looking for recycler parts, and convincing them to include their part in each memory you work through. This is one reason to keep specific records of memory processing. If you go through memories without including the recyclers, you will have to redo them, working from your records, inserting the piece which the recycler holds for each memory. It will not be as painful as the first time, but it will still be hard work.

You may ask why you will not just remember the memories you have gone through. The first time you go through a traumatic memory, you will notice it is very intense and specific, as if every sensation is being experienced for the first time. In a way, that is true: it is the first time many parts of you have had this experience. It has been stored just in pieces, and now it is put together. But when a memory has been entirely, or even mostly, put together, it enters your general memory bank of known events, and there it begins to fade in its intensity and get confused with other similar memories. So, if you want a record of it, you need to make the record that first time.

It is quite possible for you to find the recycler parts; the process is not complicated, and you can do it. Just ask internally in a casual way whether there are any parts trained to keep pieces of the memories separate. Usually, someone will answer truthfully, and then permit you to dialogue with the recyclers or those in charge of them.

Some personality systems have hidden areas in which large numbers of fragmentary parts are hidden, each group with a particular type of emotional state. These are kept for later use by the perpetrator group, and might also be used to reconstitute programmes for which they kept some of the emotions. If you have such places in your system, it is wise to find them and free their inhabitants.

Needless to say, memory work is much more efficient, and you are much safer, if each memory only has to be processed once. And, believe it or not, you can get through it. Sometimes, I look at it like mowing a gigantic lawn. When I mow, I like to go around the outside perimeter of the lawn so that the remaining square becomes gradually smaller and smaller, and eventually I have the satisfaction of seeing the tiny piece in the middle disappear completely. I have seen survivors accomplish this with memories too.

Titrate or fractionate the memory components

The goal of this work is re-association of memories, but not reliving them all at once in all their painful detail. It is important not to allow yourself to become flooded with painful memories, or to be overwhelmed by the emotions or bodily sensations when working with any particular memory. You can avoid this by using your ability to dissociate parts of experience in a helpful way.

When a memory is dissociated, the components of the experience are generally separated from one another, each component held by a different insider or group of insiders. Although you want all the insiders who were present to be present when you process the memory, you want initially to keep some of the memory's components separate.

You can look for the components by listing all the senses, thinking of the emotions as also being a group of senses. I think of the senses as organised into three groups:

- the distance senses—sight and hearing;
- body sensations—smell and taste, pain, heat and cold, sexual feelings, drugged feelings, etc.;
- emotions—fear, terror, anxiety, anger, frustration, sadness, etc.

The first time you go through a traumatic memory, you will want to allow only the first group (sight and hearing) to be present. Since sight and sound do not hurt (unless there is an unbearably loud noise), these senses can be tolerated for a fairly long time without too much discomfort. They are also essential for obtaining information about what happened, and what false beliefs, instructions, and programmes were implanted.

Bodily pain, on the other hand, is very difficult to bear. It helps to dissociate it while the *content* of the memory is learnt.

Smell and taste and touch can be quite unpleasant but not completely unbearable, unless the memory involves cannibalism or corpses, which, unfortunately, come with ritual abuse. Sometimes, it is preferable to allow those insiders present to experience just a little bit of these bodily sensations when you go through the memory for the first time, so that you can gain the information these senses provide. For example, in a memory in which a survivor was injected with a numbing drug and unable to move, it was necessary to include a small part of these sensations to make her aware of what was happening to her.

Like the bodily sensations, the emotions in a traumatic situation are very strong, and can make it very difficult to proceed with putting the memory together. So, they need to be temporarily dissociated. Sexual feelings can distract some parts, causing them to dwell on the memory rather than getting on with it. Or these feelings can be so embarrassing that you may refuse to experience them, especially if you are with someone else, such as a friend or a therapist. Feelings created by drugs can confuse you, so generally it is wisest to omit the drug sensations during the first run through the story of the memory.

Temporarily put away the feelings

When you gather together the insiders who have pieces of the memory, you could instruct them as follows.

"We are now going to put away the feelings from this memory, bit by bit, so that we can see what happened without it hurting.

"Put in all the pain, all the "owies" and hurts. (If you are dealing with child parts, use childish words as well as adult synonyms for pain and emotions, to make sure that the young parts understand you.)

"Now, put in all the fear, all the scared feelings, all the terror, all the worry and anxiety.

"Now, put in all the angry and mad feelings, and all the sad and hopeless feelings.

"Now, put in any drugs and any sexual feelings.

"Now put in anything else, anything you felt in any part of your body, and anything you felt in any part of your feelings.

"When you are sure that all the feelings are in the container, close the box (or bucket) and lock it up tightly. Keep the doggy door (or spout, or straw) ready in case any more feelings come up when you watch the film."

Remember to tailor any suggestion you read here, and any treatment in general, to your own specific needs and preferences. Some survivors like to speak out loud and name what theyare putting in. Some survivors like to have see-through containers, so they can see what is in them. Remember, however, that all of it needs to be processed later, because anything you keep out of a memory (e.g., pleasant sexual or drug feelings) is likely to cause flashbacks later.

LisaBri has a strong insider standing guard on the rubbish bin she uses to contain feelings, so that they do not leak during the memory processing.

Watching the "video" of the memory

Go through each memory at least twice. The first time, do it as if you are watching a video, with sight and sound but no emotions or bodily sensations. The parts can watch it on an internal screen in a viewing room. When you watch the video, hold an imaginary remote control, so that you can make the picture bigger or smaller, speed up or slow down, rewind, fast forward, mute, or stop. You can pause the video to take a bathroom break, or to talk about something that was on it. All, or almost all, of the feelings have been put away into a container.

Because you are not feeling the pain or the fear, you are able to describe what is happening clearly, and will remember what happened. If you do it with a therapist or friend, he or she will be able to take coherent, even verbatim, notes. But you probably do not want to be writing things down as you watch the video, since this will interfere with the process. You can ask an insider who remembers things well to help you write it down once you have completed the memory processing.

When you are watching this "video", you need to be simultaneously in the inner world which includes the memory, and in the outer present world, either alone or with a safe person, in a safe place. Stay as conscious as possible, closely enough connected to the real world that you can describe the memory while going through it. This is important for two reasons. It helps you stay grounded in the present, so that the memory processing does not turn into a flashback, and it helps you to know two important things: whether all parts of the memory are being included, and what parts were trained to do.

Be sure you include what you heard (words as well as sounds) as well as what you saw. With mind controlled and ritually abused survivors, the words usually contain the programming or training, so the parts who know what was said will sometimes omit the soundtrack, and it has to be specifically requested. They might have been ordered never to reveal what was said to them. Stay alert to whether an insider tries to skip a part of the memory, and ask them to put that part in. Be suspicious if the memory seems to have a gap, and ask whose part is missing. Even if the memory appears whole, ask whether there is anything missing or glossed over.

You (the front person or an older higher-up) can talk with the parts as they go through the memory, asking questions (for clarification only), giving reassurances that the event is not really happening now, and correcting their confused perceptions as they express them. If the abusers implanted a false idea during the memory (e.g., that what happened was all your fault), you can challenge it right there. It is extremely effective to challenge the lies and tricks right at the point where your parts are remembering them clearly for the first time.

If different parts hold different aspects of the experience, the chronological order of the parts of the memory can become confused. To prevent this, ask for someone inside who knows the content to line the parts up in the order in which their pieces come.

If the memory gets stuck, take a break to talk with the parts and find out why. Sometimes, an insider just does not want to go through with it. Sometimes, there is a piece of the memory held by an unknown part, whom you have to find. Then you need to negotiate with that part, and decide whether or not to go ahead with the memory. The feelings and needs of all parts deserve a fair hearing, and respect. Insiders can be amazingly co-operative if you just listen to them and ask them for help. Often, the only people they have spoken with (until now) were abusers, who never listened to them, so, while they might be suspicious at first, they will warm up when you listen and explain what you need. There may be parts who are ashamed of what they were forced to do, or did on their own, and now want to hide. Let them know that you need their memory pieces and will not judge them.

Often there has been "incidental training", accidental events incorporated into a training memory. For instance, in the middle of a training session or other traumatic event, someone might have turned on a radio, or a car horn might have honked outside. Incidental training is the "white noise" in the background that most people do not even notice, because they are too busy concentrating on what is happening in the room with them, but it will end up becoming part of the traumatic memory. However, it is often forgotten or left out while trying to break down a programme, leaving you unable to work out why things just are not working. It must be included in the memory processing.

During the process, be careful to monitor your emotional state. If you notice your feelings becoming overwhelming, remind your parts to dissociate them into their container. If this does not work, stop the memory temporarily to diagnose and address the problem (for example, an insider who refuses to put away pleasant sexual or drugged feelings can keep other feelings active as well).

Sometimes, a very young part will want to do the story-telling part of a memory through play with dolls, a sand tray, or other toys, or by drawing what happened. This can be useful, especially because, in some cases, it bypasses the "don't talk" programming, as the story is not told by talking.

It helps to write down what you saw and heard during the "video" part of the memory quite soon after you go through it. This narrative is probably the best record you will ever have of what happened to you, as the memory will fade once it is consciously known. The memory that returns when first putting together a dissociated trauma is far more detailed and feels much more "alive" than any other.

Special issues in memory processing

Infant memories

It is important that memories of your original splits be processed if you want to become your whole self, since, with organised abuse, most parts are deliberately split off in infancy. Abuser groups often describe a designed personality system as a tree (for example, the tree of life, the Kabbalah). A tree has a trunk from which come the biggest branches, then other branches come off those, and smaller and smaller branches off the others. Each split creates a new branch. Memories of events that occur very early in life may involve the entire personality system, as they are traumas that split a branch off the trunk. To process these, all of the parts involved might have to regress to the age at which the trauma happened while they process the memory, which is sometimes very young. You may feel yourself becoming younger as you go through these very early memories.

If, as a baby, you had already been previously split, some of your older parts might not belong to the branch whose trauma you are working on. In that case, these older parts can stay nearby and help by holding the babies internally and keeping them connected with the present-day situation. But with the earliest splits, all parts regress to infancy during the memory. So, make sure your body is in a safe, comfortable place when you do the memory work if you do not have a friend or therapist to guide you through it.

When I work as a therapist on a survivor's baby memories, sometimes I have to use word and touch signals with such memories because the survivor is unable to speak, or cannot return to the present. I squeeze the survivor's hand and ask the client to squeeze mine from time to time to indicate that he or she can hear me. I pre-arrange "stop" signals—one for the survivor to give me if he or she cannot speak, and one for me to give the survivor which will automatically stop the memory. (For example, I may hold the right shoulder firmly and say "Stop!" loudly.) I practise these things with easy memories first. If the memory belongs to pre-verbal parts, I ask a verbally fluent part to watch. Then I help the survivor process the memory in short segments, stopping to allow the older part to tell what happened. If you have a memory-processing partner (therapist or friend), you can arrange for that person to help you in this way. This person can reflect the baby's experience by imitating his or her body language, just as a caring parent will do with an infant.

Memory processing is different for infant parts. Survivor and former cult trainer Stella Katz (who has, sadly, recently succumbed to cancer) described her experience with infant parts and memory processing as relatively quick and uncomplicated.

> Processing baby memories . . . is something that can be done very quickly if you just let the person do it without verbal interference.
>
> Baby memories phase in and out because babies phase in and out during the experience. They are not like a five year old who remembers hours of torture, in that they only take in small parts of memories. That's why when training babies you use short quick things, rather than long drawn out things. What takes a five year old 24 hours to break, only takes a baby a few minutes.
>
> Baby memories are based on events that occur when life is still a complete mystery, so for a baby it is best to just take what you see as real. So, when travelling back to baby years, don't try to understand, just experience, and let it go.
>
> These memories are the hardest to get at, but the easiest to let go of.

I have found that when survivors access baby memories, they are often able to make sense of them in ways in which they could not as a baby. The memories appear in their sensory form, as they are being experienced for the first time. But now, when they cross over into the cognitive part of the brain, there is an adult brain able to understand them. One survivor remembered her mother saying "I hate you" to her right after she was born. She heard the words and felt her mother's emotions as a baby, and as an adult she knew what the words meant.

How do you find the baby memories? When one survivor had worked through all the memories of the parts on the layers in her internal structure (a tetrahedron or inverted pyramid) as well as the memories of home abuse, she was left with "the point"—the portion of the structure at the very base. It contained the infant memories, which were a conglomeration of bodily sensations and emotions. Your memories might not be organised that way; they may be divided by topic, or by emotion—but the baby memories are stored somewhere in your personality system, and someone inside knows where to find them.

Memories of dying or becoming unconscious

During memory work, you will encounter memories of times when you became unconscious or even temporarily died. This can last for some time and it can be quite frightening to you and to the person helping you. What if you do not wake up? Having helped survivors work through a large number of such memories, I have confidence that a survivor will not actually die during the memory work because they did not die, or, at least, did not remain dead, during the original trauma. I have helped my clients work through quite a few memories of apparent death, and of resuscitation by the perpetrators when the abuse went too far and the child was in the process of dying. Although it is certainly gruesome, these memories can be processed like any other.

Although I strongly suggest that these memories not be the first ones you tackle, they are necessary to address. Additionally, within these memories are the hidden gems of the near-death experiences that can give you spiritual hope. We shall look at these in more detail in Chapter Twenty.

Combining memories

You can put together a number of similar memories into one memory processing session. If you were sexually abused by your father, for example, there might have been hundreds or thousands of incidents. All the oral rapes in the bedroom, or all the touching in the television room, or all the "come-when-you-hear-the-whistle" trainings may be grouped together and processed as if they are one. I do not know how survivors do this, but I know that they can, and do. This is fortunate, because if it were not the case, trauma recovery would take forever and be so painful that people might give up.

Creating programme "wiring diagrams"

As discussed in Chapter Ten, "Dealing with triggering", some abuser groups instruct insiders about what to do if a survivor attempts to work through programming memories in order to destroy the programmes. Each programme that the survivor attempts to undo (through working through the memory) is attached to another programme, which is turned on as soon as he or she interferes with the first programme. Some personality systems have this connection between programmes built in. For example, if you attempted to undo a suicide programme, it might trigger a programme to harm your body, and if you attempt to undo the programme to harm your body, it might trigger a programme causing bodily pain, and if you attempt to undo that programme, it might trigger a programme to fall asleep. Sometimes, the wiring is circular, for instance, in the above example, working through the "sleep" programme might trigger a suicide programme.

To battle this, get your insiders to make "wiring diagrams", describing what other programme would be set off if you interfered with a particular programme. Examine the wiring diagram and select the weakest link, which might be a programme you have already worked through, or one which is minimally harmful, or one for which you know and can use the "off" trigger. Start there, and work your way through the sequence backwards. So, let us say that in the example above, you know the "off" trigger for the bodily pain. You begin to work on the memory of the programme for harming your body, and the pain kicks in. You immediately use the "off" trigger for the pain programme, and then go back to what you were doing.

Memories that have to be redone

If, later in your recovery, a part or group of parts emerges who belongs to a memory you have already done, it will be easy to reprocess the memory if you have a record of it. For instance, sometimes a programme or training you have destroyed suddenly starts working again, and you find yourself engaging in behaviours you thought you were cured of. It is important, then, to identify which programme has re-emerged, and reprocess that training memory more completely, putting in the missing pieces. When this happens, it is usually because some insider was hidden, and has now emerged, with his or her memory piece. He or she might be a recycler (whose job was to hide the piece), or simply a part who was split off during this memory.

Sometimes, there are parts who believe themselves to be computers or programmers, who believe they have the ability to create new programmes. They cannot. They can only use existing programmes and get them working again.

Adding in the feelings

When you have *completely* put together a previously unconscious memory, you have discharged the emotions connected with it, brought the behaviours programmed by the event under your conscious control, and freed the insiders separated by the event to join back together, *that is recovery.*

If you just leave the feelings dissociated into the containers, you will temporarily feel better, as I hope you did while you were putting together the content of the memory. But this reprieve will not last. The containers are likely to leak, as the memory tries to complete itself, and you may be flooded with those feelings. You are not yet healed. The programme created by this remembered event will still be capable of operating. You need to go on to the next stage.

There is an internal rhythm to this process. Once you have started effective memory work, it continues, bit by bit, as your inside leaders discover the joy of undoing what was done by the perpetrator group.

After getting the "story" of a memory, you might want to take a break in the "real world" of the present before tackling the feelings, and you might want to have some internal conversation (and conversation with your therapist or friend, if you have one with you) before proceeding. Just the information in the content of a memory is huge to digest, and the new feelings you will have in response to the content can be overwhelming.

The next step sounds easy, but it is very hard, and it can be intensely painful. Fortunately, it is brief, only lasting a few minutes or seconds for each memory, or memory segment, which is processed. It is like having a broken limb reset, which can be extremely painful but is necessary for the limb to be put back together in the right way and be useable once more. I know this is pretty unpleasant to anticipate, but the results are definitely worth it. If you survived this experience in the first place, you can revisit it for a few seconds now to free yourself from its effects. It will be incredibly beneficial in the long run.

In this step, open the container that has the feelings in it, and put the memory together with the feelings. *The feelings do not have to be experienced for the duration for which they were originally felt, but they do have to be acknowledged and incorporated into the memory along with the story and the physical sensations*. The feelings to be included are both the physical and the emotional sensations that occurred at the time of the memory; they do not include new reactions by parts (including the front person) who did not previously share in this memory. All the parts who were present during the event you are remembering need to share in the feelings.

Each survivor has his or her own preferred method of putting the story together with the feelings. It helps if you have the feelings in a transparent container, so that you can see your emotions gradually empty out of the container as you put them in with the story of the memory.

One way of doing this is counting. If your abuse does not include numbers as programme triggers, you might count upwards from one to ten, spacing the numbers about one second apart. You put the feelings in, adding more after each number. As each number is spoken, your agony increases. Usually a ten-count is enough to contain a memory, although for some very long memories it is necessary to go to fifteen, or even twenty. You will know when the feelings have all been acknowledged. Then count back to zero, putting the feelings away, now connected with the storyline of the memory. Some survivors find this brief, intense method is all they need to reassociate the feelings with the story line of the memory. Other people find it necessary to take a longer time to make sure that every physical sensation and every emotion are included.

Another method is to name out loud, slowly (or have your therapist or support person name out loud), what feelings are being associated with the memory, with a pause between each type of feeling: "Everything you tasted . . . everything you smelled . . . everything you felt in any part of your body [name specific body sensations such as pain in particular locations, electric shock, and sexual feelings, remembering to mention any sensations which would have happened in the particular memory you are dealing with] . . . everything you felt in any part of your emotions [name specific emotions such as fear, anger, anxiety, and sadness, remembering to mention any which must have been in the particular memory]."

Or you or your memory-processing partner (therapist or friend) can read out loud the transcript of what you said during the first story-telling, slowly, with a pause after each line. You then allow yourself to experience the feelings that belong to that part of the memory during each pause. Or you can go through the transcript several times, each time adding in more feelings.

Another thing you can do is to feel the feelings of the memory while you breathe in, then let them go as you breathe out. You can do this with one kind of feeling at a time, going through the storyline as often as you need to until the feelings have all been experienced and shared between the insiders who were in this event. You imagine the feelings beginning in the container into which you originally put them, and seeing it gradually empty as you allow yourself to experience them.

Look for feelings that some parts of you might be withholding because of shame or embarrassment, such as enjoyment of power, feeling special, sexual arousal, betraying or hurting someone, or sacrificing someone else to save someone you love. These must also be included, or the memory will not be fully processed, and the withheld feelings might flood you later.

As you can see, there are many ways of putting the feelings together with the rest of the memory. You can experiment with these and choose the way that works best for you.

Closure and integration of material

To complete the process, you can imagine the memory being put together by placing the whole thing in a new container, not one to be locked away, but one to be known, at least to the inside parts of you who took part in that event. It can help to mention specific things that happened in the memory, to make sure that everything is put in. You can say to your parts the final words:

"Put together:

- everything you saw,
- everything you heard (all the sounds, all the words),
- everything you tasted,
- everything you smelled,
- everything you felt in any part of your body [here, you name specific body sensations such as pain and sexual feelings, remembering to mention any sensations which would have happened in the particular memory we are dealing with], and
- everything you felt in any part of your emotions [here, you name specific emotions such as fear, anger, anxiety, and sadness, remembering to mention any which must have been in the particular memory]."

Once a memory has been put together with all its parts, a miraculous thing happens. The emotions and body sensations from the time of the traumatic memory disappear, leaving only a knowledge of what happened, similar to the knowledge of any other life experience. Finally, healing can occur. The wound is closed, though there may be a scar, in terms of your awareness that a horrible thing happened to you, but you survived. *The parts* (insiders) involved might also join with one another, depending on whether or not other memories still stand between them. This is a natural outcome of the memory barriers between them being dissolved. And the huge burden of the frozen trauma will be lifted, allowing room for joy to be alive.

There will, however, still be a need for parts, including the front person if he or she becomes aware of the memory, to experience their current emotions about what they now know happened to them, and to make sense of it.

Sending the memory into storage

In physiological terms, when the memory is reassociated, then it has been taken from the sensory and emotional centres of the brain through the hippocampus to the cerebral cortex (the cognitive processing part), and now it can be remembered like any other memory. Its vividness and emotional punch will gradually fade with time. So, if you want a record of what happened to you, be sure to write everything down or speak it into a recording device once you have the storyline, because you will not remember the details for very long.

If you had time only to partially process the memory, either leaving the feelings alone or doing just a segment of what happened, then it is important to put the incomplete memory away in one of your containers, labelling it so someone inside knows where it is. That way, it will not create flashbacks.

After all the parts of a memory, including the feelings, are joined in your awareness, you can send the labelled container into permanent storage. The way in which this is done depends upon your inner world. One survivor just threw the box into the internal river, and it floated down to its resting place. Another used her inner self helper, who believed herself to be a whale, to take the container away and deposit it on the bottom of the ocean. If she had to reprocess the memory, the whale could get it back again—but the other parts could not. Some survivors just use filing systems similar to the original ones installed by the abusers—but for completed memories. The main reason to store the memory this way is in case new insiders pop up later who have something to add to this memory. It is also useful to have it located somewhere known to the file manager parts if the front person is not yet ready to know what happened. Eventually, it will be time to let the front person know. Once the front person knows, it is likely that this memory will become just a "regular memory", no longer holding the traumatic impact it once had, although the conscious knowledge of what happened may change your life.

Completing the processing and integrating parts

At the conclusion of the process, it is helpful to have a symbolic cleansing and joining, an image of your choosing located in your inner world.

I like to use a (breathable) waterfall of soft, warm, sparkling water or coloured light, in which the parts can wash away any all remnants of the memory which did not get into the container. They can cleanse themselves, inside and out, from any dirty or contaminated feelings. They can also revitalise themselves, removing their tiredness.

Now, finally, the waterfall will wash away any boundaries between parts whose separateness is no longer necessary, and will blend them together. Any parts who still need to be separate will remain separate and have their boundaries strengthened. We shall look in more detail at integrations in Chapter Twenty-one, "Becoming yourself".

You do not have to use a waterfall. Do not use one if your abusers installed one in your inner world; use something else. Choose a setting and image which works for you, so that the parts involved in the memory can be cleansed and healed, and can join if they are ready.

Cognitive and emotional processing

Although the *previous* emotions (the ones which happened at the time of the traumatic event) have been put in with the memory, there will be new *current* emotions about what happened.

It is important, after you work through a memory, to discuss any implications the memory might have with your therapist or friend, or to write about it if you are doing it alone. All these thoughts and feelings deserve to be expressed, especially if you have just become aware of some trauma that you did not previously know about. You might need to recognise and deliberately reject the false beliefs that resulted from the dissociated trauma. You might have discovered that someone you believed was safe was a perpetrator. You need time to talk with your parts, the ones who were in the memory, and the ones who came to know about it. You need internal conversation about what this memory means, and you need to reassure the little ones that you are safer because of knowing this now.

When memories are processed and shared with other parts, sometimes including the front person, there can be new horror or shame because of parts knowing things they did not previously know about what happened to them, or what they did. It takes time to work through all these new emotions. Give yourself that time if it is needed. You also need to have time to reorientate yourself in the present. Unless you are a super-dissociator, do not go to work on a day when you have processed a traumatic memory!

Exercise 24. Steps in memory processing

This exercise guides you through the process of resolving a traumatic memory. You might need to use it with the first few memories, then it will become "second nature" and you will no longer need to refer to this guide.

1. Choose a memory to be resolved. If this is your first time, make sure it is a relatively easy one, of which you have at least partial knowledge. Do not choose it because it is creating flashbacks, but because you want some issue resolved which is connected to this particular memory.
2. As much as you can, make sure that all the insiders who contain pieces of the memory participate. Ask those inside who know to find all such parts.
3. Speak with the insiders who have pieces of this memory ahead of time (or have other parts speak with them) and get their agreement, and get the agreement of their bosses as well.
4. If this is a training or programming memory, look for recycler parts who were taught to withhold part of the memory, and make sure that the system allows them to participate.
5. Invite helper parts to be present, such as a care-taker for little children.
6. Ask other parts who might be traumatised by the memory to stay away while you process it.
7. Gather all insiders who are going to participate in this memory or help with it, in an inner safe room with a video screen and audio equipment.
8. Make sure you have ready containers for partially processed memories and for feelings belonging to the memories, such as a cave containing barrels, a bank with a vault with storage lockers, a well with buckets, or a storage room with jars on shelves, or whatever image you created. Both the containers and the place in which they will be kept should be able to be locked, but there should be a way to put things in the containers after they are locked.
9. Get the participant parts to put their emotions and bodily sensations away in the container.
10. Have the storyline of the memory (sight and sound only) projected on the video screen in the meeting room so that all participants can see and hear it. Have them watch it from "normal life", through the trauma, up until the return to "normal life".
11. If emotions or bodily sensations come up during the video, pause it and have the participants put those sensations away in the containers.

(continued)

12. If sounds or words are missing, pause the video and find the parts who have the sound track and get them to participate.
13. If the order of events is unclear, ask for someone inside who knows the content to line the parts up in the order in which their parts come.
14. If the video gets "stuck", pause it and search for missing insiders who need to participate in order to resolve it.
15. After the video has been viewed, put it in a container and take a break in the "real world" for at least ten or fifteen minutes.
16. Go through the memory again with all participants, this time adding in the feelings that were put away in the container as you get to the parts of the memory which involve these feelings. Keep checking the container to see how much is left of the feelings. You may do it once, thoroughly, or several times, adding a particular feeling each time.
17. Look for feelings that some parts of you might be withholding because of shame or embarrassment, such as enjoyment of power, or sexual arousal. These must also be included, or the memory will not be fully processed, and the withheld feelings might flood you later.
18. Put all the pieces of the memory together, mentioning specific things that happened in the memory, and asking your insiders to put in "everything you saw, everything you heard (all the sounds, all the words), everything you tasted, everything you smelled, everything you felt in any part of your body [here, you name specific body sensations such as pain and sexual feelings, remembering to mention any sensations which would have happened in the particular memory we are dealing with], and everything you felt in any part of your emotions [here, you name specific emotions such as fear, anger, anxiety, and sadness, remembering to mention any which must have been in the particular memory]."
19. Then send the labelled container into permanent storage. If the memory is incomplete and you have to return to complete it, mentally label it and file its components in temporary storage.
20. Have a symbolic cleansing and joining, through an image of your choosing located in your inner world, such as washing in a breathable waterfall.
21. Although the *previous* emotions have been put in with the memory, there will be new *current* emotions about what happened. It is important, after you work through a memory, to discuss internally any implications the memory may have for you.

Will you always need to work through memories in this amount of detail? Here is what survivor Jen Callow discovered about this.

Jen Callow: "Memory work later in recovery"

After many years of painstakingly processing every piece of a memory, my system is able to do a lot of memory work on our own. As we are not nearly so triggered by events in our daily life, and our parts are increasingly willing to work together, we have many more inner resources to draw on to help us through a memory, no matter how intense it may be. We now have more options when dealing with memories, particularly since our abusers are no longer in our life to re-programme or trigger us.

Sometimes, we choose to talk to new parts, and, when they're ready, help them leave their programme line. We do this by simply "flying over" the memory, seeing it from a distance in our mind without having to feel it all and getting drawn in. Our goal is to understand what happened, what we learnt from that event, and how those enduring beliefs and feelings are impacting our life now. We remind ourselves that we are safe and work with the old beliefs and feelings so that we can move beyond them and forward in our life. This might involve using art, affirmations, physical activity, crying and yelling, whatever feels right at the time. Sometimes, it's simply a matter of an "aha" moment where we realise those beliefs are false and replace them with beliefs that work for us now.

We can often disable a whole programme line in this manner, part by part. The disadvantage is that the line is still there. But with safety and internal co-operation, it is unlikely the line will get reactivated, since parts will not go back to it and their programmes.

Other times, we do have to process the feelings from the memory after we've flown over and understood it, as they continue to leak through. Even this takes less time than it used to, though, and the processing tends to flow smoothly with less resistance.

* * *

Along with getting to know your personality system, memory work is the core of the healing process. I hope these two chapters have given you some helpful information about how to do it. If you are working with a therapist or other helper, please feel free to share these chapters with him or her.

CHAPTER SIXTEEN

Looking at your family

This is one of the most heart-breaking chapters of this book. Most survivors of ritual abuse whom I have known had families who were involved in that abuse, and, as a result, they had to sever connections with those families.

In addition, most survivors whom I have known came from incestuous families, and the parents who were not directly involved in the mind control or ritual abuse were often sexual perpetrators. Sibling incest appears to be common, and in some cases is even taught by the abusers. Besides their involvement with the mind-controlling or ritually abusive group, parents frequently take their children to child pornography studios, or rent them out as prostitutes.

The family, which is supposed to be the safe haven in which we are nurtured as we grow from a small, helpless infant into a mature adult, has been turned instead into a frightening place where safety is non-existent, and the lessons of compliance and secrecy are well learnt. Children become dissociative because it is the only way to survive in such a family. There is not only the deliberate splitting off of insiders which abuser groups engage in, there is usually much spontaneous splitting of the child's mind, because the trauma is just too much for one person to deal with.

In this chapter, we shall look at some survivors' personal stories to see how their family life affected them. We shall also look at how to deal with your family of origin in the present, and at the situation you are dealing with if you are in a relationship and have children. Unfortunately, many marriages are arranged by perpetrators to keep survivors tied to them, and to continue the abuse into the next generation.

Let us begin with the least ominous situation.

Innocent parents

Some survivors had loving parents, but were abused outside the home, for example, through schools, religious organisations, or day-care centres. In many or most such cases, the children could not tell their parents what was happening, because of threats to kill their families if they talked about the abuse. The children might have acted out in various ways, perhaps in sexual play with other children, or temper tantrums, or social withdrawal, but it is easy for parents to write off such things as developmental stages, or just misbehaviour.

These survivors have a lot to work through, but the good parenting they received makes a great deal of difference to their resilience, and this means that after they remember, they still have parents and a family, unlike those whose parents were perpetrators.

Being angry with innocent parents is much easier for survivors than facing the way they feel about the perpetrators, who are terrifying to them. "She should have known", or "Where were they when all this happened?" are common reactions. But parents with no knowledge of organised abuse often just do not have a clue. It is not as if society as a whole knows about these things. And sometimes, the kindest and most well-meaning parents are the most clueless, because they really do not realise that human nature can be so dark, and that people can engage in such horrific acts against children.

Sometimes, it seems that innocent parents just do not want to know. If you are a survivor, parts of you were aware of the darkest events from a very early age. You have forgotten how incredibly shocking it is to discover such things. And it is heart-breaking for parents—even those who are therapists—to discover that such things were done to the children that they love. Such parents will feel incredible guilt and shame for not realising what was going on. The very act of listening to you, or reading about these kinds of abuses, is deeply traumatising to loving parents. So, when you are seeking to tell your parents the things you could not tell them when you were five, you are unwittingly causing them extreme emotional pain. This does not mean that you should not tell them. Loving parents want to know, even if it hurts.

Because of this, it takes time for innocent parents to come to grips with what has happened, and to be able to look you in the eye and listen to the horrors you have experienced. This does not necessarily mean they do not care about you. They might care a great deal. Keep up your relationship with them in all the positive ways you can, and introduce them to your experience very gradually.

When one parent was involved

In my experience, it is common for one parent to be a perpetrator involved with the abuser group, while the other parent either suspects nothing, turns a blind eye to symptoms, or is powerless to protect their child from what they might suspect is going on because the child cannot tell the authorities.

When the parents are separated, there is an opportunity for the child to tell the innocent parent, but he or she usually does not because the abusers have threatened to kill the parent if the child tells. The group might also have impersonated the innocent parent or parents. One of my first ritually abused clients, "Tony", lived with his cult-involved mother and stepfather, and had regular visits with his father in another city. Before each such visit, the cult group simulated the nature of the visit, imitating, for example, a camping trip, and the person pretending to be Tony's dad abused him. The result was that Tony was afraid of his father, kept his distance, and refused to bond with his father during these visits, and the father felt helpless to get to know his son. This father was innocent and well meaning; he had no idea why his son refused to become close to him.

Another survivor lived with both parents until her teens. Mother had taken her to the cult day-care, and introduced her to the abuser group who continued to access the child in her school years, even though mother was not present during the ritual abuse. Father suspected nothing. It was mother who "ruled the roost" in the family, father being relegated to the role of wage-earner. When the child developed depression, it was assumed she just had a mental illness, and she was treated for this illness for years before disclosing the abuse. This survivor, like Tony, remembers her father (who was in the home) being impersonated so that she would not trust him.

Another survivor was subjected to military mind-control via his estranged father during access visits. His mother, a loving mental health professional with a "positive thinking" outlook on life, simply had no idea what was going on. When the boy showed disturbance, she would accuse him of learning bad habits from his peer group. He desperately wanted to tell her "It's my father, not the kids I play with," but he could not because the abusers (including his father) had threatened to kill his mother if he ever told. Even though she did not know, the generally good parenting that she and her partner provided gave this child some resilience with which he was able to resist some of the programming his father and the other abusers intended to implant in him.

This young man believed his mother had the power to refuse access to his father. He would tell her he did not want to go on visits with his father, and she insisted he go, not realising the horror of what was actually going on at his father's home, as he had disclosed nothing. Now that he has remembered and told her about it, she has told him that she feared losing custody of him if she denied his father access, because she was in a long-term loving lesbian relationship, and the courts were prejudiced against lesbians.

Parents who are aware of their children being abused by the other parent are truly in a bind. They can actually lose custody, being accused of "parental alienation". We hear of mothers, notably Elizabeth Morgan, who have gone as far as hiding their children and eventually being jailed for refusing to allow access to fathers they believe have sexually abused their children.

It is difficult, if not impossible, for a judge to determine the truth in such a situation, because there are really some fearful parents who falsely believe their children are being abused by the other parent. They distort what their children tell them, so that the children's normal physical contact with the other parent becomes interpreted as sexual or physical abuse.

I cannot address here what a parent should do if he or she suspects that a child is being abused by or through the other parent. That is beyond the scope of this book, as it involves legal issues. The point here for you as a survivor is to recognise that you might have an innocent parent who either knew nothing or suspected abuse but was powerless to take any action. That parent might now be willing to hear your story, even if he or she finds it painful.

Paedophiles married to cult parents

I have known of several families in which one parent (usually the mother) was involved in a cult, and the other parent was simply a paedophile. This was the situation with LisaBri, who tells some of her story below. Presumably, the cult parent threatens the paedophile parent with exposure if she or he interferes with the cult activities.

Confusion about whether your parents were involved

Some adults who are aware that they are survivors of mind control and/or ritual abuse are confused about whether their parents were involved in the abuse. It is difficult to relate to your parents if you just do not know whether they were abusers. I know a survivor of very early ritual abuse in a babysitter's home who is constantly confused about this, and alternately cuts off her parents and invites them back into her life. Were they impersonated by abusers? Were they just a regular dysfunctional family, with the organised abuse having nothing to do with them? She will not know until her inside parts reveal more to her. Organised abuser groups do a great deal of work to confuse kids about what has actually happened to them, and by whom.

People who were abused as children, especially by trusted family members, often go back and forth between awareness and unawareness. One of my clients is reading a book on incest, and at times she (the adult part) says she does not know whether she was abused; at other times she says she is very angry at her father for sexually abusing her, and once she told me that her mother sexually abused her. She will only find out what really happened if she asks her insiders.

Only some of your insiders know whether one of your parents was or is involved. And some of them could be mistaken, if your parents were impersonated or if you were told by abusers that your parents were present. This can be done with the aid of drugs and hypnosis. If you are confused about this, you need to share information between your insiders so that they can work out the truth. Do not jump to conclusions one way or the other.

And, difficult and heart-breaking though it may be, you do need to be willing to face the truth. If one or both of your parents were involved, they might or might not be safe to be around now. Does the perpetrator group still exist? Were they involved willingly, or unwillingly? Parents can be told that unless they sexually abuse their children, the children will be killed. What is a parent to do in that situation? You can get clues by asking your insiders what they remember about your parents' involvement. Were they sadistic abusers on their own, apart from what the group did? Or were they trying to find ways to get free and save your life?

The same goes for your siblings. If you were abused by an organised group, there is a high probability that it happened to your siblings, too. Abuser groups use siblings against each other—to report on each other, or to put up with abuse believing it will save their little sister or brother. If any of your siblings were sadistic abusers privately, away from the group, you should be careful around them, but even in that situation they might have been acting out what happened to them—children often do.

Perpetrator families

Incest in ritually abusive families is pervasive. Father, mother, brothers, and sisters, even the dog. One of my first ritually abused clients angrily referred to "my whole fucking family". And then she stopped and looked at me, and we both laughed. Black humour. Because, yes, it was true. Every family member had sex with every other family member. This is, unfortunately, a very common situation in perpetrator families. The deliberately organised mind control and ritual abuse involves non-family members, and is strictly controlled, but within the privacy of the home, sexual abuse is endemic, and violence and physical abuse are also very common. I have heard about parents who rent out their children for sex. Cult members might casually rape the child, who they know belongs to a cult family, often gang raping. There are incest pregnancies, ending in forced adoption, abortion, or sacrifice.

In some cult groups, parents who do not want to sexually assault their children might be told they have to do it or the children will be killed. The group leaders question the children to make sure the parents have done as they were told. And of course, cult children do not know how to, and are not allowed to, lie to the abusers.

Ritual abuse survivor LisaBri has a website (www.dissociatedsurvivor.com) with several articles describing the abuse she suffered at home. She has given me permission to adapt some of her writings for this book. She grew up with a father who sexually abused her in "ordinary" ways, two older brothers who also sexually abused her, one of them for years, and a mother who was a cult leader and was vicious in her sexual and physical abuse.

As she describes each of these situations and its effects, you will notice two important things: the effects of the abuse itself, and her longing for what that family member should have provided instead. Warning: These are very sad stories, so be prepared; they could be triggering and you need to take care of yourself.

LisaBri: "Paternal incest"

Dear Dad:

Thank you for being the best dad ever.

As I entered life, you could not suppress your happiness over the tiny bundle in your arms—your first and only daughter in a house that already contained two boys.

As I matured into a toddler, you held me with your strong calloused hands as I took my first steps.

As I matured to kindergarten, we both faced our fears. I experienced the insecurity of entering a new world, somewhere beyond your presence, strength and love. And you were forced to recognise even then that your little girl was growing up.

As I matured to school age, you taught me how to make friends, and gave me the gift of learning.

As I matured into puberty, you watched me move from child to budding woman and bestowed upon me the respect and responsibility that entailed.

As I matured into a teenager, you taught me about boys and dating.

As I matured to high school, you taught me to drive, having the patience for an over-zealous student. You watched me start my first job, and as I stumbled through this new responsibility, you taught me the value of a dollar.

When I graduated, you were the first on your feet, applauding the loudest.

As I matured and left your house to make a place in the world for myself, I had all the life skills you had taught and our bond became even stronger.

As I matured in life, I gave you your first grandchild and your tears of joy were felt throughout the hospital.

And as you matured, dad, into your last days, we just sat with each other; no words needed—our love had all been expressed before.

I wish this were true, dad.

Instead, why do I remember the words you spoke to me?

"It will be our little secret."

"Don't talk about it to your friends."

"Don't tell your brothers."

"Don't tell anyone at all."

"And for God's sake, don't tell your mother!"

"If you tell, I'll go to jail."

"You don't want to see your daddy in jail, now do you?"

"The whole family will suffer."

"And it will be all your fault."

"You know you're just a little tease."

"It feels good, doesn't it, honey?"

"Daddy just wants to make his little girl feel special."

Father–daughter incest. I never forgot the incest with my father. I tuned it out, dissociated parts of it out of my mind, closed off all the feelings attached, but I *never* forgot. No one can claim my memory is the result of interfering therapeutic processes.

I came from a middle-class family, well respected in our small community. No one would expect incest in my family, but it happened and not just with my father, but my two older brothers and mother. Incest has no class discrimination.

In my generation, kids were taught not to accept rides from strangers, not to accept candy from strangers. I was never taught that I could turn my father in for sexually assaulting me. The good news is that awareness of father–daughter incest is no longer a taboo. Kids today are taught that sexual assault can and does happen in the family and it is OK to tell.

Incest takes your freedom. It ruins your life. You are labelled a victim. There are hushed voices in hospital wings where you are admitted for yet another round of self-harm and suicide attempts, trying anything to release the overwhelming pain. You're damaged goods, and no one wants you. You become a shell to be abused again and again until, if you are lucky, help arrives.

Hollywood moviegoers are warned of danger by dark, menacing, terrifying music played before a scary scene. Father–daughter incest has no musical accompaniment. There is neither warning nor escape.

Why couldn't I tell? He was my father. He told me that he would go to jail if he was caught. My mother was stuck in a marriage with no visible means of support besides his income. Having this to deal with, she turned a blind eye. How can any mother not know that her husband, her daughter's father, is sexually assaulting her child? Not once. More like once or more a week.

But more damaging and, perhaps, more shocking than all, my father's sexual assaults did feel good, knowing that it was all I would get from him. I so wanted to be my daddy's little girl. If you feel embarrassed or shocked at this, let me tell you what embarrassment is really like. It's forty years later, when you still can't let go of the sexual component in order to heal. It's years of being told by therapists that in order to heal, I have to relive the feelings, hence, let go of the frozen body. So embarrassment: try sitting in your therapist's office hidden under a blanket, shaking, hoping she can't see you as you relive those sexual feelings from your father's assaults as a child.

Given this, was it my fault? Of course not. My body is like your body. When touched in such a manner, it will respond. When a potato chip is placed in the mouth it tastes like salt. Can we stop from tasting the salt? Of course not. Our bodies respond to sensations of salt in our mouth.

This doesn't take away the shame. I don't think anything ever will. Yes, I will get on with my life, rise above it, but it is there in the back of my mind ready to remind me if something in my current life brings back the memory or the feelings.

Many years later, I came to understand we all have a choice in life, growing from the roots of our childhoods. We can either take what we are given and live in the sickness and carry it on to the next generation, or we can break the patterns and change things.

Fortunately, I found my voice before it was too late. I flew back to my dad to confront him with my new found strength that needed shots of bourbon on the five-hour plane trip to his home. Emerging drunk, I found him in the airport and with my bottle of courage, I asked, "What went on between us when I was a kid, Dad?"

There was no hesitation when he replied, "Oh, it was nothing. Just some touching and things. It was no big deal."

I have spent the greater part of my adult life running from those "Don't tell" and "It was no big deal" words, fighting them, challenging them in order to be able to embrace life. I learned in 2004 from my lawyer that my dad passed away in 2002. I can't tell him I am no longer keeping his filthy, lying, sick secrets. Or what effect his behaviour had on me. But since my dad is dead, he cannot reach out from his grave and abuse his grandchildren. And I'm glad.

I miss the dad I didn't have. The dad he sometimes was, when sex was not on his mind. I didn't see enough of that dad.

* * *

One of the worst things about sexual abuse in the family is the betrayal by someone whom you needed to love you. The loving touch which every child needs has been associated with providing sexual gratification, rather than just with warmth and cuddling and closeness. And the parent whose spouse is sexually abusing a child may be angry and punish that child out of jealousy.

Incestuous families frequently carry on the behaviours to the next generation, and this happened in LisaBri's family with her older brothers, who had been involved along with her in the ritual abuse. She writes to the brother who abused her the most frequently:

LisaBri: "Sibling incest"

My memory fades back to the beginning. I am six. You enter my room whispering, "Shh! Don't tell Mum. You'll be in trouble."

When I was nine, we lived in a rural area. I had to be protected, the mother said. I could not participate in community activities unless there was someone to escort me to the event. There were "bad" people in this world, she said, and wasn't I lucky to have two older brothers who jumped at the chance to take me to my baseball and tennis games.

But I had to pay the price. As we went to swimming lessons, I remember lying in that farmer's field, cattle all around us. As you took your due, my nine-year-old brain wondered if the cows could talk and whether they would tell on us. It was no shock to me that I didn't advance to the next level with my swimming buddies. Most times I arrived late and on that occasion I didn't show up at all. Your desires were more important.

And then the games. I owed you $20,000.00 at age ten from "go-fish". It was always "double or nothing", and I never won. But that was OK, you told me, you would take it out in trade. Then there was the paper cube game (called Origami Fortune Teller Game) where I took the cube and open a flap and read what I had to do. Things like: run up and down the stairs eight times, dial a number on the phone and talk to someone unknown for thirty seconds, have intercourse with my clothes on, have intercourse with my clothes off, suck your organ, let you undress me . . . It always seemed like I received the sexual actions from those games. I now recognise I was duped.

When you were a teenager, you let me play with you and your friends, and when they scoffed at having a "girl" play with them, you told them it would be OK. I felt all grown up playing with my older brothers.

You let me help build your fort back in the woods. As I lay on the forest bed with the smell of pine needles assaulting my senses, you gang-raped me at gun-point.

One night in the grandmother's basement, my face pressed hard against the rough plaster wall, you taught me the term "bum-fuck", explaining as you did that it was a skill I would need in high school.

At age of eleven, the dance lessons began. Disco was big at the time. You had to learn your moves for the many contests you entered and won. And you had to impress the girls—so they would think what a big man you were. But you needed a dance partner, and who better than the one who serviced your needs your entire life—your sister. For the longest time I associated sex with dance since our "dancing lessons" always ended with me holding and rubbing your organ, until surely, my hand would fall off. Complaints were met with your heavy breathing—you were too far gone in your fantasy.

You insisted I wear nylons. You liked to peel them off inch by inch and savour your heightened excitement. You made me play whore to you as I stood stock still, wishing I was the tree I could see out of your bedroom window. You told me I had a beautiful body and I believed you. You chose me above all others. I was the chosen one, not remembering I was the only girl in the family.

Today, I can't dance.

Today, I can't wear nylons.

Today, people ask me why I wear a black leather jacket, long pants and black tee-shirts with short hair. Anything to make me invisible. An entity without a woman's body.

You both played football and soccer. And played well. Night after night, practice after practice, led to road games. I was forced to attend, the family making its showing of love and support.

I was proud of you and wondered what was wrong with me. No one came to my practices, my out of town games. The excitement of earning pitcher on the Rep team for the county was exciting in itself. Earning first place standing brought tears to my eyes as my team surrounded me. The tears turned to despair as slowly the field began to empty, my playmates gathered around by their families. I was alone once again.

When you purchased your first new car my feelings ran proud. My brother, the first to drive in the family. You drove me through the centre of town honking to our friends and neighbours. I recall the many days in that car, on secluded roads, as you joked about the car's gear shift getting in the way of your own gear shift, both of them with the same purpose—driving me for your pleasure.

When you married for the first time, you insisted I stand beside you, proud that your little sister was your new wife's maid of honour. I wonder how you felt that day, marrying as society deems the norm, with me, your other "wife", the one who had taken care of all your needs for so long, standing beside your new wife. Nine months later you left her, a shock to the entire family. Over drinks, you told me how your wife would not service you the way you wanted, the way your younger sister had. You said you were spoiled, and I was the one who had spoiled you. You were forced to go to prostitutes and escort agencies. Were you blaming me, I wondered. I watched your eyes brighten as we talked of your failed marriage and new sexual alliances; your tongue caressed your lips and I saw your hands reach below the table. Minutes later, the table moved and a small gasp whispered from your lips and I felt dirty, as if I had just been raped, yet you never touched me. I was twenty-four. I was still bound to you and had I not fled the city I am sure we would have resumed the "childhood sexual contact" I had been trained for by you, and I had no voice with which to speak up and say no.

Now I have to live with this body; one that responded sexually to your acts of degradation and evil. Even though I was also ritually abused, the memories of your ongoing sexual abuse have made me feel ugly and revolting. Shame and hatred of my body has led me to harm my body and attempt suicide. Sibling incest doesn't have the programmes and rituals of ritual abuse, but it is just as devastating, and it leaves the same trails of destruction behind. And it is a daily event.

In 2004, I gathered strength and with help, I filed a police report. An investigation was conducted with the conclusion that it was the "natural curiosity of children", "kids playing doctor", "It's part of growing up". The assault upon my body all those years was minimised to "childhood sexual contact". No charges were laid. When the detective who investigated my police report was questioned during a Victims Compensation Hearing, she stated, "He was out of the city and he never returned my phone call when I phoned him." The two board members representing the government just shook their heads as I paraphrased to the detective: "You are telling me that my brother who sexually assaulted me on a daily basis from the time I was six until age sixteen, was not interrogated for these crimes because he was out of town and didn't return your phone call?" Her answer: "Yes." Hell, I wouldn't have returned the call either! It sounds horrendous when placed on paper. How should any brother get away with such acts of sickness?

Any children still at risk will not be interviewed. I have spent sleepless nights and wakeful days wondering whether any nephews or nieces are being assaulted. After all, the message I received from that particular police force was: "Abusers have rights, too."

Dear brother, I am not alone. The community of survivors speaking out is increasing at an enormous rate, ensuring that abusers will no longer be able to hide behind '"childhood sexual contact". And when that day comes, dear brother, I will be the first in line to protect the next generation.

* * *

The worst of LisaBri's abuse in the family was by her mother. Sexual abuse by mothers is thought to be rare, but in my experience it is common in families who are involved in ritually abusive cults, whether their children are boys or girls. LisaBri's story about her mother reflects not just incestuous abuse, but the devastation of emotional abandonment by the one person we all expect to be there for us.

LisaBri: "Maternal incest and emotional abandonment"

My brain stops. All functioning inert. Years piled with emotional abuse have taken their toll. I don't want to remember that it was my mother who broke my spirit.

My gait is a half-hearted attempt to walk. I don't want the flooding of memories to reveal that my handicap is the result of my mother's physical abuse.

My heart breaks and tears roll down my cheeks. I don't want to remember abandonment by my mother.

My mind recoils and my stomach lurches. I don't want to remember childhood sexual abuse by my mother.

My mother and I were very close. People always commented on our relationship. Envy filled their eyes watching us interact as if we were sisters or best friends. I defended my mother to the stars. Nobody spoke ill of her around me. Then I moved away from home, put time and space behind me, and I started to remember.

She was an at-home mother, giving up her potential career to bring up her children. I went to her for everything: the time I fell and cracked open my knee, all the times she made me a soft boiled egg in an eggcup when I returned home early from school with cramps, the time I went to her confused over what to do with my life. These are the things a mother should respond to with care, love, nurturing and understanding. And she did. At times.

I thought she and I were very close, but I did wonder why I hated to be in the same room with her, or why I would flinch when she touched me. I discovered that the "closeness" with her which I once thought came from me was actually from a single part inside me, Lise. This realisation shocked me. I would never let anyone call me Lise. Except my mother. I had hit people, yelled and screamed at them, told them my name was Lisa not Lise, and if they expected to keep their teeth they would remember my real name. This violence against innocent people calling me a common nickname seemed a little harsh—I should have known.

In our small rural community, where everyone knew my mother, she took extreme measures to prove no favouritism towards me as the only girl in the family. She often iterated, "I brought you into this world, I can take you out just as easily." When most kids were scheming to find ways to stay home from school, my mother snatched me from school, leaving us the privacy of the empty house.

The times of love shared with my mother are overshadowed by abuse. Many times I came home from school, work or an outing and held on to the doorknob leading into the house thinking, "God, please let her be in a good mood. Let her be a mother." She would switch in a second from a happy person into a monster, ugly to the core. I have finally realised that my mother is dissociative. It is the only explanation for the mood swings, the inconsistent acts of sometimes mothering, sometimes abuse.

I endured endless fits of her screaming at me for things like not staying at work when I came home sick. The next time when I fought through sickness to stay at work, I was brow-beaten for not having the common sense to come home. When my best friend died, I wanted comfort and an outlet for my grief. All my other friends had found places to grieve. Hoping for a shoulder to cry on, I went to mum and was humiliated for my apparent lack of strength to endure this small tragedy. I never went to her again. The message became very clear—my mother couldn't give me the love I had desperately craved.

Eventually, after I became aware of my inner parts, Lise told me of ongoing sexual abuse by my mother involving giving and receiving fondling, inserting objects into the vagina and oral sex. Throughout all of this, Lise loved her mother. The body responded to pleasure and Lise wanted to give this back to her. It was the only way she could gain her mother's love and affection. At other times, the body was tortured from her mother's assaults. Once, in the long grass field behind the house, Lise was left bleeding and in shock after the mother rammed and twisted a carving knife into her vagina. After such vicious and brutal sex my mother told Lise that she made her do it, and that she was "dirty and bad". Because of this, I have deep feelings of shame, humiliation, and disgust. Consequently, I have never had any sexual relationship other than childhood sexual abuse and rape as a young adult.

My mother was the High Priestess in the Satanic cult I was forced to participate in. From age five, I was trained to continue on in her footsteps. There was a simulated surgery in which my mother's brain was supposedly transplanted inside my head. In another simulated operation at the age of seven, fake ears were attached to my real ears and the same done to my mother who (we were told) would hear everything we thought or said, and any action we took to reveal the abusers. It was my mother who took me to the pornography studio and to the dentist who pretended to cut the tongues out of the little girls who had to take part in the pornography.

Most likely my ritual abuse was generational. She had no therapist and if I thought speaking out about childhood abuses was taboo in the twenty-first century, I can only imagine the pressure she was under to not speak of the horrors done to her growing up. Yet, she had the same choice as me, and she could have chosen not to pass on what was done to her, regardless of the time period.

I have not seen my mother for over twenty-five years, nor do I wish to. She continues to exert her power by sending others to bring me to her. All her attempts have failed and will continue to do so. She is old and will die soon. Perhaps, this is the one act of kindness she will ever give to me, Lise, and the other parts of me who lived with her: the physical freedom to live our life our own way, knowing she can't touch us.

* * *

Emotional and physical abuse—the minefield

Many of the organised abuse survivors that I know have grown up in families where not only incest, but also emotional and physical abuse were the norm. In fact, two clients' near-death experiences (see Chapter Twenty, "Overcoming spiritual abuse") occurred after severe beatings by their mothers. Perhaps the strain of parenting while involved in violent perpetrator groups taxes a parent's personality system to the point that he or she can't "hold it together", and attacks the children. Survivors report living in a "minefield" in which small actions can lead to violent repercussions by their parents, particularly mothers. The constant threat of violence erupting poisons the entire home atmosphere. The children become scapegoats for all the unbearable emotions erupting inside their parents, who are themselves multiple.

Children learn to be wary and to watch their parents closely to see whether they are close to the breaking point when they will break out into physical violence. Often they develop parts who become their parent's care-takers, soothing and placating the parent to prevent that parent's emotions from breaking through and causing violence, or comforting the parent after such an incident.

Emotional and verbal attacks diminish the children's self-esteem hugely. It is very hard to forget words which are repeatedly thrown at you, not just swear words, but attacks on your character, physical appearance, and intelligence. I know one survivor who is very physically disabled, but will not stop working and accept a disability pension because her violent mother constantly called her lazy when her physical injuries prevented her from doing housework properly.

Family members who are multiple

LisaBri is now aware that her mother is multiple. Her mother had some external parts who presented to the neighbours and community as normal and caring, but she also had other parts who came out at home and were violently abusive, as well as parts who were active in the cult.

Not all multiple mothers abuse their children, of course. If you are a mother or a father, and are dissociative, it does not mean that you have abused or will abuse your children. Multiples, like everyone else, come in all kinds. Some engage in violence on their own (without being forced to by other perpetrators) and some do not.

One of my early DID clients, "Jennifer", severely abused by her mother, recognised her mother's multiplicity when she wrote this Mother's Day poem:

> M is for the many times you hurt me.
> O is for your orders to obey.
> T is for the trust I've never had.
> H is for the hope that it would stop.
> E is for the evil that's within you.
> Oh Mummy that I love, I wish you would Remember.

What is life like when you are multiple, and your parent is also multiple? You switch in tandem. You put out whatever part of you is necessary to deal with the particular part of your parent who is out at that moment. This means that the little girl who loves her mummy is unaware that her mother has abused her. And the child who underwent the abuse is unaware that her mother has a caring side. In public, as a child, you can only access the parts of you who have had positive experiences with your parents. So, you cannot tell anyone what your parents are doing to you, not just because of threats, but because you are genuinely unaware of it.

Jennifer had no idea her mother was an abuser when I first saw her. She wrote the poem after she became aware, both that her mother had abused her, and that her mother was multiple. She also recognised that her everyday "mother" had no idea of the things that her mother's other parts had done to her children. There are abusive parents who genuinely believe they are innocent, because they do not remember the abuse they perpetrated. They might be genuinely outraged, and accuse their children (and their children's therapists) of making things up. If you remember abuse, and have parents like this, recognise that they might not be just lying, they might really not remember. One client of mine confronted her father, who said, "I hope I didn't do it." What a peculiar response. He was probably aware that he had periods of time he could not account for.

Survivor therapist Arauna Morgan writes,

> My mother's participation was literally not to know. When family came and abused us, her job was just to make sure that they didn't kill us; later her job was just to be oblivious to anything that happened to us. Some of my younger clients told me their mothers turned into "zombies". I think this is a very accurate description.

Internal mothers and fathers

Some multiples have internal representations of their parents inside. I discovered that Jennifer did. I asked to speak to her mother. She replied, "Just a minute, I'll go and get her." She went out to my waiting room and came back—as her mother. When she later drew a map of her personality system, I discovered that she had within her not only each of her family members, but that these insiders were themselves multiple, having within them copies of her actual family members' insiders.

I do not know how common this is. What I do know is that if you hear a voice that says it is one of your family members, it is not. It is some child part of you who believes itself to be that parent or sibling. Or, possibly, it is some other insider replaying a "tape" of something that family member used to say to you. You can recognise this by the fact that it always says the same thing.

Betrayal trauma

Psychologist Jennifer Freyd wrote a book titled *Betrayal Trauma,* in which she argues that one reason people do not remember much childhood trauma is because it involves significant betrayal by care-givers. A child needs to rely on her parent or other care-giver for food, shelter, love, even life. In order to keep trusting that person, she needs to see that person as trustworthy. So, she dissociates the awareness of any abuse by that person. Many survivors of incest or other forms of childhood abuse dissociate the memories (usually into inside parts of them) in order that they will not recognise the betrayal. This inability to recognise the abuse means that survivors can be vulnerable to ongoing abuse. Adah Sachs has written about this in an article entitled "Still being hurt" (2013).

It is very hard to come to terms with the fact that your loved ones, the people who were supposed to care for you, abused you (and, in some cases, could be still abusing you). It takes time. It involves considerable grief.

Note, of course, that your not remembering abuse by your parents does not mean that they abused you! But it also does not mean that they did not abuse you.

Do you talk with family members about the abuse?

This is a difficult and complicated question. In some families, the original perpetrator group has dissolved, and the present generation is no longer engaging in the abuse. In such cases, it might be safe to spend time with your siblings—though it is wise to be careful how much you disclose to them about what you have remembered, in case some of them are still in contact with perpetrators.

If you are pretty sure your family members are no longer involved with the abuser group, and your higher-up insiders confirm this, it might be safe for you to remain in contact with your family of origin and attend family gatherings. This way, you will retain some semblance of family. But even this can be difficult. One survivor knows her siblings are safe to be around, but is very frustrated by the fact that she is the only one of them who remembers the things that happened, and that when she confronted her father about abusing her, one of her older brothers supported him. The family gatherings have superficial happiness, but they gloss over what really went on in their childhood. This survivor keeps an ongoing relationship with her sister but finds it too difficult to have much contact with those siblings who forget or deny her reality.

If family members are still involved with a perpetrator group, your talking about your memories is likely to alert the group that you are remembering, and they will take steps to stop you. Survivor therapist Arauna Morgan writes,

> My experience with asking siblings or family members is very bad; not only does the family get triggered but the cult is immediately brought in to stop the remembering. I have found that individuals are grudgingly allowed to get free and remember, but where the whole family is stirred up, there can be drastic consequences for disturbing the whole unit. You can't tell if it is safe to ask until you do; I had no idea that I would get the reactions that I did! If someone is just recovering these memories and either confronts a parent, still active or not, and/or brings charges against them before recovering enough memories to gather the evidence they need, then there could be big problems.

Arauna's parents were only minimally involved in the perpetrator group, which was led by distant relatives, and since the time when she tried talking with family members about the abuse, the cult leaders have become ill and are no longer capable of the reprisals which they could once perform. She knows that her whole family is dissociative, and she writes,

> For me, a big consideration was: what kind of relationship would I like with my parents now, and what am I willing to let go of to have that? I chose to leave the past behind, as far as confronting and talking about the past, so that I could have a healthy relationship (if you disregard what happened in the past) with my parents now. This has been exceedingly hard for me, but in order to forgive what has happened, it has forced me to look at generational family dynamics, DID family dynamics and cult family dynamics. I know that neither parent was inherently cruel and each dealt with family in the context of themselves having experienced extreme abuse as children and adults. I choose to teach my family now how to be a functional family.

If you make this choice, it means giving up on getting your family members to remember and validate your experiences, in favour of keeping the few good things in the present. Even if the abuse and group involvement have ended, usually those family members are in denial (and probably do not remember) about what happened, and it is very difficult to be around people who were present but will not acknowledge the abuse or the depth of your pain. How can you forgive something that has never been acknowledged? Even though Arauna has chosen to remain in contact with her family, she has chosen not to talk about the abuse with them. Talk about the "elephant in the room". But at least she has some semblance of family.

Furthermore, it is only safe to have this kind of contact with family members if you know that they are no longer involved in a perpetrator group. Can you be sure of this? Only if you know your entire personality system well enough that your insiders would tell you if they had such contact.

Arauna's is (in my opinion) an unusual situation. Most of my survivor clients had parents and siblings who engaged in horrendous abuses, not just during group activities but on their own, even if they were multiple and did not remember those things. It is just not safe for these survivors to be around them.

Ongoing risks from perpetrator family members

The programme which one of my early clients labelled "Return for Hallmark™ holidays" requires you to see your family of origin on family birthdays, Christmas, Halloween, Easter, Thanksgiving, and other such dates, the times when most ordinary people get together with their families. Those are the times when you and your children are most at risk if your family is still involved in an organised perpetrator group, because they will expect you to continue your involvement, and to make sure your children are properly programmed. They will take advantage of these innocent-seeming family gatherings to access you and your children.

If your family continues to be with an organised perpetrator group, they will naturally expect you—and your children—to remain involved, too. If the group has already discarded you, perhaps all they will require of you is that you keep the secrets. But if you were not discarded, it will be very difficult for you to spend time with your family of origin without being abused, reprogrammed, and forced to perpetrate. And the scariest thing about this is that you might not remember this happening, since this is done to child insiders who are not supposed to let the main adult know it is going on.

Cult groups, and other mind control perpetrators, arrange marriages. They select spouses on the basis of genetic abilities and predispositions, and belonging to the "right" race or genetic grouping. Sometimes, they select spouses who will not be involved in the group but will bring in the genetic qualities they want in the children. At other times they select spouses whose families of origin are also involved. That way, they continue to control you in adulthood. They might even choose a generational cult spouse for you as punishment.

Those who grow up in such groups are expected to participate in the training (which means abuse) of their own children and grandchildren. If they refuse to do so, a trainer may take over or may force them to take part. The groups work hard to break the parent–child bond, taking a child away from the mother if the bond is becoming too strong, making her abuse her own child (by a threat to kill the child if she does not abuse), or impersonating her and abusing the child. One young mind control survivor began to get his abuse memories just before the birth of his first child, remembering having his father teach him that if he had a child, he had to suffocate it whenever it cried.

Teresa, one of my first ritual abuse survivor clients, courageously and selflessly gave her daughter up for adoption when the child was five, when some of her inside parts realised they could not protect the little girl from abuse. Teresa grieved for years, but she did the right thing. After the child was gone, the cult group had nothing to hold over her, and she could do her healing work.

If you have already raised children while involved in a perpetrator group, you have the most agonising experience of all: seeing your own children become perpetrators, and pass the abuse and involvement on to your grandchildren. You remember trying to love your children, and you see what they have become, and what they continue to do. Sometimes you have to recognise how little you can do to save them, or their children, at this point.

If you have specific memories of the grandchildren being abused you can report these, and if those children can be made safe for long enough that they feel able to tell what has happened, they can be taken from the abuser parents. I knew a stepfather who worked hard on raising ritually abused children and keeping them from their real cult-involved father. I knew a grandmother who rescued her grandson from his ritually abusing mother, and got him into a safe foster home. But often those children will not tell because of fear of themselves or their non-abuser relatives being killed, so reports of abuse fail. A foster mother once said to me, "If a child says that daddy touched her pee-pee, the authorities take it seriously and remove that child. But if the child says daddy and mummy and granny and grandpa went out into the woods with some other people and sang strange songs and had sex with everyone and killed a dog, the authorities think that child is making things up." Sad, but often too true.

Severing ties

What can you do if your family of origin is still involved in an abuser group? Most such survivors I know who are in recovery have moved a long distance away from that family, and severed ties. In some cases they maintain superficial contact through cards and phone calls, but are alert to triggers and the presence of reporting insiders, making sure the reporters tell the family nothing of significance.

In most cases, they have just completely cut off contact. In some such cases, perpetrators have travelled across the continent to find them and programme them back to loyalty, but if this does not work, the abusers cannot afford to keep doing it. They have jobs and families and lives, so they are likely to write off the distant survivor, as long as they are not getting evidence that the person is disclosing their secrets. It is very helpful for a survivor who is cutting off contact to have a non-offender and non-survivor spouse or roommate, for safety. The person is not likely to be harmed, as the abuser groups place a priority on not being seen or noticed.

You need to consider your options carefully. I cannot advise you on what to do.

Dealing with the loss

Whether or not you maintain superficial contact, the reality is that if your family members are or were perpetrators, you have to grieve. You need to grieve both the past and the present, as well as the future you cannot have with a supportive family. Regarding the past, it is what they did not provide for you—nurturing, attunement, safety, encouragement, all those things which a family is supposed to provide for a child and a young adult.

Your child parts hold the unfulfilled longings. Recently, I was for the first time with a very ill child part of a client of mine. She peered up at me and said, "I don't want to imagine you." She believed me to be just a figment of her imagination. When she was being abused and neglected, she had imagined a woman coming to rescue her and comfort her, but no one had come. Now, forty years later, this child part needed both to experience my real presence and to allow the sadness to come out, the sadness she had felt when no one came.

Regarding the present, there is the experience of being an orphan, without parents or siblings, or even aunts or cousins. If you have children, they do not have grandparents, at least on your side of the family. When other people get together for Thanksgiving dinners, you know that you cannot get together with your own extended family, because they are dangerous. You do not get to see your siblings' children grow up. If they are being abused, you know you can do nothing about it. They would not tell the truth to the authorities if you reported that you suspect abuse. They would probably get punished just for being questioned, and it would alert the abusers to the fact that you were talking, and put you (and your present family, if you have one) at risk. If your children grew up in the perpetrator group, they are also a risk to you, and seeing your own grandchildren puts you at risk both for being abused and for being forced to abuse them.

There is a hollow loneliness for the disconnected survivor, especially at the times when other families are celebrating their togetherness. You might feel you are all alone, on your own in the world, as if you do not belong here.

Grief is hard. It comes and goes in waves, even though it is always there. You just have to ride the waves, and allow yourself and your insiders to experience the grief of all you have lost.

It is important to comfort yourself as best you can. Here are some ways survivors can comfort themselves:

you can rock yourself;
sit by the fire;
stroke yourself;
eat a small bit of chocolate;

take a walk in nature;
a bath with Epsom salts;
tell yourself how much you love yourself;
be proud of yourself;
do something nice for someone else;
read a novel;
do work with your hands;
clean a counter;
pet your own or someone else's dog;
talk with a calming friend if you have one;
have a small glass of wine;
cook a healthy meal;
make a contribution to charity.

Pets

One very comforting relationship almost anyone can have is with a pet. Even if your abuse included rape or physical attack by animals, you know the animals were coerced to do it; it is not their real nature. If you saw pets killed, you know this was done because it is so natural to love a pet, and for a pet to love you. You can have this loving relationship again even if you do not have any family. Pets love you no matter what, they do not engage you in arguments, they just cuddle up.

Here are a few quotations about pets, taken from www.paralumun.com/catquotes.htm and www.brainyquote.com/quotes/keywords/dogs.html.

Dogs and philosophers do the greatest good, and get the fewest rewards. (Diogenes)

What greater gift than the love of a cat. (Charles Dickens)

Histories are more full of examples of the fidelity of dogs than of friends. (Alexander Pope)

A cat has absolute honesty. (Ernest Hemingway)

Dogs never bit me. Just humans. (Marilyn Monroe)

The smallest feline is a masterpiece. (Leonardo da Vinci)

Dogs are not our whole life, but they make our lives whole. (Roger Caras)

There are many intelligent species in the universe. They are all owned by cats. (Anonymous)

Dogs are my favorite people. (Richard Dean Anderson)

I got rid of my husband. The cat was allergic. (Anonymous)

If dogs could talk, it would take a lot of the fun out of owning one. (Andy Rooney)

The cat is the only animal which accepts the comforts but rejects the bondage of domesticity. (F. A. Paradis de Moncrif)

> If I have any beliefs about immortality, it is that certain dogs I have known will go to heaven, and very, very few persons. (James Thurber)

Even if you are unable to have a healthy relationship with your family of origin, you can, I hope, build other relationships, with a partner or supportive friends, to partially make up for it. Chapter Eighteen, "Succeeding in friendships and relationships", is an introduction to relationship skills. With a pet, you do not even need these skills; you just need to be kind, and provide it with the food, comfort, and exercise it needs. It will reward you with love and devotion.

Parenting

I could write a whole book on this topic. In fact, I did, along with my friend Dr Allison Rees. (Two books, which you can order from www.lifeseminars.com.) *Sidestepping the Power Struggle: A Manual for Effective Parenting* (2006) covers understanding children's temperament, developmental stages, why they behave as they do, and healthy ways to manage their behaviour. *The Parent–Child Connection: A Guide for Effective Family Living* (2008) covers the parent–child bond, handling emotions, healthy families, boundaries, and communication skills, specifically with children. Although I have given you plenty of tips in this book, you probably need to learn much more if you come from a very dysfunctional family, as most survivors do. One ritual abuse survivor client had several children after completing her healing from the abuse. Her parents were both cult-involved and very abusive. I was delighted with how tuned in she was to her children, and how she knew them each as an individual. I asked her how she learnt to be such a great parent, and with a smile, she answered "From a book." I was flattered when I realised she meant our books.

You do need to be careful which parenting books and courses you choose. Some approaches to parenting treat children as if they are animals to be trained to obey and produce appropriate behaviours on cue. You probably grew up with an extreme version of this, at least during the mind control training, and when this same approach comes in a milder version (without torture), you might not recognise it as unhealthy, but it is. Children are living creatures who grow when given the healthy resources they need; they are not meant to be made into what their parents think they should be.

I would like to mention some particular dangers for parents who are survivors in the following sections.

Recognising when children trigger you

I remember one woman who attended my parenting course years ago. She confessed to me that when her children left messes, she became enraged, and yelled and screamed at them and even hit them. I asked her what had happened if she left a mess as a child. Her face went white, and she said, very slowly, "My dad . . . would get out . . . the whip." The sight of a mess left by a child triggered huge anxiety in her, and the anger was a protective response to that enormous anxiety. She had to get rid of the mess at all costs, because her inner child, living in the past, was terrified that her father would come and punish her. As well, she had probably believed that her father's response to her normal childish messiness was appropriate, which it was not.

If you find yourself triggered into feeling like mistreating your children, you need to flee the scene and take time out while you work out what is going on inside you. You cannot help being triggered, but you can take charge of what you do when it happens. You can go into a room and close the door for a few minutes. You can ask someone else to take care of your children while you calm down. You can walk around the block if your children are old enough to be left. You need to make sure that your insiders' reactions do not lead you to be abusive to your children in any way, including verbally. Cruel words stay in a child's mind long after the physical bruises are healed.

Survivor therapist Arauna Morgan developed a unique solution:

> When my children were babies, the sounds of fussing and crying were very triggering. I was able to refrain from doing anything bad to them, but I was frantic about trying to find what was wrong and fix it so they would stop. At the time I had no idea why I had this reaction, but I solved it by wearing foam earplugs that shooters wear. (I worked in a high noise environment and we had to wear them at work and I realized that you can hear people talk perfectly, but they filtered out all the other noise.) It offended my husband that I wore earplugs around my kids, but my anxiety went to zero when I did and they could make all the noise they wanted!

Now, I am not suggesting that you wear earplugs whenever your children cry. They need to know that you are responsive to their expression of their needs. But as a stopgap measure, if programming is kicking in and you are in danger of hurting them, it is all right to do this kind of thing for a short time.

Overprotectiveness

Some people who were abused as children become overprotective of their own children, seeing danger everywhere. To grow up healthy and confident, children need to face surmountable challenges, and to gradually expand their control over their own lives. It is a tricky balance to recognise when your children are in genuine danger (for example, if they spend time alone with the grandparents who abused you as a child), and when they are not (for example, if they walk home from school in a safe area). If you are not sure, consult with other parents.

Danger of role reversal

Adults who are multiple have child parts inside. These children can come out, or come through the adult, and relate to other family members in child-like ways. If you have a nurturing spouse who understands the situation, this may be fine with him or her. But many spouses do not understand, and many are not capable of dealing with their partner being a child. One multiple client of mine said to me plaintively, "The little boy in me needs the adults in his life to be strong and understanding." But this man's female partner is struggling with having a new baby, and she needs him to be a strong man for her; she cannot be a mother to his inner child. For the most part, parenting of the inner children needs to be done within the personality system, not by outside people.

As for your actual outside children, it is not all right to make them into parents or older siblings for your inner children. If they have to look after you when you turn into an anxious or fearful child, this is placing a burden on them that will delay and interfere with their emotional development. You might have friends with whom you can be a child, but this should not happen with your own children. Sometimes, you can play with children and your inner children can enjoy the play and even contribute to it, but you should not allow them to take over completely, as they are still children and might not understand such issues as safety.

You can learn to be an effective parent, but you might need to work at it.

Exercise 25. Facing the facts about your family

Each question in this exercise might cause you to grieve. Take it very slowly, meditating on each question, and allowing your emotions to be felt and your insiders to express themselves about it. Stop and take a break if it is too much for you. This can be devastating material.

Do you believe that one or both of your parents was involved in the organised perpetrator group that abused you? Why? Would you say that your parents are innocent of the abuse, one parent was involved, or both parents were involved?

If, after communicating with all your parts, you are sure that a parent or sibling is innocent, what is your relationship with them like? Are you able to talk with them about what happened to you? Would it help to try, or would it damage your relationship?

Was your family incestuous? Who in your family had sexual contact with you? At what ages?

If there was sexual abuse within your family (apart from the organised abuse), how do you believe it has affected you?

Did you live in a "minefield" at home, where physical and emotional abuse was likely to explode from one or both parents?

If so, do you have parts who have the primary memories of this, or who adapted to a violent parent? How did they adapt? Do you have parts who were your parents' care-takers?

What words do you or your parts remember being hurled at you when a parent was violently angry with you? Do you believe what your parent said about you? What can you do to disprove what that parent said?

What positive things did your mother provide for you during your childhood? What should she have provided but didn't? Allow your insiders to express their grief about her.

What positive things did your father provide for you during your childhood? What should he have provided but did not? Allow your insiders to express their grief about him.

What positive things did your siblings provide for you during your childhood? What should they have provided but did not? Allow your insiders to express their grief about them.

Were any of your family members dissociative or multiple? What makes you think so? What are they like on the outside (in the regular world), and what parts have you seen in private? Do the parts of them that deal with regular life have awareness of what the other parts have done?

Do you have ongoing contact with your family of origin? If so, what do your insiders remember about this contact? Have you been safe? Will you be safe in the future if you maintain contact with this family? Why or why not?

(*continued*)

If you have a partner, is that person part of the perpetrator group, or an outsider? If an outsider, to what extent can you share your experiences with him or her? Can your partner listen to your tales of your painful experiences?

Do you have a pet? If so, how does he or she enrich your life? If not, how could a pet provide companionship and comfort? Do you need to work through any memories first?

If you have children, are they safe? Do they spend time with your parents or siblings, and if they do, do you believe they are safe? Ask all your insiders about this. If your children are grown, have they been involved with the perpetrator group? Is it safe for you to spend time with them during your recovery? What could you do to protect yourself, if they have such involvement?

Is there anything you can do to protect the children of your relatives if they are at risk? If not, you might need to grieve this.

If you have children, do you switch in their presence? Are you aware of what happens when you are alone with your children? If not, ask your insiders about it, and be prepared to make some internal changes if parts of you are not behaving like loving parents.

Do you find your children looking after you or consoling you in ways a parent should do for a child? Do you know this behaviour is unfair to your children? If this happens, how can you change this dynamic so that your children can just be children and not feel they have to look after you?

Do you find that certain of your children's behaviours trigger you to rage? If this happens, what do you do about it? Are you able to take time out so that you do not become emotionally or physically abusive?

For each behaviour of a child that makes you angry, identify what in your own childhood may be behind your overreaction. Plan to work through these memories.

Are you overprotective with your children because of what happened to you? (This is most likely with survivors whose abuse happened apart from their families.) Consult with other parents to see whether your fearfulness is appropriate or inappropriate.

Are you underprotective and blind to other people (such as relatives or teachers) abusing your children, because you have learned to dissociate such information? Are you both over and underprotective?

CHAPTER SEVENTEEN

Healing your sexuality

I am sure this is a chapter some of you would just like to skip. Many survivors do not talk about sex with their therapists because the whole subject is embarrassing and possibly repulsive. Often the front person knows little or nothing about sex, and does not recognise or acknowledge sexual feelings.

This is just a book, and you are reading it alone, not telling anyone else what you are thinking or feeling. So you do not have to be embarrassed—I cannot read your mind! I know that just mentioning some things might trigger shame, feelings of humiliation, and possibly flashbacks. It is also possible that reading this could arouse sexual urges and fantasies, even violent ones. It is important that your inner leaders find a way to manage your emotions and behaviour as you read. This might mean deciding who inside should read this, and who should not.

Sexuality, like pain and emotions, is actually a good thing that abusers have distorted for their own purposes. I am including this chapter to give you hope, because it is possible to heal your sexuality, no matter how badly it has been damaged. Meredith Sharman's story later in the chapter shows how.

Many years ago E. Sue Blume wrote *Secret Survivors: Uncovering Incest and its Aftereffects in Women*. Although at that time she was unaware of the particular sexual violations involved in mind control and ritual abuse, much of what she wrote is still relevant. Every survivor (male or female) of these abuses has experienced extreme kinds of sexual abuse, and this has had a profound effect on his or her sexuality.

Blume wrote a moving passage about how sexuality should ideally develop. If you have a male body, please change the gender:

> A baby girl touches her genitals because the touching *feels good*. She *chooses* whether, when, and how to touch her body. It is within her control. But for many women—not just incest survivors—

> this moment of sexual self-determination is soon eroded. In an ideal scenario, as the child begins sexual exploration, she chooses as her partners other children, whose bodies and personalities are like hers developmentally. She touches and is touched; she learns what gives pleasure and what does not. Later, her sexual experiments become more focused, progressing from the joys of holding hands to more overtly sexual activities. She learns to distinguish friendly kissing from sexual kissing, affectionate feelings from sexual desires. She experiences kissing, deep kissing, necking, petting, and finally intercourse or other intense, genitally based activities whose purpose is orgasm.
>
> Step by step, she learns which sexual activities she enjoys and which she does not; she decides when she wants to pursue a certain sex act and with whom. And she decides when to lose her virginity. (In an ideal world, this decision is hers, and not the result of pressure or date rape.) She learns to value her body and its sexual expression, to engage in sexual activity for her own pleasure and (maybe) for bonding with a partner. And she learns that this is hers, this experience of sexuality, to do with as she wishes. (Blume, 1991, p. 205)

Somehow, I doubt that this is your experience. It is not the experience of most people, particularly women and girls. Blume states (p. 207) that "the primary message incest sends is that the victim's sexual life is not her own". Nowhere is this more true than in mind control and ritual abuse.

Not only have survivors experienced sexual abuse by relatives at home, they have almost all been forcibly involved in child prostitution and pornography, and often the sexual experiences they have had to endure, and the sexual skills they have been forced to learn, involve not only gang rapes and sadism and masochism, but also pairing sexual arousal with extreme violence, sex with animals, sex with dead bodies, and killing. Some children have inside parts who have been taught to abuse younger children.

How does a child endure having to go through such things? Only through dissociation; it would be unbearable for a single mind. The abuser groups, including those who specialise in child prostitution and child pornography (including the violent kinds), train children through manipulation of their insiders.

Every sexual training experience involves some parts who experience sexual pleasure, and others who at the same time experience physical or emotional pain, either their own or the pain of others who are being abused. These two kinds of parts are both present for the experiences without being aware of one another. So, for example, masochistic parts feel sexual pleasure while pain is being administered to their body, but do not actually feel the pain, which is held in another part of the system. Similarly, perpetrator parts do not feel the pain of the other person being harmed, and sexual abuser parts might even believe the child they are abusing is enjoying the experience, because they are disconnected from the insiders who hold their capacity for empathy. All this is deliberately designed by the perpetrator groups. They use sexual stimulant drugs and pain-killing drugs to train children to enjoy pain. Some parts are taught to need pain in order to achieve sexual release, and they feel this pain as pleasure.

Besides dissociation, there is also pretence. Children forced to be involved in prostitution and pornography have parts who are good actors or actresses; they have to be, under threat of extreme violence or death. Do not assume that your child parts necessarily enjoy what they say they enjoy.

One thing I find horrifying and disgusting is the fact that the groups who produce and sell child pornography, and who train and sell child prostitutes, produce their own market. Some of the children they have trained and used grow up and become their customers, their sexual responses having been trained to be connected to children and to violence.

I am not going to dwell any further on the details of these abuses. What you have gone through is for you to discover through inner communication. You do need to know, however, that if you find yourself having disturbing sexual thoughts or feelings, those are probably a result of what you have been through, and not the natural, organic you.

I am also not going to repeat all the excellent descriptions of what sexual abuse survivors go through, or all the excellent advice given to them, which is in other books such as *Secret Survivors* (Blume, 1991) and *The Courage to Heal* (Bass & Davis, 1988). I encourage you to read these books. I am just going to talk about specific problems related to the warped sexuality practised by many mind-controlling groups, including, in particular, organised crime, and some ways you can deal with these problems.

What your parts learnt about sex

When a child is brutally raped, he or she learns to fear any physical approach to his or her genitals, or anus, or mouth. When a child is taught to perform particular sexual acts to please "customers", but never to become attached to those customers, he or she learns to be a good actor, but never to be truly present during sex, and that he or she is valued only for sexuality, not for intelligence or kindness or any other quality. When a child has to provide sexual gratification to a parent's needy young parts (in a parent's adult body), he or she learns that the only way to have any intimacy, physical contact, or closeness is to meet the other person's sexual needs, at his or her own expense. When a child has been sexually stimulated and brought to orgasm while being violently abused, or watching someone else be violently abused (in person or on film), he or she learns that sex is inevitably connected with violence, or is the only way not to be killed.

When a person has experienced mind-controlling abuse by an organised group, he or she has probably experienced all these things. As a result this person has insiders representing each of these different attitudes to sex and insiders who are angry about it all, viewing anyone with a sexual or romantic interest in the person as an abuser. This can make it very difficult for a survivor to develop a relationship with a sincere romantic partner.

Regardless of the type of abuses you have experienced, the core of your learning is eloquently expressed by Blume (1991, p. 208):

> The incested child or adolescent . . . learns that the purpose of her sexuality is the gratification of the other person. She learns that she cannot control what sex acts she becomes involved in, that her body does not yield sexual pleasure, but shame, embarrassment, pain, entrapment, and betrayal: ultimately, she learns that sex is dirty.

So probably the most important new learning you need is that your body is your own, and only you should be in charge of what it experiences.

Learning to accept the body you have

Many women who have been sexually abused hate having female bodies, believing that only girls get abused. When they are old enough to menstruate, they might hate having breasts and having periods, especially if their abuse started at puberty—or if it ended at puberty, they might be glad.

Male insiders in female bodies hate the fact that their bodies are female; they, too, often believe that only girls get abused (which is actually not true).

Do your insiders see themselves as having different bodies from the front person? My experience is that many insiders in the survivors I have met believe they are still children or teenagers, see one another with bodies of that age in the inside world, and have difficulty accepting that the "old" body they now inhabit is really theirs. They also frequently believe their body to be the opposite gender from what it actually is. I often hear "What happened to my body?" and "How did I get this body? It isn't mine!"

There are many reasons why a girl may want to believe she is a boy. Although Western society has made some changes recently, girls have always had a harder time being recognised for their abilities and allowed to pursue their interests. I tried deciding to be a boy when I was seven years old, as I saw the future of girls being housewifery, a career I did not want. I disguised my appearance as best I could, hiding my hair inside a cap and rubbing dirt on my face when I went out to play. Eventually, in my twenties, I decided that I would not have been given my abilities and interests, along with my female body, unless it was all right for me to follow these abilities and interests and be myself, regardless of what kind of body I had. I have a client, a man in his seventies, who has inside him a girl, who chose to be a girl because he was a creative, artistic, and physically small man born into a rough, tough fishing family who valued only traditional masculinity. He is not gay.

If a girl is being sexually abused on an ongoing basis by a man or men, she might believe it would not happen if she were a boy, so parts of her could split off who imagine themselves to be boys. If a boy is being sexually abused by a man or men, the parts of him who endure the abuse might imagine themselves to be girls or women, because they feel it is less humiliating.

Mind controlling abusers assign gender to parts of you, regardless of the gender of the body. They might tell the "soldier" parts that they are boys or men even if the body is a girl. They also make internal copies of abusers, and these parts believe they are whatever the abuser is—usually a man or a woman.

Parts in women whose abusers told them they were boys or men see themselves as boys or men, complete with penises. This is especially true if they were made to wear a strap-on vinyl penis for pornography. Parts in male survivors who were told they were female might believe their anus is a vagina.

All this confusion often leaks through to the front person. I do not know what proportion of people who are looking for gender reassignment surgery do actually have hormones which belong to the other gender, and what proportion have had child abuse experiences which lead parts of them to very badly need to be the other gender.

If you have a strong urge to be the other gender, it would be wise to talk with your insiders and discover who feels this most strongly, and why. If you are multiple, a big decision such as gender reassignment should only be made with the agreement of all your major insiders. Do not allow a few panicky parts of you push you into something you might regret later when you have gone further in your recovery process.

Figuring out your sexual orientation

There is more and more scientific evidence that genuine homosexuality or heterosexuality, or possibly bisexuality, is inborn, and cannot be changed by social pressure or child abuse. There is, however, also evidence that if a person's earliest sexual arousal and gratification is paired with certain stimuli, these stimuli can continue to produce sexual arousal for that person. So, as a survivor, you have both your inborn sexual orientation, and the experiences that for your insiders may have been linked to sexual feelings, producing arousal—or revulsion—or both. If the sexually responsive parts of your body were touched in an arousing way, they would have responded, regardless of who or what touched them. That does not mean your own natural sexuality is orientated towards whoever or whatever touched those parts. If a girl, for example, knows that her body is about to be violated by a woman, she might produce lubrication in order to ease the situation, but this does not mean she is a lesbian.

You might be confused about your sexual orientation because not only do you have opposite-sex parts inside, you also have parts who believe they are gay or lesbian, as well as parts (most commonly the front people) who believe they are either straight or completely asexual (having no interest in or desire for sex). What are you to do about this?

First of all, talk with your insiders about why they believe themselves to be male or female, and why they believe themselves to be heterosexual or homosexual. Some insiders in a woman might see themselves as lesbian when they are really just afraid of penises because these have been used to hurt them; they need to learn that some men (and their penises) can be gentle and kind. As Blume says, "A woman who hates men because she was molested by a man does not gain the capacity to be aroused by women". This is true for male as well as female survivors; being molested by a man does not make a boy gay, but it also does not turn a genuinely gay boy into a heterosexual man.

You might be surprised at what you find out from your insiders. One heterosexual male survivor was extremely embarrassed and humiliated because he had insiders who kept urging him to have sex with men he met. When he talked with these inner teenage boys, he discovered that they had been forced to perform sexual acts with men in order to earn the reward of sex with a woman. They were not gay; they believed that the only way they would ever get to be with a woman was by having sex with a man.

Although it is thought that the vast majority of adults who molest both female and male children are men, in the Satanic and Luciferian cults and in the organised criminal groups, it is common that children are molested by women as well as by men, often in violent ways, but sometimes as the only experience of relatively gentle touch which the child has experienced. No wonder survivors are confused about their sexuality. Survivors who come out as lesbian and then remember abuse by females become especially devastated.

Sometimes, survivors of abuse by men believe that women will be different. I have known several survivors who made friends in the lesbian community without being at all sure about their own sexuality, only to feel extreme social pressure to "come out" as lesbians. One survivor moved in with a woman who said she loved her, and had no idea that this meant they would have sex. The partner became abusive when she tried to resist.

What is a natural sexual orientation? It appears that some people are attracted only or primarily to the opposite sex, some to the same sex, and some to the person regardless of their gender.

How do you figure out your own genuine sexual orientation, given all the confusing experiences you have had? I would say, cautiously. Do not rush into identifying yourself in any specific way. Learn to notice your own and your other parts' emotional responses to different kinds of people and different acts. Resist social pressures to define yourself the way other people want you to be. Be careful of translating the desire to be held as a sexual preference, or the desire to at last have the love of a certain parent as a sexual preference.

Dealing with sexual acting out

This is not a problem for all survivors, but it is for some. Many survivors have some insiders who, either on their own or through influencing the front person, engage in sexual behaviours that could get them into trouble. Some are compulsively seductive. Some engage in impersonal, "promiscuous" sex with strangers. Some work as prostitutes, strippers, and porn actresses, using the training given them by the perpetrator group. They might rationalise, "I may as well make money from it." Some use their sexuality as power, or for revenge against men. Some try to sexualise all their relationships. Some might be involved in sadomasochistic relationships or groups such as whipping clubs.

There are also private problematic sexual behaviours, such as self-harm, which bring on sexual arousal, and addiction to violent pornography or child pornography. I have seen these behaviours more often, but not exclusively, in male survivors.

Before you judge these parts of you too harshly, talk with them. Find out what they know about why they do these things. Some behaviours may be programmed: for example, attempts to seduce therapists, attempts to get pregnant, and sexual self-harm. Sometimes, the abuser groups continue to use adult survivors for prostitution or for seduction and political spying. Do not assume all this behaviour is spontaneous. Find out whether any parts of you are still being used in some way, and if so, have your internal leaders talk with them about how they might plan an escape.

Many survivors have inner child parts who assume that every adult wants to have sex with them. One such part made me an offer, and when I declined, saying I do not have sex with children, that part was indignant—"Why not? That's what kids are *for*." He (a male part in a female survivor) did not understand why it made me sad that he actually felt rejected by me when I refused sex.

Your inside children do not necessarily want what they say they want. For example, an abuser told a little girl that if she did not pull his hand towards her genital area, he would hurt her there. So she did what he said. Then he told her that the fact she pulled his hand to her body meant that she "wanted it". All she wanted was not to be hurt.

As I mentioned earlier, some survivors also have insiders who use sex for revenge, and a way to have power and to express anger. All survivors have plenty of buried anger—but it would be better to aim it at your abusers, not at anyone who attempts to have a sexual relationship with you. There are many innocent people for whom sex is an expression of affection as well as attraction. Although some paedophiles do look for single mothers in order to abuse their children, more men have no interest at all in having sex with a child.

Working out your sexual values

When your body has been used as a sexual commodity, it is tempting to just write off sex as meaningless and perhaps evil. Or the opposite—to believe that your sexuality is the only thing about you which has value, so you need to maintain that value by being seductive or even by earning your living through it.

What do you really believe about sex, its purpose, its value? Many people who have not been used sexually regard it as an expression of emotional intimacy. Whether they confine it to marriage, or believe in "polyamory" (loving more than one person), they associate it with love and committed caring for persons with whom you have a deep relationship.

Other people believe that sex is just an enjoyable physical experience, and consenting adults can do whatever they feel like doing. This is also a valid moral stance, as long as your sexual partners have the same belief. Too often, a person who enjoys casual sex takes advantage of another person who believes sex belongs in a committed relationship.

Some people believe that BDSM (bondage, domination, sadism, and masochism) is all right between consenting adults. BDSM groups try to govern themselves by ethical standards. I have a problem with their ethics, because of what I know about dissociation. What exactly is consent between adults, when the front person consents to experience sexual enjoyment through pain without being aware that a child insider is bearing the pain? By abusing children sadistically, and coupling this violence with sexual arousal and orgasm, organised perpetrator groups produce survivors who are attracted to the violent pornography they produce or who continue to participate in sadomasochistic activities as adults.

You might have some insiders whose sexual responses are connected with pain, or with harming others, with young children, or even with animals or dead bodies. This is not your true nature. These conditioned responses come from what was done to you in childhood, when your body was made to respond while you were giving or receiving pain, or coupled with another child, an animal, or a dead body.

If you have parts who have been made to be sexually attracted to children, they may mistakenly believe that children enjoy having sex with adults. This is because little children in perpetrator groups are trained to fake enjoyment. Let me tell you loud and clear: children do not want sex with adults. They want attention, caring, and closeness, and often even cuddling, but not sex.

I have seen survivors who become sexually aroused while harming their own bodies. This is a programme, taught in childhood. If this happens to you, you need to say "No" to the behaviour and make sure that you work through any memories of this training.

Many survivors have sexual fantasies that are actually representations of their memories of abuse. Every human being has sexual hormones that lead to sexual responses. People in whom sexual release has been linked with cruel or bizarre practices by abusers may have parts who believe they need to do these things in order to have an orgasm. Rather than focusing on the shame and degradation of what these parts want, you can educate them about what makes an orgasm happen, explaining that these learned behaviours are not necessary. One male survivor used to torture himself anally. He had to teach those parts of him who did it to discover his penis and see that it could respond sexually without any need for torture.

Sexual fantasies are one way of finding out what happened to you sexually. You are not actually harming anyone when you are having a fantasy. But you do not have to spend time dwelling on the fantasies in the process of discovering what was done to you. And, of course, you cannot act on any harmful fantasies. Doing harm to people (even with apparent consent), including yourself, doing harm to animals, having sex with children, and violating the dead are behaviours which I find hard to justify in any situation. If you did these things, it was because the perpetrator group forced you to make a choice of the lesser of two evils. Some survivors might turn to pornography because it resembles their victimisation experiences. If you purchase such films, you should realise that you are aiding the perpetrator groups to continue to abuse people to make money. You also have to be careful that your fantasies do not become addictions, which take the place of developing real relationships with real people.

How do you begin to deal with the violent and perverted sexual desires which some of your parts might have? You can develop your own values about sex, based on treating other people the way you wish you had been treated. Your internal leaders can insist that all parts of you live by those values, even though some may want to do otherwise. To truly heal those desires, however, you need to work through the memories that created them. There is no way around this. And the good news is—it works!

Sexual avoidance and celibacy/chastity

In my experience, it is common that a survivor's front people (and other parts as well) have little or no interest in sex, especially if those parts remember being sexually abused. Sex for such parts is simply being used for someone else's gratification, and has never been an expression of love, or caring, or mutual enjoyment. If all your parts were that way, you could probably be fairly contented without any sexual relationships, and some survivors seem to manage this, perhaps suppressing those of their parts who hold the sexual feelings. I have seen more than one incest survivor who is not gay but has knowingly married a gay person in order to avoid sex. Their partner is their good friend, or their household management partner, but sex is not expected.

Sex, when it has not been interfered with, is actually a good thing. Sexual attraction brings together people who will make healthy children. It can create close bonds. Because your abusers perverted sex, you do not have to omit it permanently from your life. But you need to restore it to its rightful place in your life.

Blume writes (1991, p. 229):

> For many incest survivors, the only safety can be found in saying no to sex entirely. At the same time, she may or may not want to cuddle, be naked, or share affection in other, nonsexual ways. ... The incest survivor may feel guilty (for not giving her partner what she feels he wants) or

> cheated (of her own sexual birthright) or angry (at men who want her to satisfy them). She may want closeness, though not sex, and may not see the difference. She may be afraid she must sacrifice closeness to say no to sex, or she may discover that there hasn't been any closeness except sex. The partner also suffers from this aftereffect, especially the most caring partners.

Blume suggests that many incest survivors need a period of choosing chastity. Then "After she is free of sex (and violation), she can journey through the adolescent tasks of developing sexuality that she was robbed of by her early abuse". Ellen Bass and Laura Davis, in *The Courage to Heal* (1988), suggest "time out from sex", then beginning with making love to yourself. I shall let you read those other books to get more of an idea of what this means. Essentially, it is reclaiming your body and your own sexual responses by touching the sexual areas of your body lovingly and allowing yourself to respond in safety, discovering that sex can involve pleasure without pain or violence. See whether you can stay in your body while being touched, knowing that the touch is not abuse.

If you have a sexual partner

If you are in a relationship with a spouse or partner who wants sexual relations, you probably need to face the question of sexual healing, at least for your partner's sake. This is especially true if your partner sees sexual relations as an expression of deep intimacy, which is the opposite of your own past experience.

What happens to survivors when they have sex with a partner? Some "space out", trying not to be present. Some find that child parts of them come out during sex because these are the parts who had to go through their sexual abuse experiences. The partner suddenly finds that he or she is making sexual love to a child—possibly a very experienced child, but also possibly a terrified and traumatised child. Some survivors suddenly switch from sexually greedy and enthusiastic parts, who initiate sex, to parts who hate sex and experience it as rape. One male client of mine who was married to a survivor told me about how confusing it was for him to believe he was making love to his wife, and have "some other woman" get up out of bed and walk away without any awareness of who he was or what had been happening.

Many survivors find that sex brings on flashbacks, or "emotional flashbacks" of strong feelings of revulsion or anger. One partner of a male survivor reported that although the sex itself seemed fine, her survivor husband would go into a very angry state right afterward, and become emotionally and physically abusive to her.

Developing your healthy sexuality

I know I am repeating myself here, but sex can be a normal, healthy part of life for an adult. This might be hard to believe after the experiences you have had. So, if you want to, you can reintroduce sex into your life gradually. Meredith did this in stages, beginning alone, then with a safe and supportive partner. At one point, she recognised that she was allowing herself to be used for sex when she did not want it, and she corrected this by refusing when she did not feel like it. The final stage, for her, was allowing sex to be connected with love for her partner, as the parts of her who had been sexually used (in child pornography and prostitution) had been taught that they should never love a "customer" (that is, a sexual partner).

The reality is that you, like everyone else, are a sexual being. You have hormones. If your body is female, you have (or had) a monthly cycle and you might feel sexual desires particularly at certain times of the month. You might find yourself sexually attracted to certain people, and you might find yourself aroused by the sight of certain types of bodies. This is not shameful, it is normal humanity, the way nature ensures the survival of our species. If you are not ready to be in a sexual relationship, you still may need to acknowledge your sexuality. Jen Callow (see her section in Chapter Twelve) found a creative way to deal with this by giving her sexual inside parts loving sexual partners. Other people learn that it is all right to masturbate, as long as you are not being violent to yourself. For one thing, it can provide a release of tension.

The Courage to Heal, as well as other books for sexual abuse survivors, has many practical suggestions for various stages of healing. I suggest you consult those other books.

Steve Frankel has developed a method of helping survivors develop their healthy sexuality, as follows.

1. Find out if there are any insiders who were not personally involved in sexuality. Rather, their jobs may have involved other aspects of abuse and functioning, but not sexuality directly.
2. Ask if any of those insiders would be willing to try to develop sexual functioning and interest. If any agree, have them try sexuality out for a while, seeing if they can explore the body's sexuality alone or in a safe relationship.
3. If they are able to do this, and only once they have been able to do it for a while, then address the trauma-sexualised parts' feelings about sex. These parts are then free to withdraw from sexuality completely without impairing your whole person's sexual functioning.

This is a practical solution for survivors who are in a relationship and want to make their partners happy. However, it cements your splitting, meaning that you have to stay split indefinitely, or at least until you work through the memories of sexual trauma. This is only worth doing if you truly love your partner, and if making love to you is for that partner an expression of intimate connection, rather just using you as a sexual object.

Pregnancies

You might have heard that cults make teenage girls pregnant, deliver the babies prematurely but late enough that they will be born alive, then sacrifice them. Is it true? It appears so, judging from the experience of survivors who have remembered. In the Satanic and Luciferian groups, it appears to be a standard practice to sacrifice the firstborn as the "child of Satan". The supposedly "Christian" ritually abusing cults also sacrifice babies on Christian holidays (Christmas and Easter). Certain teenage girls are selected to be "breeders", to give birth over and over again only to have their babies taken from them for the cult's purposes, either for immediate sacrifice, for being kept as an unregistered child and sacrificed later, for trade with other groups, or for sale. Breeder girls are given hormones to bring on premature puberty so that they can provide babies for sacrifice or sale.

According to what I have been told, traditional organised crime is also in the business of breeding babies, sometimes with particular genetic characteristics, for adoption. Some survivors have memories of being kept in brothels where abusers impregnate them, deliver their babies, and then take those babies away.

This is a source of much grief if it is remembered. Regular-life pregnancies can bring back memories of prior pregnancies and of what happened to the babies. Bereaved mothers always carry the pain in their hearts.

Perpetrator groups also use children and babies to control survivors: a mother with a child can be controlled by threats to that child. There is programming for certain insiders to want desperately to be pregnant, to have a baby to love. These parts do not recognise the reason why they want a baby so much. Mothers whose children are being accessed by perpetrator groups are often only vaguely aware of this fact, though they might be aware of the threat of harm to the children if they leave the group or make disclosures about it.

So, even the sacred experiences of giving birth to a child and nurturing him or her have been contaminated by the evil of groups who see babies as sacrifices or as commodities to be sold, and see women as commodities and as baby-making machines.

Is it even possible to heal your sexuality? It does take courage. Many survivors do not even try.

Meredith Sharman (a pseudonym to ensure her safety) is one courageous survivor who has pursued full healing, including healing of her sexuality. Here is her own story of her healing process.

Meredith Sharman: "My sexual healing process"

Some people say you can never get over sexual abuse. They're wrong. Some people say it takes a lifetime to heal. They are wrong, too. You yourself might find healing and enjoying a healthy sex life unimaginable, but if you are reading this book, you have at least a glimmer of hope for improvement. You have to start with at least a little bit of hope. It is possible to heal; it is possible to be whole and healthy, and it's possible to do it in a reasonable amount of time. There may be permanent scars, but even they will fade over time. These healed scars are insignificant compared to the festering sores that keep you up at night and prevent any semblance of a healthy relationship.

The things that happened to me left me with problems in virtually every area of personal functioning, but much of that was hidden because my real life and the "other life" were fairly neatly segregated—dissociated from each other, with experiences divided up into a very large number of inside parts. That was before the walls started to crumble when I was seventeen. It's a bit hard to remember now which part knew what or did what when. They are all me now. I did it all and I experienced it all, the good and the bad. There was a lot more bad. While there was a wide variety of types of abuse and damage, here I am going to focus on healing my sexuality.

Therapy

The first thing that happened on my road to recovery was that I fell apart completely. I was at boarding school and went home most weekends. I spent those weekends cycling to the library to read diagnostic books to try to find out what was wrong with me. I began experiencing flashbacks and nightmares. I became withdrawn and had difficulty sorting out the past from the present or even working out what was real. There were voices in my head, lost time, and feeling like a stranger was running my life. The structures and systems that had kept me so organised and controlled for nearly eighteen years were beginning to crumble and the external me, who knew only normal life, could not cope with the floods of horror scenes in my head. Some of this deterioration was fuelled by physical health problems and some of it by the recognition that this was an opportunity—possibly the last—to get out.

At some point in this personal disaster, I worked out that there were different "parts" of me and started to label and map them in my journal. At the end of the school year, I had a total breakdown and ended up in the psych ward diagnosed with a psychotic break. This, plus some involvement with the criminal justice system which will be detailed later, led to psychotherapy and therapeutic foster care.

I was optimistic about therapy from the start. I expected my therapist to be able to help me and I figured then that it could not take longer to undo the damage than it took to do it. I got better comparatively quickly, in about four years for the bulk of it. This is not because the abuse was mild—at least, I don't think it was—it is because of several factors that made things more straightforward or faster for me. Other people may take longer, but with a supportive guide (probably a professional therapist), motivation, and a willingness to face some of the scariest things in your life, it won't take forever. One of the factors that helped was that I was young and at first had no responsibilities. Several people told me they wish they had done their work when they were my age. I hated hearing that. Now that I'm their age, I suppose I see their point. It is easier when you don't have children, a job, a marriage or various other complications. It's a lot easier when you don't have to worry about maintaining functioning day to day and keeping things under wraps so no one suspects how really screwed up you are. Still, I spent my transition to adulthood with only professionals to care for me and trying to get away from that crazy mixed-up life, figure out who I was, and learn to be independent all at the same time. It was hard. I felt as if I had lost my entire life. In some ways I did. It was worth losing, but still, I have regrets.

In therapy, I learnt more about my personality system and how it worked. I learned about dissociation and how dissociating protected me from events I couldn't cope with, but may have outlived its usefulness. I learned to process memories of abuse by going to a nice place with all the parts who had pieces of it. We would talk through it, put it together and then put it away where it was allowed to blend and fade like any other memory. And that's what we did every week for four years.

Being a victim

From very early in life, I was used and abused sexually by everyone in my family—my parents and my brother. My older brother had been taught by others that having sex with me was the right thing to do. For the most part, I enjoyed these interactions. He didn't have to really force me into it; he bribed me with good feelings. Sometimes he got too forceful and wouldn't stop even if I didn't want it or it hurt. I didn't know there was anything to be ashamed of. I guess I was too young and oblivious. I stayed oblivious for a long time. We knew it was a family secret, but not why.

As we got older, things got more complicated. From later childhood, my brother was "selling" me to his friends for sex. I saw little or none of the profit from this, but I went along with it because I was fearful of him and didn't know there was any other option. I felt exploited, but still possibly not as horrified as it seems now that I should have been.

I also remembered things about being hurt, including being hurt by a group of people. They taught me to do as I was told for the men and the filmmakers, and they taught me to associate sex with both pleasure and pain. It was too much for me as a little kid to cope with all that, so I went away. But I couldn't really go unconscious at will, so there was part of me left behind even when "I" wasn't there and that part experienced things and got overwhelmed just as the first me had and she went away as well and then there was another. Dissociation. Lots of it. So I never had much idea of what was what when I was living my life and I was never too surprised when some new weird thing happened. These events were planned and organised to train me to dissociate in certain ways and to respond to cues without conscious awareness.

It turned out that my brother was not my first or only pimp. The same thing was being promoted by my mother from a much earlier age. As a small child, I learnt to take on various roles mainly with men, who were surely paying considerable sums for my services. I could do a great act. I could be a sexy young vixen or an innocent victim or anything in between, so long as it was what the man wanted. I was trained to make them feel pleasure and that their approval of me was the most important thing. I was terrified of the customer being dissatisfied in any way because the consequences for me would be severe, even torture. I was taught to put away the pain the men caused me by dissociating it. Another part of me was always bearing the pain somehow, but for those parts that remained "out" and were successful at pleasing the men, this experience made them feel loved and valued. Some parts thought sex was the only possible way anything good could ever happen. True love, however, was banned. If I developed a true affection for one of my abusers, that could cause him to do things he shouldn't, like try to steal me. The interaction had to remain detached at the same time as intimate and passionate. A hard juggling act for a young child, but perfectly suited to dissociation.

I wasn't just prostituted, I was also used in child pornography very early in life. These events, the acts, and the training that led to them caused me to mix up pleasure, pain, love and exploitation. They gave me long-term drives to hurt or be hurt in sexual interaction or play.

Being an offender

My breakdown when I was seventeen was in part a release of long held secrets. Among the first to surface was that between the ages of nine and fifteen I had been sexually abusing my little brother. I did the same type of things to some boys that I babysat, although not as much. I never threatened them and I always tried to make them feel good too, to pay them back for using them and to make them less likely to report it. But I knew it was wrong even though I could not quite understand how something that felt good and didn't scare them could be harmful.

Two months before I turned eighteen, I confessed to my doctor about what I had been doing to my brother. Part of the reason was that I had decided to tell on myself so that I would be tried as a juvenile. I was also tired of the constant threat that at any time our mum could find out. I had tried to tell her a few times, but she didn't get the hint. I thought she knew at one point, but it turned out that was when she found out that he had been molested by a friend of the family. So eventually I told on myself. I went to court and pleaded guilty, against my lawyer's advice. I was given the strongest non-custodial sentence they could. Actually, it was longer than they were allowed, but it included mandated therapy, which was probably the point.

The first step in therapy to make sure I didn't hurt little boys any more was to make me not feel like doing it. This was achieved in the short term by the parts of me who remembered what it felt like to be abused sharing the memories with those who felt like abusing others. This gave me enough empathy for my victims to prevent me acting on any impulses I had to do it. The next step was to put together all the parts of the memories that made me into an abuser. First, we had to find out why I was sexually attracted to younger children. One of the origins went back to what I had been doing with my older brother. After having sex with me from as early as I could remember, my older brother, in turn, introduced me to sexual activity with our younger brother. There was more of a power differential there because the age difference was much greater, and I think this is important. This is why I consider what I did with my younger brother to be abuse whereas it is a bit more ambiguous with my older brother, who was closer to my age.

Processing the memories was a lengthy and stressful process that involved recounting and then briefly reliving every aspect of the memory before putting it away, integrated and whole. At the same time, sometimes the parts involved would integrate if there was no longer any reason for them to be separate. In the end, when the memories were together, I didn't feel like abusing boys any more. Even if the thought crossed my mind, it was just a thought and not a drive.

Pregnancy

As pregnancy is a natural outcome of sex, and involves a lot of invasiveness by medical staff in otherwise private body parts, I think coping with pregnancy and birth is relevant to my sexual healing. When I was being abused as an adolescent I became pregnant a number of times. Most of the babies were forcibly aborted before they could survive, although at least two of them were born alive. One of them lived for years and was then killed in my presence. These experiences left deep scars and made me fret about the impact of having any more, but I desperately wanted children.

My first was conceived under unusual circumstances. The group that had abused me as a child continued to do so whenever they could catch me, and tried to get me to return to them. When I was twenty they decided they wanted me to have a baby so they could manipulate me better. By triggering scripts that had been implanted a long time before, they made me seek out a man to father a child. It didn't matter who he was, as long as he wouldn't be involved. So I found someone through the personal ads in the newspaper. When we met, I lied and told him I was on birth control. When we went back to his house and things were heating up, I switched to an inside part who did not want to have sex with a stranger and tried to get away, but he forced me to continue. It only took once. When I told people I was pregnant, it was hard to explain who the father was or why I'd gone and got pregnant as a young woman on my own with no partner or family. Although I had been manipulated into getting pregnant, I was happy because I had already wanted a baby for years.

The pregnancy gave me very strong motivation to get completely free from my family and to put the past behind me. I didn't want it negatively affecting my child. I worked harder than ever in therapy and on my own outside of sessions and put together all the memories and inside parts we could find at that time until I was whole and together.

I had the usual prenatal care, including quite a few internal examinations. I must have endured those by dissociating. As the birth approached, I became afraid of how I would manage the pain and whether I would end up dissociated and either acting in a way that would make them take my baby away, or simply missing the whole experience. So I decided in advance on a number of things that should help me stay present and focused—a picture, music, key words—and I decided that I wanted an epidural as soon as they were willing to give me one, to keep the pain from getting to an unbearable level. My baby was induced at one week overdue, perfect and healthy. One and a half years later I had a mental health crisis, including self-injury, and she was taken away by social services, but after two years of waiting for a court date and then fighting for her in court, I got her back. Several witnesses, including those from social services, said that I was a loving mother with good parenting skills who always put my daughter first. Also through the process of the court case, I had external acknowledgement by the judge that I really had been abused by a group of people. This helped with my acceptance of my past and moving on with my life.

I had two more children with my now ex-husband and then a further two with my current partner. At certain points in all the pregnancies I would struggle for a while when they got to the point when one of the earlier babies would have been terminated, but I got through that with support from my partner.

So I now have five children, from an almost grown teenager down to a not yet one-year-old baby. All are doing well, none have been abused to my knowledge, nor have they more than the vaguest hint that there was anything amiss about my past. I have made a conscious decision not to keep secrets or deny events from their own histories, but there is no need to burden them with my story. My eldest knows that she was in foster care for a while, but takes that in her stride as just part of her own history. The only thing they ask about is why they don't have any relatives on my side, and I still struggle to come up with honest answers to that.

Relationships

After beginning to remember all these nasty things, I went off sex altogether. I found it an embarrassing topic to discuss with my psychologist, especially when it was about real world current issues rather than about being abused as a child. So I did a lot of the healing necessary to go from "solo only" to sex with someone else on my own. To some extent this was processing more memories by myself, but it was also a process of coming to terms with what had happened to me and deciding that it didn't have to affect everything about me for the rest of my life. I know that some therapists wouldn't recommend it or even believe it it is possible, but for me sometimes the best way to get over something is to just steel myself and blast right through as if it isn't there. I have been through so much, I'm sure I can tolerate a bit of anxiety. Once I have tolerated the discomfort of doing something I find scary or uncomfortable, it does not get such a big reaction the next time, and even smaller the next. Eventually, I can do the thing I was once terrified of just as if it isn't a problem.

By the end of this process, I didn't have a therapist and mostly didn't need one. First, I had a boyfriend who was so gentle and slow and uncertain that he was the ultimate in non-threatening and gave me plenty of time and space to be the boss. That's just what I needed. We did quite a bit of fondling and hand jobs and not so much full on intercourse. Next, I got another boyfriend whom I eventually married and divorced. He was rather more enthusiastic with plenty of initiative. He was the first man I lived with. We went through some tough times together when things from the past would bubble up again and we had to endure it and put it away again. On many occasions, he convinced or coerced me to have sex with him when I didn't really want to. I was so used to being used, I just allowed this one more situation for that to happen.

Finally, I found my current partner. I had an eight-year crush on him online before I finally professed my feelings for him and found they were reciprocated. He surprised me by never forcing himself on me in the slightest. If I wasn't in the mood, even if it was just because I was tired, he would stop and back off, maybe altogether or maybe just to cuddling, depending what I wanted. With him it was possible to have physical affection that didn't always lead to sex. This sort of respect for me and my body was something I had never experienced. It shed new light on the behaviour of my ex.

Things were a bit tumultuous at the beginning, to say the least, but he was kind and patient with any issues I churned up for him. There were times when I would have a wave of past issues and I would become afraid of him, confuse him with an abuser, or act as if he was going to hurt me. This hurt him, but he stayed by me at whatever distance I was comfortable with, and talked me back into the present, reminding me that I was with a man I loved and would never be hurt like that again.

Long after I thought everything was resolved (again) I had the emergence of another inside part. This one was a child who loved sex. She wanted to please and pleasure men and put some considerable effort into doing so for my partner. He was torn about the ethics of allowing a part who thought she was a child to have sex with him, but together we decided that as it was really me, an adult, it was acceptable. Others could decide differently if a similar thing happened to them. It would have been okay with me if he decided he wasn't comfortable with it and wanted to call out an adult any time she appeared. But to be frank, even the best man isn't going to go out of his way to avoid a good blow-job. This is something I had never really been able to do before, and I suddenly wanted to do it all the time because that was this part's speciality.

When that child part began to feel true affection and love for my partner, she became terrified. I was flooded with frightening memories and she was interfering with my ability to function in day-to-day life. That young part had been taught that if she loved any man she was supposed to be pleasing in the child prostitution scheme, she would be tortured or even killed. She was also helping to maintain a dissociative separation between "me" and all the events of my past. With the help of my old therapist from fifteen years ago consulting by phone, my partner helped me to process the relevant memories, and to take sole ownership of my life. It was arduous, but worth it in the end. I am now truly whole and I know that "the other life" (the bad things) is also "my life", even if it's not constantly in the forefront of my mind now.

The final inside part became part of the whole that is me now. I retained some of the sexual interest and skill that I previously had not had access to when they were dissociated. I have not had any further issues since except for the occasional bad memory briefly resurfacing.

Where am I now?

Far away. Over a decade ago, after therapy and getting my daughter back from foster care, I moved thousands of kilometres to another country to live with my now ex-husband. Often, such moves are an attempt to run away from unresolved issues and problems, but in my case those things were as resolved as I could get them living under the oppressive cloud of my past. I was able to leave behind my past and its legacy, the fear of being recontacted by the people who abused me, my psychiatric records, and the contamination my mum had left everywhere by telling churches, community groups and anyone else she could that I was a sexual predator.

I have a loving partner. Ironically, I think that some things that made our relationship work in the beginning are no longer quite as good now that I am a little too stable and not needy enough. We are boring and a bit bored and intolerant. Yet one of the things that does work, surprisingly, is our sex life. There's a lack of frequency, but that probably comes from too many babies and hormonal birth control. Our physical intimacy is working. I don't cry or feel bad. I don't feel taken advantage of. I respond. He responds. We trust each other. There is no force or coercion. No instances of "I really don't want to but . . ." Occasionally, I will go along with it even when not totally into it, but I am freely choosing to do that as a gift to my partner, to make him happy, but not in a submissive way. The only thing still very quirky about me would be some of the thoughts I find arousing. They are not things I would talk about with anyone and they would not be possible to carry out, which I wouldn't anyway.

With the exception of my partner and my ex, no one in my current life knows the extent of what happened to me. I like it that way. It's not relevant any more and I do not want it to be part of my identity.

The person who asked me to write this is hoping that it will give hope to others. If my story is anything to go by, you can hope that one day you have a mundane yet enjoyable, stable yet sufficiently exciting sex life. You can hope to have children who grow up with healthy natural sexuality. You can hope to get rid of compulsions to act on desires you don't want to have and to keep the ones you do. You can work out what your genuine sexual orientation may be. This can be so confusing when you're multiple. I don't think there's any particular reason to have a goal to integrate. My goal was to heal and for me integration was a side effect of that, but maybe it doesn't have to be.

Where am I now? Here. In normal life. I hope you can join me one day.

* * *

Steps in sexual healing

There are many things you can learn from Meredith's story. The stages of her sexual healing included:

- getting to know her personality system;
- accessing her history of sexual victimisation;
- facing up to her history of sexual perpetration;
- having victim parts share their feelings with perpetrator parts (This was a turning point for Meredith.);
- working through all the memories of victim and perpetrator parts;
- dealing with her history of "breeder" pregnancies;
- exploring solo sex;
- noticing and permitting unusual arousing thoughts or fantasies without acting on them in inappropriate ways;
- sex with a kind and non-threatening partner who had patience;
- learning not to allow herself to be used;
- giving sexual parts permission to love her sexual partner without fear and dread;
- allowing herself sexual enjoyment—and tolerating boredom—with this partner.

You might notice that the first few stages involve internal work to access her personality system and sexual memories. The last few stages involve sexual behaviours in the real world.

Finding your sexually experienced insiders

Very often, the front person is embarrassed and ashamed about sex, so he or she might not want to acknowledge that there are insiders with sexual experiences and training, especially if some of this was of a distorted and perverse nature. If you look at the very beginning of this chapter, you will see a brief description of some of the kinds of sexual experiences which mind-controlled or ritually abused children are forced to endure. If you have had any of these experiences (which, unfortunately, is likely), you will have insiders who went through them.

If your body was made to feel sexual arousal, pleasure or satisfaction during any of these experiences, you will have insiders who felt these sensations. Just as you would taste a strawberry if it were placed on your tongue, you would experience sexual feelings if your genitals were stimulated in certain ways, whether or not you wanted to. You might feel ashamed of this, but it is perfectly natural. It simply means that the body was working the way it was designed to work.

If you were being hurt during sexual experiences (including not only pain but choking or other forms of violence), you will have insiders who hold that pain and discomfort, and who consequently hate anything to do with sex. If other people or animals were being hurt during those experiences, you will have insiders who hold their pain empathically.

All these parts will eventually need to co-operate in the sharing of the memories, if your sexuality is to be healed. And, initially, they will have very different attitudes about sex. It is important not to argue with one another about this, but to accept all parts as having had different experiences that shaped their outlooks.

Perhaps you can have some objective insider make a list of who inside has what kind of sexual experiences and desires. Then you can prioritise your sexual healing work according to what things are most important to change.

Preventing sexual perpetration

You might not want to know whether you have sexual perpetrator parts. Not knowing will not make these parts magically disappear. If you have them, it is wisest to know it, or at least for your inner leaders to know it, so that you can address the problem.

Meredith entered therapy when she began to remember sexually abusing her little brother. She was unaware of all the training that had led to this, but she was aware that some of her parts still wanted to engage in it. Before she could work through all the memories, she needed a stopgap measure to make sure no part of her would act on those impulses again. So, her inner system leaders decided to ask the parts who had been sexually abused to share their feelings about it with the abuser parts. This was unpleasant for the abuser parts, but forced them to recognise that being sexually abused was not really a pleasurable experience for a child, even if that child pretended to enjoy it.

Most sexual perpetration for survivors of mind control and ritual abuse happens either at rituals or in the home. I have been told that cult-involved parents are told they must sexually abuse their children, or their children will be killed, and the children's reporter parts are interrogated to make sure this is happening. At rituals, sexual orgies often involve violence. So, if these things are still happening in your life, your priority must be to end your (and your children's) current contact with the perpetrator group.

Working through traumatic and training memories

You cannot fully heal sexually without working through the memories. These include memories of "spontaneous" abuse in the home, rapes in rituals, and the sexual training of your parts who were supposed to perform sexually and/or to become offenders. These are very difficult memories for the front person to face, but you deal with them no differently from the way you deal with any other kinds of traumatic memories. Some people are too embarrassed to do this work with a therapist, and choose to do it on their own, although that can be very difficult. Other people find the presence of a safe person whom they know will take it in his or her stride reassuring.

Full sexual healing is not the highest priority for survivors of mind control and ritual abuse. As long as you are not acting on impulses or fantasies that could harm yourself or other people, you might decide to work on other things before you tackle sexual healing.

Be aware, however, that working through the memories brings relief for those of your insiders who have been stuck in these memories for years. You might want to have compassion for them and free them by processing their memories rather than just leaving them shut down.

Exercise 26. What needs healing in your sexuality?

This may be a difficult exercise, and you may want to keep the results private. Your answers to these questions can guide you to which insiders you need to work with, and what kind of memories you might need to work through.

Does your front person (or persons) want to avoid sexuality altogether? If so, does this create any difficulties in your life, or does it make things easier?

(continued)

Do you have opposite-gendered insiders? Does this have anything to do with their sexual preference, or is it more about the "masculine" or "feminine" jobs they were assigned, or names they were given?

Are you clear about your gender identity?

Are you clear about your sexual orientation? Do you have parts who are homosexual and parts who are heterosexual?

Do you have a life partner? What difficulties do you have in that relationship regarding sex?

Are you able to be sexual with yourself (your own body) without harming it or descending into shame and humiliation?

If you have sex, does it create any of the following.

- Anger?
- Feeling dirty?
- Disgust?
- Spacing out?
- Flashbacks?
- Needing to get drunk?
- Crying or feelings of grief?
- A feeling of power?
- Switching into child parts?
- Odd or violent fantasies?
- Having to please the other person regardless of what you like or dislike?
- Discovering you have sexual skills you do not remember learning?
- A feeling of being drugged?

Take a moment to stay with your emotional response to this question.

Do particular sex acts bother you? Which ones? Ask your insiders why this is.

Do you have insiders who act out sexually? What do they do? Does this create problems for the front person?

Have you been promiscuous? If so, how do you understand your promiscuity?

Have you (as an adult) been involved in the sex industry? How do your different parts feel about this?

Have you been involved with sadomasochistic groups? If so, how do your various parts feel about this?

Have you worked out your sexual ethics? In what situations is it good to have sex? What kinds of sex are permissible?

Do you have violent or abusive sexual fantasies, or fantasies which disgust you?

Do you find you or some parts of you have sexual responses to children, animals, or weird things?

Do you engage in any form of sexual self-harm, such as cutting your genitals?

Have you used religious artefacts such as crosses during sex acts?

Do you have strong negative feelings, or sexual arousal, at the sight of cameras?

Are you able to say "No" to sexual advances?

Do you respond to any romantic or sexual pursuit as if the person were an abuser?

What is triggered by your being pregnant or giving birth?

Is it difficult for you to be sexual with someone you love or for whom you feel affection?

(If you are female) have you had babies whom you were not able to keep? What are your insiders experiencing regarding this?

Your answers to any of the above questions give you clues about what your insiders have been through and what needs to be healed. If you want to proceed with this healing, your internal leaders can now make a plan regarding where to begin.

My sexual healing plan:

CHAPTER EIGHTEEN

Succeeding in friendships and relationships

Mind-controlling abusers are concerned about security, so they want their victims to keep their distance from outsiders and to be dependent on the abuser group itself for any friendships or relationships. If you have had to separate from your family in your attempts to get free from participating in an abuser group, you might find that you are living an isolated life, having difficulty getting close to and trusting people. Perhaps you wonder why.

Programming for isolation

Organised perpetrator groups indoctrinate children that safety only exists within the confines of the group, and they can never trust anyone who is not part of the "family". They tell children that people they know and like or love will always leave them and will end up hating them. They tell children that anyone who finds out about the abuse, as well as their families, will be hurt or killed. They tell children not to get attached to people, because something bad will happen to those people, sometimes because of contact with such an "evil" person as a cult child.

This group of lies, which many of your insiders may believe, includes both general training not to trust or bond with people, and specific lies to prevent you from connecting to helpers such as therapists, police officers, and medical professionals.

As with all the mind-controlling lies, scenarios are set up to "prove" the "truth" of the perpetrators' statements. For instance, a young child is asked to choose between two groups of people, one group wearing hooded black robes, the other group wearing ordinary clothes. Naturally, she chooses the people in ordinary clothes, and they assault and abuse her. She is put back in the choice situation, and chooses the robed cult members, and they pretend to welcome her with love. Years later, the adult who has that child part inside will become afraid if she begins to develop friendships with regular people outside the cult.

A worse scenario occurs when a child is paired with a "disposable" child (an unregistered child, unknown to the outside world, bred for the purpose of sacrifice). The child who will be allowed to stay alive is permitted, for the first time in his or her life, to have a friend, and then is forced to participate in the real or simulated murder of that friend. This horrible event is a basic part of the training of cult children not to make friends.

Although your front person does not consciously remember it, this indoctrination into an "upside-down" system of reality might prevent you from breaking free from the group and developing real friendships with outsiders.

Ask your insiders about what they were told and what experiences they had to make them fear getting close to people who are not part of the "family". You might find that some of them were set up with childhood experiences to make them remain fearful and isolated from people who are not part of the perpetrator group. Realise that these experiences were deceptions designed to maintain the security of the perpetrator group. While not all "outsiders" are trustworthy, many of them are trustworthy, kind, and capable of being loyal and supportive friends or partners.

Survivors' isolation is, in part, a result of this deliberate programming, but much of it is a result of your everyday experiences in childhood. Programming is a series of calculated experiences delivered to particular child parts in order to control their beliefs, behaviour, and emotions. These experiences, though they may be horrendous, only take up a relatively small proportion of a child's time. The rest of the time consists of living with your family and attending school or being around other people. This "regular life" also has a strong impact on your future relationships.

Healthy love and attunement

Parents are the most significant persons in children's lives, and the ones with whom children usually spend the most time while their personalities are being formed. Therefore, they are the most influential in building or destroying both the children's self-esteem and their basic trust in other people and in life. A close nurturing parent–child love bond is essential for a child's healthy development. Although adult relationships must set boundaries and require equal amounts of giving and taking, a baby needs unconditional love from a parent who sees, respects, and esteems the child's true self and underlying nature. This kind of love does not require that the child measure up to certain standards. It does not ask for anything in return. With such love, children become people who fulfil their true potential. The nature of that potential is, of course, different for every individual. We are meant to be different from one another, each having something unique to contribute to the world.

A baby's first care-giver, usually the mother, holds and rocks the baby, and looks into the baby's eyes. The baby is calmed by the sound of her heartbeat. When the baby gives off distress signals (cries), different ones for hunger, for anger, and for pain, mother responds to those cues and is "tuned in" to the baby's needs, and an attachment bond is formed. The bond is formed not only by physical closeness but also by *attunement*—the way in which the care-giver tunes in to the baby, understands and responds to his or her signals of need. Rather than forcing infants to be what the parent wants them to be, attuned parents sense their infants' true natures and encourage them to develop these real selves towards maturity.

A securely attached baby relies on mother to keep him safe. A bond of affection develops. As the child becomes mobile, he or she begins to explore the environment, but constantly runs back and checks on mother's availability and attentiveness. Using mother as a secure base, the infant explores the world. If there is any sign of danger, he or she runs back to mother. This happens in all animal species. The young animals who get separated from the flock because they do not have a strong attachment are the ones who get eaten by predators.

Prevention and breaking of bonds

Organised abuser groups deliberately interfere with the mother–child bond in order to make all parts of the child know that they can rely on no one to care for them. One common scenario is to have the child in distress and then have its mother walk by and ignore it. Another is the parent suffocating or hitting the child when it cries. Even before the baby is born, abusers give some mothers strong electric shocks to make them withdraw their emotional connection with their unborn children.

Once the bond with the mother has been broken or prevented from forming, the abusers try to create a bond with them. They tell children "You are only safe with us", and "We are the only ones who will want you". But, of course, the child is not safe with the group members at all. This means there are parts of the child who believe what they have been told, while other parts know that they are not safe with the abusers and have been lied to. There may be parts who are aware that their mother was forced to abandon them. But the need for someone to attach to is so basic to survival that many parts of the abused child run to the perpetrators when they feel threatened.

Psychologist Adah Sachs, in an article entitled "Still being hurt: the vicious cycle of dissociative disorders, attachment and ongoing abuse" (2013), says that "attachment" signifies

> *a survival instinct* (not an emotional longing): the young of every species instinctively holds on, follows and acts in ways that engage the adult's attention, to maintain their close contact . . . The survival of the young depends on their ability to draw the closest attentiveness from the parent that he or she has.

She says that in some cases "the deepest and most powerful engagement between the child and the attachment figure occurs during abusive acts".

A child who learns that closeness involves abuse might return to an abuser over and over again, and will most likely get into abusive relationships later in life, mistaking the focused attention of abuse for a true connection. Cults and other mind-controlling groups want their victims to maintain this kind of connection with them for life, while they deny those victims any nourishing attunement and actual safety.

Probably because of the deliberate breaking of the mother–child bond, survivor therapist Arauna Morgan's experience was that her own and other cult involved families were distant and dismissive:

> Children are mostly left to their own devices; they are expected to comfort themselves, siblings are allowed to 'work things out,' and can do anything they want to each other that does not result in blood on the rug or furniture (bleeding outside or in the bathroom is fine) and does not result in questions from people at school that cannot be easily answered. Children do their chores and if in a middle class family, they also do their homework with no adult supervision. Children do not interfere in the affairs of the adults and do not ask questions about what the adults may be doing. There may be occasions when the adults are interactive, but this is so rare that it is viewed with suspicion by the children and the adults pretend they act that way always. Adults will tell other adults that they are aware of the things their children do and the children will agree with them, even though they know their parents have no idea of what happens in the home, even while the adults are there.

Contradictory parenting

A survivor of mind control and/or ritual abuse knows by painful experience that not all parents are properly attuned to their children. I have heard the most horrendous stories from my ritually abused clients regarding the kind of parenting they experienced. Ongoing bad parenting was in addition to the deliberate controlled abuse in the formal training of their inside parts. Parents who are members of these abuser groups are usually dissociative themselves, and often have sadistic parts who come out in the privacy of the home and abuse their children physically, emotionally, and sexually. And parents who truly love their children may be required to sexually and physically abuse them, believing that the alternative is having them killed.

The parents' contradictory behaviours lead to the child developing spontaneous insiders whose purpose is to deal with the different parental states—some apparently loving and trusting, others fearful, and others care-givers for the parents. These splits are in addition to the deliberately created splits made by the perpetrator group.

Adult results of early attachments

The nature of a person's early attachments affects his later attachments to friends, partners, and children, and even pets, and his capacity to love and be loved. Attachment researchers believe that much mental illness and psychopathology result from disturbed attachment in childhood.

Although its primary importance is in infancy, attachment theorists believe that the "attachment system" continues throughout life: people of all ages regain a sense of security when they are anxious, afraid, ill, or tired, by establishing contact with someone they love and trust. The extent to which they love and trust other people and themselves depends on their attachment history, beginning with that all-important first attachment in their infancy.

Parents, peers, siblings, friends, and sexual partners may all operate as attachment figures over a person's lifespan. Most adult love relationships include the same defining features as infant–mother attachment: a desire for closeness, especially under stress, a sense of security which comes from contact, and distress or protest when threatened with loss or separation. Sue Johnson, the founder of Emotionally Focused Therapy for Couples, believes that adults' ability to have secure intimate relationships depends on their capacity to form interpersonal connections, which in turn depends on their early experiences with parents.

Psychologist Kim Bartholomew has studied attachment styles in adults, and has divided people into four categories, as shown in Table 1.

The people in the first two columns (secure and preoccupied) have a positive view of other people, while the people in the second two (dismissing and fearful) have a negative view of other people; they do not trust easily. The people in the first and third columns (secure and dismissing) have a positive image of themselves—they like themselves, while the people in the second and fourth columns (preoccupied and fearful) have a negative view of themselves—low self-esteem.

Bartholomew writes of the preoccupied category: "Children who experience inconsistent and insensitive parenting, especially if accompanied by messages of parental devotion, may conclude that their own unworthiness explains any lack of love on the caregiver's part" (Griffin & Bartholomew, 1994, p. 431: see Bartholomew's writings at www.sfu.ca/psyc/faculty/bartholomew/research/publications/attachment.htm). She says that these people will be overly dependent, and have "an insatiable desire to gain others' approval and a deep-seated feeling of unworthiness".

Of the fearful category, she writes, "Rejected children would tend to conclude that others are uncaring and unavailable and perhaps, in addition, that they themselves are unlovable . . ." She describes these people as experiencing "pervasive interpersonal distrust and fear of rejection". They are generally unhappy and oversensitive to what others think of them. In social situations and close relationships, they expect and tend to perceive rejection.

Bartholomew speaks here only of rejection, not of abuse. But abuse, especially by parents who are not consistently abusive but are sometimes apparently loving, can make children very fearful. When psychologists speak of children's attachment styles, they talk about a category of "disorganised attachment"—approaching the parent then freezing or trying to escape. This should be a red flag for identifying abusive parents. The child desperately wants the parent's love and support, but knows that coming close to that parent sometimes results in being hurt. And, especially with a parent who switches between kind and abusive parts, the child has to be constantly alert for which aspect of that parent he or she is dealing with.

Finally, Bartholomew describes those in the dismissing category as maintaining a positive self-image in the face of rejection by attachment figures by distancing themselves and seeing themselves as "fully adequate and hence invulnerable to negative feelings", as those feelings might lead them to want to depend on others. "Individuals with this style passively avoid close

Table 1. Categories of attachment styles in adults.

Secure	Preocccupied	Dismissing	Fearful
Comfortable with both intimacy and autonomy	Insecure, needy, dependent Has difficulty being separate Expects partner to meet all his or her needs	Denies attachment needs Values independence highly Tries not to need people	Afraid of attachment Avoids closeness Avoids relationships

relationships; they place much value on independence and assert that relationships are relatively unimportant."

This is more characteristic of persons whose parents were too busy, ill, or preoccupied rather than abusive. Sometimes, children are vulnerable to abuse outside the home because their parents are inattentive. But cult families can also leave children to their own devices when not abusing them, resulting in those children knowing they have nobody to rely on except themselves.

So, we see that your view of yourself as good and lovable or bad and unlovable, your view of other people as trustworthy or untrustworthy, the way you handle your emotions, your capacity to form secure and healthy relationships with peers and partners, and your self-confidence, are all strongly affected by how your parents treated you. Do not despair, however. The beginning of positive change is recognising what needs to be changed.

It goes without saying that survivors of mind control and ritual abuse probably have all four attachment styles in various inside parts of them, though not many would have a secure attachment. It is common that, in close relationships, survivors switch between different parts and therefore show different attachment patterns, confusing their friends and partners, who might

Exercise 27. Identifying your attachment issues

Do you find that you are unable to become close to other people, or when you become close to them, you begin to panic and pull away or criticise or provoke them to make them reject you?

Ask your insiders whether they were trained or have programming not to get close to anyone. Are they acting on that programming?

Ask your insiders whether some of them feel that when they are stressed they must make contact with persons (family members or others) who are part of the perpetrator group? If so, have other insiders let those parts know why that might be dangerous, if necessary giving them memories to demonstrate this reality.

What do you see as your front personality's main attachment style (secure, preoccupied, dismissing, or fearful?) What experiences led him or her to develop this style?

Do any of your insiders have a secure attachment style? If so, who are they attached to in this way? Is it realistic, that is, is that person really trustworthy? If not, educate these insiders. If it is realistic, perhaps these insiders can teach the rest of you some things about how to make a relationship work.

Do some of your insiders have a preoccupied (needy) attachment style? Have they driven people away by being too demanding? Does their neediness leak through to the front person? Infants and babies need this kind of care and attention, and it is a sad fact that it is not available to someone in an adult body.

Have you developed relationships with unsafe people because the needs of some young parts have taken over and led you to ignore signs that these people are not safe? If you have, arrange for some insiders to watch for signs that a person is not safe, and inform everyone inside if this is the case.

If you have young parts who need more care than is available in the world, see whether you can provide it in the inner world. What could you do internally to meet these childhood needs? Can you provide internal caregivers, or can some older parts volunteer for this job?

Is there anything you can do in the real world to provide nurturing for your young abandoned internal children, such as getting a pet or a rocking chair?

(continued)

Do some of your insiders have a dismissing attachment style, believing they don't need anyone and that the only persons they can trust are themselves? Identify which insiders feel this way.

Are some of your parts fearful of any relationship at all? Can you help these parts see how their childhood experiences have led them to believe all people are untrustworthy, rejecting, and abusive, even though this is not really the case?

What will all of you be missing if the fearful and dismissive insiders prevent you from having any friedships? How can you achieve a balance between those parts who need love and connection and those parts who need safety and autonomy? Can you rearrange the jobs of your insiders so that some strong insiders will guard against you being re-abused, while permitting trust to develop with trustworthy people?

One important principle in relationships is that trust should not be given unconditionally; it has to be earned, and not just by a kind word or two. Do you give people a chance to earn your trust? What would it look like if you did this?

Are any parts in you anxious as a result of reading this section? Can they express their fear, or can someone older express these fears for them? Can an older part reassure them?

begin to feel they cannot do anything right. All the distrust learnt appropriately in childhood is carried forward into adulthood and projected on to people who might not really deserve it.

Principles in developing friendships

Developing friendships gradually

People (in fact, all mammals) were designed to live in relationships, having family and friendships. Many survivors of mind control and/or ritual abuse are, of necessity, cut off from their families, because their families are involved with the abuser group or are themselves abusers. But good friends can fill the void left by the family, which is why abusers try to prevent survivors from having close friendships.

Friendships come at many different levels: casual acquaintances, work colleagues, buddies who share interests and activities, relatively close friends with whom you can share some struggles of your everyday life, and, finally, best friends who can handle most or all of the history and difficulties you share. The latter are hard to find, but that does not mean you should not have friends at all the other levels. Each kind of friend can meet a different kind of need in you. Not all friendships have to be deep in order to enrich your life.

The deep friendships generally develop over time from one of the other kinds of friendships; they are not instantly deep. You need to be cautious about people who get too deep too fast; it might indicate that they lack personal boundaries and a sense of what is safe to be shared and what is not.

Many survivors just do not know how to develop friendships. They tend either to avoid sharing anything with people they meet, or they blurt out their entire life history, frightening off people who could be supportive friends. This often comes from child parts who are tired of keeping the secrets, are lonely, and want to be understood and accepted. It can also come from child parts who are programmed to sabotage friendships by making you look crazy.

The first thing to know about developing friendships is that it is a gradual process. You do not share everything at once. You share little bits of your life at a time, observing how the person reacts to your disclosures. What you observe will give you information about what kind or level of friendship you want with this person, and what kind or level of friendship he or she wants with you.

Some people cannot take you sharing much about your life history. There are many reasons for this. Some people who have not had much personal trauma are genuinely shocked and traumatised by hearing about child abuse, even the milder kind. When it happens to someone they know, it is as if it happened to them. You may have no idea how overwhelming it is for someone who has not suffered much to hear about mind control and ritual abuse. Even therapists go through this. I know I did with my first few ritual abuse survivor clients, and I still sometimes feel shocked and overwhelmed by the things people tell me.

Just because people are shocked and horrified does not mean they cannot become good friends or they do not care. Just the opposite; it may mean they are sensitive and caring. You just have to go slowly with them. Share one small thing at a time, so that they will not be overwhelmed.

Other people have walled themselves off in a view of life which will not allow for the fact that terrible things happen in the world. They want a constant positive rosy glow. Such people are likely to say that the past is past and you should move on, or to react to disclosures with scepticism, or to say that God makes it all happen for a purpose. Or they suggest that you are stressed from events in your present life and, therefore, are imagining the things you are remembering. Such people are fine for going bowling or to the cinema with, but do not share anything personal with them. When your abusers told you "No one will believe you," they were right—about some people, but not about others. You do not need to risk the disbelief of people who are not open to hearing about the bad things that happened. Seek out those who will believe you.

It is also boring and unfulfilling to try to have friendships with people who just do not know about trauma and do not want to know. Perhaps they are all right to go to see a film with, but they will not fill your need for connection.

A true friend is a healthy role model, something that survivors desperately need, since their role models in childhood were badly flawed. A friend who accepts all of you as you are is the most wonderful source of healing. This kind of acceptance can come from therapists, but it can also come from friends.

Whenever I meet a new client with a trauma history, I tell them I do not expect them to trust me. Trust takes time, and it has to be earned. This is as true in friendships as it is in therapeutic relationships. Allow people to earn your trust. Keep your vigilant parts listening for signs of disbelief or untrustworthiness in potential friends, and get them to bring these things to your attention. However, make sure they are not just overreacting to small behaviours which do not mean anything, on the basis of their childhood training. If your whole system works together, you can keep safe while developing friendships.

Friendships with other survivors

Many survivors dream of a friendship with someone who really understands what they have been through—and that ideal person, of course, is another survivor. I have seen such friendships be very supportive, and I have also seen them be very destructive. Be very, very careful.

Many survivors are not consciously aware that many or most of their friends are cult members and still actively involved. Some survivors of mind control and ritual abuse are still involved with perpetrator groups, and some have programming to report on other survivors and get them reinvolved. I have seen survivors taken back to cults other than the ones they escaped from.

I have seen friends who were both survivors being accessed and reabused at the same time by cult people. If survivors live together, they are particularly vulnerable to this.

I have seen survivors have programming triggered by things said or done by other survivors. There is a greater chance of this with another survivor, especially if that person has parts who are trained to trigger others.

What if both of you have achieved physical safety? There are still some risks. I have seen survivors become inappropriately sexually involved with one another, and hate themselves afterwards. I have seen two survivors have their "get pregnant" programming triggered at the same time, and go out into the streets offering free sex to anyone nearby.

I have heard of survivors spending all their time together coddling one another's "littles", living primarily as children, and not getting on with their recovery.

I saw two survivor clients of mine begin to develop what could have been a real friendship, but then one of them accused the other of making sexual comments to her, an accusation that deeply wounded the other person. They stopped seeing one another, and I worked with both while not knowing which one was mistaken. After several months, the one who made the accusations discovered that some of her own insiders were imitating her friend's voice and making the comments in her head. It was a great shock to her to discover they were doing this, acting on programming not to get close to anyone. She felt very ashamed, and had to apologise to her friend. It was too late for the friendship to resume.

Despite all this, I know some survivors who have developed deep, supportive, and abiding friendships with one another. Part of what has made this work is not spending their time together in child states, and not talking about the abuses they have experienced. The focus of such friendships has been on helping one another manage present-day life in a healthy way. And, of course, you do not need a fellow survivor to accomplish this.

Respecting and maintaining boundaries

It is not enough just to be close to someone else. We need to feel that the other person sees us as we are, appreciates the unique person that we are, and does not try to make us different. If the person, in "loving" us, needs us to be someone that we are not, we can feel both smothered and abandoned.

Every person needs both to be loved and to be himself or herself. This is possible only when there are healthy boundaries in the relationship. Personal boundaries are imaginary lines that separate people within relationships. You can imagine your boundaries as bubbles, fences, or walls. They work best when they are flexible rather than rigid.

Boundaries are essential for healthy relationships. Without boundaries, each person has no separate sense of self, and one person's identity can become submerged in that of another person. Intimate closeness is normal and essential between a mother and her infant, but as the child grows, he or she gradually becomes separate from the mother. Both child and mother begin to assert their own boundaries and some degree of independence. This process is called differentiation. Unfortunately, in the dysfunctional families involved in cults and mind control groups, children are not generally allowed to differentiate and become separate selves.

At different times, any person has greater needs for closeness or for distance. This happens on both a physical and an emotional level. There is a continual dance back and forth as people express their needs for intimacy and for separateness, and people respond to others' needs by moving closer or further away. A healthy friendship, relationship, or family is one in which you can be loved and be yourself at the same time. When you are multiple, this is more complex, but still each part needs to be accepted for who he or she is, and each part has a unique set of likes and dislikes and interests.

In a healthy relationship, people learn to hear no and say no. Boundaries are discussed, respected, and maintained. There is closeness without sacrificing the freedom of each person. Being in a loving relationship involves compromises, since not everyone's needs can be met at the same time. It is possible for one person to put his or her needs aside temporarily to respond to the other's needs, because he or she trusts that the other person will do the same at another time. No one is taken advantage of on an ongoing basis. Caring is not an obligation but a matter of free choice.

In a healthy relationship, the "fences" between the people are both strong and flexible, and they are respected. A person can extend her personal boundaries (or open her gates) by asking the other person to meet her needs, responding to his or her needs in turn, and sharing things in her life. A person can pull in his personal boundaries (or close his gate) by withdrawing, taking time alone, keeping personal information private, or indicating that he is unable at the moment to respond to the other person's needs. When he does this, his boundaries are respected, and his gate does not get kicked in. This makes the person feel safe to extend or soften his boundaries on other occasions.

Relationships that are too close: enmeshment

"Enmeshed" is the technical term for a family or a relationship in which everyone is involved in everyone else's business. Often, such families describe themselves as "very close". In an enmeshed family, the parents do not know how to have closeness with their children and allow them freedom at the same time. Presumably because their own boundaries were not respected when they were children, they do not recognise and respect either their own boundaries or those of the other family members. Each family member is, therefore, torn between his or her need for closeness and his or her need for separateness. Enmeshed families are very common in families where abuse occurs.

When a child's personal boundaries are not respected, there is too much closeness in the relationship and the child does not have room to grow. Yes, it is important that there be a healthy, close attachment between parents and children, but in an enmeshed relationship, the parents are over-involved in the children's lives and the children feel that they do not have privacy, their own space, or the ability to make their own decisions based on their own preferences and values. The children cannot develop personal boundaries. Parents who had anxious, insecure, or fearful attachments to their own parents are the most likely to give their children too little space. They might use their children as confidantes, and want to keep them as their care-givers all their lives, making the children give up their own ambitions. They might also push their children towards having the life they (the parents) wanted.

Friendships, like family relationships, can be enmeshed, with the people doing everything together. When this happens, frequently one person becomes dominant and the other person's preferences are squashed.

Relationships that are too distant: disengagement

Children who have had to deal with intrusive parents often respond by trying to create distance in later relationships. They keep their distance in order to feel nobody will violate them. However, in doing so they give up the possibility of emotional intimacy. If you can learn how to have firm but flexible personal boundaries, you can have intimacy without giving up your own unique self (or selves, if you are multiple).

A person may attempt to disengage from an enmeshed relationship by putting up very rigid, wall-like boundaries, remaining in contact but keeping out the other person's "invasions" by anger outbursts. Or he or she might do it by silent withdrawal, removing the gate altogether and putting up a "wall of silence". There are entire families that exist together with no real relationships, as all members have emotionally disengaged. Disengagement makes relationships very unsatisfying; it is preferable to break off the relationship altogether if you cannot talk it out.

Boundaries around relationships: triangles

For relationships to be healthy, there need to be boundaries not only around individuals but also around relationships. Adult family members and friends need to be able to have one-to-one relationships with one another without other people interfering. In healthy families with strong boundaries, individuals are allowed to work out their own conflicts without interference. However, children first need to be coached in ways of relating without violence or sexual intrusions. In families where boundaries are weak, many of the relationships are not respected and the result is triangles in which people "take sides". Many sibling rivalry conflicts are made much worse by a parent who interferes.

People who grow up with this situation carry it through into their adult friendships. A triangle occurs when a third party enters a conflicted two-person relationship to alter the balance of power. People who have grown up in families where triangles were common are likely to intrude into others' relationships as the third party who takes sides, ganging up and often becoming the "rational judge" who says who is right and who is wrong. When this happens, it prevents people from working out their own conflicts and learning to communicate assertively and kindly.

It is important, as you develop friendships, to keep boundaries around those friendships and not begin gossiping with one friend about another. And do not allow others to intrude into your friendships.

Boundary blindness

People from enmeshed families of origin are often insensitive to invasions of their own personal boundaries. They are not able to say no to requests, and might give in to a request which could easily have been denied with a "NO". Then they feel resentful of whoever made the request. If you are unassertive like this, it leads people to think you are all right with whatever they suggest or request, and then they are surprised to learn you are not, since they cannot read your mind or even the subtleties of your body language.

It is common for an unassertive person to become suddenly depressed or angry and irritable without knowing why, and to stay in that state for some time. Usually, this is traceable to a boundary violation. Someone has intruded into your life in a way that violates your personal boundaries, but you were not consciously aware of it at the time. However, if you are multiple, some of your insiders will know that you feel invaded, although they will not necessarily tell you.

It is important to learn

- how to perceive your own boundaries and assert them;
- how to respond to requests and probes;
- how to respond to outright invasions.

Assertiveness is the ability to maintain your own boundaries without invading those of other people. If your parents taught you to always obey and say yes, *no* is probably not part of your vocabulary. Survivors of mind control have great difficulty saying no, because insiders who disobeyed the abusers were often punished with torture. So, feelings from these insiders will leak into the person if he or she even contemplates saying no to anyone. It is important to reassure your insiders that the punishment they experienced in childhood will not happen now if they say no to regular people. It is also important to know that even people who normally do not like to *hear* "No" are able to accept it if you say it to begin with, rather than later changing your mind.

Having boundaries does not mean that we do not have love and compassion for others. It does not mean that we stop doing things or caring for others. When you have healthy boundaries, you can give *whole-heartedly* from a loving place. With poor boundaries, giving feels like an obligation and is shortly followed by resentment.

As people begin to recover from growing up in an enmeshed family, they are often oversensitive to boundary violations, perceiving them where they are not intended at all, or overreacting to minor unintentional violations. In normal negotiations, a person asks for something (such as some time together, some help, or a personal disclosure), and the other person can respond with "yes", or "no", or "not yet". Boundaries are being tested and respected rather than violated. People who are just learning to perceive their boundaries go back and forth between two extremes: unassertiveness (not standing up for oneself) and aggressiveness, rather than following the sensible middle road of assertively maintaining their own boundaries and respecting those of other people.

People who have grown up in an enmeshed family might also be insensitive to others' boundaries. Not knowing how to see self and others as separate, they begin to control the people they "love", telling them how to live, taking over their responsibilities, and insisting on being involved in every aspect of their lives. It is important to realise that such people are not consciously aware of their enmeshment with family members or friends. They just lack empathy for how the others may feel about this, and are unaware of others' need to be themselves and make their own decisions.

If this is you, you need to learn to recognise the clues (often subtle), which indicate that another person is asserting his or her boundaries, recognise that this is not a threat, and respect the privacy and autonomy of those you love. They can only trust you if they know you will not try to control them. This might be difficult for you. People who have been controlled a lot feel safest when they are in control themselves, but in taking control of others they put those others in the same disempowered position they themselves used to be in.

Dealing with neediness in friendships

A survivor of severe child abuse, who did not have attuned parents, has lots of abandoned, hurt, and needy child parts inside. These parts really want someone to care about them. They might have unrealistic expectations of what a friend, even a very close friend, can provide. It is up to the older parts of you to take care of them, and to meet as many of their needs as you can.

Be careful not to let needy child parts take over your friendships and demand more than your friends are able to give. For a friendship to succeed, it must be two-way. That is, you must give as much as you get. If you are always taking and never giving, your friend may withdraw—unless he or she is also full of unmet needs and will put up with anything in order to have a friend. That also is not healthy, and the resentment your friend stores up might one day come out all at once.

Some survivors go to the other extreme, and believe they should always give and never receive. A friendship is for both people. If you have a friend and they are always taking and never giving, you need to set some limits. Do not give more than you get. It is important to have empathy for other people, and there are times in everyone's life when they are needier and deserve to have more attention and help. But it should not remain that way for ever. If it does, it is no longer a friendship; it is a volunteer job.

Couple relationships

Except for the possibility of sex, couple relationships work much the same as friendships. To summarise: you have to allow the relationship to develop slowly, seeing how much you can trust the other person with increasing levels of sharing. You need to respect one another's boundaries, and to maintain your own boundaries so the other person does not overwhelm you. You need to be able to rely on the other person to support you when you need it, but if you have hurt and needy children inside, you need to recognise that you, or your older parts, are their primary parents, and you cannot expect even a life partner to meet all the needs which a young child should have had met by loving attentive parents.

All the challenges of a relationship intensify when you live with someone, even a roommate. And it is even more with a partner, because you expect more of them, and you are more easily hurt when they do not come through for you. So SLOWLY is the best way—let a friendship develop slowly, and if it ripens into a deeper love, you will have plenty of time to enjoy that; you do not have to rush into it before all parts of you are ready.

In developing new relationships as an adult, you might need to unlearn much of what you learnt in your family of origin. You need to become aware of what was violating, and teach yourself not to do those things. It is all right to make a few mistakes along the way. It is hard to learn as an adult what you should have learnt as a child.

Exercise 28. Assessing your boundary awareness

Would you describe the family in which you grew up as enmeshed, disengaged, a combination of enmeshed and disengaged, or having appropriate boundaries? Describe what boundaries were like in that family. Did the parents respect the children's boundaries? Did they respect children's relationships with one another and with friends, or did they intrude? Did they treat their children differently, being enmeshed with one and distant from another?

Are you aware of your own boundaries, and when someone crosses them? What signs indicate that your boundary has been crossed?

Are you able to say "No" when you do not want to do something someone asks? Why or why not? Can you say it firmly but respectfully?

Think of a situation in which you want to say no to someone. How could you say it to affirm your own boundary without being rude to that person?

Are you aware of other people's boundaries? Do you intrude upon them, or are you respectful of the subtle signs that they want privacy or more distance?

Think of your friends and acquaintances. Is there anyone who seems excessively needy, and expects you to be there for them all the time? What could you say to that person?

Are you ever that person? How can you prevent yourself from overwhelming your friends with your neediness?

Do you have any friends who are mind control or ritual abuse survivors? What differences do you notice in their boundaries, *vs.* those of your other friends?

When you have had friendships or relationships that have gone wrong, can you say what went wrong? Did it involve boundary violations?

How quickly do you develop friendships? Do you think this is too quickly, or too slowly?

What level of intimacy do your friendships have? Superficial (doing things together), relatively deep (sharing about present life), very deep (you can share your trauma history freely)? Are you happy with the level of each friendship? Would you like to share more with some person, or less with some other person?

The workplace

If you work outside the home, as most people do, your workplace is probably a setting where you have to deal with people. Everything I wrote above about boundaries in relationships applies in the workplace. Unfortunately, many workplaces are dysfunctional in terms of the relationships between people. One survivor, who had just returned to work after a period on a disability pension, had her first experiences of sexual harassment (a supervisor persistently trying to make friends with her and finally kissing her) and bullying (colleagues criticising her and making remarks about her). It helped her when she learned the names for these behaviours, and that what these people were doing was not all right. She reported the sexual harassment to the supervisor's own boss, who put an end to it pretty quickly. She realised she would have to stand up to the bullies, and when she did, they stopped their behaviour.

You probably had to deal with bullies when you attended school. Bullying is more obvious when it is a child who pushes you or calls you by an insulting name, but it is quite common in workplaces. It is perpetrated often by supervisors, and sometimes by co-workers. Types of bullying include threats to your professional status (belittling your opinions, public professional humiliation, accusations regarding lack of effort, intimidating use of discipline), threats to your personal standing (undermining your personal integrity, destructive innuendo and sarcasm, making inappropriate jokes about you, persistent teasing, name calling, insults, and intimidation), isolation, pressure on you to overwork, and destabilisation (failure to acknowledge good work, allocation of meaningless tasks, removal of responsibility, repeated reminders of your blunders, setting you up to fail, and telling you there is more to be done when you think you have finished).

Many people, not just survivors of child abuse, have to deal with difficult bosses. But people who spent much of their childhood being bossed around might take it for granted that bosses are unkind and allow themselves to be verbally abused or taken advantage of in the workplace. A childhood of slavery does not prepare you for a life of freedom and autonomy. However, be careful not to overreact to slight difficulties at work. LisaBri writes:

> Innocent directions from your boss can bring up the feelings from memories of rituals ordering you to answer to a higher power, such as Satan. It is important for you to distinguish between the two.
>
> If your boss, on the other hand, is demanding, threatening, or overbearing, you have the choice not to deal with this tyrant. Quit, and if that is not an option, do not let them get the best of you. Sing to yourself under your breath, changing the cadence of the boss's voice to a ridiculous sound that you can laugh and share with inside others, later. Also, learn your boss's voice. Know it is on the outside. If a programme was set to have a part mimic someone's voice and set off havoc in your system, recognise that it is a programme and dismantle it.

How do you know when it is time to run from a job? One survivor who quit her job provided me with the following list.

When to run from a job

1. When Administration overworks staff to exhaustion.
2. When Administration requires complete subservience.
3. When you are punished for expressing yourself and especially for pointing out unethical practices in the agency.
4. When they pick on you and blow up possible mistakes.
5. When they blame you for things you did not do.
6. When they do not acknowledge your strengths or minimise them.
7. When they practise partiality and favouritism to others (who have mastered subservience).
8. When the organisation is run by greed rather than service.
9. When they try to blot out your individuality and ability to think.
10. When they inhibit any initiative.

In other words, when the workplace is as coercive as the abuser group you grew up in (though without the torture). If this is your workplace, recognise what it is like and start looking around for another job.

You also need, however, to be careful that you are not reading underhanded motivations into people on the basis of your past experience. You might have parts who think everything is an insult, and cannot handle even reasonable authority. While such parts can be helpful, they should not be allowed to run the show.

Communication skills

The most important communication skills are listening in a way that attempts to understand the other person, speaking in a respectful and clear manner, taking turns, and conflict resolution. There are courses in communication skills, and if you have difficulties in this area it might be wise to take such a course.

Dealing with anger in relationships

The biggest reason for conflict in relationships is anger. I explained in Chapter Thirteen that anger is a normal emotion that tells us our boundaries might have been violated. Unfortunately, most survivors have inner child parts who can become very angry at very small things which are reminders of their trauma.

Researchers Matthew McKay and Patrick Fanning, who wrote *When Anger Hurts Your Kids* (1996), discovered that parents with high levels of ongoing anger were using certain kinds of "trigger thoughts". These anger-fuelling thoughts consisted of three categories: magnification (making something bigger than it is), labelling (calling the person names in your head), and assuming intent (assuming they did the annoying thing on purpose to harm you). When we are stressed, these trigger thoughts can start a downward spiral toward aggressive behaviour. Becoming aware of not only our feelings but also our thoughts has been proved to be an effective way to defuse emotional build-ups and overreactions.

Think of some behaviour of your friend, partner, or child that upsets you, then see which of the thoughts outlined below fit you. Notice how your emotions about the situation change when your thoughts do, and how the behaviour you might engage in changes when you understand the situation differently.

Trigger thoughts

Examples of magnification

Your supervisor at work gives you a last-minute assignment that you have to scramble to get done.

Magnification: She's really mean. She doesn't like me. I can't work under her. This is too stressful. I should quit this job.

Realistic view: She might not know how much work I already have to do. She may be under pressure herself. I can handle my workload, or if I can't, I can ask her which things are the priority.

A seven-year-old child has a temper tantrum when you say "No" to her.

Magnification: I can't stand it. She never listens. She's getting out of control. This is manipulation. She doesn't care how I feel. This behaviour is intolerable.

Realistic view: She can't help doing this; it's how she tries to cope. Children have to go through these stages. I don't like her behaviour, but I can accept it. I'm the grown-up; I can handle this. I can get through it without blowing up. I need a plan to get her attention without anger.

Examples of labelling

Your doctor keeps you waiting for forty minutes.

Labelling: She only sees me for the money. She's inconsiderate.

Realistic view: Something delayed her. Since it bothers me, I can ask her why this happened.

A ten-year-old girl has stomach-aches at night and becomes anxious.

Labelling: She's a drama queen. This is manipulation.

Realistic view: Something is bothering her, and I need to pay attention, comfort her, find out what's wrong, and give her ways to cope.

Examples of assumed intent

A two-year-old pours his milk all over the floor from his high chair.

Assumed intent: He's doing it to annoy me. He doesn't care that he makes work for me.

Realistic view: He isn't really trying to annoy me. It's just how he's coping right now. He doesn't have the words to express himself. He's much too young to understand my workload.

Your best friend doesn't mention your birthday.

Assumed intent: She's doing this deliberately. She doesn't care about me.

Realistic view: Birthdays don't mean as much to her as they do to me. She doesn't know it matters to me.

Coping with unexpected trigger thoughts

1. Think of other reasons why the person might be doing what they're doing.
2. Figure out how important this situation is.
3. For each negative label you have used in your mind, try to find a neutral description you could use instead.
4. Remind yourself of ways that you can cope and keep your cool.

Of course, there are special issues for survivors of mind control and ritual abuse. Triggered emotions and the associated thoughts often come from child insiders, even when the adult on the outside is unaware of it. These emotions can be strong and even overwhelming, just like the emotions of children who are going through severe trauma. It is important to keep these children well looked after on the inside, and for some older insiders to reassure them and help them know that you can cope with the situation and they do not have to handle it themselves. Children do not have to deal with adult situations. If programmes are triggered, inside higher-ups need to make sure they are turned off, so that you do not react inappropriately.

These inappropriate thoughts and reactions are especially likely to happen when you are dealing with children, because of the way your parents and other adults dealt with you when you were a child. If you are a parent, it is a good idea to take a parenting course and/or read some good books on parenting (such as my own), so you can learn how to parent children in a different way from the way you were raised.

Exercise 29. Working with the anger chart

The following chart (from our book, Miller and Rees, 2008, *The Parent–Child Connection*) might help you know what to do if your anger begins to take over. It uses the letters A – N – G – E – R to identify steps towards awareness of your anger. However, you can use it when other very strong emotions are triggered.

Whenever you have a situation in which you notice yourself becoming irritated, upset, anxious, or angry, find a way to be alone and think through or (preferably) write out the answers to the "Steps to awareness" in the left-hand column. Then make plans for the actions in the right-hand column.

	Steps to awareness	How this can be effective
A	Attend to your early signals of anger. What do you feel in your body? How do you behave?	You can catch anger before it escalates. When you increase your awareness of the early signals, you can choose how you will react. Annoyance is an early stage of anger.
N	Negotiate with those around you about your anger, not about specific issues. Choose distance and time.	Discuss this strong emotion with your family or friends. Come up with a signal that means you need time out: *Give me five*; *Grumpy guy alert*; *I need a break*. Calm down, remove yourself from the situation, and take some time to to reflect. Even turning your back and breathing deeply can be effective.
G	Gear down from taking action and explore your feelings. Identify them if you can. Pay attention to your own triggering thoughts that might provoke anger.	G = Get alone E = Express your emotions A = Analyse your thoughts R = Recognise your needs. Catch negative trigger thoughts and replace them with healing ones. Use your feelings to explore what your needs are.
E	Express your feelings and needs assertively.	When you _____, I feel_____ because _______. I want/would like you to __________.
R	Resolve issues if possible. It might be as simple as making a positive request. It might mean engaging in conflict resolution. It might mean resolving the issue within yourself.	Resolving conflicts stops the vicious circle of old issues and patterns recurring. Resolution does not have to be complicated, but it cannot happen without the preceding steps. Often, we need to feel anger to know there is a boundary that needs to be addressed.

Learning to be alone

As you become more discriminating in your selection of friends, you will find yourself lonely at times. It is rare to find the kind of friend who can be there for you consistently and can understand and accept what you have been through. You can still have superficial friendships, however, and I hope you do so, while you look for true friends.

What can help with the loneliness? Well, if you are multiple, you can have friendships within your own personality system (see Chapter Twelve). A pet can also be a tremendous source of companionship for anyone who lives alone or with people who do not understand. Animals, especially dogs, make wonderful companions. They are designed to live in community, to be close to their owners, and to enjoy your presence. It really is true that "a man's best friend is his dog"—or a woman's, or a child's.

But even if you are comfortable being alone, do not close off the possibility of close friendships. Look at your attachment style, and see to what extent it is a result of your childhood abuse and neglect. A close relationship can be very rewarding, and can give you an anchor in difficult times, if there are respect and clear boundaries in the relationship.

This chapter has covered most of th*e important issues in friendships and relationships, but, of course, only briefly.* Many of these issues are problematic for anyone raised in a dysfunctional family, not just for mind control and ritual abuse survivors. Besides *The Parent–Child Connection*, there are also many other helpful books, such as Harriet Lerner's *The Dance of Anger* (2009a); *The Dance of Connection* (2009b); *The Dance of Deception* (2009c); *The Dance of Fear* (2009d); *The Dance of Intimacy* (2009e). For couple relationships, I recommend Gottman and Silver's *The Seven Principles for Making Marriage Work* (1999), and Sue Johnson's *Hold Me Tight: Seven Conversations for a Lifetime of Love* (2008).

CHAPTER NINETEEN

Therapy and therapists

Healing from mind control and ritual abuse takes a long time. It can help to have a companion along the way, especially one who understands what you are dealing with and is caring rather than shocked or disbelieving.

Many survivors of ritual abuse and mind control see therapists. One survivor, who had been to both bad and good therapists, listed for me the benefits of having a good therapist.

- It gives all parts of the survivor the experience of being near somebody who is good, which is an antidote to all the evil they have experienced.
- It is better not to be alone in healing, the way you were alone in the abuse. It gives support, a companion as you enter an unknown world of horror.
- It makes you feel as though you are worthwhile when someone else is this interested in you.
- The therapist can keep you on track, with a relentless pursuit of what is necessary for your healing, when you are tempted to retreat from the pain and horror of what you have to deal with.
- The therapist can record what you remember as you go through it, so you do not have to use any of your own energy or attention for record keeping.
- Since your controllers programmed you to forget every time a trauma occurred, it helps to have a witness to your remembering, someone who encourages retrieving and not flushing away the memories.
- A wise therapist knows how to distinguish what is important from what is trivial, ignore irrelevant information, disinformation and fraudulent information, and focus on what matters.
- A knowledgeable therapist can be more thorough than you would be on your own: asking questions you would be blind to, looking for the root of each problem, the first instance of

each programme training, the missing pieces of each memory, the incongruities and inconsistencies which need to be pursued for the information they hold, searching for the insiders who hold each emotional or physical state belonging to a memory, and the words used by the perpetrators when programming your insiders.

However, even without a therapist, you can heal, so do not despair if you cannot afford therapy.

Programmed resistance to therapy

Knowing that therapy can not only help a survivor, but also unmask the secrets of the perpetrator groups, the groups take measures to ensure that therapy is ineffective with survivors of their abuses. They pay special attention to disrupting their victims' potential relationships with therapists.

Here is a story more than one survivor has told me. As a child, her parents took her to see someone she believed to be a therapist, who invited her to tell the story of a recent cult event, giving a visual signal to reporter parts of her that they should talk. She was not allowed to look up at the therapist and see his or her face, until she was told to. The therapist was wearing a devil mask, and raped her.

Many survivors have a similar experience with the family doctor, who is usually a cult member. After the child has been injured, he or she is encouraged to show the doctor the injuries, and the doctor then abuses him or her. The message is "Never tell a doctor when you have been hurt."

In another type of training, the "therapist" to whom the child is triggered to disclose the abuse tells the child that he or she is crazy for talking about such things, and takes the child to a "mental hospital" or a "loony bin". In the hospital, people put the child in restraints and administer strong drugs which make him or her feel ill and unable to think. Inmates or staff of the "loony bin" or "mental hospital" abuse the child. The person may or may not be a real therapist, and the hospital may or may not be a real one.

If you are a survivor, you probably have insiders who hold the memories of these or similar experiences, and as a result are afraid of doctors, therapists, mental hospitals, and making disclosures. If you go to a therapist, specific insiders have been taught to bring up these beliefs and the associated memories and fear. Your insiders also bring up reminders of the supposed devices (microphones in your teeth, Satan's eyes or mother's ears on the walls) that tell the abuser group what you have disclosed. These were, of course, just tricks.

You might notice that if you go to a therapist or a doctor, you are unable to look at him or her. Child parts are trained (via the "doctor" or "therapist" with the demon mask) not to look at a therapist, so that the perpetrator group can later impersonate an actual therapist more effectively, since the client does not really know what the therapist looks like.

If a survivor is in therapy and is disclosing the perpetrator group's secrets to the therapist, and at the same time still reporting to the group, the group is likely to impersonate the therapist. When I was seeing my first few ritually abused clients, I discovered that I was being impersonated frequently by a woman who sexually abused these clients. The local cult found a way to get into my office (via a cult member who attended another therapist's sexual abuse survivor group in our shared office building), and one of my clients became very afraid of my office. I had to meet him instead in the coffee shop across the street. Once I worked out what was happening, I asked each client to instruct certain insiders to memorise the appearance of my one crooked finger, and to compare it to the hands of the person they were told was me to see whether it was really me. They quickly learnt to tell the difference.

I had surgery on that finger, and saw a new ritually abused client shortly after the surgery. She kept staring at the bandaged finger, and when I asked her why, she said, "You didn't have that the last time I saw you." I had never seen her before. The cult was one step ahead of me.

When I moved to a new office that was not shared, with a good alarm system, the cult had to find another office space nearby and pretend it was my office. Then, with a new client, they decided to use a subtler approach. Instead of having "me" sexually abuse the client, they just had "me" do really bad therapy, yelling at the client and accusing her of bad behaviour. It worked, and she fired me, accusing me of doing things that I had not done. In the weeks before this happened, this client told me that she kept drawing my office, and did not understand why.

If there is a chance that your therapist has been impersonated, you can teach all your parts to find some unique thing in your therapist's appearance or voice or manner which the cult group is unlikely to be able to create in the imposter. Do not use anything about the face, as the chances are you will find yourself unable to look at the impersonator. One survivor had a blind insider who could tell the therapist by her smell, although if your therapist wears perfume this is easy to simulate.

Crime Victims or Criminal Injuries funding for therapy is often dependent on you making a police report about the crimes committed against you. Unfortunately, most survivors of organised abuse are terrified of talking to police, often believing many police are members of the perpetrator group. This fear comes from insiders' experiences with uniformed people they believed to be police officers. The group triggers a child to talk to a "police officer" about a memory, usually one in which another person was tortured or killed. The supposed police officer accuses the child of being the perpetrator, arrests the child, and puts him or her in a jail cell with abusive guards and "inmates".

Of course, this is all a setup, a deception to make your child parts scared. Even if some police officers are actually cult members, most are not. However, since many police are trained to be suspicious about reports of ritual abuse, it might be wiser to just report sexual or physical abuse by a relative, since this is sufficient to get therapy funding.

"Don't talk" is the goal of all kinds of programming. So, even if you recognise that your child insiders were deceived about therapists and police all being perpetrators, you still have to cope with the more general "Don't talk" training of your insiders. Many of the kinds of training your very young parts might have received are designed to make sure you do not talk to anyone about the abuse. See Chapter Nine for descriptions of some of this training.

Another common training, especially favoured by military/political mind control groups, is to change the meanings of words commonly used by therapists so that those words instil terror or anger in your insiders. These include such words as "love", "care", "forgive", "think", "light", "life", "truth", and "free". Often these words mean their opposites to some inside child parts. When a therapist or other helper uses such a word, some insiders believe it means what the abuser group meant when they distorted it. For example, "free" could bring back memories of being chained, "think" could bring back the sensations of being punished for thinking, "love" could mean sexual abuse. If this is happening to you, you can try to find the inside children who had this training, and gradually help them to know that things are different now, and these words actually have good, positive, helpful meanings.

Remember that the child parts on whom these deceptions are perpetrated are deliberately kept at the ages at which they believe such things and accept the "proof" of them provided by the abusers. If you attempt to find out what happened to you, the fear coming from these young parts may flood you, no matter how old you are. *It is important to recognise what may be causing this fear, and not let it deter you from finding good help.*

Do bad things really happen when you get into therapy? Well, it depends on who your therapist is. In Chapter Six, you saw how Sally's higher-ups were able to act on their programming and defeat the intent of her first few therapists, who were uneducated about mind control and ritual abuse. In Chapter Seven, you saw the mistakes made by LisaBri's first long-term therapist, who became overinvolved and then abandoned her, and who increased the hostility between LisaBri's insiders rather than helping them all to work together. You might find it helpful to review those stories now, if you do not remember them clearly.

You might have noticed that with both LisaBri and Sally the early therapists had difficulty maintaining clear boundaries, and became overinvolved with their dissociative client. In Sally's case, her system was acting on programming to overwhelm the therapist. There is some evidence that dissociative people do need different (looser) boundaries than singletons (non-multiples) do, probably because they have so many children inside, whose unmet childhood needs emerge when they have a nice therapist. Adah Sachs (2012) researched this and found that therapists who treated DID and non-DID people more frequently offered DID clients time outside normal working hours, outside the office, and during practitioners' holidays. However, with some therapists, unclear boundaries can lead to bigger problems. The following section is a story of what went terribly wrong in a long-term therapy.

Adriana Green: "Downfall"

"This is how some people say goodbye to each other," Derek, my therapist of ten years, says. We sit as still as possible. He pulls the red chair close in front of us, until there is only a small space before our knees touch. He leans forward, kisses lightly, as if a feather has just brushed against our lips.

I'm closer to the foreground than earlier when we were in the midst of memory, yet the other parts of me are still here, watching, waiting what will happen next. He kisses us a second time with his eyes closed. "I can't stop kissing you."

We're dazed.

He opens his eyes. They are bright and shining. He smiles wide until his ears lift. He appears different, younger than his forty-something years.

Our session is coming to a close. We are suddenly too open, as if air falls through us. Derek pushes the red chair back in an angled position, where he begins and ends each session, taking meticulous notes, giving thought to what is needed by the small population that comprises me.

The younger ones are so still, like small statues lined up, each with their own frozen expression, each clutching their part of the story—a line, a tear, an unspoken word.

From the backdrop of my mind, I do not feel threatened, only numbness. I think of father, who held a firm grip on the shoulders and pressed hard on my lips like a blowfish, demanding more than what a child could bring.

I am not fully back, struggle to come forward. I can't yet talk. The others are beside me, the fourteen-year-old in front. She's smitten, more shy than earlier.

She thinks, *he must really love me.*

"Ready to go?" he asks, stands and stretches his arms towards the ceiling. He straightens his tie, his cabled sweater that is askew from the child parts of me that he held earlier in the session, before the kissing. He held the three-year-old, and the one who is six, and spoke with the eight-year-old, but she is too grown up to be held. She would rather tell him about how everyone is doing, because she is the one who sees almost everyone. Once trust took hold, there was little refusal to be embraced, to be loved. They came forward in his consolation, they showed their pain in his presence, their need for human contact—now that danger was gone.

But not all want closeness. Some do not believe in the notion of belonging. They keep far in the distance, and watch.

Lately, Derek has spoken of how the world of therapy is changing; how we are nearing the end of the 1990s towards a new era, a new approach. Now there is a question, an ear to the ground, as to whether therapists should comfort the patient in their arms.

What was once acceptable might soon become grounds for misconduct.

The thought of such change frightens the younger selves. They do not look to me for comfort. They do not consider me as someone that can be relied upon. I am considered the one to watch out for, not to be trusted. For some, I do not even exist.

They do not come out fully at my home, where Adriana, the wife, the mother, lives.

He looks at us, raises his brow. "Make sure the adult is here before you leave. You can have the room for a while to come back. I'm off to have lunch."

I don't know how long it will take to come back, to unfold and once again fill the space I retreated from earlier.

I'm anxious to take the puzzle home, to make sense of what has happened. *This is how some people say goodbye to each other.* I wonder, is this true? Where? Here, in our country? In Canada?

We curl on the couch and face the door, which stays closed. And then, as if the zoom lens is turned on, I notice more sharply the open knit of the comforter around me, the jacquard pattern of the pillows. I notice the green black broadleaf plant in the corner that climbs to the ceiling, how it takes a turn to the right from where I sit, and travels halfway across the room. I am back in the forefront, yet sense the others are still here with me.

I think about the kissing, try to bring the act, the still warm memory, into focus. But it remains tangled in confusion. I want to believe that the trust is deep enough, that nothing can rock the foundation of safety built over the years.

I remind everyone that we are safe, and tell them, *Derek is not the father. He will not hurt any of us.* None the less, when I pull on my jacket, my hands shake.

The kissing holds different meanings for everyone. I know the younger ones do not understand. They have now left altogether. I walk down the street, two city blocks away from Derek's office.

Someone yells in the corridor of my mind, blots out the traffic, the spray of wet from the road. *You are a fool.* I recognise the voice, the protector—the one that will cut the body, so pain will not be felt; the one that regrets trusting. I am cautious of him, of punishment. His temper flares from the confusion. *Now look what happened. You knew he would change. That is why you kept asking him, will you change?*

The fourteen-year-old is here as well. She interrupts, tells me, "I don't want anybody to be mad at Derek." Her voice is timid, yet carries a distinct mingling of shame and infatuation. I know she adores Derek. How he came and sat with her, understood her not wanting to be in the world. How she did not want to belong, before she met him. He spent painstaking sessions befriending her. Last summer, she painted her toenails a coral pink, dared to go barefoot in sandals to a session. She did not tuck one foot behind the other to hide them from sight. Rather, she did not mind her feet being noticed.

She was beginning to like the idea of being a girl.

I want to believe that the kissing was only a show of genuine affection. But after all these years, why now the close attention to the lips? I try to shake loose from the spin of surprise. I need to talk with Derek, to make some sense of this push beyond the simple comfort of a held hand, of encircled arms.

And then I wonder, *why do I feel the terrible push to keep silent? . . .*

I wait for the window of time and space to ask about that which bewilders me.

"Your body is waking after all these years," Derek says, and stretches his legs out in front of him, crosses his hands behind his head. "You can be more in your body, feel what you might not have before." I am uncomfortable when he talks about the body, as if it is yet another separate identity—one that is given far too much attention. I do not want to hear the theory, his point of view about where I am in the process of recovering my sexuality. "Do you notice any changes, Adriana?"

"I'm not sure," I say. "But I am confused about the time you kissed me."

He sits tall, his back a straight line to the ceiling, looks at me without speaking, long enough to heed warning. I hear my breath, my heart beating in my ears. Everyone inside is quiet. They draw further inward. But I know they can still hear.

"You remember?" He stands and walks a few feet away from me, then stops. He turns to face me. "Well?"

"Yes," I say. "I do remember." I want to shout at him, *How could I forget? Did you not know that I was there, in the backdrop of my mind? Was it not you that explained I would always be there, so that I could understand, so that I could listen?* But instead, my voice fails me.

"What do you *think* the kissing means?"

"I don't know," I say.

I look in his eyes, but they are flat, withholding.

Humiliation is hot on my face, dampens the palms of my hands.

He stands with his feet together, puts his hands in his pockets. I hear the muted jingle of coins.

"Tell me what you think," he says.

I think of lips touching, the warm breath that exhaled on the face, the faint smell of washed hair, scent of morning coffee. I think what this means to me, to the others; how still everyone was.

We are not in a country where we kiss on the lips to say goodbye—unless of course we are with family, and even then . . .

He squints at me as if I am suddenly hard to take in. In this instant I think of father, of avoiding being near him; how I disappeared early in the morning and evening, the time of day that gave justice for a kiss. He was disgraced with my clever escapes, tricked by my ghostly existence.

"I think it was sexual," I say, but do not know whether I am asking or making a statement.

One look at his face, and I see that a decision has been made as to my perception. The deep lines that cross his forehead are deeper still, his eyes turn from me to the wall as if to say, *enough*. And so I fall quiet. He looks out the window that is fogged with the heat in the room and the cold outside, where only the high branches of winter trees can be seen. Where life carries on the street two storeys below.

I want to yell at him, *You seemed younger*.

Instead, I return to the place where speaking is impossible.

Pain is a rock, hard and round in my chest.

He walks to the other side of the room, near the door, leans his back against the wall and slides down until he is sitting, then draws his knees upward to where he rests his elbows. He runs his hands through his coarse black hair, puts his head against the wall and shuts his eyes.

I dare not breathe.

"I'm depressed," he says after a long silence, then opens his eyes, keeps his gaze averted, looks out the window again. I don't know how to comfort him. I want to ask him what we can do to make this right again.

He lowers his eyes until they are level with my own, unwavering, and says, "Don't tell anyone. They may not understand."

My pulse quickens.

I do not know where I can find room for this secret.

He lifts himself off the floor, walks over to the red chair, and picks up his black notebook and pencil off the floor. We are back in our places, therapist and patient. I want to tell him he was not at all like father. There was no wrongdoing. We can make this right. This is what I need to believe.

But he has already made up his mind to let it drop, as if the first part of the session did not exist, and says, "Tell me about your week. What do we need to work on today?" His voice is like cold metal.

I work to bury the image of what he wants me to forget.

At the end of our session he stands and pushes back the red chair. The scrape of wood on carpet is like a reprimand. He puts on his jacket, pulls at the zipper as if he is already standing in the winter air. I get up from the couch, my legs like water, and walk towards the door. He holds it open, stands to the side.

My mind reels with unanswered questions. I need to talk this out, to come to a place of understanding so that we can repair the safety net.

"What now?" I dare ask.

"What do you mean?" He pushes the door shut and faces me.

"I still don't understand," I say.

"I want you to be careful," he says. I notice the twitch in his right shoulder, the ever so slight rise. I do not miss the slowed tempo of his words that carry the weight of meaning.

"Of what?" I ask.

"Of what your father did to you, Adriana. What your father did to you is not who you are, but he still may have control inside over what you do. He might be inside of you."

Stunned, I try to make sense of what he is saying. And then it dawns on me. I know what he's saying. I must be on watch for what lies inside even if it isn't clear. I must be on watch for what can happen under the influence of the past. I wish I could see beyond my fear. My heart beats hard. I can't trust this. I can't risk the hurt it can create. What has happened and what is unknown stir in my stomach like a sickness. I'm terrified—but not for my own safety. I pray in quiet desperation. I pray that harm will not befall my ally from the cost of my actions.

* * *

This is a very disturbing story. In the first many years of therapy, Adriana's therapist, Derek (not his real name) did not exploit her but worked to gain the trust of her younger parts, and they gradually disclosed their memories of sexual abuse in the home by her father, along with her mother's blaming her for this abuse. Derek put himself in a position of the loving rescuer to the little child parts, and physically held them, in an era when therapists were less afraid of being accused of sexual exploitation of their clients. Adriana became very dependent on Derek to help her feel better when emotions or body sensations came up from the abuse, since he was not able to teach her adult self how to work with her own inside parts.

While holding the child parts, it appears that Derek misinterpreted their response to this closeness, since they were in a woman's body, and came to believe that they represented a woman's wanting to enter a sexual, or at least romantic, relationship with him. When he asked what she thought the kiss meant, Adriana gave the answer she thought he wanted without understanding its meaning. Her little child parts had no concept of sexual feelings, but they craved the close cuddling which they had been denied in childhood. The fourteen-year-old had the kind of chaste crush which a young girl can have on an older man. She wanted only to continue the loving, close relationship she had with Derek; she had no concept of sex other than as abuse. They all (except the protector) felt loved by Derek.

You may have noticed that Derek asked Adriana whether she remembered his kisses. It seems that knowing she was dissociative, he was hoping that she would not remember his inappropriate boundary-crossing behaviour.

Although it does not come through in this excerpt, Derek's "memory work" encouraged discharge of bodily sensations without finding the parts who remembered the content of what had happened, so it did not resolve the problems. He did not even know Adriana had experienced ritual abuse, although if he had enquired about what experiences led to these bodily sensations he would have quickly found out.

It was Derek's words that did the most damage. When his own feelings led him to behave inappropriately, he blamed his client, accusing her of being like her sexually abusive father. This resonated with the ritually abused parts, who were told by the abuser group that it was they who were evil once they had been forced to participate in the group's evil acts. Years later, there are parts of Adriana who still believe it is she who is evil, and Derek's accusation is for them the proof of it.

You may notice that Adriana's protector part was aware that people change, having grown up with dissociative parents, and was constantly watchful for Derek changing from a loving, nurturing helper to something else. This part of a person is important, as it often sees the truth that other parts want to deny.

If you have had a therapist become sexual or romantic with you, know that it is not your fault. This is true even if you have a part who has attempted to seduce a therapist. (Some groups programme child parts to do this.) It is always the therapist's responsibility to make sure that the relationship never becomes sexual, and to deal with his or her own sexual or romantic feelings without involving the client or blaming the client.

There is another risk that is worse than inept therapy, and even worse than a therapist sexualising the relationship: that is the risk of getting a therapist who is still part of a perpetrator group. Wendy Hoffman, who is herself a therapist as well as a survivor of mind control and ritual abuse, tells the story of her attempts to deal with her memories with the therapists she has seen over many years. The therapists' names and locations have been changed.

Wendy Hoffman: "My life as a therapy patient"

If I had not sent my child to a specialised private school, been disobedient and fought my cult husband, who was also my handler, launched a successful performance on incest that toured, started one of the first lawsuits exposing incest, mounted a group art exhibition on satanic ritual abuse that attracted the press, went to graduate school without their permission, written a clinical book on satanic ritual abuse that had a publisher who had featured the book in its advertising, tried to help survivors get free of this mind control and abuse—if all that had not happened, then they would not have sent me to their own therapists. I would have been one of their many obedient automatons sent for tune-ups and maintenance now and again, but not for punishment and close-down.

Three cult therapists: a psychiatrist, a psychologist, and a Christian counsellor, in three different cities, reprogrammed me before my last one, Ann, who was a Christian counsellor with a master's degree in education. I will just tell you about my last series of punishments here, for, although the circumstances were different for each set of therapy, the close-down procedures were similar.

Every few months for almost one year, I commuted to this last therapist for week-long intensive therapy sessions. I (that is, my front person) believed it would be excellent therapy with a specialist in ritual abuse who was recommended by one of the leaders in the field. My New York handlers had tricked me into thinking the cult was programming me against Ann. In one of their programming rooms that had torture instruments, and electricity for electroshock and visual effects, they showed me wall-sized photos of Ann with steely facial expressions and changed her name to "Abominable". That interference persuaded the outside me that she was safe. I remembered and reported this mind control to Ann and she pretended to be outraged. My inside parts, who knew what Ann really was, thought of cheating spouses who feigned to despise the person they were sleeping with, but my front person thought she was sincere.

During the therapy sessions, Ann did something strange with her eyes, moved her hands back and forth, spiralling upward—hand signals that meant "if you ever tell, we will kill you." In her guesthouse, where I stayed overnight, Ann and her professional partners, Lenny and

Marge, drugged, hypnotised, tortured, and threatened me: "If you ever remember this—kill yourself when you are back in New York." They didn't want any mess on their land in Freeport. And so I was programmed with the foundational cult training that I could never be free of my oppressors and never consciously aware of my programmes and personalities who held the programmes and the structure that embedded them.

Even though other parts in my brain knew what these impostors were up to, they did not tell the rest of me, including my front person. I should not be exasperated with my insiders. They had their reasons. But it irks me that I fell into treacherous hands again. I have searched my mind to ascertain how it happened. Two of my ruler-insiders tell me that they believed that once the cult assigns you to a close-down specialist, it's a done deal. Even if I had been more aware of my inside reality, changed my name, run to another country, disappeared, other parts of my brain were still reporting on me. Until the internal reporters understand the ramifications of what they are doing, there can be no safety.

Drugs and torture take away the ability to think and have a will. Because she had possession of the volumes of my 'black book', Ann knew how to draw out and intimidate vulnerable pieces of my dissected brain. "You will never remember, tell or write about what we do or we will kill your only living child, of that you can he certain." No one inside me doubted it. In retrospect and without the drugs or brain concussion, I can see that it is doubtful they would have taken the chance of killing my daughter. My protective act was most likely for nothing.

Lenny called out my inside babies who couldn't resist his tyranny. "Take your book about cult abuse off the queue, never give it to anyone, it's a finished project. Write to the publisher and say you don't want it published." His orders went to the adult me but the babies felt the torture and intimidation. He held a gun.

Another time, I was asleep but some parts of my brain heard the guest-house door lock turn, the door open and close, footsteps through the living room and hall. Rita, one of the clients they co-opted, was in the other guest bedroom. Physically strong, she was being prepped to be a torturer. Ann, Marge, and Lenny surrounded my bed. One of them tasered my left nipple and my body leaped a foot or two off the mattress. After injecting my arm, Ann said, "Come forward," to a young part who held the memory of the original nipple torture. Ann raised her left hand index and third fingers, made a circle with her thumb nail and index finger and pushed her hand toward me, meaning "We will kill your child if you ever tell." She did the sequence four times and then the two straight fingers one more time. "If anybody tries to help you, don't listen to them. You will never be free, you are only slave material."

When I was born, my maternal grandmother had put a needle through my left nipple at an initiation ritual. Ann had the record of this torture in my "black book". On the floor of this Freeport Counseling Center, Marge did the same thing as Ann chanted:

> "Snatches, batches, you are a waste,
> snatches, batches, you have no face.
> snatches, batches, go from this place,
> snatches, batches, you are to be erased."

In unison, they all said "a waste." They love to chant and rhyme as they programme.

Ann took me to her church where I learnt about the Baptist beliefs of Christianity. Instead of getting to mind control programmes, parts, and structure, Ann focused on Jesus, demons, human spirits, and spiritual warfare. And in her therapy sessions, Ann liked to slap her thighs four times while saying "lies, trickery, deceit, illusion" over and over, meaning that the cult practised deception and that I shouldn't be tricked. But in group programming sessions at night, she and her entourage used the same movements and rhythmic beat to say "You will never escape, you belong to us, forever and evermore."

In 1993, I lived in New York City, my psychotherapy clients were making progress and I had begun working on a multi-media performance about ritual abuse. In 1994, they commanded me to stop commuting, leave my city, and move to Freeport. If I didn't, I thought they would kill my child. About six months after my move, at an outdoor ritual, Ann showed me the tarot card with the death angel in blue and said that after I got home, on February 4th at midnight, I was to slit my wrists sitting on the seat in my shower and that there was a razor already placed in the bathroom near the sink. I must have handed over a key to my house during a mind control session or someone could have climbed through a window. Although I did feel suicidal, just as they had programmed, one of my internal leaders picked the razor up carefully, another wrapped it in paper towels, and a third inside part threw it in the garbage. My insiders were in turmoil because some of them wanted to take this opportunity to die but others, especially the leaders of my internal world, felt victorious. Despite the elaborate ritual and all the programming, my handlers did not win. My front person's having no conscious memories of this mind control or ritual, I continued in therapy with Ann. She had by now, through hypnosis and drugs, made me emotionally dependent on her.

One day, Ann telephoned me to say that she got word from God that I should watch the movie, *Papillon*. In *Papillon*, two men are exiled to an island surrounded by mountainous cliffs. One figures out a way to escape by diving into the water at the seventh sequential wave. The other man contents himself with being a prisoner by starting a garden on the barren rocks and keeping his mind distracted. Ann and her colleagues drugged and tortured me as the score from *Papillon* played in the background. "You will never escape us. You will always be the man trapped on the rocks. You will never be free of us. God wants that. You will never jump on the seventh wave like the other man. You are caught here with us. It is God's will."

Ann taught that demons held programmes in place and kept the personalities separated; hence the need for deliverances. When an inside part is first coming out, it can feel like a wave rising, almost like levitating. Ann persuaded me that these were not parts of myself, but human spirits and demons or demonised human spirits. She convinced me that the levitating feeling was proof that these were demonic beings inside of me. Ann performed weekly exorcisms to rid me of these "supernatural beings", but what she was doing was closing down the courageous parts of myself that tried to come forward and speak. The hand movements she used during the exorcism gave trigger signals to cult-trained insiders to lock away the part she was talking to in a sealed container. I felt temporary relief after each of these parts was put away and, therefore, believed that I had had a successful exorcism. By the time she finished with me, all the inside parts who knew their and my story had been sent away, and I thought that I had been mostly filled with evil entities.

Whenever I related a memory to Ann, she said "Really?" Once I complained to her that it stopped my process. Without knowing it, I was complaining about the programming. Ann, Marge, and Lenny did not have a special black electrified chair in their offices in Freeport, but they had hand-held electric shock devices with sticky glue and electrodes, and shocked my body as they said to my hypnotised parts, "Whenever you tell anyone anything, they will not believe you and think you're crazy. They will say 'Really?' which means 'You're nuts.' Protect yourselves by not telling anyone what you know of your past." Again they employed a combination of settings. In an outdoor ritual in the woods, I lay on the altar with electrodes over my body. Ann instructed me to tell Marge, Lenny, and three of the co-opted ritual abuse victim-clients a memory such as "Ann tricked me into moving here." I told the same memory to every person, one after the other; the person replied 'Really?' and I was electro shocked, then stoned. Drugged, my body frozen and bruised, I almost stopped breathing and stayed in paralysis. Then Ann reinforced the motto of this training: "It doesn't pay to tell people anything because no one will believe you." I remember feelings of despair that crawled around and never stopped until I ceased remembering who I was.

Another night, I was in the front office of the Counseling Center and Marge had a large pad of paper on a stand. She drew my internal structure on it, outlined the sections in bold black lines which meant I was never to go there, drew arrows by the Illuminati section and said "Never, never enter there on penalty of death." This Illuminati section is the core of my programming.

Here is some advice from a duped person. When you go to a therapist, your front person could pick up clues: if the therapist makes you feel bad about yourself or if s/he alternates between making you feel bad about yourself and grandiose, then you should be on the alert. If you are chronically angry with the therapist, honour your anger. Your inner people will have the facts, and it would be wise to ask them about what they know about the therapist(s). If they tell you the therapist(s) call inside people out by words, images, hand or foot signals, numbers, or any kind of mind control trigger, or push down or send away parts of your mind, or administer drugs and torture, then you know you are in the hands of a double agent.

Although I am now working with a skilled and trustworthy therapist, I still have scars. Now whenever my honest therapist does anything at all even remotely reminiscent of something Ann and her gang may have said or done or gestured, waves of mistrust sweep over me. The scars of being so tricked have long-lasting tentacles.

After seven years, Ann and her entourage deemed that I was sufficiently closed down and were disgruntled that it took so long. She needed my space for other unwitting survivors making progress in their quests for freedom and was anxious to discard me. But first they had to make sure I would have no future therapy. After all, it is possible to find a safe and helpful therapist.

Right before I was sent away, Ann drugged me and Lenny put a head vice around my now fifty-seven-year-old head, squeezed it more and more tightly until someone agreed to be a seven-year-old girl who was in charge of a whole schoolroom of internal children. "All the children have to be told there's no point in seeing other therapists because they are all Ann. If you need a therapist, you have to go back to Ann. You must never tell anyone about Ann."

Just before I left Freeport, Ann and her colleagues were in her programming room, which she called a therapy room. They flipped through my black book deciding which memories to flag. They planned to take pieces of crucial memories out and block them so that I would never be able to complete and therefore resolve certain dissociated sequences. She would call out a part of me from a memory, torture and shock that part, and move it into storage in what she called a "morgue". There the parts remained in cold storage, separated from the other parts of the experience. These programmers considered each memory for selection, and chose important rituals and programming sessions. They left out everything before the age of three, as well as memories that they thought would be too humiliating for me to remember.

They then recruited ten previously created child parts of me to stand guard at the door to this imaginary "morgue" and not let any other parts of my mind enter or leave. Finally, they got a four-year-old part and her helpers to agree to hide a piece of pain from each subsequent abusive event after I left therapy with Ann. Then they beat me up and discharged me. They were sure they had sealed me off for good.

* * *

Wendy's piece speaks for itself. I do not know what percentage of the therapists who specialise in working with mind control and ritual abuse are "plants", but for certain some of them are. If a therapist has been recommended by a family member, be wary. If the therapist has been recommended by another survivor, be wary too, although it is possible that the other survivor has actually found someone competent. Be wary in any case—Wendy's last cult-involved therapist was suggested by a leader in the field, who was not (to my knowledge) a plant. You need to ask your insiders to be watchful, as Adriana's protector part was, and to tell you the truth about any therapist you might consider. It is also wise to help your reporter parts understand as soon as possible how they undermine your safety, so that they will not report that you are on your way to healing.

You might have wondered what happened to Sally ("Old Lady") after the experiences written about in Chapters Six and Eight of this book. She did find a therapist who understood what she was dealing with, and here is what she wrote about it after three years with the new therapist.

Sally's higher-up insiders: "The new therapist"

The new woman was a therapist and so we were supposed to get rid of her too, either kill her or give her a hard time so she wouldn't accept Old Lady. When we kept emailing her, she just set down clear strict boundaries and was not a pushover or scared of us or weak like the other therapists. She was firm, which we liked because we were used to being trained that way. We were intrigued and scared and determined to make her fire us or we would kill her. But first we wanted to see her and test her. Who was she? Why did she want to help us? She told us that she was here to listen to us and learn from us and to help us to be free. Could we trust her? Why should we trust her? Why didn't she appear weak? Why couldn't we push her around? Hmmmmm . . . she was a challenge, we thought. With each test that we performed to see if she would fire us, abandon us, or even get mad at us, she passed.

We always let the littles come out before any of us higher-ups because they were expendable. If the new therapist was going to trick us like the other therapist or doctor or the bad lady, then she would hurt them, not us. The new therapist did not hurt the littles when they came out, and did not get mad at them. She treated them with respect, like young children who had the right to think for themselves, laugh, be creative, and play and learn. She didn't hurt them or hate them even if they did their jobs. We could see that they were not as afraid any more. They were happy—smiling, laughing, and having fun. This was strange for us higher-ups to see and we wanted it too, but we were torn about being loyal to the cult, and also scared to try something different, even having fun. They shared some information with us so we know we are safer now and can maybe come out too, because none of us really likes being stuck in our memories, or in pain, or doing our jobs all the time.

Some of us higher-ups are scared to come out and talk about this stuff, too, because we don't like being exposed or naked, and we do not like to lose any power. Thinking we have power helps us to stay safe, and feel big and strong and brave like our cult leaders, powerful and bad. But we do not really like to be bad or hurt people. But we still got scared to give up all our power because it was like being naked. So we told her that it was like taking a card from a card house we had made, and the card house was us, and when you take the card away the house falls down. It is gone forever because it's dismantled, every last code and job and secret, and that scares us because then what would we do? And do you know what our therapist said? She said "Why don't you play cards then?" and it made us laugh because it was so funny. We used to have the power to turn on programmes or make the body sick and remember things, but we were really just hurting ourselves for the cult's purpose and not our purpose. Now we have power in a different way, power to do good and help others. This is why we turned the programmes off.

Our new therapist taught us that we are not bad people, we are kids who were messed up and taught to hurt without thinking, but not any more. She kept asking us things that made us think, and it surprised us that we could think. Sometimes it hurts when we start to think because our heads aren't used to thinking. It was freeing for us too, and empowering. We began to question what we were taught, to wonder if what our leaders told us were lies. She asked us to check on the Internet and read books so we could practise thinking for ourselves and judge for ourselves whether what she told us was true or not. We found out that we do have minds and can think for ourselves and make choices without being told we are bad or needing to be punished or killed. She said it was all right to disagree with her, that sometimes she would be wrong because she wasn't perfect. She also would apologise if she was wrong about something or if she hurt us. We were not used to this.

And very soon she began to help some of us work through our memories in a way that all the insiders who had a part in a memory could work through it together, so that we all could relive the memory to be free and feel without being overwhelmed and in pain. Then we could be free and be able to welcome the other insiders and protect them, dress them, or take care of them and start to work together as a football team and then as a family that values mutual respect and democracy.

And we see now that we can think and decide for ourselves what we want to do, like play or sleep or protect the body and the littles, and help others be safe and heal and have fun, so that's why we are speaking today about what we know. Instead of being like a caterpillar, with so many legs that it cannot decide which way to go, we are becoming free like butterflies.

* * *

Transference and countertransference

One of the experiences known to be common in therapy is transference. Transference is the word for what occurs when a client has an emotional reaction to the therapist that actually belongs to a parent or other significant person in that client's life. Transference can be positive or negative. Organised abuser groups make sure you have plenty of negative feelings to transfer on to any therapist you might see. Not only is there the anti-therapy programming I described earlier in this chapter, there are the negative experiences of daily life. Many of your parts have only encountered adults who were rejecting and abusive, or who switched from kindness into abusiveness, so it is natural for them to expect this behaviour from a therapist. It takes time to be sure that someone will not treat you the way the adults in your childhood treated you. So, you are bound to have negative transference to your therapist.

A good therapist needs to be able to detect negative transference and not take it personally, and also to detect when a client is genuinely having trouble with the therapist's behaviour, and be ready to examine that behaviour and apologise if necessary. Even good therapists do make mistakes, and clients perceive them.

Survivors are filled with young insiders who have unmet childhood needs for nurturing, appreciation, comfort, and friendship. If the therapist is kind and caring, these child parts emerge. Some of their needs are too vast to be met in a therapy relationship, because infants need a loving mother full-time, not for an hour or two per week. Healing comes through grieving for what you did not have when you should have had it, not through trying to replace it later in life. Your therapist—and even your partner—will "burn out" if he or she tries to be a parent for your infant parts. A common reaction for therapists working with survivors is feeling like the mother who was unable to protect her child, and becoming overly involved and guilty. This can lead to the young parts wanting more and more, not understanding the limitations of the therapist, who cannot provide the constant availability and physical holding provided by the loving parent of a young child. The parts who were told they were "special" by the perpetrators may also feel entitled to special attention beyond what a therapist can give them. The therapist is unable to set clear boundaries, the programmes to harass the therapist are set off, and chaos ensues. We saw this in both LisaBri's (Chapter Seven) and Sally's (Chapter Six) stories about their therapists.

Countertransference is the word used to describe what happens when a therapist projects something on to a client, reacting to that client emotionally because of a resemblance to someone else in the therapist's life. Whether it is the therapist's own past traumatic experience, or the therapist's present needs, anything projected on to the client is detrimental to the client's recovery process, as you will see. If a therapist cannot acknowledge these projections, examine them, and take responsibility for them, he or she is actually dangerous to the client, at least on an emotional and psychological level. We see this illustrated in Adriana Green's story.

If you do find a truly competent therapist, your recovery can most probably proceed much faster than if you do it alone. There is something wonderfully healing about having an ally who truly cares about you and understands what you have gone through and are going through now. Wendy states that "Just knowing this person is there fortifies the survivor, and the other person's objectivity about what may be the effects of mind control is invaluable."

What I would want in a therapist

I have something to confess to you: I have never been in therapy, except as a therapist. So, I can only imagine what it is like to be a therapy client, just as I can only imagine what it is like to be a survivor of mind control and ritual abuse. However, I have been a therapist for over thirty years, and I have observed what my clients go through. Several of my mind-controlled and ritually abused clients have come to me after years of failed therapy, and I have learnt from what they have told me about what went wrong.

Like every human being, I have needed basic medical care all my life. Recently, I had a bad experience with my primary care physician, who tried to override my concerns and decisions (I had brought a list) in favour of her own. Now, I recognise that physicians know what symptoms to look for, because they have training in recognising serious illnesses, and there is a place for asking about things that the patient might not have considered. But this does not excuse her failing to listen to me, and attempting to refer me for procedures without respecting my opinion, since it is my body and my health being considered.

It made me think about what I want in a doctor. I need that person to be (1) knowledgeable and competent; (2) respectful of me as an intelligent participant in my own healthcare decisions; and (3) kind and compassionate, able to reduce my anxiety and my actual and potential suffering. My doctor needs to listen to my concerns, take the time to answer my questions clearly and respectfully, be reassuring when I am anxious, and explain his or her reasons for tests, referrals, prescriptions, or advice. I need my doctor to know that I, not she, am in charge of my own health, and I will make the decisions, although she is there to assist me. What I want is the basic minimum that is the right of every patient or client. Being a patient who was not heard has given me some insight into what clients and patients frequently go through with therapists, no matter what the therapist's academic training or discipline.

The research shows that it is the character of the therapist that makes the most difference in the effectiveness of therapy. Patterson (2000) summarises:

> The magnitude of the evidence is nothing short of amazing. There are few things in the field of psychology for which the evidence is so strong. The evidence for the necessity, if not the sufficiency, of the therapist conditions of accurate empathy, respect, or warmth, and therapeutic genuineness is incontrovertible . . . The effectiveness of all methods of counseling or psychotherapy may be due to the presence of a therapeutic relationship. (p. 436)

That is one reason the mind controllers work so hard to try to destroy that relationship.

What would I want in a therapist if I were a survivor of mind control and/or ritual abuse, struggling to free myself of the programmes and their consequences? The first qualities I would want are those I want in my doctor, and in any therapist I would consult about any issue: knowledge, respect, and compassion. In addition, I would want my therapist to be a stable person, emotionally healthy, able to set clear boundaries, tune in to his or her own feelings, and remain grounded while I went through the ups and downs of the recovery process. I would especially want my therapist to care about me, for real.

Knowledge

I stated that my doctor should be knowledgeable. The main way a doctor acquires knowledge is in many years of university training, plus on-the-job supervised training. This is not very different from a therapist. Different therapy professions (psychiatrist, psychologist, social worker, counsellor, art therapist, etc.) have different emphases in their training. I believe it helps to know family systems theory (since a dissociative person is a system), child development, and play and art therapy (since a dissociative personality system contains children), and attachment theory (since the therapy relationship attempts to repair the broken attachments of childhood). Many other theories and skills can be helpful.

Although there are many things therapists can learn during their formal training, no university programme that I know of yet teaches its students how mind control works or how to work with a mind-controlled client. The main way in which I have learnt about these abuses and their effects on survivors is through listening to my clients, listening to the content of what they disclose, and listening to what is unspoken, their agony. A therapist needs to listen with respect, knowing that the only real experts on what a person has been through are the parts of that person. That is still the case, even though I and others have begun to write about what we have learnt and to teach others. So, knowledge in a therapist is deeply intertwined with the ability to listen to what the client is saying and experiencing.

This is not to say that knowledge is not important. If you look at the list of advantages of working with a good and knowledgeable therapist on the first page of this chapter, you will see that a therapist's knowledge about how mind control and ritual abuse work can be very helpful. Someone who understands these matters will not be shocked or overly traumatised by your traumas, or overly intrigued by your multiplicity. He or she will understand about parts having jobs, about symptoms being caused by these jobs, about the lies the abusers tell you, about how a programme training is repeated at different ages, about how a traumatic memory belongs to a whole group of insiders rather than just one—and many other things. The competent therapist may know the road map of this abuse, which you might not be aware of until you meet all or most of your internal parts.

If you do not have such a person available in your area, you might find someone who is willing to learn, both from you and from those more knowledgeable therapists who discuss these matters online and write books and articles about them.

Respect

A recent pilot study by Ellen Lacter and others (2012) looked at the most and least helpful approaches in dealing with ongoing victimisation of ritually abused clients. The participants in the study, who were ritual abuse survivors who were in training to be therapists, said that disbelief and "abusive neutrality" were among the least helpful approaches, while believing the client and understanding the subject matter were among the most helpful. To me the essence of this is respect for the client and his or her experience. Even if a survivor is completely confused about whether or not anything happened, even if he or she is "remembering" things that appear impossible, and even if he or she appears psychotic, it is respect for that survivor which will enable the person to look inside and discover the truths to be found there.

Mind control is a tricky business. I believe each survivor has the right to determine the validity of his or her own memories, while being aware that much of what he or she has experienced might involve deliberate deception. I was fortunate in that the one and only really useful course in my graduate programme was essentially a course in scepticism, a course in which we analysed all the then-current approaches to psychotherapy and looked at their assumptions and their validity. This scepticism has provided a firm base from which to approach the maze of information and disinformation regarding ritual abuse and mind control. As I have struggled to make sense of it, I can assist my clients to learn to think in ways that will enable them to make sense of their own experiences. Listening to the content of what my clients tell me requires me to be both curious and sceptical—believing my clients' experiences to be real, but looking at a larger picture to explain these experiences. That is how I discovered much of the trickery embedded in the programming. I believe a healthy scepticism is a really important quality for a therapist working with survivors, as well as compassion for how it might feel to discover you have been deceived all your life.

One of my major goals in working with survivors of mind control is to free their minds, so that they can decide for themselves what is true and what purpose they want to have for their lives. I do not want to replace one kind of mind control with another. You want to make sure that any therapist you see has sufficient respect for your understanding and your right to make your own decisions. Your therapist should empower you, not rescue you or take away your rights by hospitalising or medicating you against your will.

Stability

Every survivor has some inner parts who are exquisitely tuned to what is going on in the therapist. They notice every sound and perceive every innuendo in the therapist's wording or tone of voice, looking for judgement, or disbelief, or rejection. This is different from parts who are trained to distrust all therapists just because they are therapists. In Adriana Green's story, you see the value of her protector part. Trust these parts in yourself, listen to their messages, and take them seriously.

The survivors I have worked with reported that many of the adults in their childhood were multiple. Anyone who has grown up around adults who are multiple has parts who are looking for switches, or the precursors to switches, when a person who was being kind or attentive suddenly becomes abusive or self-centred. You may notice that Adriana said that Derek "appeared different, younger" when he crossed her boundaries. It is all right to watch your therapist for switches. I always tell my clients that I do not expect them to trust me at first; trust has to be earned. This is nowhere more true than in the therapeutic relationship. I also tell them that I am incapable of switching because there is only one of me, and they can watch me to see whether this is true.

Every therapist is, of course, a human being, and will have times of difficulty and possible inattentiveness when he or she is going through something personal which is unrelated to you. If you notice such things, ask your therapist what is going on, and see how he or she responds. While the therapist is unlikely to tell you the details of what goes on in his or her personal life, it is important that he or she is aware of when it is affecting his/her therapy. You need your therapist to be essentially stable.

You might have noticed in Sally's story that it was very important to her that the new therapist was "firm" and "didn't appear weak", as her higher-ups tested her in various ways. Therapists are only human, and our own fears can be triggered by the fears of our clients. We find this material very disturbing, and we can feel incompetent because nothing we were taught in graduate school gave us a way to deal with the horrors and the complexity of mind control and ritual abuse.

Many therapists run quickly to any easy fix which is offered us by those promoting a "one-size-fits-all" solution, which does not require us to accompany our clients through the living hell they have been in. Many graduate schools encourage students to learn various models of therapy, and apply them to clients regardless of what the clients are dealing with. Many newly trained therapists are afraid to venture out on their own, and follow models or techniques they have learned at workshops uncritically. "If your only tool is a hammer, everything is a nail." This is particularly true when we are anxious. You do not need a therapist whose anxiety and need to appear competent leads him or her to slavishly copy someone else's method. Every technique is valuable only as a tool in the hands of someone who can look at the big picture and choose his or her tools carefully.

Emotional contagion can affect therapists. Over the years, I have observed how some therapists working with survivors have been taken in by the abuser groups' disinformation, coming to believe that there is one gigantic cult that controls the whole world and knows everything, or that therapists' families are in mortal danger, or that survivors (or certain parts of them) are evil and controlled by supernatural forces of evil. You saw how Wendy's cult-plant therapist persuaded her she was filled with demons. Clients can convince therapists of such things, too. Your therapist needs to be able to realistically assess danger without panic, since parts of you may panic easily. He or she needs to offer a safe ground when you feel unsafe.

When I listen to a client, I have to be solidly grounded in myself and in the present, while opening my heart to hear the client's experience. It is a delicate balance. If I am not fully with my client, he or she will know this at a deep level, and will be unable to trust me, and I will be unable to hear what is unspoken, or the deepest reality of what is spoken. If I am not fully in my own experience, knowing the world to contain both good and evil, knowing why I have chosen compassion, knowing everything I have learned in seventy years of living and growing, I will be drawn into my client's panic, and will resonate with it so much that I will be unable to provide a solid ground to steady the client, and I might be overcome with terror and susceptible to believing the lies the abusers told my client.

Compassion

Literally, the word "compassion" means "to feel with". Therapy is, above anything else, a real (though one-sided) relationship, a relationship within which I come to know another person deeply, sense the places where they are hurt or where their growth has been halted, and bring healing to those places. Listening to my client's heart, with my own heart, allows me to detect what is unspoken, and to provide that connection, that attachment bond, without which the wounded young parts of my client cannot come alive and move beyond their trauma. The essence of that bond is compassion, along with appreciation for the survivor's courage and tenacity in pursuing recovery.

One woman saw me for a whole year without speaking in sessions. I observed and connected with each young part of her as she switched, and I spoke what I was detecting in her mind, usually an emotional state. I began to perceive her insiders moving around inside her head; she encouraged me to do this, and I would speak about each one that I saw, what that one felt and what it believed about people. Over time, our relationship has progressed, and now she is working through very early memories of sadistic abuse in a backwoods cult, as well as years of brutal abuse by several family members. Sometimes, it feels as if I can see what she is thinking or seeing when she goes through a memory, as if I am there in her head. Her young parts describe me as "reaching in".

Sometimes, I am with a client who is going through a traumatic memory, and she is unable to cry because of the brutal "don't cry" training. I find myself with tears on my face, although I do not feel weak and helpless—tears because I care about that client and what he or she went through.

Recently, I did an "intensive" with a client—an entire week during which we worked to resolve her mind control memories. The first or second night, I had a dream in which I went down many levels of a waterslide inside a tall building, enjoying the ride, but missed the last two levels because there was a red curtain over them and the water in there was red. I walked down the stairs instead, but then decided to do those levels I had missed. I had to get up to the top of the building and go down a different waterslide in another section of the building to reach those forbidden levels. When I described the dream to my client, she gasped and said that the building I had described was her system structure and the waterslide was the "river of blood" by which we could be transported to the important deeper levels of the structure. My dream guided our work. I had three other dreams that week, all relating to what my client and I had to work on. In the last one, I saw a group of people who were looking together at some pathways, and each of them had brought a different pair of spectacles. As they looked through one another's glasses, they could all finally see the pathway clearly, and what had appeared to be several different pathways turned out to be just one. I believe this is what was happening within my client. It seems that the process of attunement between us allowed my subconscious dreaming mind to gain crucial information for our work together.

It is important that your therapist be capable of connecting with you lovingly on a deep level, connecting with all parts, no matter what feelings and what memories they hold. You have parts who can sense whether or not the therapist is capable of this kind of connection.

Why I choose to work with survivors

I believe we all have the same basic choice in life. Those of us who grow up with poverty or abuse or deprivation can choose to become bitter, and pass on the abuse to another generation, or to learn and grow and turn things around for the next generation. Those of us who grow up with safety and comfort and privileges can choose to take those things for granted, and turn our faces away from the less fortunate, or to take on the challenge of helping others and making the world a better place, even though it will have a personal cost for us. Choosing not to choose means we become blind to whatever evil we see, and make no difference to the world.

I had been a practising psychologist for over ten years when I encountered my first mind control and ritual abuse survivors. Very little of what I had studied had prepared me for this work. Working in the "mental health" system had deepened my distrust in the "medical model", which saw all serious difficulties as illnesses to be medicated away. I could see that my survivor clients were receiving little or no help from traditional mental health services. Could I take on the challenge of finding a way to help? Nobody would have blamed me if I had continued to just do what I had been hired to do, which was provide mental health services to children. But I would know that I had shirked an important challenge.

My survivor clients have enabled me to learn much more about how the human mind works than the few basic and often mistaken things I learned in university. Unfortunately, much of what I have learnt is information that organised perpetrator groups have known for many generations but not shared with the visible "mental health" community. In addition, I have come to know and admire people who have fought bravely against many obstacles to regain control of their own minds and lives. I recognise how fortunate I have been not to have to go through childhood torture and mind control, which could have been my lot if I were born to a different family. I have learnt how to use my "mirror neurons" (some people might call them psychic gifts) to tune in to what was going on in my clients' very complex minds, in order to help them. I consider it a great privilege to be able to work with survivors and to learn from them.

In this work, I have also had the exhilarating experience of seeing miracles happen. I have seen people cured of bulimia or chronic pain in a single day, when we worked through the memory of the events in which this symptom was created. I have seen clients who were weighed down with hopelessness gain new hope, regain ownership of their own lives, and go on to make the contribution they want to make. This is very satisfying.

But the horror never goes away, not for me, not for the survivors I speak with. The things they-you—have endured are at the farthest limits of human endurance. I have to renew my commitment daily in order to not look away from these horrors and be able to reach out a hand to those who have experienced them through no choice of their own.

Exercise 30. Assessing your therapist(s)

The following questionnaire goes into detail about your therapist and your relationship with him or her. If you do not have a therapist at this point, it will give you important questions for assessing any potential therapist.

Professionalism

What special skills or education does your therapist bring to your work together?

Does your therapist seem to you to be a stable, mentally healthy person?

Does your therapist pretend to have knowledge or expertise that he or she does not really have?

Is your therapist consistently reliable (on time, remembers appointments, rarely cancels or reschedules, responds to crises, keeps accurate records, gives you advance notice of vacations, remembers important facts about you)?

Does your therapist answer questions honestly?

Does your therapist maintain clear boundaries?

Has your therapist become over-involved with you, inviting you into his or her personal life, or having more than one kind of relationship with you?

Agenda

Have you agreed with your therapist on the goals of your therapy?

Is your therapist following a set agenda or methodology regardless of where you are at and what you say you need?

(*continued*)

Is your therapist more concerned with your functioning than with finding the internal causes of your difficulties, and getting to know your insiders?

Is your therapist only focused on giving practical advice about life?

Does your therapist try to push his or her religion, or dislike of religion, on you?

Whose needs predominate during sessions, yours or those of your therapist? Do you ever feel used?

Danger signs

(A "yes" to any of these danger signs indicates that you would be wise to have serious doubts about remaining with this therapist.)

Has your front person noticed any odd behaviour (such as hand signals) which might indicate that your therapist is involved in an abuser group?

Does your therapist's office contain items (such as pictures or magazine articles or particular dolls or toys) that appear to be triggers for some of your insiders? (This could be deliberate or accidental.) If so, does your therapist readily remove the items when you tell him or her about your discomfort?

Ask your insiders whether any of them have seen or heard your therapist do or say anything that would indicate he or she is involved in an abuser group. Has he or she called out insiders, or pushed them inside, through abuser-created triggers?

Has your therapist ever been sexual or romantic with you, overtly or covertly, told dirty jokes, or looked at your body or touched you in inappropriate ways?

Has your therapist ever used or threatened to use physical force with you?

Has your therapist ever spoken highly of cult practices such as members wearing beautiful clothes or admiration for people in high rank? Has he or she ever seemed envious of cult rewards and pay-offs?

Have any of your insiders seen your therapist at rituals?

Does your therapist see you as sick or "mentally ill" rather than mentally injured and traumatised?

Do you find you are chronically angry with your therapist?

Does the therapist make you feel grandiose (too special) or ashamed and really inadequate?

Has your therapist ever shamed you, humiliated you, or put you down? Do you feel that he or she looks down on you?

Does your therapist blame you if you are not progressing in therapy?

If any of these things have happened, are there any indications that your therapist has been impersonated (as I was) by a cult member? If so, how can you learn to tell the difference between the real and the false therapist, and how can you avoid this happening again?

Do different parts of you have different kinds of experiences with your therapist? Ask inside and do not take silence for an answer. Does your therapist have more than one way of being? Do you have parts who remember being abused by the actual therapist, not an impersonator, as Wendy was?

Therapeutic relationship

Does your therapist make you dependent on him or her for rescuing or preventing self-harm or relieving your painful emotions, or encourage dependency in more subtle ways?

What kind of transference do you have with your therapist? Do you see him or her as the all-powerful saviour, or as just a well-intentioned human being?

Do you react to your therapist as if he or she were one of your parents, or one of your abusers? What behaviours of your therapist trigger this reaction?

(*continued*)

How does your therapist respond when you test him or her? Do you dare test him or her?

Has your therapist ever reacted to you, or to something you have done, from a transference of his or her own? If so, did he or she own up to it and apologise?

Does your therapist respect your decisions, even if he or she disagrees with them?

Is your therapist a good listener, able to listen to all parts of you and gain an accurate understanding of what you are communicating?

Do you feel that your therapist is truly with you during the sessions?

Can your therapist admit to mistakes and apologise sincerely?

Does your therapist show compassion for the hurt parts of you?

Does your therapist's body language match his or her words?

Is your therapist resilient, able to remain strong and not panic when you may be panicking?

Effects of programming

Do any of your insiders have programmed reactions to any words your therapist uses? If so, discover which words, and what these words mean to them.

Do you find that your insiders' training to fear therapists, or to fear disclosures, is making you unable to trust a therapist who might be trustworthy?

Do you experience physical pain or extreme fear while making disclosures to your therapist?

Expertise with multiplicity

Does your therapist understand multiplicity and switching? Does your therapist notice when you switch and bring it to your attention?

Does your therapist accept all of your insiders, no matter what they believe about themselves and no matter what they may have done or been forced to do?

Does your therapist speak respectfully to insiders?

Does your therapist have favourites among your parts, liking some and rejecting others?

Does your therapist encourage you to reject or isolate those of your insiders who are loyal to the perpetrator group, are named after perpetrators, or believe themselves to be evil?

How does your therapist react if your immature or needy parts come out?

How does your therapist react if your angry or aggressive parts come out?

Understanding mind control and ritual abuse

Does your therapist have a good understanding of what mind control and ritual abuse are?

If not, is he or she prepared to do the hard and time-consuming work of learning about these things?

Does your therapist understand why your parts might feel they have to do their assigned jobs?

Does your therapist recognise when your feelings or behaviours indicate you are acting on programming?

When working with memories, does your therapist understand about involving all the parts of you, all the emotions, and all the sensory experiences including especially the "sound track" and what was said?

Is your therapist astute enough to help you detect the deceptions in what you experience or were told by the perpetrator group?

Does your therapist respect and appreciate your survival, your coping, and your desire to recover and to have a meaningful life?

Does your therapist respect your despair and not wanting to have lived?

So, is it worth it to have a therapist? You can see from all the examples that it can be very harmful, mildly harmful, mildly helpful, or very helpful indeed. It depends on the therapist and the relationship. If you do find a therapist who is able to provide the support and insight that enable you to work with your personality system to undo the mind control, it will speed up your recovery process immensely, as you will not be alone in it. If you can afford therapy, I believe it is worth the search for the right person, despite the risks.

Looking at all your answers to this exercise, are there issues that you need to raise with your current therapist, if you have one? Do you need to seek a new therapist? Or if you do not have a therapist, would it be a good idea to look for one? If so, what professional knowledge would you like your therapist to have? What personal qualities would you like your therapist to have? Can you afford a therapist? What funding options are open to you? Is it possible to find a therapist in your location who meets your criteria? What, if anything, do you need to do about finding a good therapist? Do you need to relocate? (See Chapter Nine regarding the risks and benefits of relocation.)

I am hoping this chapter has given you ways to evaluate both your present therapist, if you have one, and any potential therapist you might consider. It could also give you guidance as to how to treat your selves if you have to be your own therapist. Perhaps some strong insider in your personality system would like to take on the therapist role for other parts. If you have to be your own therapist (because you cannot afford one, or because no one suitable is available in your location), what have you learnt about how a therapist should respond to your different parts and their experiences?

CHAPTER TWENTY

Overcoming spiritual abuse

I am not myself a survivor of mind control or ritual abuse. I can only imagine what survivors have been through when they tell me about it. I had to stop frequently while writing this chapter, because the horror of the events I discuss here overwhelms me. What does it mean for me to live in a world where these things happen? And for you, what does it mean that you were there and had to undergo these experiences?

This chapter contains graphic detail which can cause memories to flash back, including some that bring on considerable guilt and shame and possible self-hatred, so make sure you have parts inside ready to put away any memories that come up, until you are ready to deal with them (See Chapter Ten, "Dealing with triggering".)

Throughout your childhood, and possibly throughout your life, survivors have experienced an extraordinary amount of abuse, exploitation, and betrayal. You have seen the worst horrors known to humanity, perpetrated by human beings who might even have been your care-givers when you were a vulnerable child. And you have been forced to participate in those horrors as a perpetrator. What you have endured is a hidden holocaust (a term I first heard from survivor Anne Earle). The horror is what makes recovery take so long, and go so slowly. There are no shortcuts to recovery.

Am I evil?

I have heard this question many times from survivors. Sometimes, it is not phrased as a question, but just as a statement: "I am evil." It is often followed by "God hates me. I am going to hell." These beliefs are deeply ingrained in survivors, particularly of ritual abuse. There are two reasons for this, one true, one false. The false reason is the things the abuser group told you, and the scenarios they set up to make you believe these things. The true reason is that evil was committed, and you were made to be part of it. Every survivor has to come to terms with this.

The guilt and shame of every abuse survivor

Mind control and ritual abuse universally include sexual abuse. The sexual abuse alone is enough to bring on considerable guilt and shame in survivors. E. Sue Blume (1991) describes some of these effects. (Note that although Blume says "she" for the victim and "he" for the abuser, it could be the other way around.)

> Many survivors of childhood abuse draw a simple inference from their experience: "If all of these bad things happened to me, then I must be bad; if I didn't fight and scratch to the death, I must be responsible." This is truly *survivor guilt*: "If I lived, I must not have done enough." And in her guilt, she turns her anger on herself, removing it from her abuser and blaming herself . . .
>
> The child victim of incest feels *soiled* and *spoiled*. She feels contaminated by the dirty act of incest that she "permitted" or even "asked for." Because the event(s) occurred in childhood, while her self-esteem and her identity were still developing, and often before she was even verbal, these feelings weave their way into the very fabric of her being . . . She grows up feeling as if something inside is putrid, disgusting . . . Simultaneously she feels both bad and responsible. (pp. 111, 112–113)
>
> Although powerless to stop the abuser, the child believes that somehow she should have been able to stop him (p. 110)
>
> By blaming herself, the incest survivor blocks her awareness of her victimization. "I was not *abused*," she tells herself, "it was *my fault*." (p. 108)
>
> And if, God forbid, her body responded in any way with arousal, even as the rest of her wanted to puke from the violation, then she must have *loved* it, the most awful guilt of all. (p. 109)
>
> The child victim of incest often sees herself as a participant rather than a victim . . . Actually, in incest one person is active and one passive, one dominates and one acquiesces. The incest survivor herself often fails to make this distinction . . . The alternative would be even more difficult to face: *powerlessness*. It is less threatening to see oneself as somehow responsible and, therefore, guilty than to admit that one has been basically powerless and, therefore, the victim of a situation out of control. (p. 110)

Over the past thirty or so years, society has come to recognise that adults having sex with children is abuse. However, when adults sexually abuse children, they frequently blame the children for being seductive or wanting the relationship to be sexual. And, if a child's body responds, the adult points that out as proof that the child wanted this to happen. It is likely that your sexually abused child parts still feel very dirty and contaminated, especially if abusers told them it was their fault.

Perpetrators who abuse children physically and emotionally also blame and shame them. Children believe they are being hit because they are bad, or did something wrong. The words of verbal abuse stick in their minds, and they believe those words rather than recognising that there is something wrong with the adults who speak or shout the shaming words.

Physical, emotional, and sexual abuse are common in the homes of mind-controlled and ritually abused children, so those of their insiders who live daily life in the family home often believe themselves to be dirty, bad, stupid, and whatever they have been called. But more sinister things happen in the hidden part of survivors' childhoods.

Forced perpetration

Probably the worst spiritual abuse for victims of abuser groups is being forced to take part in both physical and sexual abuse, especially killing of animals and real or apparent killing of infants and people. Ritually abusing cults engage in sacrifice of animals and, sometimes, people, including the "Black Mass", in which the flesh of the sacrifice is devoured by the cult members. Racist groups murder members of despised groups. Most mind-controlling groups force children to take part in these events as perpetrators.

Initially, an adult holds the child's hand around a knife and makes it stab the victim. By a certain age, the group requires children to do this without adult assistance. Parts who refuse are discarded, and the coercion continues with the child being tortured until he or she fully realises he or she cannot resist. Finally, a part is split off who will do the stabbing without being physically forced. The adults similarly assist each child to participate in rapes. For a girl, this is done with objects. The group splits off successive parts until they get one who will perform the act, often with little or no understanding of what he or she is doing.

Group members are expected to take part in sacrifices, rapes, and murders on a regular basis. Some of the murders are no doubt simulated, but they are real to those who are forced to participate in them. Persons who steadfastly refuse to perpetrate have to watch others harm someone or kill an animal, and are told it is their fault. "Kill this rabbit or we will kill your baby brother" is the kind of forced choice a child must make. He or she might have to choose which other child will be sacrificed.

Perpetrator groups also set up simulated "psychic killings", leading children (and later, adults) to believe they have the power to kill psychically. They make a child angry, then show that child someone he or she can kill psychically. The victim appears to die, and the child is told that he or she succeeded in killing that person, and has special powers that can at any time destroy people's lives. When someone in that child's life dies or becomes seriously ill, the child is told that he or she caused it.

A note about psychic abilities: my belief, after having had such experiences myself and reading several books about the research on these, is that psychic abilities such as telepathy and clairvoyance are natural abilities. Many animals as well as people have such abilities. However, in most people they are weak and inconsistent at best. If you want to know more about the scientific investigation of psychic abilities, you might read Chris Carter's *Science and Psychic Phenomena: The Fall of the House of Skeptics* (2007). He has also written similar books on the scientific evidence for near-death experiences and the afterlife (2010, 2012).

Wendy Hoffman says, "extreme suffering makes one more psychic and enhances one's natural ability. As soon as we were born and before, we were on the alert for danger. So existing on the non-earthy realm was second nature and practiced". At the same time, perpetrator groups lie to children about the psychic killing as well as about actual killings.

Some survivors have an added horror. Women often give birth to infants who are sacrificed at birth (sometimes by their own insiders), or kept hidden and later sacrificed. According to Stella Katz, a former cult trainer, each girl (aged 11–13) in a Satanic or Luciferian cult is made pregnant and required to sacrifice her first-born male child. These groups also use "disposable" children, who are raised in secrecy for a few years and then sacrificed. Children of cult members are encouraged to form their first permitted friendships with disposable children, and then forced to sacrifice those children.

Stella has shared this story from her own life, as an acknowledgment of what she was forced to do as a young girl and a tribute to the (other) victim. She states that Miranda was a disposable child bred within her group, and was used to train Stella in sacrifice, by being the sacrifice. (Caution: If this personal story is too much for you, you can skip to the next heading.)

Stella Katz: "For Miranda"

This is for you Miranda, and for all the other Mirandas who came before you and who have come after you. May your souls be forever at peace.

Miranda was four years old when she died on an altar of Satan, at the hand of her five-year-old friend.

The only difference between Miranda and the other little girl was the family she was born into. The five-year-old was fortunate, or not so fortunate, depending on the way you look at it, to be born to a family of the inner circle. She was destined to be "great" and was groomed to be so, and Miranda's death was part of this hideous grooming. Miranda was born to the lower circle. From the moment of her conception she was fated to die. She was probably conceived during an orgy, paternity unknown. Her birth would have been at home, or in the home of another coven member. She would never have seen a doctor unless he was of the coven, or anyone, for that matter, outside the group. She never went to nursery school, or the zoo, or any public place. No outside human being would have known of her existence.

From the moment of her birth she was neglected and abused, physically, emotionally, sexually, and spiritually. She was given only the bare necessities of survival. She was never allowed to associate with other little children or have any kind of friends. About six months before her death, she was, for the first time, allowed to have a little friend. The bond created between these children was unbreakable.

For those six months the friendship was encouraged in every way, and it flourished, neither child knowing what was to come. When someone is starving to death, and food is offered, they do not often stop to ask the cost. When children are deprived of love, any affection is welcomed. When that child suddenly has someone, the bond that is created is everlasting.

For Miranda and her little friend, the bond that was created was nothing more than a deliberate cruel joke. The children were told that something special is coming, and that they are to be a part of it. They got excited as children do, talking and whispering and giggling about what it might be. As the day approached, they were primed and pumped and hyped up, just like children anticipating a special gift from Santa.

On that special day, they were bathed in sweet-smelling soaps, and covered in sacred oils. Their hair was neatly curled and groomed and their bodies were painted with sacred symbols.

For those six months, they had been inseparable. And now they were to join in a big celebration at which they would be the honoured guests. They were dressed in ceremonial garb, the little friend in white satin, and Miranda in a beautiful red chiffon dress, all soft and flowing. She looked like a princess and felt, for the first time in her little life, like someone special. Her blonde hair fell in ringlets flowing gently over her shoulders and down her back. Hand in hand, Miranda and her friend were led into the centre circle by the High Priestess. The bell rang nine times, and chanting began. The High Priest began the offerings, and then, after what seemed like forever, he picked up Miranda and carefully placed her on the altar. Her hands and feet were bound, and as the fear welled up inside her, she began to cry. The priest then picked up her little friend and held her as she knelt beside Miranda. When Miranda saw her friend she immediately quieted and smiled. The priest picked up the sacred athame and placed it into the hand of the little friend.

Holding her hand in his, he raised her hand, and, with one swift thrust, pierced Miranda's heart. Miranda looked up at her little friend and smiled through her pain and tears, and said, "You was my friend", and died.

The little friend was left kneeling on the altar at Miranda's side holding the knife with the blood of her friend dripping off the end of it, knowing that she had just killed her best friend. The High Priest picked her up again, and raised her to the crowd, and said, "You are forever ours." They cheered. She was passed around the circle and praised. The shock of what had happened was so great she couldn't even cry.

Well, Miranda, thirty odd years later, your friend is finally crying and canot seem to stop. There are too many Mirandas. There are TOO many children that society doesn't know about, or care to know about. They turn their heads away and pretend that this stuff just does not happen. And worst of all, some are claiming that our memories of Miranda and kids like her are false.

Well, Miranda, I know that you existed. I know that my memories are very real and so were you. I promise to you here and now that as long as I am alive, the world will know that you and others like you are not figments of our overactive imaginations. And Miranda, I swear to you that the voice I silenced so long ago, your voice, my friend, will scream through mine, until somebody finally hears, and puts an end to the slaughter of all the little Mirandas.

No one on this earth will ever tell me that you never existed. Be at peace, my little friend.

* * *

Stella's tale of her little friend not only shows the horror of forced perpetration, but exposes the horror of the brief lives of unregistered children, born into cults and kept for a few years solely for the purpose of sacrifice. In some groups, each cult child destined to live is paired with a "friend" whom he or she has to sacrifice, as Stella did. Besides forcing a chosen child to participate in a killing, this experience teaches him or her never to make friends. And, of course, this initiation is designed to make that child believe that he or she is evil and a killer, acceptable only to the cult.

(Caution: Here is another horrifying story which you can skip if you choose to.) My most personally traumatic experience in all the years of working with ritual abuse survivors happened when I discovered that one of my clients had an unregistered five-year-old child. The client's reporter part told the group that I had found out, and she was forced to kill the little girl before anyone could locate her. She had to work through this very recent memory with me. The part of her who performed the killing had already integrated with the mother part and was aware that this was her own child. The group told her to perform the sacrifice quickly, and when she refused, began to cut parts off the child, killing her slowly, until the survivor did what she had to do to end her daughter's suffering. As the therapist she had told about the child (before she or I knew about her internal reporter parts), I felt guilty and responsible both for the murder and for my client's having to endure such a devastating trauma.

How does a person come to terms with having experienced such things?

Women and men who continue to be cult-involved while parenting find they have raised cult-involved children who have been abused and programmed, and who will carry the horror on to their own children. Some military/political mind control survivors discover they have been programmed to carry out assassinations, and have done so, and they, too, might have involved their own children, or recruited other children, for the purposes of the group who abused them.

As survivors come to awareness of what they have experienced, it rocks their view of the world, of humanity, and of themselves. It rocks therapists' view of the world, too.

Survivors must face massive guilt and shame for having been forced to participate in rapes, murders, and cannibalism, which to them are very real, whether or not there was trickery involved. For this, they often feel they are too evil to be forgiven, even by a "higher power".

Shaming of victim-perpetrators

After a victim is made to participate in an act of evil, the people in charge put a lot of energy into convincing that child or adult that he or she is evil and a perpetrator rather than a victim, just like them. The perpetrator adults tell the children that God hates them and will punish them because of the evil they have done, that they are children of the devil and belong only to the coven and to the devil, that they are going to hell, and their only choice is whether they will be hurt there or will hurt others. This indoctrination, combined with forced perpetration of acts of extreme cruelty, serves to make such children believe they are different from the rest of humanity in the extent of their evil. They are certainly different in what they have experienced.

Ritually abusive groups also convince children that something evil has been put inside of them. For example, a child is made to believe he or she has a "black heart"—seeing the abuser holding an animal heart and then feeling severe chest pain while it is supposedly inserted. In "brain transplants", the brain of an abuser or of a despised animal such as a rat is supposedly put into the child. Children are told that they are demons or monsters or aliens, or internal copies of an abuser whose "seed" has been implanted by rape.

A programme for flooding of offender memories is set off when a survivor begins to remember the abuse. The survivor suddenly finds himself or herself remembering being the perpetrator of all kinds of horrible acts, and wanting to die because of it. If you have experienced this, know that some insider is acting on his or her programming, making you remember bad things you were made to do without giving you the important information about how you were made to do it and what alternatives you had, if any.

Simulated religious scenarios

Ritually abusive groups are religious organisations, in service to their deities. They resort to trickery to convince their victims that their beliefs are true. They simulate religious scenarios for the children they abuse to make the children believe that the only way to be safe in life is to worship their deity and become a lifelong member of their group. Some genuine, above-ground organised religions do similar things, but not to the same extent or with the same degree of deliberate deception.

The ritual abusers use scene settings and costumes taken from traditional religious imagery to make children believe they are in heaven or hell, and in the presence of God, Jesus, Satan, Lucifer, or other supposed religious figures.

God, Jesus, and heaven

Children are drugged to the point of passing out, placed in a coffin, in some cases buried, and told they are going to die. They awake in a place they are told is heaven, with staged scenery that looks like traditional images of heaven.

God is represented by an old, white-bearded man. Depending on the effect the perpetrator group wants, he might rape a child, or he might verbally abuse that child, telling that child how bad and evil he or she is, that he (God) will never accept the child, and that the child must go to hell for his or her crimes.

Jesus is represented by a younger bearded man who dresses in a robe like the traditional pictures of Jesus that children might have seen in Bibles or on the walls of churches. He might turn his back on a ritually abused child, spit on the child, or rape him or her. He might be tied to a cross, and the child forced to stick a spear into his flesh. Or the child might be tied to the cross, sometimes upside down, and Jesus, along with his followers, tortures that child.

Many cult rituals, including the Black Mass, which includes cannibalism, are conducted in churches. At Christmas time, members of ritually abusive "Christian" cults sacrifice a child who may be said to be the baby Jesus.

I have heard of priests being in charge of the rituals, conferring "forgiveness" through raping the "sinful" child. Because of this, some survivors are very afraid of the notion of forgiveness.

Costumed perpetrators who say they are God or Jesus rape children to make new parts, who are given the job of making the victim remember the rape and the words the abuser said. Sometimes these parts are given the name of "God" or "Jesus".

If you hear the voice of "God" speaking to you, investigate further, but please do not assume it is actually the creator of the universe! It is probably one of two things: (1) a memory of someone who impersonated God, or (2) an insider who has the job of saying "God's" words to you. Do not believe or do what it says, but if it is an insider, speak with it and learn more about its job and why it does it.

Abuser groups use very bright interrogation lights, saying they are shining the "light of God" on the abused child, to make him or her terrified of God. One survivor's inner children all have their eyes closed when they come out because of their fear of the light.

When your inner children experience extreme terror in hearing someone talk about God, it is likely that they are remembering the "God" they had to deal with in the cult. They might also react to religious organisations, buildings, and symbols.

Child victims being tortured are told to pray to God or Jesus to rescue them from torture, and when they do, nothing happens. The cult group mocks them, saying such things as "God doesn't want you", or "See, your God has no power, Lucifer has all the power." Then they are told to pray to Satan or Lucifer, and someone in that costume comes to help.

Angels are also frequently simulated in abusive religious cults. Persons disguised as angels abuse children. In some Kabbalah-based cults there is a blue angel (the angel of the sunset) at the end of each pathway (a very stressful experience for a child), who offers the child peace through drugs. This is part of programming the child to take a drug overdose to reach that peace—and die. If you begin to see or imagine a blue angel who invites you to come to it, tell all your insiders to run fast in the other direction: this is a trick put in by the abusers to get people who are remembering and telling too much to kill themselves. Then ask who inside is showing you the picture of the angel, and when they were taught to do that. "Angel of the sunset" programming begins very young, so it may be coming from very young insiders who do not realise it was a trick. Secrecy is so important to abuser groups that they want to make sure that those who remember die by their own hand before they can disclose the secrets.

For many survivors, Christian beliefs (such as God forgiving) and words (like "Suffer the little children to come unto me") have been so perverted that they cannot even be heard. So, if your outside adult is a Christian, make sure that for the insiders "forgive" does not mean "rape", and "God" does not mean a sadistic abuser. Until your insiders can recover from their terrified reaction to these words, you can use different words for the ideas, and teach your therapist to avoid trigger words. Instead of God, you (and your therapist, if you have one) can say "the compassionate life force" or the "great spirit"; instead of "forgive", you can say "understand and accept".

Satan, Lucifer, and hell

Ritually abusive groups give children heavy doses of drugs, place them in coffins where they pass out, and revive them in a place they are told is the afterlife. It might be "heaven", as discussed previously, or it might be "hell", a place with darkness illuminated by fires, and people in demon costumes with pitchforks and instruments of torture. I have heard of both outdoor and indoor simulations of hell, but please know they are simulations.

Lots of programming goes on in simulated hell. In "hell", the victims are tortured as punishment for their "crimes" and/or are made to participate in torturing others. They are told their destiny is to go to this hell, they cannot escape it, and they have to choose between being tortured there and becoming torturers. Painful rituals are conducted in "hell". Those children wanting to be safe in this life and the afterlife through loyalty to Satan or Lucifer may have to sign "contracts" giving their souls to those beings.

Many more scenarios are set up to make children (and, therefore, the adult survivors they become) believe in the reality of demonic beings. In Satanic or Luciferian groups, demons are simulated through various means, including puppets, films, and costumed people. According to Stella Katz, when a child is three or four years old, people in demon costumes sexually assault him or her, tell the new inside parts split off by these rapes that they are demons or devils, and teach them how to behave in these roles. If you hear the voices of demons or devils, they are likely to be these little child parts of you talking or thinking.

In addition to the Judeo-Christian God and demonic entities, perpetrator groups also simulate ancient Egyptian and other deities. Military/political mind control groups simulate "gods" (for example, wearing togas and standing in misty places) to tell insiders their "true purpose in life" and lead them to believe they are serving the divine when they do the group's bidding.

It is important for you as a survivor to realise that you probably have children inside who believed all these things to be real. Many of them may still be "stuck" in these scenarios: for example, terrified of God and wanting to die, or believing they are already dead and are in hell. It is important to gently bring those child parts into safe places in the inner world, then gradually introduce them to the real, present-day world, where these things are not happening and they can begin to experience some of the good things in life, and eventually to help them work through their spiritual abuse memories so that they can be free of their overwhelming terror, guilt and shame.

Exercise 31. Identifying religious trickery

Ask your insiders about the following religious experiences. Ask for an observer who can tell you and the other insiders what really happened (look for zips in the Satan suits, Halloween costumes and masks, the trick which made the devil appear out of the fire).

God
Jesus
Baby Jesus
Jesus on the cross
Other gods
Angels
Other spirits
Dying
Burial
Resurrection
Heaven
Hell
Forgiveness
Damnation
Anything else
Voices inside saying they are God, Satan, Lucifer, other deities
Insiders with those names

Gaining perspective

It is important for both your front person and your system leaders to recognise that the gods and demons your insiders have seen were all fake, staged and simulated through trickery, even though the little ones inside might believe they were real. The evil was real, but the creatures and entities they saw were not; they were humans, or technologically created to appear real. The crimes of rape and torture and murder might have been real, but the circumstances that made you participate in them were those of deception, cruelty, and inescapable forced choices.

Mind control and ritual abuse survivors tend to believe that they are more evil than any other person, and unforgiveable. Before you judge yourself too harshly, it is important to become aware of the whole context of the things you remember which make you feel evil.

Your discarded and "garbage kid" parts will remember your attempts to refuse to do the evil that was demanded of you. Look for these insiders. For every insider who stuck a sharp stick inside a vagina, plunged a knife into a living body, or took "communion" with the heart of a sacrificial victim, there are usually several who refused, and were severely punished, one after the other, until a new one was created who would commit the required act, often without understanding its significance. Even in events where it appears that one insider performed an act of unspeakable cruelty, it is likely that the insider had previously been split from another, who had been split from another, who had in turn been split from another, so that the eventual product was a part who was out of touch with his or her humanity and believed the adults' lies.

Let me give you an example. Many groups have an important initiation ritual in which a twelve-year-old child has to kill on his or her own, without someone else's hands using the child's hands to perform the killing. I recently worked through the memory of this event with a survivor. This survivor begins with reliving the bodily aspects of the emerging memory, and only explains the story later. I watched in horror as she choked, seemingly to death, losing consciousness three times. Finally, a new part emerged who suddenly sat up and announced, "I'm the new one, I came from the dead one, I can kill." After I had introduced myself to the new one, the survivor told me that her whole system had rebelled against this killing, with the result that the "killer" refused to do it. She was punished by being buried alive, and what she was reliving was the experience of choking to death from dirt in her throat, then being revived after a new part had split off. My sense was that her whole system, including her core, recognised that the punishers were not going to allow her body to remain dead, but they would persist until they got a part who would do the evil that they wanted. "The new one" asked me whether I hated him because he had killed.

The mind-controlled child is frequently given "lesser of two evils" choices. All of these choices, and the resulting perpetration, are memories I have watched survivors in agony work through:

"Take your part in the ritual, or we will go out and find everyone you love and kill them."

"Kill this rabbit, or we will kill your little brother."

"Stick this poker into this girl, or we will stick it into her and into you as well".

"Kill your child quickly, or we will kill her slowly and painfully."

Survivor therapist Wendy Hoffman writes,

> My job as an Illuminati princess was to choose the infant to be slaughtered. A man held three infants up. "Choose one or we will kill all three," he said. I froze and did nothing. This standoff went on for a few minutes. Someone inside me said "Be sensible". An eight-year-old male came forward. Older females inside me whispered to him which one to choose based on whom they thought was the least likely to survive. This setup was frequent. As time went on, someone jumped out sooner.
>
> My friend Jeannette, who lived across the street and who did not attend school, had already been sacrificed when she was sixteen in a ritual in the woods adjacent to our families' properties. Her strong, robust brother was a little younger than her. They were both blond with blue eyes. The members strung him up on a crucifix and were bleeding him slowly at the same ritual site. His blood dripped from his ribs into a bucket. He went in and out of consciousness. In a black robe, I

> lay on the ground, on my stomach with my hands tied behind my back. Someone was stepping on my back as he whipped me. His foot moved closer to my neck.
>
> "Say you worship Lucifer.
>
> "Say you worship Satan.
>
> "Say it now or we will start skinning."
>
> I didn't want to and I could get stubborn. For minutes, I resisted. Minutes during torture is eternity. Then several things happened all at once. I could not take the pain, I saw Jeannette's brother's glazed eyes and someone inside said to me, "This is ridiculous." A chorus of girls who were about eight years old jumped out together and said, "We worship Lucifer. We worship Satan." My father looked pleased. They untied my wrists and let me stand, then they swiftly stabbed the brother.

Some mothers are told that their children will be killed unless they abuse them sexually and physically. Others are made to choose between personally abusing their children or having their children taken away. One survivor wrote to me, "I told them that I would not abuse my children. They told me that the only way that this could happen (me not abusing my children) was for my children to be taken away. I agreed to this, thinking that this would save them from abuse. It was arranged that my husband kidnapped my children and I was unable to get custody. I realised decades later, when I recovered my memories, that they were abused anyway, but at least not by me."

These are all unbearable choices, but many survivors have been given such unavoidable apparent choices. If you made such choices, what else could you have done? And how can you blame yourself?

Accountability, remorse, and forgiveness

Survivors still have to face the fact of having perpetrated, even if they had no choice other than the lesser of two evils. Remember that guilt, remorse, and shame are not good or bad, but normal and human. We feel guilty and remorseful when we commit evil acts, acts that harm others. We feel shame about who we are when we have violated our own deepest sense of morality. Even though abuser groups work hard on turning children's guilt into shame, the guilt is real, and the shame for having perpetrated is also real.

It is important to recognise that if a person were truly evil, he or she would not feel remorse, guilt, or shame. The fact that you experience these things means you have not lost your inner core of goodness, in spite of all you may have been made to do.

Full healing includes taking responsibility. Even if he or she is forced to do it, a child whose body is involved in an evil act, for example, holding a knife which hurts or kills, is violating his or her own core spirituality, that human ability to have empathy for other living creatures. The child might have created a non-empathic insider in the process, but when that part joins with those who feel empathy and compassion, guilt or remorse will result. This guilt needs to be accepted and confessed, at least to yourself.

Even if you were a trainer or programmer, or raised your own children (consciously or unconsciously) to be part of an abuser group, the same principles apply. My understanding is that doing evil is possible only through dissociation, when a part of a person is separated from the core who understands the moral truth. This is even true for "conscious" perpetrators, who are often designated for high positions within the perpetrator groups. There is a programme which ensures that when they reach a certain age, their everyday-life parts join with their perpetrator parts, while their internal pain-holders and empathy-holders remain locked away, hidden from their view, so that they cannot consciously feel the pain of those whom they hurt, and they do not remember their own pain. They believe they remember everything that happened, but they do not.

Full healing involves coming to understand how you were made to become the person who did what you did. Allow the parts of you who perpetrated to become connected with the parts who took the pain, so that each can understand what the others went through. This will bring on remorse and regret, and perhaps also an ability to understand at least some of the persons who hurt you.

Forgiving yourself

What happens when you forgive another person? It does not mean excusing or glossing over their behaviour that harmed you. It means looking that harm straight in the face, and accepting that it did happen and was hurtful. After that, it means giving that person another chance when (and only when) he or she truly and genuinely wants to be free of such behaviour. This is also what it means when the creator, or a person you have harmed, forgives you. And when you ask someone to forgive you. And when you forgive yourself.

Whether or not he or she intended it or wanted it, every mind-controlled or ritually abused person has done acts of evil, and needs to face it. This does not require specific religious beliefs; it only requires recognition of innate morality and how it has been violated. It can be done in private with the creator, or in a one-to-one relationship with an accepting and forgiving person. It is a very freeing experience to confess your guilt, and accept forgiveness from a universal spirit or creator who is greater and more loving than you can possibly understand. And if you do not believe in a compassionate life force, you can still come to an understanding of how your mind was split in order to enable you to do those things you would not otherwise have done.

It helps survivors who are immersed in shame to have a real relationship with a person—their therapist, or partner, or clergy person, or friend—who accepts them even knowing that they have done these things, and does not just excuse them but recognises the extent of the evil in which they have been forced, coerced, or tricked to participate.

Apologies

Should you approach persons you have harmed, to apologise to them? This is a difficult question, particularly if the persons you have harmed do not remember it. It might do more harm than good to awaken traumatic memories in persons who have them put away. And if those persons are still involved in a perpetrator group, it is risky for both them and you. One ritually abused client remembered sexually abusing her stepson. She decided to tell him, and fortunately it was at the time when he had just remembered it, so she was able to provide a genuine apology, which was accepted. Perhaps if you know that someone you abused is now physically safe, you could apologise and, if you are able, offer to pay for that person's therapy. But you have to consider what is best for them at present, and if you make an apology just to relieve your own feelings it might not be helpful to them. Your concern now should be for their current and future wellbeing.

Arauna Morgan writes,

> I have found a way to make general apologies to people I believe that I have harmed, even though they do not remember. I do not reference specifics, only time periods where, "I believe that I may have done things in the past that were hurtful/harmful to you and I am deeply sorry for doing these things. I'm sorry, but unless you remember specifics, I will be unable to explain further, but please accept my apology now".

What about persons who died? Some survivors have conducted their own memorial services for those whose deaths they remember. You should know, however, that many deaths are simulated and the persons could still be alive. It pays to have an internal search to see whether any of your parts remember those "killed" persons being alive after the time they were supposedly killed. And you might use the Internet to conduct an external search as well.

Forgiving others

The following excerpt is taken from Aurora Levins Morales' piece, "Torturers", 1998.

"Torturers"

> Several years ago the media was full of the story of two ten-year-old English boys who had beaten a toddler to death. The coverage dripped with revulsion and hatred toward these children. They were described as inhuman, as evil, as bad seed. Reporters exclaimed, enraged, that they showed no remorse and wished aloud that there was a death penalty for ten-year-olds. The complete rejection of the boys couldn't be said often, or loudly or vehemently, enough. They are not of us. We are not like them. If we don't destroy them, we will never be safe. What I didn't hear anyone ask was what had to happen to a pair of children that by the age of ten they could batter another child to death with a brick.
>
> Torturers are made, not born. We know enough about the repetitive cycles of violence, enough about the training of secret police and death squads, special military units and spies, to know that the way you learn to torture is through torture. As a child I had an intimate view of this process. For a period of several years, without the knowledge of my parents, I was periodically abused by a small group of adults who practiced physical, psychological and sexual tortures, mostly, though not exclusively, on children. It was clear that their treatment of me had several goals. They deliberately confused and intimidated me so I would not reveal what was happening, but they also were attempting to reproduce themselves in me and the other children, to separate us from our own humanity enough to turn us into torturers as well.
>
> I understood that the first step in becoming like them was to learn to dehumanize others and that part of the goal of their cruelty was to make us hate them, make us want to hurt them, make us see them as monsters we would be willing to torment. To plant in us the seeds of their own pain.

> Part of the way I prevented this was to envision my abusers as young children, before they became this cruel. I would imagine that imprisoned within the adult bodies that hurt me were captive children who had themselves been tortured. I would pretend I could catch their eyes, send them signals of solidarity to give them courage. Imagine how horrified they were at the actions of their grown-up selves. This was what enabled me to survive spiritually.
>
> If we have nothing but retribution to offer the perpetrators of the world, we will, in an important sense, become like them. The urge to punish, to execute, to wipe them out is the refusal to consider what we ourselves might be capable of.
>
> I speak for the torturers because they are the tortured who did not survive intact. I speak for the ones who were so numbed by the world they saw and the part they were told to play in it that they cannot understand the reality of the harm they do. Of the men who tortured me, I wrote:
>
> There are people in this world
> so terrified that they hunger, night and day, for the fear of others.
> There are people in this world
> who can show their wounds only by inflicting them,
> and the story of my body
> is also the map of their unspeakable pain.
>
> There is nothing more moving to me than the stories of people who had the courage to reclaim their humanity even after full participation in the shameful. Too few people know that the beautiful hymn "Amazing Grace" was written in gratitude by a slave trader who suddenly, mid-Atlantic, awoke to the horror of what he was doing and refused to participate any further.
>
> Until we confront the moments when we have been co-opted, coerced or seduced into harming others, we will be vulnerable to becoming defensively self-righteous. Like those English reporters, we will exclaim in horror over the crimes without taking responsibility for the world that keeps turning children into criminals.
>
> I am holding out for a radical refusal to compromise on the possibility of any one of us to heal, make new moral choices, make amends and reclaim kinship with those we have harmed. There is a place for righteous rage at the torturers, and a place to demand accountability and hard work. But punishment is not a tool of liberation; it is the powerless exercise of violence by those who can think of nothing better. It is the refusal to acknowledge our kinship with those who hurt us. (pp. 111–112)

No one knows better than the survivor of mind control and ritual abuse that any person can become a perpetrator, even a torturer. This happens through dissociation. Child selves do indeed become imprisoned within adults when children are tortured. But they are not all innocent children. In my experience it is, for the most part, child selves who torture. Perpetrators in adult bodies, even those who believe themselves to be adults, are often split-off parts who have very little life experience, often none outside of the perpetrator group. They do what they do as a result of choices they were forced to make when their bodies were still small and under the control of deceptive torturers—or when they had no choice at all. Incidentally, that is why they often seem to behave childishly—because they are actually still children, frozen in their development. And this may be the case with many of the people who abused you, as it was with you.

Do they understand the reality of the harm they do? Well, did you understand this reality when you did such things? The answer is probably "Part of me did." I believe that some part of them does, though in many cases the part who is doing the harm does not have full understanding, or believes he or she is doing it in order to save a life. One recovering survivor says, "It would have been better just to refuse and let everybody die." I do not know whether every part of her agrees with that.

I have heard of some perpetrators who appeared to be wholly dedicated to evil, to inflicting as much pain as possible, for their own enjoyment. Perhaps they were the "conscious perpetrators" I mentioned previously, whose front people were joined with their perpetrator parts, while their hurt and empathic child parts were locked away, unknown to them. Whether or not this is a result of programming, it is important to continue to keep safe from such persons, and to recognise that you cannot forgive them until and unless they are truly remorseful, even if it is your father, husband, brother, sister, or mother.

Should you forgive those persons who perpetrated against you? Only you can make that decision, and it may be different for every perpetrator. When you put together all your memories of those people, perhaps you can determine how free they were to refuse to harm you, and whether they harmed you to save your life, or with glee.

You do not have to forgive someone just because he or she apologises. Many apologies are insincere. You need to assess their sincerity as best you can. And, most important, you do not have to let them back into your life, especially if they remain connected to a perpetrator group and could endanger you again. Survivor therapist Arauna Morgan writes as follows.

> To me, forgiveness is mostly beneficial to the person who forgives. When I have forgiven someone, I was the one who felt the relief and the other person, not so much. When people have told me that they have forgiven me, it was evident to me that *they* were the ones who benefited most from the exchange. I do not ask for forgiveness, I apologise and if I need to, I forgive myself.
>
> To me, forgiving someone for something that happened does not mean that I have to like the person or that I intend to spend any time with them or that I would not put them in jail for abusing me. To me forgiveness is for my peace of mind, not theirs. I do not care if my abusers had the insight to recognise that what they did to me was from their own abuse or not; I forgive the child parts, who were abused and forced to perpetrate until they found a way to abuse without external abuse to themselves first, and who I am sure that perpetually internally abuse themselves. I forgive the part that lives in an internal hell of his own making. However, I will do whatever is legally necessary to ensure that the body of this person no longer abuses me or anyone else.
>
> It took a long time for me to come to this place. I think that trying to get somebody to forgive before all of his or her parts have had a chance to relate what happened to them and how they were hurt will slow down the whole healing process, making it necessary to back-track to allow parts that were skipped over to be heard. Other steps need to come before forgiveness.

Exercise 32. Guilt, responsibility, and forgiveness

If you remember being sexually abused, who do you believe was responsible for it? Why? Would you say the same thing about another child to whom this happened? How much power did you actually have to control whether or not this abuse happened to you?

(*continued*)

Do you have parts who perpetrated in any way on other people? How do those parts feel about what they did? How do they feel about who they are?

What did the abusers tell them to make them feel shame? Do they still believe it? Do you?

How do other parts feel about them? Does the rest of the system reject your perpetrator parts? If so, this leaves them alone and either not understanding the harm they did, or sunk in the shame the abusers poured on them.

How much do you know about what led these parts to do what they did? It might take a long time, but it will be helpful to see what led up to this perpetration, whether there are others who refused, whether the perpetrator parts knew what they were doing, and what lies they were told. What, if anything, were they attempting to prevent?

Is there anyone whom you can tell about these things, someone who will believe you, accept you, and also accept the enormity of what you were made or taught to do, someone who can offer forgiveness without shying away from the reality or abusing you? If so, perhaps you can begin by telling that person about one thing.

Do you believe in a loving and forgiving force in the universe? If so, would you tell that being about what your parts have done, and allow yourself to be forgiven and freed from ongoing shame? You can do this even if there is not a human being whom you can tell.

If you do not believe in any being other than your own highest humanity, are you able to choose to accept your perpetrator parts and acknowledge that they were coerced/forced/tricked/conditioned into harming others? They can then be transformed by connecting with your kind and empathic parts.

Will your perpetrator parts agree to stop participating in the harm of self or others? Can they have a new purpose now? What will it be?

Are there any persons in the real world to whom you need to apologise, and who would benefit from an apology?

When you remember each of your abusers, do you see him or her as having been wholly dedicated to evil, enjoying hurting you, or as split and acting on programming without full understanding? Which of them can you forgive, and which of them can you never forgive?

Developing your own spirituality

If you are a survivor of mind control and/or ritual abuse, it is important that you develop an approach to spiritual issues which is truly your own, and not externally imposed by any group.

If you are multiple, as I believe all such survivors are (including "conscious" ones), you need to develop an approach that satisfies all parts of you.

I am going to review different possible approaches that are offered to survivors, and give some critique for each. This will require thinking on your part (something you were probably told not to do). You do not have to agree with me. I only want you to think about it rather than blindly following what some "expert" has told you, even if that person is a clergy person, or therapist, or any other kind of expert in religion or healing.

Supernaturalist approaches

Ritual abuses are so horrendous, and divine or effective human help for victimised children so vividly absent, that they make us question any faith we might have had in humanity or in a benevolent deity.

Many ritual abuse survivors in particular (at least, their everyday life parts) adopt evangelical Christian belief systems, in the hope of finding an answer to the noise in their heads about Satan and demons and God, or out of a hunger to find something good which is stronger than the evil to which they have been exposed. As well, many sincere, well-meaning Christians want to help survivors, and seek out Christian leaders to help them know how to help.

Ritual abuse survivors whose front people are Christians often have inner parts who hold similar beliefs to Christians about God and demonic entities, but believe that Satan or Lucifer rules the universe and has claimed these insiders for his own. One of my first ritual abuse survivor clients, "Tony", was a very strong Christian; his insiders called him "religious Tony". Tony was a religious Christian, but among the parts who controlled his personality system were Satanists, who believed as they had been taught, and others who disbelieved everything.

As we have seen, cult and mind-controlling perpetrator groups use stage magic and trickery to simulate religious experiences, dressing people up in costumes to simulate demons and deities, making "Satan" appear out of flames, and putting children in a fake hell or heaven. These experiences make survivors seek belief systems that focus on the battle between good and evil but teach that the good side will win and can intervene in our lives.

However, these survivors most likely have inner parts who know that neither deity really rescued them from extreme suffering (even if a man dressed as Satan or Lucifer got them out of some particular situation). These insiders may be atheists, or may believe they are too evil to be rescued or loved even by a loving God.

Survivor Chrystine Oksana, in *Safe Passage to Healing*, says,

> Until the early traumas around supernatural phenomenon are resolved through recovery, survivors may continue to be drawn to "magical" solutions outside themselves. Recovery is realizing that the solutions are within yourself ... Once your sense of self is regained, you are in a position to sense deceit and manipulations. There is less likelihood of confusion by external influences. You are less susceptible to revictimizing by people claiming to have 'the answer,' when their interest isn't to empower you but rather gain power for themselves. You will know who you are and your own truth. (1994, p. 258)

Now, I do not believe that evangelical Christian therapists are all after power for themselves. Although some may be following a laid-out agenda and more interested in conversions than in compassion, most of them are very sincere in their beliefs, and genuinely want to help survivors. But in the search for answers to these horrendous abuses, which involve the invocation of supernatural powers, they often tend to look to their outspoken leaders for answers. So do many survivors whose front people are Christian.

Attachment of demons and spirits

At this point, the primary outspoken Christian leaders seem to have only one viewpoint: that the demons are real, are "attached" to survivors (they prefer this word to "possessed"), and have to be expelled, generally by a professional in the field. Among those professionals who have written about these issues from an evangelical Christian perspective are the late Pastor Tom Hawkins of Restoration in Christ Ministries (2010), and Reverend Tom Ball (2008). These leaders do recognise the existence of dissociative disorders, but believe that demons attach themselves to internal parts of survivors and form the barriers that keep the parts separated.

The belief systems put forward by these Christian leaders in the field have a lot in common with those of the cult groups in which some have been raised, as both Satanists/Luciferians and fundamentalist Christians believe in specific controlling deities and other entities who interfere in human life and expect loyalty and obedience. The primary difference between these "mirror image" world views seems to concern who will win the battle and control the universe—God or the other side—and who is right and, therefore, deserves people's loyalty.

The late Pastor Hawkins described one of the methods that ritualistic abusers use to get those demons into the person:

> Most [ritual abuse survivors] were forced to engage in rituals that included vows, oaths, sacrifices, or covenants made with the evil spiritual realm. These "legal transactions" gave evil spirits, or demons, the right to "attach" to the specific alters involved and to exert varying degrees of influence and control over them. They may play a role, for instance, in enforcing programming; blocking memories; and re-traumatizing any alter who fails to fulfill cult purposes, tells secrets, or seeks outside help. These demonized alters have essentially been brought under bondage to Satan and his agenda . . .
>
> Connections can also be made to evil entities of a higher echelon than demons . . . Many of the more sophisticated cult perpetrators also claim that dissociated identities can be . . . held "captive" by evil cosmic beings and covertly used in Satan's worldwide agenda that is being directed from the spiritual realm. Within the person's system, these alters generally maintain a seemingly out-of-body perception and may be considered absent or even 'dead' by the other identities. (2010, p. 62)

Here, he is talking about at least two kinds of insiders: the ones within the internal hierarchy who have been given the names of supposed evil entities, and what I call in Chapter Five the "outliers", the parts deliberately deceived by perpetrators to believe that they do not belong to the body. I believe that their out-of-body perception has been induced by drugs, not by anything from the spiritual realm. In that chapter, I also included an excerpt from the writings of recovered programmer Stella Katz about how, in her experience, very young demon insiders are made and trained. You might want to review that chapter before you go any further, because it is important to know that ritual abusers deliberately create parts who tell you they are demons or other spiritual beings, whether or not they believe it. (Some might believe it, and some might not.)

Mind controllers of all kinds, military as well as religious ones, use the notion of "legal" agreements and rights a great deal. They "enlist" children in armies that they did not choose, and make them sign (often in blood) agreements committing them to give their lives to Satan or Lucifer, or the Third Reich, or whatever or whoever the group believes in. They tell those children that they are "married" or are bound for ever.

Steve Oglevie is a well-known "deprogrammer" and expert in mind control systems who gives workshops on the different kinds of mind control programming. Like Hawkins, he is married to a ritual abuse survivor. Many therapists have attended his trainings. Here is how one day-long event is described:

> Recognizing Spiritual Evil, Recognizing Dissociated and Disembodied Foreign Human Spirits and "Installed" Personalities. Understanding of Spiritual Evil and how it Interferes in the Therapy

> Process. The therapist will be introduced to the very complex field of dissociated and disembodied foreign human spirits including their level of attachment to the client and ways in which they can be successfully disentangled from the true humanity and sent away. Therapists will be introduced to understanding installed personalities and how to differentiate between installed and genuine personalities.

When Oglevie speaks of "disembodied foreign human spirits", I believe he is referring to the deliberate creation of insiders who believe themselves to be specific perpetrators the child knew. An abuser will rape the child, saying that he is putting his "spirit" or his "seed" into him or her. The resulting new split-off part is then told he is that abuser. This is a common event in ritual abuse, and also in other kinds of mind control, and I have met many such insiders. Sometimes, the person who makes the new part is costumed as a demon or beast, and the child is drugged to unconsciousness and then costumed like the abuser. The new part of the child wakes up to see himself in the same costume as the perpetrator. In military/political abuser groups, parts made in this way can believe themselves to be such entities as Hitler, generals, and various doctors or military leaders. Abuser groups also use drugs that make the body numb or unable to move, then tell the drugged parts that they are dead, ghosts, or aliens. They tell these confused parts that they do not belong to the body—and if they kill the body, they will not die themselves.

So, how do you differentiate between insiders who have been deliberately deceived into believing they are demons, devils, abusers, political leaders, and deities, and actual demons or "foreign human spirits"? And how do you distinguish between a "demonised" insider (one to whom a demon is attached) and an actual demon?

Reverend Tom Ball states that other Christians working in the field "assert the best method [by which] to be sure a demon is present is to exercise the gift of discernment of spirits". This appears to leave it up to the Christian expert to decide whether any given entity is part of the person or something external. Some of the sources Ball cites suggest that you can tell a demonic spirit if it slithers like a snake, or has rolling eyes, or looks hateful. But "demon" alters (small child parts) are taught to do exactly these things. Another expert in the field asserts that states who do not belong to the person are not motivated to feel better, are hostile to therapists, and do not make a human connection with them, expressing scorn for the rest of the person and hatred for the therapist; the person feels much better when he or she believes these states are gone.

I recently met a new insider in a long-term client. It was very hostile, and very much acted the role of a "spiritual attachment". I asked the part whether it thought I was a member of the cult and was testing it to see whether it remained loyal. Its reply was "*Yes, of course.*" This part simultaneously believed that I was an outsider who would destroy it, and that I was a cult member who would punish it if it showed any signs of disloyalty. What a set of feelings to juggle. I got the system leader to explain to it why she had become a "traitor", and that she had known me for several years and they really were safe. Then it relaxed, and began to behave like the child it was.

These parts are really no different from any other part. You (or your therapist) cannot judge that some part is external to your personality system just because of its behaviour, no matter how "evil" that behaviour, or its attitudes or self-identity. These are usually very important parts in maintaining the inner hierarchy of loyalty to the abusers. When I met twelve-year-old "Lucifer Immortal" in a client of mine, he maintained he was in charge of all the others. I asked him whether he had met the other Lucifer Immortal, who was eight and had also been told he was in charge. He quickly became indignant at the way the abusers had deceived both of them, giving them the illusion of power and lying to them.

In my view, it is important to view these parts with an extra dose of compassion, and not collude with their own view (and that of other insiders) that they are really evil external entities. It is not hard to see that such reactions are normal for a part who has been told (1) that it is not part of the body and should kill that useless and traitorous body, and (2) that it is an evil spiritual being and if it talks to a therapist or other outsider it will be destroyed, either by that outsider or by the abuser group. Banishing these parts might make them feel they are being destroyed. It takes patience, persistence, and kindness to break through their defences and help them know they are now safe and do not need to continue to do their jobs. In my experience, exorcism or "deliverance" attempts simply alienate important parts of the personality system. I have seen many survivors in whom the "demonic" parts went into temporary hiding as a result of rejection by therapists or religious authorities, and, consequently, they could not recover fully because some of their important insiders were not involved in the recovery process.

Tom Hawkins stated that

> Successful resolution of the major spiritual bondages occurring in RA survivors requires ... an understanding of the spiritual principles relating to the cosmic struggle between the forces of God and the forces of Satan as found in the Bible ... Releasing the person from bondage to the spiritual realm can only occur through the power of God. Therefore, this part of the process needs to be facilitated by a pastor, Christian counselor, or prayer minister who has thorough training in working with the dissociative disorders. ... Disconnecting RA survivors from the spiritual entities holding them in bondage is not a simple process. The specific legal rights claimed by the demons and/or evil cosmic beings must be ascertained and renounced by the identities involved. (2010, p. 62)

This approach takes power from the survivor, giving it to the trained Christian worker, the only person who can remove attached entities. I find it far too much like that of the abuser groups, who tell these insiders that the group members are the only ones who can understand and accept them. I would like to tell you that you do not have to give your power away any more, not to anyone. No one but you should be in control of your mind.

Why do some Christians accept that there are genuine legal agreements made in some heavenly or hellish court? If such agreements, especially when made by under-age children under coercion, were made on earth, no genuine court would regard them as legal or binding in any way. We have seen this with regard to forced marriages with child brides, where the older "husbands" have been charged with sexual assault.

Once you let go of your belief in them, such agreements are nothing but evidence of how a child was deceived by cunning adults. You do not have to believe the lies your abusers told you! You might find it helpful to deliberately renounce agreements that were made, but simply as a statement of your own free choice, not because they are actually legal agreements.

There is also a more sinister side to this. Survivor therapist Wendy Hoffman (who tells part of her story in Chapter Nineteen) had many years of therapy with someone she believed to be a kind Christian therapist, sending "attachments" and "human spirits" to "the throne of Jesus" for judgement. When the "Christian therapist" was ousting these parts, she was actually using cult-created hand signals to have them put away inside, and as a result all the programming was intact and Wendy's recovery was halted. Wendy's front person experienced a sense of relief as the "deliverance" happened, as parts who were doing their supposedly evil jobs went into hiding. It was easy for her to believe that the warfare was outside her, between her and external spiritual entities, and these entities were actually leaving her. However, without their co-operation, she could no longer discover how her personality system worked and what had been done to her. The "deliverance" was just further mind control.

Now, I do not believe that all Christians who take this approach are members of evil cults, but this one was, along with her whole treatment team.

If you (the front personality—or any other part) are a Christian, must you accept the approach recommended by the most vocal Christians working in this field? I do not believe so. Many Christians do not believe in "possession" as a literal fact, or in "legal agreements" between coerced children and external spiritual entities. Jesus' teaching is that "by their fruits you shall know them"—in other words, an evil or a good being is distinguished not by its appearance or its supposed loyalty, but by its actions when it has an actual choice, not a fake or forced choice.

You can exercise your free will by rejecting and separating perceived attachments, but, in my opinion, that is likely to continue the internal war within your personality system, a war which was deliberately set up by your abusers, who knew that if they told part of you that they were demons or evil spirits, those parts would believe them, particularly if they were made to commit acts of evil. To be truly free, your whole person, including those parts, needs to assert that you will no longer be part of any religion or belief system that does evil.

The following section gives the perspective of a Christian counsellor (and professor of theology) whose approach is, in my opinion, more understanding of survivors of mind control and ritual abuse.

Heather Davediuk Gingrich: "A Christian therapist's perspective"

My initial reaction to reading Dr Miller's cautions about Christian therapists is that she is rather hard on us! Unfortunately, however, I think that many of her criticisms are justified. I have seen too many dissociative people retraumatised through well-intentioned, but none the less misguided attempts at casting out evil spirits. To my horror, one such client reported that the deliverance prayer she underwent was experienced by her as more traumatic than the ritual abuse she survived! What recourse, then, is available to those of us who believe that demons are actual spiritual entities (rather than always being dissociated aspects of self), which can derail therapeutic process? This is a complex question, one which I cover more extensively in my book *Restoring the Shattered Self: A Christian Counselor's Guide to Complex Trauma,* but the following paragraphs are an attempt to hit the core issues.

Many years ago, I was reminded by the pastor of a church which had an extensive deliverance ministry that when people are demonised, the evil spirits influencing them probably have been around for many years, if not decades. Therefore, he concluded, there is not necessarily a need to be in a hurry to get rid of them, particularly when attempting to do so could put the individual at risk for greater harm.

The term "spiritual warfare" can be confusing to ritual abuse survivors. Simply put, it means fighting against evil, which we evangelical Christians see as involving actual demonic forces that are not part of a person. Exorcism-type rituals, sometimes called power encounters, are only one way of doing spiritual warfare. The one that excites me the most as a therapist is that counselling itself can help free people from demonic influences as they reject the lies they have been told (or forced to accept through torture) about themselves, others, and reality, and begin to make choices based on truth.

The "armour of God" talked about in the Bible (Ephesians 6: 10–18) includes nothing violent. The belt is truth, the coat of mail is integrity or honesty; the shoes are the good news that God wants to make peace with you; the shield is faith in the reality of a loving God; the helmet is the awareness that God accepts and forgives you. The only offensive weapon, the sword, is words from God that speak the truth, when evil forces want you to believe lies.

Sometimes, Christian counsellors want to temporarily "bind" the power of perceived evil entities. This does not mean putting literal ropes or chains around any of your inside parts! If you have parts who have experienced this, be assured they are not really demonic entities. The term simply means holding back any evil powers (external to you) who might be making your life difficult.

In my role as counsellor, I am always aware of the possibility of demonic influence, and know that at some level my clients and I are engaged in doing spiritual warfare. However, I also know that explicit discussion of this in therapy is very risky due to the possibility that dissociated parts of a client could misinterpret what is being said because of the way in which abuser groups often distort Christian concepts. For example, a particular dissociated part could connect a phrase such as the "armour of God" to soldier training, or "the blood of Christ" to a ritual involving killing. Specific Scripture verses and words commonly used in Christian prayers could have been given a malevolent meaning. So, a wise Christian counsellor will ask you what you think something means, and make sure that you understand the true meaning of any words they use. If my counselees desire explicit use of spiritual resources in counselling, such as prayer and Bible reading, I will certainly incorporate them into the process, but very carefully, watching for distortions of meaning and recognising that there will probably be varying reactions from dissociated parts of the person.

Dr Miller's concerns related to Christian counsellors are broader than the danger of misidentifying dissociated parts of a person as demons, attempting to cast out evil spirits, or inadvertently creating problems by using Christian language that has been given a different meaning by an abuser group. She is afraid that Christian therapists are sometimes not appropriately respectful of their RA/MC clients' own spirituality. This is a tough one, partly because the part of you that seeks out counselling may identify as Christian, but you might not even be aware of the worldviews of other parts of you! In a sense, both your therapist and you need to tread gently, making sure that all parts of you feel understood and respected, regardless of what each part believes in a given moment. One of my DID clients invited other parts of her to learn about Jesus, having adult discussions with the older ones, and reading children's Bible story books to the little ones. Over time, and one by one, all parts of her decided they wanted to follow Jesus, but did so without coercion. To be honest, I would love all of my clients to have a similar experience. But I realise that I always need to be mindful that that it is not my job to evangelise my counselees, that I must be aware that they may end up with a very different view of spirituality than mine, and that ultimately the decision is theirs to make. The decision *is* yours to make.

* * *

I cannot emphasise enough how important it is to accept those parts of you who were told by the abusers that they are demonic. Restoring the human dignity of insiders who have been forced to perpetrate and have been told they are evil and damned is one of the most important parts of recovery. For this to happen, the parts who performed the evil acts need to see how they came into being and the double binds involved. But if these parts are rejected and ousted as demons, or "attachments", they lose this chance for recovery, and are, in a sense, put in a permanent grave.

In twenty years of working with ritual abuse survivors, I have never met a single real demon or "attachment", although I have met lots and lots of insiders with impressive demonic names (many of whom thought they were demons), as well as names of various leaders of perpetrator groups. I believe that evil is about what we do, and its essence is doing harm to other people and living things. Raping little children and teaching them to kill are evil. It only muddies the waters to add notions of external forces. Evil done in the name of Jesus, or God, or Mohammed, or Buddha, or Hitler, or Stalin, or Satan, or the "free world", or democracy is still evil. In Chapter Four of my book for therapists, *Healing the Unimaginable* (Miller, 2012), I have a piece by Sally (called "Old Lady" in that book), in which her young insiders tell about ritual abuse, including sacrifice of babies, done in the name of God and Christ as well as in the name of Lucifer.

Some people do appear to be entirely governed by evil and to enjoy doing it. I do not believe this can happen because of legal agreements with demons made under coercive conditions, or because of being forced to choose the lesser of two evils. It may perhaps happen if a person consistently chooses power over others rather than equality and compassion. We all, whether or not we are ritually abused, make such choices, daily, in big or small ways, and each choice moves us further along the continuum between devotion to evil or to truth and justice.

Dissociation offers a powerful explanation for the existence of relatively autonomous and destructive entities within someone's mind. A part of a person, separated from that person's capacity for empathy, is more able to do evil than a human being whose inner parts are all connected to their empathy and wisdom. Recovery is moving toward a state of wholeness, whether it comes in the form of literal "integration" or internal co-operation and co-ordination and living for a positive shared purpose. In my view, approaching evil as a set of disembodied evil entities interferes with your ability to achieve that goal.

Ritual abusers, who might for centuries have believed they were attaching real demons to children, now recognise they are creating dissociative conditions. They still *tell* the children they are attaching demonic spirits, or their own spirits, or the spirits of dead relatives, but they now know they are actually splitting children and naming and training the newly separated parts. Should we continue to subscribe to the belief system the abusers have implanted, even when they themselves know that it is dissociation that gives them power over their victims?

In one sense, all humanity, indeed all of creation, is a single entity, a very complex multiple. Some people believe that all living beings on the planet are parts of that entity, which is sometimes called Gaia. When we choose to live and work for the good of that entire entity, we are choosing good; when we choose to live for the supremacy of ourselves or some small part of it such as our religion or our race, we are choosing evil.

Karmic belief systems

The standard fundamentalist Christian approach is not the only way survivors try to sort out their spiritual beliefs. Some survivors maintain belief systems that reassure them that "everything happens for a reason", and "God never gives us more than we can handle", although "God's ways are not to be known by mortals". These beliefs provide them with the perspective of a just, or at least a protected, universe, which is not the way the world appears to a child being abused. These sunny beliefs may often be held by the front person, who knows very little of what went on in childhood, but are often not held by the abused insiders, who experienced overwhelming physical, emotional, and spiritual pain, enough to split their psyches repeatedly.

What can you say about a God who is all-powerful but would allow children to go through such brutal experiences without intervening? Who would tell them that this terror and horror are for their own good? No wonder many insiders are opposed to God, if this is the kind of God they believe exists.

Some try to make it all right by adopting new-age approaches that include a notion of past lives and karma, defining the trauma they have experienced in this life as something they earned in previous lives. This notion of karma allows a belief in a just universe even for those who have perpetrated and/or have suffered severely. It makes everything appear to be just. One survivor I know believes she has had memories of past lives in which she did evil, and this evil is the reason she had to make up for it by suffering in this life. Another survivor who developed cancer said it was her karma because of all the evil she had done while in the cult, especially as an adult. (But some scientists believe that cancer can be caused by unexpressed grief.)

If this is true of mind control and ritual abuse survivors, it must be true of everyone. Are all illnesses then the result of our own bad behaviour in this or past lives? Does the experience of being abused only happen to those who deserve it? This approach also denies the reality that people have the power to harm others. It suggests that everyone who gets hurt deserves it.

It is very difficult for anyone looking at suffering from the outside to believe that, for example, all the children who have died of AIDS in Africa are suffering the results of karma accrued in previous evil lives. And if those children are suffering unjustly, how can we say that the suffering of mind controlled and ritually abused children is just? I have often heard a survivor say, "Other children don't deserve to be abused, but I'm different, I'm dirty, I'm evil, I deserve it." These are things the perpetrators have told you. I cannot accept this. No one is that special, that much more evil than anyone else. Yes, many ritually abused kids were made to participate in evil acts, but it was through adult coercion and deception. I know that if I had been there, I would very probably have done the same things. Would that have made me especially evil? I would feel very contaminated, as you probably do, but really it would be the situation that had made me do those things, not my own nature.

The belief that the abuse was a consequence of your own past behaviour is a way of making you feel you had more control than you actually had. It denies the consequences of earthly and political realities, and gives every believing individual the illusion of power over what happens to him or her. It saves you from the experience of powerlessness, and the associated feelings of despair. But powerlessness is a reality in some situations, in particular mind control and ritual abuse.

How honest is a perspective that makes everyone responsible for his or her own suffering, denying what other people can do to us?

Some people have a karmic belief system that does not blame the victim. Arauna Morgan writes, "I believe in reincarnation, but also free choice. I believe that if you just 'go with the flow', and do not reflect and struggle for insight and enlightenment, then lives of 'tit-for-tat', where revenge and suffering are the theme, will continue. To break the cycle, one tries to awaken and treat themselves and fellow human beings with compassion, which still allows for stopping perpetuators from harming others. It is insight that allows for forgiveness.

"There is much more, but while someone is still hurting, it is hard to justify anything that happened and I think that, at that point, there should be no attempt to justify anything that happened. The survivor should be allowed to question everything, reject all religious thought and concentrate on healing the trauma. At some point, the survivor will be ready for a religion or faith that feels right, even if this is atheism. I, for one, have been abused in the name of several religions and resent people touting one or the other as 'the religion'. It is a personal choice, thank you."

Nihilism, atheism, and humanism

Many survivors, however, fall into despair, believing either that they are truly evil or that there is no good in this world. If there is a God, and even He does not care, how can they find the strength to fight for themselves? Sometimes, they find that strength by rejecting all spirituality, especially notions regarding a God. Yet, they are still left with the question of good and evil, and the awareness that what happened to them (torturing little children and forcing them to participate in harming helpless others) was evil. Agnostic and atheistic humanism has a respected tradition of developing a value system in the absence of the supernatural, and I believe it is one of several valid options for survivors. If you are not familiar with it, you may want to Google it and learn about it.

Choosing good and seeking truth

It is possible to develop a spiritual approach that does not follow the currently popular options that I have described above. And I believe it is important for every survivor to engage all his or her parts in working out the meaning of their experiences and an approach which makes sense of what happened and what they are doing in the world.

In *Reaching for the Light*, ritual abuse survivor Emilie Rose has a helpful chapter about spiritual abuse. She believes that spiritual abuse is perhaps the greatest wound. An important part of Rose's spiritual healing was rejecting the false notions of the divine which she had been taught, not only by the abusers, but by the conventional religion which she had at the start of her journey:

> I don't believe it is possible to be a survivor of ritual abuse without undergoing a deep, spiritual crisis . . . My realization that I was a ritual abuse survivor profoundly affected me. In some ways it totally shattered my old ideas about God. Who was this loving God I had heard about all my life? How could God be loving if God would not save those children I saw sacrificed? How could God be all-powerful, all-protecting, omnipotent? Obviously God could be none of these and also be good. Good Gods didn't watch the massacre of innocents when they had it within their power to act. Good Gods did something. How could I place the heinous reality of ritual abuse into a spiritual framework while still embracing the God I know? The answer was that I could not. Instead, I railed at this God. I hated this God—"the bastard God," as my friend said. Finally, in the midst of the deepest spiritual crisis of my life, I renounced this God. . . . I had to create a completely different vision of God. Today I think of God/Good as a light energy, an energy of creation that flows within and without so that it is a part of me, as I am a part of it. (Rose, 1996, pp. 102–103)

These questions, she says,

> . . . come from a part of us that knows that nothing like ritual abuse should ever happen to anyone. They come from the part of us that knows that what happened to us is contrary to the way the world was intended to be. That part of us is outraged and sickened and horrified. Our questions come from the place within us that cries out against such evil, that life-clinging part of us that helped to keep us alive. That tiny spark of justice within us could not be put out even in the most horrible, degrading experiences a human being can go through. (pp. 109–110)

But she sees hope:

> Every ritual abuse survivor has an inner part that somehow stayed connected to life even in the midst of torture and death . . . It may have many names: the strong one, the keeper of the spirit, the healer, the mystic, the grandparent, the wise one. Whatever we call the part, we can assist in its healing by seeking that part of us, inviting it out, befriending it, nurturing it, and assisting it to develop further in our life . . . This strong one within has a natural longing for life and healing. It is wise beyond years. It knows about pain and healing and spirit. It may be the place where our connection with a higher power resides. It guides us in the healing journey if we give it room to do so. (p. 146)

She talks about survivors, including herself, having transcendent experiences of joy and love, even during the years of the abuse. This, to her, is God:

> There are many things like that in my life, that I can point to or experience, and say, "This is real. This is good. This you did not destroy, and will not, ever, no matter how hard you try. This is God, the transcendent, the holy. This is what matters, and it is with this that I will cast my lot, *not evil.*" I know evil, intimately, and I reject it with everything in me. This does not mean that I reject those parts of me that were made to do bad things. I accept them, condemn the ways they were violated, and am thankful for the ways they helped me survive. And so, I see my life, as a kind of ongoing prayer. It goes on all the time, because in every moment, every thought, every action, I feel confronted with that choice between good and evil. It is not merely a theoretical choice. I know I really could go either way. And I continually constitute myself by consciously choosing the good. (p. 165)

My experience as a therapist for survivors of mind control and ritual abuse has been similar to that of Rose, the survivor. I can no longer easily embrace the idea of a God who is both all-loving and all-powerful, and who intervenes in people's lives to prevent disasters. I am aware of too many horrors. I know also that I, too, could have been a ritual abuse survivor and yes, a perpetrator, given different circumstances in my childhood. I was not, but countless other people—people with no less value than I—were. What that demonstrates to me is that God does not micromanage.

Survivors' genuine spiritual experiences

Spiritual experiences do happen to ritually abused children, even though no deity intervenes to stop the abuse. Ritual abusers frequently bring children to or near the point of death, and they have no control over what happens in the person's experience at that point. They can restart a stopped heart, but they canmot prevent the near-death experiences. Over the years, with the clients who were brave enough to work through the most horrific of their memories, I have encountered amazing near-death experiences (NDEs) that address the truth of what the client has experienced on the deepest level.

One six-year-old girl experienced the usual components of the NDE, including the presence of a being of light, and a life review in which she recognised she was not responsible for the perpetration which was forced upon her, only for the events in which she made an active choice to harm someone. Some of these events had nothing to do with her ritual abuse. Another child of five, while beaten almost to death by her mother, found herself in a new place with a loving angel. When brought back to life by the cult doctor, she said something about wanting to stay with the angel, and he told her mother, "Don't mention it, she'll get over it." Once she had accessed this memory, the client has been able to go to this happy place to be with her angel when she needs it. Another client, too, found some of her most damaged parts had angels accompanying them.

Now, I do not know what an angel is, and explaining them is beyond my scope as a psychologist, but I do know that experiences of angels have happened to a number of my ritually abused clients, none of whom have a specific religious faith. (I am not, of course, talking about the angels who are simulated as part of ritual abuse training, for example to invite a survivor to suicide. Perhaps these groups simulate angels because they have experience with survivors who talk about them. They use the "angel of the sunset" deception because they know there will be angels present if the victim actually comes to the point of death, and they want to block out the experience of the genuine divine.)

Another survivor's Satan part was enduring some training in a simulated hell, when the drugs were too strong and the child almost died. "Satan" split off another part, "Satan's ghost", who found himself in a beautiful place with a being of light. He encountered a dog and a baby whom he was to be forced to kill, and both told him that they forgave him. When he returned to fake hell, he knew it was not really the afterlife.

Another person remembered a near-death experience in which a little boy she knew, whom she had been forced to kill in a ritual, was waiting for her at the other end of the tunnel to the afterlife, and told her he would remain with her as her helper. Recently, I was with a survivor whose killer part was grieving for a boy she was made to kill, after which she was told she was going to hell. It occurred to me to say, "The boy is somewhere now. What would he say to you?" She listened, and then reported that the boy said three things: that he forgave her, that he was in a place where there was no pain, and that she would not go to hell because there was no hell. I asked whether she and he could be friends in the afterlife, and the answer was yes.

These accounts give me hope. If you do not remember such an experience, it might be helpful to know that they have happened to other survivors who, up until that point, believed the perpetrators' lies about how evil they were.

Many survivors have spiritual parts such as "Essence", or the wise part which Emilie Rose talks about, who remain spiritually connected to a higher reality, the compassionate life force, who seem to guide the recovery process, and who will communicate if asked. Perhaps you have such a part, too. Perhaps everyone has, but singletons have more difficulty recognising it.

Exercise 33. Your spiritual beliefs and experiences

What kind of spiritual beliefs does your main adult part have? Why? Who have been the main influences for your beliefs?

Have your spiritual beliefs changed? What changed them? What is the history of your spiritual beliefs?

What kind of spiritual beliefs do your insiders have? (There may be a variety.) Ask each one who responds why he or she holds a particular belief. Remember the trickery that you looked at in Exercise 30.

What emotions hold each part of you to his or her present spiritual beliefs?

What loyalties or personal connections with people hold each part of you to his or her present spiritual beliefs?

If you have a therapist, does that person have a particular spiritual viewpoint? Has it influenced you?

Do you have any insiders who have gone into hiding because someone tried to get rid of them? (You may also have insiders who really want to get rid of them, believing them to be demonic.)

Do you have any parts who have had genuine near-death experiences in which they crossed to the afterlife? If so, what can they tell you?

Do you have an Essence, or other spiritual parts? Can you communicate with them, and if so, what do they say?

Have you had experiences of angels, or persons who died, speaking with you or accompanying some of your inside parts?

Have a discussion between the parts who have different spiritual viewpoints, and perhaps out of that discussion you can begin to develop your own spiritual perspective.

CHAPTER TWENTY-ONE

Becoming yourself

You might have difficulty knowing who you are, especially if you are multiple, and have different insiders, each of whom has a different sense of identity. I have titled this chapter "Becoming yourself" because, for me, it is my most important goal with my clients. Every species of animal or plant has an essential nature. You cannot make a kitten into a dog, or a cedar seedling into an oak tree. Mind controllers try to make children, at least parts of them, into things of their design, rather than developing each child's essential nature by providing the spiritual nutrients from which the child can grow into who he or she really is. If you have experienced mind control, either the systematic, organised kind, or just the programming provided by controlling parents and/or a society which wants people to be a certain way, you might have abandoned your essential nature in order to avoid pain or to please people whose acceptance of you has been essential to your survival.

You are a living being, not a machine

A child is not a machine to be programmed with others' ideas and plans. A child is a living being, like a tree, only vastly more complicated and with more potential. A tree needs water, sunlight, nutritious soil, and a chance to put down roots that will sustain it through each winter and draw nourishment to enable it to make leaves, then flowers, and finally seeds, in the other three seasons. If it has begun its growth in hard dry ground or in a dark place, it might have struggled for life, and taken on a shape which is not what nature intended. However, if it is transplanted to a good location and well looked after, it will once again grow towards its full potential. So will a person. A child who grows up in a dysfunctional or abusive family might have tried to become what that family wanted, just to survive, but once away from the family, he or she can begin to grow into his or her real shape. This can begin at any age.

Self-help writers talk a lot about self-esteem, as though having it is basic to happiness and to mental health. It is, as long as it is on the right basis. Too many people base their self-esteem on "conditions of worth", valuing themselves if they measure up to some externally imposed standards of wealth, beauty, success, or character. This does not just happen in families who harm children for their own ends; it happens everywhere. You can see how worth is measured if you just watch the advertising on television. Basing your self-esteem on conditions of worth makes you very vulnerable if you are unable to measure up to these conditions.

I believe that true self-esteem means simply esteeming, accepting, and liking who you are, with weaknesses and mistakes and even failures because you are a learning, growing human being. Rather than striving for self-esteem based on measuring up to some standard, you can learn to be authentic, real, true to yourself. When you are authentic, self-esteem follows naturally.

However, something comes before self-esteem—knowing and allowing yourself to be who you are.

But how do you know who you really are, if people have worked hard to make you what *they* want? To have the right basis for self-esteem, you first have to have an awareness of your own self. This awareness comes through experiencing your likes and dislikes, your positive and negative emotions, the joy of using your abilities and the distaste for doing things that do not fit with your true nature.

How do you know who you are if you are multiple? Some of your insiders might be crying out "But we're all different! I don't even like some of the parts inside this head; I'd like to get rid of them." Well, the reality is you all occupy different electrical and chemical circuits within the same brain. Although you experience yourself as different people, and may have different images of what your bodies look like, you are all living within the same head of the same body. If that body becomes ill, you are all ill, even if some of you do not feel the pain or sickness. If that body has grown up, any of you who come out into that body will find themselves in an adult body, with signs of maturity and aging. Each of you only uses a few of the circuits that make up the immensely complicated brain you inhabit.

Who you really are is the whole thing together, all the learning and feeling and experience contained in that complicated brain, with many capacities beyond those that each one of you believes you have, and that adult body, with its size and strength and also its limitations. If you think of people as trees, a singleton may be like a conifer which has one main trunk and just little branches out the side, and a multiple may be like a tree which has several or many main limbs, and branches out in a very complicated manner. If one of you, even the front person, insists he or she is the main person, this is not true, as each one is using only a very small part of the potential of that powerful brain. The more all of you communicate within that brain, which means communicating with the other parts, the closer you come to being who you were meant to be. It will be up to you whether you eventually choose to integrate fully, so that you experience a single identity, but even if you do not, it can only benefit you to become more connected to one another, so that all of you have access to all the abilities and insights and intelligence and experiences available within that brain and that vast mind.

So, how do you get there? It begins with recognising the effects of indoctrination, by your family, your abusers, and society. Besides the specific indoctrination for the purposes of the abuser group, there was also your family's home environment, which for most survivors was a place where adults required unquestioning obedience from children, and told them how to be and what to do. To combat that indoctrination, you need to learn about your needs through your emotional reactions (which are often contained within inside parts), learn about your body through how it feels and what it can do, and learn about your gifts and abilities through trying new things in a playful way, with different parts coming together in those new safe experiences.

Rejecting the lies they told you about who you are

If you were raised within an abuser group, the adults in your life saw you as a commodity rather than a person who needed nurturing and psychological and spiritual food for growth. Some parts of you were accepted or even praised, but only when you sacrificed your own needs and wants in order to obey the adults and become what they wanted—all the different things they wanted. Although the group might have put considerable effort into assessing your abilities, it was only for their own use, not to allow you to develop to your full potential. They might even have deliberately given you disabilities to prevent your entering a fulfilling career. Or they might have insisted you excel in areas which do not really fit your natural interests or abilities.

Every part of a mind-controlled survivor has been told lies about who he or she is. Whether you believe you are a high-level programmer, or a demon, or a copy of your handler, or your father, or a seductress, or a soldier, or a robot, or a worthless piece of garbage, or someone specially created for a job without which you will not exist—you have been deceived. So, you need to begin all over again to discover who you really are, apart from those lies.

Children who are not abused or mind-controlled discover who they are in childhood, through exploring their abilities and interests. Even though it has been delayed, you can still do this. You will probably find that those of you who were given "jobs" by the abusers had certain interests and abilities of theirs used in carrying out those jobs. But those of your insiders who were told they were worthless pieces of garbage had abilities and interests too, such as the capacity for standing up for the truth. They are just as important parts of you as the ones who were told by the abusers that they were important. They often contain the most important qualities of kindness, empathy, and courage, which can benefit the whole of you.

Tuning in to your own needs

If your parents were members of an abuser group, they were not allowed to be attuned to you; the group deliberately broke any bond they might have developed with you. You learnt very early that people would not respond to your expressed needs, but they intruded upon you at times and in ways of their choosing. No adults spent time with you just to be together, letting you take the lead in play and exploration of your environment. So, you probably do not know how to play and explore your world and your interests.

Children whose parents have not been attuned to them often cannot "tune in" to themselves. They become adults who do not know what is going on in their bodies or their emotions. They do not know how to soothe themselves when they are upset, because nobody was tuned in enough to soothe them when they were upset children. They do not develop their own mature, thought-out values, but rely on others to tell them what is right and wrong.

When you have been neglected and rejected in this way, it is natural for you to abandon yourself and your own needs and desires, especially when these are held in other parts of you and you therefore do not feel their pangs. How good are you now at recognising what you need and how you feel? The way we learn what we need, and how to meet our needs, is through listening to what our emotions tell us. (See Chapter Thirteen on "Emotions".) Our emotions were designed to give us information about every need of ours, about what is happening to us psychologically. Do you invalidate your own needs? If your needs and strong emotions are tucked away in inside parts, do you listen to those insiders and try to let them know their feelings are valid, and that you will hear them, protect them, and try to meet their needs?

Learning about your interests and abilities

A child brought up in a loving family, with attuned parents, gets to try out various activities and continue with those which they like and are good at, while discarding those that do not fit who they are. Although the school system insists we all learn certain things, whether or not they are the most important to us, it is important that we not lose sight of which things "turn our crank" and make us happy, which things we are naturally interested in and/or good at, and which are things we do not much like and need to learn only minimally.

Children normally learn about their interests and abilities through trial and error in childhood. They try painting, writing, various sports, singing and musical instruments, and various school subjects. Wise parents do not force a child to continue for years with something he does not enjoy or is not any good at, but encourage him to develop his own abilities and interests. Sometimes, that goes "against the grain" of society's prescribed roles. I was a child in the 1950s, and I remember praying nightly that I would not have to become a housewife, since none of the skills involved in that career (other than, perhaps, enjoying children) fitted my abilities and interests. I was a complete dud at cooking and sewing, and had absolutely no interest in clothing or house cleaning. My thinking, writing, and intuitive abilities would have been wasted if I had followed the path of my female classmates.

Depending on your body's age, you might or might not be able to direct much of your life into areas that fit with your abilities and interests. If you are older, this might be difficult, except for hobbies. But even hobbies can bring some satisfaction. If you are younger, you might be able to find and pursue a life direction that truly fits you, rather than fitting what your parents or your programmers intended for you. If you have numerous insiders with varied interests and abilities, perhaps you can find a life direction that allows for a bit of time devoted to each area of interest and ability.

Learning what we like and are good at begins with play. Children try out various life roles through play. Let your inner children do the same. Give them chances to paint, draw, write, be athletic, study science, take courses—whatever enables them and you to find out who you are, what you like, and what you are good at.

It might help to discover what ordinary children are like so you can relax a bit more with your inner children, allow them to behave like children again, and enjoy them. Watch comedies such as *The Simpsons* (an excellent critique of American culture) with your inner children, and shows which depict children (and teenagers and adults) making mistakes and accepting themselves, or having other people accept them as they are, with all their flaws.

Learning through mistakes

Abuser groups bring up children with the goal of complete, unquestioning obedience. Parents who are involved in illegal activities want to maintain an appearance that their family is perfect and successful. So, in some such families, the push for children to excel is very strong. Parents who are members of these groups, as well as handlers within the groups, are often perfectionists, insisting that tasks be done immediately and be done right, no matter how the child is feeling. Mistakes are simply not allowed.

If you grew up with these demands, you probably have some parts who are ferocious inner critics, insisting you do everything right, and not accepting mistakes, tiredness, sickness, or even just plain disinterest in a task. It is important for these critical insiders to learn that mistakes are all right. If you are really a perfectionist, set yourself a goal of making a certain number of mistakes a day, and laughing at them. It is fine to make mistakes. We learn through trying things we do not like or are bad at, and once we are in charge of our own lives we do not have to continue doing those things. We also do not have to base our self-esteem on doing everything perfectly.

High standards are good. They can motivate us to grow and to do excellent work. But if they are too high or are perfectionistic, they lead us to be constantly dissatisfied with ourselves. If you are dissociative, you might actually hear the voice of an inner critic, perhaps sounding like one of your parents or trainers. You need to get to know this part and speak with it about how its job is no longer necessary.

When we are being our authentic selves, failure is not devastating because we do not need to please others and our self-esteem is not dependent on their approval. So, we can afford to take risks. We can try new things, explore our gifts by using them, and speak up when something needs to be said. We can be motivated by the hope of success rather than the fear of failure. I know this is difficult for mind control survivors who have been programmed to fail, but this is the goal.

Developing a sense of humour is one of the most important parts of this process. If you see mistakes as funny rather than devastating, this gives you permission to laugh at your own mistakes, recognising that you are only human and are learning. Everyone makes mistakes; they are allowed; they can even be good. When you do make a mistake, especially an embarrassing one, you might want to take a break until you can see the mistake from a different angle.

Developing values instead of "being good"

"Being good" in groups who engage in mind control means obeying whatever the abusers tell you to do, even if it is a criminal act, or something completely against your own conscience and nature. Most survivors have inside parts who were consigned to the "rubbish dump" because they refused to "be good" and do things they believed were wrong. But they also have parts who were "good" and did these things in order to save their lives, or those of others, and avoid torture or something worse.

If you are a survivor of mind control and/or ritual abuse, you are sure to have been conditioned to be "good" in the terms that your abusers defined. And you are likely to have inner child parts who push you to continue to be that way, out of fear of punishment. There is often an inner war between the ones who implement the instructions of the abusers and those who rebel against these instructions, each group believing the others are "bad". It is important to mediate between these groups of insiders, helping each to understand the other and why they did what they did.

One important task in becoming yourself is to develop your own values. You have been given upside-down values by the abuser group. Most cultures and religions give at least lip service to the Golden Rule—"Treat other people the way you want them to treat you". There is much wisdom in this. It avoids all the petty rules and goes to the heart of the matter. One version of the Golden Rule says, "Love your neighbour as yourself." I like this because of the *as*. It suggests that it is all right to love yourself and treat yourself as well as you treat your neighbour. Both you and the other person are valuable human beings, and as you share a common humanity, you can recognise what the other person might be going through and would benefit from, and they can do the same for you. (Note: One survivor says she was told that Silence was the Golden Rule. Maybe it is the most important rule in some cults, but that is not the real Golden Rule.)

What are your own deepest beliefs about what is right and wrong? You need to consult all your insiders to find these, especially those who were discarded by the group. One thing I have learnt from survivors is that even very little children know it is wrong to kill and torture other living beings. Adults have to use very strong means to make them do it, because children just know that it is not right.

Exercise 34. Steps to becoming your real self

When you were a child, did your parents expect you to "be good"? What did this mean to your parents?

Did members of the organised abuser group also tell you to "be good"? What did this mean to them? What happened to the parts of you who were not "good" or correct?

What can you do to get away from "being good" and obedient, and allow yourself to follow your own instincts and your own conscience?

Do all your parts accept that you all exist within the same brain and the same body? If some do not, why not? Talk with one another about it. Help one another recognise how powerful a united brain can be. When you are connected, you will have all the knowledge and abilities and experience of every one of you to draw on, and you will be able to see through tricks and make wiser decisions.

Do your parts realise that what they believe about themselves was mostly indoctrination (which means it was not true)? Identify the parts who believe those lies. Find the parts who are old enough to think logically, and ask them to help the ones who were deceived to recognise the lies.

Are some of your parts ashamed of who they are? Find out who, and why. If this shame is a result of abuse, including verbal abuse, help them realise that just because it was said to them does not mean it is true.

Do some of your parts feel ashamed because your involvement in the perpetrator group led them to do and think things that they now know to be wrong and false to your true self? Encourage those parts by pointing out how they have learnt and grown and become more authentic.

(continued)

How much ability do you have to recognise your needs, your wants, and your likes and dislikes? Are some parts better at it than others? Is it frightening to think of yourself as being allowed to have needs and wants, and likes and dislikes?

What is the basis of your self-esteem? That is, when you like yourself, why is that? (Or, if you feel you never like yourself, what are the reasons?)

Are you a perfectionist? If you are, what areas of your life do you tend to stress over the most? How did you become a perfectionist? What can you do to allow yourself to try new things and make mistakes?

Ask each of your insiders (and ones who live in the outside world, too) what are his or her biggest interests. Then try to find a way to incorporate these interests into your daily life.

Ask each insider about his or her abilities. Give all your insiders a chance to develop those abilities through activities that rely on these skills.

Do you have time in your daily life for play and art and physical activity like sports, through which the younger children can work out what they like and what they are good at? If not, could you plan scheduled times for these activities?

The question of integration

When therapists began working with dissociative persons, the explicit goal was generally integration or fusion, a term that was used to mean fusing all the insiders into one person. This was usually conducted through a ceremony that joined the entire system or major parts, and was artificially induced by therapist-directed hypnosis. It often did not work, or created more problems than it solved.

My experience after twenty years of working with dissociative people, including those with mind control and ritual abuse histories, is that parts often naturally join with one another when there is no longer a need for them to remain separate, to protect secrets, or to keep toxic emotions or body sensations from flooding the whole person. There is no need for you to deliberately make it happen, unless there is a special reason to hurry.

As small joinings happen at the close of each piece of memory work, they become the natural evolution of the system—and they hardly ever come apart. The real barriers between the insiders are the separately held secrets and the intense feelings that belong to the memories; once these have been shared, there is no need for parts to remain divided.

Fragmentary parts, who only have little bits of memories, join easily; more complex parts have to process all their distinct memories before they are able to integrate.

If you or your parts are very invested in separateness, integration will become more difficult. But it will still happen, at least with some groups of parts. Several survivors have told me that it is impossible to keep parts separate when the traumatic memories that divide them have been fully processed.

Temporary blending

It is possible for parts to choose to temporarily blend with one another to see what it feels like, and then come apart again. Here, psychologist and lawyer Steve Frankel describes how he teaches this process to his patients (clients).

Steven Frankel: "Learning to blend"

I teach blending as a skill. I want my patients to learn how to do it and undo it, so they have control over whether/when/for what purpose(s) to do it. It happens to be a skill that provides experiential learning of what fusion feels like, so they will have a referent for that experience and not be so afraid that fusion means that some will die or disappear (the most common concerns about fusion). Blending also gives them an experiential lesson in the difference between being "not alone" (blended") *vs.* alone (unblended). For many who have not already had spontaneous blending experiences, this will be the first time they will have felt "not alone", but what this is like cannot be explained in advance, as it is experiential in nature—sort of like trying to explain three dimensions to a two-dimensional creature (I do not mean this in a devaluing way—just a descriptive way).

One of the neatest things ever to happen between the USA and what used to be called the Soviet Union was the US–Soviet Space programme. The reason it was so neat was that it took one astronaut/cosmonaut from each country—countries that had deep and abiding distrust for each other—and put them in a common space, with common problems to solve. Each country could be assured that if the other was pulling a fast one, their countryperson could radio back to them to warn them, and they had constant contact with their person to make sure everything was all right. While sharing the space together, the individuals found that they could appreciate each other and work together effectively to solve problems of the universe. That's what blending is like.

Blending is helpful with many problems. The two for which I most frequently use it are:

1. Conflict resolution where the parts in conflict do not have the empathic connections with one another to be able to talk through solutions/accommodations to problems. For example, one group of parts says that daddy loved them, valued them, made them feel special, never hurt them. They resent the parts who keep telling them that their daddy was a bad man who hurt them and abused them. Neither group can convince the other of the rightness of his/her views; they just can't imagine what it feels like to have that different belief about something so important.
2. Establishing "teams" of insiders for the purpose of solving life tasks. This approach can be applied to a great variety of life tasks. The dissociative way to solve problems is to have each part do a single task. A more productive way is to have teams that do life tasks, making life problems "our" problems rather than someone else's problems. The task could be assertiveness in the workplace, for example, or sexuality with a partner.

I have three rules before blending can be tried: (1) permission, (2) willingness, and (3) omitting the trauma.

Permission: I suggest that if there were permission from the group that thinks daddy never hurt them, and also from the group that thinks that daddy was a bad guy, for one representative of each group to blend together, maybe they could understand each one another better. I then ask for permission, which is non-negotiable rule no. 1. If one or the other side says NO, I ask what the objections are, and if I can't meet them, I don't teach the skill. End of story. If there are no objections, I ask for two volunteers.

Willingness: Non-negotiable rule no. 2 is willingness. The parts that blend must be willing to try it. No one gets dragged, kicking and screaming, into a blend.

Once we have permission and willingness, I announce the third non-negotiable rule: neither part can carry toxic trauma material into the blend—they have to take it out and put it on the floor before entering the blend. This, I explain, is due to the fact that parts are separate for very good reasons, one of which is that the toxic trauma material they carry is so powerful that it is too much to bear and must, therefore, be divided up. I tell them that if, as they blend, they feel a burning sensation, someone hasn't taken all of their trauma material out of them, so they have to unblend and repeat the step of taking the toxic trauma material out of them and putting it on the floor.

Then I give the blending instructions: everyone watch and listen please, as this is a skill for you to have and use as you see fit. Then, to the blending parts: please face each other, take the toxic trauma material each of you carries and put it on the floor. Now, I'm going to count slowly from 5 to 1. As I count, I'd like you to walk toward each other very slowly, taking deep breaths between each number. When we get to "3" you'll be nose to nose and I'd like you to keep walking right into each other. When we get to 1, the boundary will close around you. Five (breath), four (breath), three—nose to nose now/keep going (breath), two, right into each other and 1, feel the boundary close around you.

Now, is either of you feeling too cramped in that space? If so, take a deep breath and the space will expand. Is either of you feeling a burning sensation? If so, step back out of the blend and put all toxic trauma material on the floor, then walk back into the blend.

Part A, can you announce that you're there please? ("I'm here") and Part B, can you announce that you're there please? ("I'm here"). I do this to assure everyone that no one dies or disappears when they are in a blend.

Can each of you tell me what you are experiencing? I never tell them what I think they will experience. In my experience they often report feeling thicker, denser, and stronger (I ask them to move the body around, make fists, etc., to help them experience the body with them blended), and they report being amazed at how much stronger (and SAFER) they feel, and that they now understand/appreciate one another's feelings.

* * *

You can adapt what Steve has taught here for your own purposes. Discuss it internally before you try it. Blending is something you can practise to see how various parts feel about it. It is not the same as fusion, especially as the trauma that forces the parts to remain separate has not been worked through. But, as I said before, parts naturally join together and remain joined when the trauma has been resolved.

Stella Katz, the cult trainer who had the courage to escape from her abuser group, work through her traumatic memories, and recover, here tells the story of her recovery, including her eventual integration:

Stella Katz: "Reclaiming me"

I am writing this for one reason only, and that is to prove to others with DID that there really is LIFE beyond the dark tunnel.

I spent the better part of forty years fragmented. I had one stable alter personality who lived everyday life, went to school, took dance and skating lessons, dated, married, and had children. That person knew nothing of what was going on in the rest of my life. All I knew was that from a very early age I would go to bed at night and wake up with dirty feet, or completely clothed with unusual makeup or markings, and bruises. What I found odd, though, was that I only did the sleepwalking at my Grandmother's house, and never at home until after my Grandmother died. As a young child I assumed it was because I missed my own bed, but I had no explanation for it happening later on. I was told that the horrible things I remembered in the morning were just bad dreams and to forget about them and not to tell anyone because they would think I was insane and lock me up in the home for bad crazy people.

At the age of thirty-five, when all came to light, I was horrified. I was told to go to a group for people like me, only to find out that most of the people never really got better, or ever integrated, and were in therapy for most of their lives. Being stubborn and pig-headed, I was not going to hear of that. I wanted to get well. I wanted to know every detail of my secret life, and, moreover, I wanted the loud, opinionated, taunting voices in my head to shut up.

So began the journey that helped me reclaim "myself".

I can still remember the feeling of horrific physical pain of the memory that first brought it all to light. Although it was only a memory, the pain was so intense I was sure my foot was broken. I could barely walk on it for days after. I still remember the smell of wax from the burning candles and leftover incense that permeated the room where the memory all took place. Even now it was like yesterday. It was all so horrid but it answered a burning question I had had since I was five years old about how I broke the heel of my foot while I was supposedly sleeping.

The more I learnt, the more I wanted to learn. I wanted forty years of unanswered questions answered. But the more I learnt the worse I felt about myself, because the one thing I learnt was that I was still going somewhere where these things happened. I needed to find the people inside who knew the most and I knew that once or twice a week in a therapist's office, no matter how good she was, just wasn't going to cut it. I needed to get out of the group not years from now, but right now, and unless I learnt more about my internals, I would never be free of the group. So, I began my version of homework.

On the days of my sessions, after my children were in bed and my husband safely tucked in front of the television for the night, I would go down to the recreation room where I could be alone and go over the therapy session of that day. I would try to figure out what seemed to be missing from what I had learnt or worked on during the session. It meant that I had to go back into myself and try to talk to those who had been out that day in the therapist's office. My biggest fear was that I would get in and get stuck. So I bought myself a silk rope, and a timer. I would set the timer for thirty minutes, tie the rope to the chair and hang on so tight you'd have thought I was dangling from a ten-storey building. Somehow the rope gave me safety, as if it was a lifeline to pull me back from falling over the edge. I would close my eyes and visualise a dark tunnel and step by step I would walk through into my inner world still hanging on to my rope, calling out to the name of the last insider I remembered from the session.

As I got to know each member of the Clan, as they called themselves, I began to see them as real people. Some were easy to talk to, while others were so dark and scary it was all I could do to look at them. There were adults on the light side and the dark side, and children, oh so many children. Some rather happy, some so terrified they would only peek out of little holes in the fabric of our mind. I saw houses and places that were familiar, and places I was sure I had never seen before, yet felt strangely familiar. At times I was so terrified I just wanted to run. I felt so foolish because I knew I shouldn't be scared of these people—after all, they were part of me. I equated it to being afraid of my own arm. It seems so silly now, but then it was terrifying.

After a few years of twice weekly therapy sessions and twice weekly homework, I finally realised that though I liked my therapist a great deal, I didn't want to grow old with this woman. So I stepped up the work I was doing on my own. Along the way, something happened, and the therapist and I parted ways. I went on to another who was sweet but useless, and then to another who was both unpleasant and incompetent. All that forced me to work harder on my own. So I left therapy altogether, for a while.

Night after night I worked getting to know my system, one alter at a time, or sometimes in little groups. It was amazing and intricate and I didn't think I would ever get to know everyone in it. Just when I thought I was through most of it, a little floater child would introduce me to a whole new level. A floater child does not actually belong to the structured system created by the abusive group, but is "born" by accident. As Fiona the floater didn't belong to the structure, she was free to travel throughout the system and was no threat to anyone in it.

After about six more months, I was taken on by another wonderful therapist. I got to know so many more in my system with her help, but her office was too far away. The beauty of living in your head is that you can do things you cannot do in the real world, such as creating a holodeck like the one on *Star Trek*. When I became afraid of a memory or a dark Clan member I was dealing with, I would simply "freeze programme" and go around and look at the entire situation from every angle. I discovered that so much of what had been done to me was nothing more than smoke and mirrors. I was able to see the Devil who had abused me from all angles. I saw that he was not eight feet tall; he was just a grown man while I was a small child. He did not have scales and claws and a tail, he wore a stretch suit with a zip up the back, and you could see the line of his boxer shorts under his costume. It made me laugh. The fear I had was now gone. The more comfortable I got with processing my memories, the more I increased the period on the timer from thirty minutes to forty-five, sixty, and eventually two full hours.

I became friends with my Clan, with the help of Fiona, the little floater child who knew every single member of the clan. I was able to get through to members who would have been blocked otherwise. Fiona trusted me, and because she trusted me, the others came to trust me as well.

I was often in awe of the structure of the system. I learnt so much about the missing years and answered so many of the burning questions of my life. I discovered the reason my real life children spoke languages I didn't. The Clan had an internal nanny who cared for the internal children. She had the ability to come out and take care of my real world children when I slipped inside. She spoke Gaelic to them and sang songs with them, and they learnt and had a great deal of fun. The only thing that bothered me was that she was a better mother than I was. In time I found out why I hated highly textured food, and especially raisins. I won't tell you why, but I can tell you it was disgusting. I came to love the little internal children, and animals, and even my little demons, who were all under the age of five. I came to understand that my black heart was not black as in evil, but black as in a mix of all the wonderful colours of the world.

I knew that every member of the system had to be in agreement about integrating. They had to be able to decide for themselves and choose to join the healing plan because they had never had any choice about what had happened to them. I knew this could only be done by helping the little ones grow up, or at least to understand what we were hoping would take place. So, after the real-world kids had gone to school, I would set the timer, bring out the toys and cookies without raisins, and let the children out to play and watch television and read books. Once they were allowed out into the world, they grew quickly, not like real children do, but years in a matter of weeks. One by one they grew. One by one they joined.

All through this healing process, I still had one big problem, which was that I still belonged to the group. I was still a high priestess; I was still part of the inner circle. I was still a trainer. I knew I had to get out of it but I knew they were not going to let me just walk away because I knew too much.

For the next couple of years I was stalked and harassed daily. My children were threatened. I had dead animals put in my car, snakes in my postbox, and dead kittens nailed to my door. I was driven off the road at night and raped. I didn't think it would ever end. I got tough and looked at the rapes as just lousy sex. Once I was sent a photograph of a person dead and mutilated with a threat saying that would be me. I called the police and an officer came eight hours later. I gave him my statement and the picture. I took his business card, only to find out when I called to talk to him it was fake.

The more I worked on my system, the less use I was to the group. Eventually, they got tired of stalking me, and let me go. It took a few more years, but I was free, or at least felt I was relatively safe.

Once I was free, it did not take long before I was pushing through the system, had everyone catalogued, knew where, when, and how each had come into separate being. With that all done, I was able to get everyone in the system to set a date and time that we would join as one. Some were afraid they would die. Others were afraid that the body wouldn't remember them, others were afraid it would hurt, but we worked through the fears. We planned the day it would all happen, and so, on a beautiful day while the children were in school, I gathered the members of the Clan, had everyone line up in order of their birth, hold hands, and form a circle. One by one, in a very ceremonial manner, the newest member stepped into one who came before and so on down the line until we reached the child whose body had been born. It felt wonderful and frightening and strange, and a little like a house of cards ready to collapse at any second. It felt like the house's foundation had been built on jelly, but it felt right.

I was one with myself. I wasn't who I thought I would be. There were a few times when I was sure we would fall apart, but I hung on. No one died, no one was forgotten, and I had to fight to get rid of the Celtic accent I had acquired unexpectedly. In the first few months, when I recalled something I saw it through the eyes of the person who had experienced it. As time went on, all the memories became mine. And it was an amazing feeling, though a little lonely at times to have only one voice in my head. The thought I was thinking was my thought and mine alone, and to know that I would no longer hurt little children or animals or wake up with muddy feet was amazing.

I was not prepared for what came afterwards. I was stupidly under the impression that all would be well once there was only one of me. I could not have been more wrong.

What I did not expect was the unbearable remorse for what I had done. The faces of every child I had hurt, their cries, and their anguish kept flooding through. It was a dam that broke in my moral conscience.

I no longer had a therapist because "I was well and integrated". I really could have used someone at that point, even if it was just to cry on her shoulder, but I had no one. I had to hang on and let myself feel the pain. It went on for two years. There were rivers of tears, torment, and guilt. I had never been so depressed. I had known the pain while fragmented into mini me's, but now I understood that all the pain I had felt in those years of abuse had been dulled by an imaginary coating of Novocaine brought on by the fragmentation; now it was just the raw pain of remorse and I had only one of me to feel it.

I also went through a spiritual crisis. I didn't know what I believed. I had the guilt teaching of the Catholic Church running through my head, telling me I was going to hell. I had the Satanic beliefs that God is weak and worthless. I had my mother's Pagan beliefs that Dark and Light are equal and balance life. I had Jewish beliefs of the group I had belonged to, and I didn't really feel any of it was worth my time. I think this was the hardest part to try to work out in my mind.

It all came to a head at a stop light one sunny afternoon when a song triggered a memory that forced me to ask the question "What do I believe?" Between stop lights and stop signs, I went through the list. The questions were everything from my belief in a god to my personal beliefs about life in general. I gave myself ten seconds to answer each question. I felt that what I answered in ten seconds was what I truly believed without the process we all have of over-thinking, and justifying what we say. By the time I got home, I felt as light as a feather. The weight of the world had been lifted off my shoulders. I could not stop grinning. I finally knew who I was, and what I truly believed in. I found my life at the end of that long tunnel. I was integrated on all levels. It had been a long, long road.

It's not my dream life, but it is mine. I now have terminal cancer, but I worked through what I believe about death, and I'm all right with it. I don't know how long I have left, but I see every day that my name is not in the obituary column as a great day, and more so as a gift. I have made my peace with myself.

For all of you who are still going through the torment of memory and the chaos of an untamed system, know that there is Life at the end of your tunnel. Know that you are not alone because we are all connected in the universe. Know that every member of your internal self is part of the whole and worthy of love and of being heard. And know that it's all right to remain divided if you can get your system to co-operate. No one member is more important than another in the long haul. The tunnel to yourself is long, painful, and, more often than not, extremely frustrating, but it does have an end. If you all work together, even through the chaos and pain, there can be peace.

* * *

You might notice that Stella integrated all her parts through a ceremony, and had considerable difficulty afterwards. It is possible that this was because the insiders' emotions, particularly guilt and shame, had not been fully worked through when she processed the memories. Stella was in a hurry, because of her high position in the cult and the ongoing harassment she was experiencing. She warns us that, for survivors who are still being accessed by perpetrator groups, it is unsafe to continue to have child insiders remain separate, because the groups can re-split them to create new parts, whereas they are unable to do this to a fully integrated person.

However, as you may be aware, guilt and shame are, unfortunately, an effect of your front people and some insider parts coming to know and take ownership of things you have done because of your involvement in the mind-controlling perpetrator group. There is no way to avoid dealing with these feelings and the spiritual issues that they raise. Because of this, I recommend working through the emotions gradually as the memories are accessed a little at a time. Generally, it is helpful for the parts who are just memory fragments or partial "people" to join with stronger ones, and it is easier for a personality system to work together with a smaller number of parts.

Full integration is not *the only* healthy resolution of dissociative splitting. Survivor Jen Callow has thought a lot about the process of integration. In this article, written two years ago, she demonstrates that there is no formula for how parts, individually or in relationship, will respond to this process, for what will change, and how parts will feel. She also shows what can happen if insiders are not fully involved in, and prepared for, the process. She explores the value of keeping out just a bit of a memory until all parts involved in that memory are really, really ready to integrate. "Integration," she says, "is more of a journey, and doesn't have to mean total fusion." On the other hand, it "isn't about losing who you are, it's about becoming what you were meant to be."

Jen Callow: "To integrate or not to integrate"

I started out with over 700 fully and partially developed parts, although only a handful spent time in the outside world. Partially developed parts are ones that carry memory fragments, but do not have a clear identity and personality, unlike fully formed parts. Now I have about 150 parts, since many times two or more parts have merged into one new part that is a composite of these original parts. With merging, the walls completely disappear and there's no barrier between certain parts anymore. This can lead to a stronger sense of self. When parts were really ready to merge, my merges happened effortlessly without my full awareness. I sometimes felt a new energy coming into me, the outside part, but normally only noticed a shift in my perceptions, feelings, or beliefs afterward. Often, I felt stronger and more whole inside. For a number of my parts, integration like this is just "something that happens". Some are quite positive about it, seeing it as becoming stronger and wiser, gaining in life experience. I have child parts who look forward to "growing taller" through merging with another part.

For parts who are unprepared or do not understand what is happening, or who do not want, or are not ready, to merge, this merging can be terrifying. All parts respond to integration differently, depending upon how close they are to the parts being integrated, whether it is happening directly to them, and their beliefs around what is happening. With my system, it also depends upon whether they are fully or partially developed parts. Merges between partial and full parts seem to be easier, with the partial part being strongly pulled toward the full part. Merges between fully developed parts have the potential to be more emotional.

Many of my parts still fear integration. Some parts see the inner world decreasing, with a physical loss of playmates, friends, and care-givers as various parts merge. This can result in a huge sense of loss, and parts may need time to grieve. This reduction in numbers can also be interpreted as people "disappearing" and parts might be afraid of disappearing, too. Others see integration as a loss of self, and are terrified at the prospect.

Just as integration can be a welcome event, it can also be traumatic when parts are not ready to integrate or merge. Once, I had a part crying as he merged, resisting all the way. Pete (the name he chose) hadn't realised he would merge when he helped process a particular memory, and it was an awful experience for him. He was not prepared for what was happening to him. He had just processed a long and terrifying memory on the assurance that it would help him and my system feel better. Afterward, he fought the merge, moving in and out of the other part involved. Eventually, I discovered he was still trying to keep out a piece of the memory so he could stay separate. But by this point he hated being half in and half out, and realised he could not go back to being fully himself. When Pete released the memory piece, we processed it, and he merged with the other part. This took only a few minutes, now that he was ready. The new part still contains elements of Pete, and he tells me everything's all right, although he still carries some of Pete's anger and sadness about the merge. Had we made it clear that he might merge if we went through the memory, and offered him the opportunity to address his feelings and perhaps, in his case, the choice to stay separate (see next paragraph), merging would not have been so traumatic.

It might be helpful under some circumstances to arrange to leave a small piece of a memory unprocessed until resistant parts are ready to integrate. The memory piece could be a smell, a sound, an image, or even a short scene, whatever works best for you and will create the least disturbance if it is left in your system. Regardless, whatever is left unprocessed needs to be something that was directly held by the part, otherwise the part could merge. If a part chooses to leave a piece unprocessed, it is important to set the piece aside in such a way that it won't get added into the memory, or affect the rest of the system. For example, the part could put the memory fragment into an inside container, label it for easy retrieval should the memory need to be finished, and then put it in a safe spot where it can be found, but will not be accidentally opened.

Use this technique sparingly, though, as each memory piece dramatically increases the chance that one of the associated memories could be opened again and negatively impact you, regardless of how much of the memory was actually processed. Only when memories are fully processed are they gone and carry no risk of impacting you.

Parts that have merged might also need support to adjust. It might be hard for them to fit in, to find their new role in the inner world. A merge may suddenly result in a part becoming older and no longer at the same developmental level as his/her playmates, or any number of other changes. My merged parts seemed to adjust fairly easily because I had made a point to help all of the parts involved find new roles in my inner system, whether they had merged or not. So, parts often had fairly clear roles before they merged, and afterward their roles were simply amalgamated or expanded.

For a number of my parts, integrating is scary because it means giving up their identity and becoming someone new and unknown. In my view, merging is a micro-version of spiritual bliss, or nirvana. In both of these situations, giving up the self or ego to a higher power is called for, in order to achieve a greater unity and sense of inner peace. With integration, I am achieving a greater unity within myself, as opposed to merging with a greater spiritual force, although I find my spiritual connection deepens, as well. Many books have been written on the subject of spiritual enlightenment and a common theme is how terrifying and difficult it can be to give up your sense of self, your individuality and identity—in other words, your ego. This fear exists even with the promise of an incredibly joyous and peaceful state. Each part's thoughts, feelings, and personality will not be their own any more. Integration, in both a dissociative and spiritual sense, is a leap of faith.

If you have not experienced integration yet, it can be hard for you to imagine what it might be like. If some parts have merged successfully, it can be helpful for parts that are scared of merging to talk with them. Some parts may need to understand that it is not a painful process and that they will be all right in the end. This should never be done to coerce parts to merge, but, rather, to help alleviate their fears so they can make a good choice for themselves.

I believe my fear of merging is, in part, due to never being allowed to develop a separate sense of self growing up. To survive, I had to adapt myself to be whoever people wanted me to be, and as I developed my sense of self in my recovery process, I became scared of losing it or having it ripped away. This fear also came from abusers forcing me to switch (change parts out in the body) at their whim, and not knowing if I'd ever be able to bring any given part back or for how long. As my sense of self became more secure, I became less scared of losing it. Integration is not about losing who you are, it is about becoming who you were meant to be. This doesn't mean that I want to fully integrate all my parts, or that none of my parts is afraid. Rather, it means I have a stronger foundation to draw upon when integration does happen.

Integration is more of a journey than a specific goal, and it doesn't have to mean total fusion. During the course of my recovery, I found that the "walls" between my different parts grew thinner. At first, my parts became aware of one another's presence. Then it got easier to communicate with each other and to work together to build a community. More parts were able to participate in my daily life and to feel that they mattered. It also became easier to find and rescue parts that were still in unpleasant situations inside.

My personal choice has been to integrate, but not completely. My system is now cohesive enough that I can experience a high degree of personal safety and I have come to view my inner world as my family. Someday, I may become "one" person, but that's not my goal. I am happy in my life and enjoy the company of my inner parts. I have come to love and cherish them in a way they didn't experience in the outer world, and would miss their distinct personalities and spirit should they fully become part of me. They have taught me how to increasingly love myself as I come to love each of them.

And the parts that have integrated have taught me how to trust, to know it can be safe to connect deeply with others, and that as I connect within, I am also connecting with the divine.

* * *

Whether or not to fully integrate is up to the person—or is it? Stella chose full integration. Trish Fotheringham, as reported in her DVD (2009), did not choose either way. All of her parts remained for a long time as separate parts inside her, but then one day, when she was experiencing anguish and despair about her life, all the parts came together and integrated into a single identity. Like her, Jen chose to integrate some parts but allow others to remain separate. This is a valid choice. However, even if that is what you plan to do, it is not always what happens, or at least not what remains the case throughout your life. Here is what happened to Jen (and also to Trish).

Jen Callow: "Life after integration"

About six or seven months after writing my first piece on whether or not to integrate (above), I unexpectedly integrated. A friend was doing some energy healing on me and cleared a lot of stuck energy, particularly in my abdomen. I felt my energy shifting and changing; the top of my head was tingling. When she had finished, my parts had merged and the inner "lines" holding my programmes had vanished; I had integrated.

The irony of my integration wasn't lost on me, considering I had chosen to remain multiple and some of my parts feared losing themselves through integration. In reality, integration itself was both powerful and natural. Afterward, I felt stronger and more peaceful, and a knowing that it had been time to integrate. The biggest challenge was adjusting to being whole. Integration is not a common outcome of energy healing and I was not prepared for it. Just as people who are multiple are unique, I suspect there are many ways of integrating. I offer this piece as a rough guideline to what life after integration can be like, and as help to adjust to this change.

Over the coming weeks, I did my best to adjust to the quiet inside me. I felt hollow and lonely without the chatter and activity that had been there up until integration. Before the integration, I still had around 100 parts, I think, although I cannot properly remember now. They had provided company, unique ways of seeing the world, and a chance to take breaks from everyday life by switching with one of my older parts for short periods of time. I found it exhausting to be "out" all the time and wished I could escape the way I used to, even for a few minutes. I still zone out for short periods, even now, in order to keep from getting over-stimulated—often on walks, or somewhere safe.

I also had to adjust to feeling many emotions at once. Although I had experienced this to a lesser extent as my system became more cohesive, I now experienced mixed emotions over many things that had seemed very straightforward. It took time for me to realise this was normal, and even healthy. It also took time to learn to sit with myself, to feel all the emotions as I breathed and tuned into my body's messages and my intuition. This was the only way I seemed to be able to make clearer and wiser decisions for myself, in addition to it being a coping mechanism. Gradually, sifting through my emotions became easier. It is definitely one thing to learn to manage differing emotions as you grow up, another to get a crash course in it through integration.

My biggest challenge was adjusting to the loss of my kid parts. I hadn't realised how much I had drawn on their energy and ways of being in the world in order to survive. Although they were still within me, and were not "dead" or lost, they were no longer separate. Their unique energy had merged into the larger whole of "me". Without them being separate, my energy felt flat and I felt very old. I had no reference for being my actual adult age in the world, even though I had been capably dealing with adult responsibilities for many years. Months later, I am finally learning to generate energy without relying on my inner kids; when I am living in my passion and joy, fully in the moment, a lot of that energy returns. Only now it feels different, deeper somehow, as it is sourced from my whole self. I believe this will help me learn to be an adult in the world while retaining the enthusiasm and wonder of my inner child.

I remained in a state of full integration for at least several more months, until one day I went inside myself to deal with some strong feelings coming up and discovered another part. She was a young girl who had been buried deep inside of me. From other people I know of who have integrated, it seems common to find one or more parts and to still be, essentially, integrated, as the rest of me was energetically still in that state of "oneness". Thankfully, my inner structures were still intact, so the girl had places to live. When I wondered how I would properly support her, given I spend most of my time out in the world and she would be living alone inside, some of my parts spontaneously re-separated. I still cannot explain how this happened. These parts were sad to do this, missing the feeling of being integrated, but were also willing to help. It was empowering to realise I now had a true choice about whether to be integrated or multiple.

Interestingly, although I can still have parts, it is harder to create any helpers inside. Helpers differ from my parts and were a significant part of my system before I integrated; when I integrated, they disappeared. Created from my imagination, helpers provided what felt like a very real presence and help inside. We (myself and my parts who separated to be a support system) no longer have extra healers, mother figures and the like, to draw on, though we somehow managed to re-create our main healer, who performs her same duties. She is less substantial than she was before, though not exactly a ghost, either.

The young girl I found inside was in a lot of pain, although she was no longer attached to any programme line (my system was like a spider web of coloured lines, each one a programme with parts locked on to it). I held her inside, as a caring adult, and listened to what she had to say, witnessed the scenes she showed me. I let her feelings move through and out of me, acknowledged her pain, and when she was ready to hear it, showed her how things were different now and reassured her I would keep her safe. There was no need to run through the memory over and over, as in the past, or to specifically link up each part of the memory with a feeling, sound, etc. Because all of the other parts involved had already merged with her, a lot had been processed through other memory work (including related memories with similar feelings, sounds, etc.), and this memory wasn't as intense or charged as it would have been in the past. Once she had been reassured, she also had some feelings to express over being deceived. After that, she continued to live in the inner world for some time, feeling more safety and love than she had had before. When she had worked through whatever remained, she simply integrated. It wasn't something I was aware of, I only noticed one day she was gone and I think she had integrated sometime before that.

Most of the time, I find what's left from the abuse is body memories and core beliefs. When I have feelings that are overwhelming, or out of proportion to the event, I make a point of tracing them back inside. Sometimes, the feelings are truly an in-the-moment reaction, but usually they are from inner parts. Sometimes, I trace them back to what "normal" people describe as their inner child. We are all dissociative to some extent, and many "normal" people would say they have an inner child; practically everyone has areas and parts of themselves they hold separate. These inner children don't feel as if they were separate to begin with, in the way one of my actual parts would feel separate, and I do not remember them being a part of my system. They are less substantial than actual parts, and appear more translucent to me, although just as real as any other part. (My actual parts were solid in my inner world, both visually and to the touch.) After I listen to the inner children and support them in working through their concerns, they hang around inside for a while, and once they have had whatever corrective experiences they need and released all their feelings, they tend to integrate, or reintegrate, on their own. Integration isn't the big deal it used to be.

Recently, I did find a group of three actual parts still attached to part of a programme line. This caught me by surprise. The young girl had a wisp of green coming out of her back, the remains of the programme line, and was upset at being tortured and poked. I soothed her as best as I could and, because of the green wisp, traced the "line" back to another young part who was doing the poking. He was also being encouraged by a third part holding a lot of rage. These parts were living in isolation and could not do much damage due to the lack of a whole programme line and related parts; however, they were attached enough to still affect each other. Their shared memories were emotionally charged and intense. I've had to do a lot of processing, and have worked with them similarly to when I was in therapy, just with fewer parts holding larger pieces of the memory. I have had to link more of their feelings, sounds, sights, etc., in a movie of sorts, and to watch it several times with all of these parts present. The third part has a lot of anger, which we are helping him with inside. This group of parts has proved more challenging to help, due to the strength and complexity of their beliefs and feelings. With fewer of us inside, there is more room for individual attention, which can help parts such as these. My hope is that over time, they will come to trust us more and be willing to release their pain. The difference now is that their pain doesn't overwhelm my system or, since I have integrated, me, and we are concerned for them more as individuals than from any agenda of our own (e.g., making our life easier, integration, etc.).

A focus in my healing now is helping my physical body release trapped energy. This is energy still stored in it from the abuse, which has created imbalance and illnesses over the years. Now that I have done so much emotional and spiritual healing, it finally seems possible to heal physically (much of the imbalance is still emotionally based). I do guided meditations, breath work, and various forms of energy work, along with regular exercise and movement. I often visualise the stuck energy moving, leaving my body as a cloud of smog, and visualise my being filled with light. When I do this work, my body feels progressively lighter.

The most challenging thing for me now is dealing with the deep-seated core beliefs left over from the abuse. These include: "I'm not worthy", "There's never enough", "I'm a bad person", "Everything good gets taken away", and "I can't keep myself safe". Since integration, I've realised how much these beliefs permeate my life and influence how I both show up in the world and take care of myself. After years of therapy, and finally feeling done with that, I didn't realise I'd still have this piece ahead of me.

Sometimes life provides corrective experiences where it is clearly shown that the old beliefs are not true, and if I am ready to accept a new way of seeing myself and the world, I will have an "aha!" moment that dramatically shifts things. I am deliberately choosing ways of being that shift behaviour patterns no longer serving me. For example, instead of allowing myself to feel hurt and not speaking up, increasingly I take the risk to speak my truths. I also might choose to reach out and have fun with a friend when I'm feeling unloved, or to look for ways I can give love that day, which opens me up to receiving it.

I also spend time, ideally each day, going inside and communicating with the inner children who send feelings up to me, building a strong relationship. I ground/breathe into my adult self so I can be strong and present, listen to the child's (or even teenager's) feelings, let them express without interruption or judgement and let them know they've been heard. I notice what core beliefs have been triggered, and with the child's help, determine how the feelings and beliefs were triggered in the present, and what they are related to in the past. I commit to taking action when and if I can, and reassure the child with concrete examples that things are different now. I also increasingly make a point to spend quality time with my inner child in play, quiet time, or whatever it is they need. This all goes a long way to clearing core beliefs, I find, when coupled with positive affirmations. It is a long process for me and some days I feel like giving up in frustration, but when I can step back from my perfectionism and desire to be completely free of the abuse, I know I've come a long way and it's worth it. Once a detrimental belief is changed, it is as if a whole new area of the world opens up to me.

I have changed a lot since integration. My sense of self is deeper and stronger, my body feels amazingly whole and I can feel the energy flowing from my feet on the floor all the way up to the top of my head. Although I still have an underlying anxiety about life, which comes from the core beliefs and few remaining parts, I am not overwhelmed by programming any more. Even when I am triggered, it is usually feelings with maybe some brief flashbacks, and they are easier to clear. It is more stable, secure, and peaceful inside, and I think that's reflected in the fact that integration isn't even an issue any more. My inner world is becoming my inner sanctuary. More and more often, I am able to find a place of power, expansiveness and joy within myself. I am finally able to be more of who I am, to more fully express myself in the world.

Although people will label my inner state as they wish, I feel and identify as integrated and "one" person. I don't fit the world of "multiple" any more; I'm creating my own new world now. Although integration wasn't what I wanted, and I feel I am moving through largely uncharted territory now, it is worth it to feel so whole and solid. I would never tell anyone to integrate, and still truly believe being multiple is a perfectly valid and good-feeling way to live once parts are connected enough. For me, integration feels natural, like the birth of the person I am meant to be.

* * *

You might notice that Jen's experience of spontaneous integration, later finding one or more hidden parts, and then their integration, is much like that of Meredith Sharman (in Chapter Seventeen). They and the other integrated survivors I know are content with the way things developed, as it was natural. As I read Jen's account of life since integration, I see that there is some loss in integration, the loss of the child parts and their energy as separate, and the internal noise and conversations. There is, however, a strength and a peacefulness and a sense of wholeness.

There is also the experience of ambivalence and mixed emotions, as well as the stress of being "out" all the time. We can see that integration does not mean there is nothing left to heal. Jen names trapped energy that needs release, core beliefs such as "I'm bad", and experiences of out-of-proportion emotions related to present-day post-traumatic triggers. These experiences are no different to those which regular non-multiple people, singletons, have to deal with. You might notice that her way of processing her emotions and triggering is much like what I have recommended in Chapters Ten and Thirteen. Therapy can be helpful for singletons as well as multiples—but you may find that you have developed such skills at inner work that you no longer need professional help.

A client of mine, an older man whose childhood trauma did not include ongoing mind control or ritual abuse, is in the integration process. After finding himself being clearly assertive in a situation in which he would previously have just given in to others' demands, he wrote to me:

> I tell you this to confirm that integration allows assertiveness and action. When faced with difficulties, a small child is not left to deal with the problems. Shifting moods keep a person from making decisions and carrying them out. A consistent mood state allows thinking through problems, taking into account the various thoughts, feelings, without being overwhelmed by one of them. Difficulties don't have to result in despair. Time and energy can be budgeted.
>
> How much easier is life for the integrated.

However, he also says:

> Integration is very painful and difficult. I think the dominant feeling of integration is sorrow. Dissociation, while an immediate solution to a problem, pain, fear, when maintained, creates endless losses. Consistency is required for success and productivity. You can't be successful when constantly changing mood states, personalities. Dissociation does not allow adaptability. It keeps a person from understanding other people. It makes it very hard to create and maintain friendships, professional relationships. It maintains and gives power to the past. I have been unable to shake free from my mother yelling "You are nobody and nothing and don't you ever forget it." It's always there.

As you heal, you feel sorrow about all the years during which you could not take charge of your own life because parts of you were trapped in the past.

There is no "right" way for all multiples. Keep in mind the goal of recovery. It is not to make a multiple into a singleton, but to become more functional and free of disabling symptoms. For a mind-control survivor, the goal is to remove all the external controls over your mind so that you can be a full human being—free, in charge of your own life, choosing your own life goals.

Each system will naturally blend to a smaller or greater degree as memory work goes along, and, at the end, find its own resolution. As someone once said, survivors may integrate, or become a corporation, or become a collective. But what happens will happen naturally, and that is as it should be. In the end, the choice is yours.

I use two different images in explaining integration to my clients. The first is two rivers joining. All the water that was in each river is contained in the new, larger river, which contains both of them. The only thing that is gone is the strip of land between them, which represents the secrets that they did not previously share. The new river will probably carry the name of one of the original smaller rivers, but it will contain all the water—all the memories and experiences—of the other small river, too.

The other image I use is that of a stained glass lamp. Many coloured pieces come together to make a beautiful lamp through which the light can shine, displaying all the colours and making a picture that could not be seen as long as the pieces were separated. This image can be used for co-operative co-consciousness as well as for integration.

I have been asked "What happens to your memories after integration?" Once a memory is known to your everyday consciousness, it starts to mingle with other similar memories in your brain, and the details fade. It is hard to remember exactly when something happened, though the fact that it happened remains clear. An event is never so clear in its sensory details as when it is first *experienced*—and, for delayed recall, that means when the memory is first put together, even though this might be years after the event happened. If you want to know exactly what happened to you, you should write it down or tape your account right after you first put the memory together, or after each piece comes out. Then you can refer back to the account you made when the memory was fresh.

What about the feelings from the traumatic memories? After integration, they will be less raw than when you first experienced them, but they can probably be triggered to some extent by life events that resemble the original traumas. If and when this happens, you will need to revisit those traumas as well as the triggering situation, search for hidden parts or "inner children" whose feelings have been triggered, and offer love and security to those parts of you.

As Jen discovered, you might also need to work on changing the beliefs you acquired during those years when you were so unsafe. Of course, you will not end up with the naïve, sunny outlook of someone who has never suffered. The goal is to put the bad things in perspective, as part of what happens in a world which contains both good and bad, and still has many wonderful experiences to offer, especially as you move forward.

Exercise 35. Internal consultation about integration and life direction

Do you have parts who have merged with one another? If so, how and when did this happen? What seems to have caused it?

How do the merged parts feel about what has happened to them?

How do the other parts feel about what has happened to those who merged? If they are upset or confused, give them a chance to communicate with the joined parts to see whether the parts who seem to be missing are still there within the new people, and what it is like for them.

Consult your main outsiders about what their recovery goal might be. Do they want everyone inside to remain separate? Or to have a reduced number of parts who co-operate with one another? Or to achieve full integration?

What might you need to do to reach this goal?

Do you, or some of your parts, have an idea about what is the most important thing to do with your life, once you are in charge of your own life? If you do, what is that idea? Does everyone inside agree with it?

What stage of life are you in? How do you feel about having those years prior to recovery taken away from you? How are you handling this grief?

Maintaining your emotional and spiritual health

Much of what I have covered in this book is repairing the damage that the mind control and ritual abuse did to you. If the damage were physical, you would need a series of surgeries to repair the breakages caused by a series of severe physical traumas. But after the surgeries, you would need to maintain your physical health through exercise, healthy eating, regular check-ups, rest and recreation. Good health is more than repair; it requires ongoing maintenance. The activities Jen talks about in "Life after integration" are all ways in which she maintains her psychological and emotional health. Chapters Twelve, Thirteen, and Eighteen of this book are full of suggestions for ongoing work which will help you become a fully functional, mature, and developed person. In addition, once the "repair" part is completed by working through your traumatic memories, you can learn and grow in many new ways as you become your authentic self.

Finding a life direction

Most survivors who are in the recovery process are not able to be content with the petty values they see in the general population around them; they want to contribute to the world and to others through their work or creative output. Our abilities are meant to be used, to contribute to the world. Many "normal" people are bored, and lack self-esteem because they feel useless. Their jobs are meaningless, their recreation is adequate but boring, and they feel they are just marking time. An authentic person wants to take it further and use his or her gifts for the good of others. This gives deep satisfaction, not just for survivors, but for anyone.

As you work towards integration, or co-operative co-consciousness, and become more functional and more in touch with your feelings, needs, and abilities, the question will arise of what you want to do with your life. That is a big deal for someone whose right and ability to think independently and make choices has been derailed.

Some survivors will choose to become outspoken survivor advocates. For them, recovery might resemble what it means to alcohol and drug addicts, whose sobriety requires that they "pass it on", or they might find the meaning they need to attach to their suffering, and the suffering they were forced to cause, by bearing witness to the truth in a public way. Some will choose to "go public" through publishing and telling their stories to the world, by helping others through such forums as web discussions, by "fighting back" through lawsuits against their abusers, or by making their survivor status publicly known in other ways. If you are not fully integrated, however, there are considerable dangers in this. Programming can still be triggered through words, non-verbal signals, or what appear to be innocent questions. One of my clients who was involved in a court case recently had programmes reactivated when a lawyer (who had access to my clinical notes) asked him about certain alter personalities (probably on purpose to trigger him). Another had programmes triggered through words spoken to her by a participant in an online forum she was helping to lead. As I mentioned earlier, I lost a client when a man found her in an online discussion group and worked out her personality system. I have also, on two different occasions, seen well-known public speakers on the topic of ritual abuse use deliberate triggers as part of their talks.

Never forget that these abuser groups have a strong interest in keeping their secrets, and survivors who expose their status publicly, even by attending lectures on the subject, need to be alert for triggering events. I recommend that survivors be very cautious about "going public", and only do it if they truly feel it is their calling.

Many, perhaps most, survivors might decide of their own free will to leave all those awful experiences in the past and get on with lives that have nothing to do with mind control or ritual abuse. The *choice*, the *decision*, is entirely yours. You can have a life outside of mind control and ritual abuse. Meredith Sharman, who tells her story in Chapter Seventeen, has chosen an entirely different life direction, one in which she contributes to society, but has nothing to do with the abuses of her past.

* * *

Well, dear reader, that is it. I have shared much of what I know about the process of overcoming mind control and ritual abuse. It is almost as if I were ending therapy with a long-term client, with whom I have travelled a great distance, through many ups and downs, to a successful conclusion. If you have actually read through to this point, you have learnt a great deal, and if you have done the exercises, you have changed a great deal. Ending is sad, but it is also an accomplishment! And a beginning.

I know that you did not choose what happened to you, but I also know that you can choose what you make of your life now. You can accomplish this, regardless of what abusers did to make you believe otherwise. All your experiences have given you strengths that most people do not have, since you have survived unimaginable challenges and emerged dedicated to recovery. You have developed wisdom along the way, and as you share among your parts what you have learnt, that wisdom will provide practical guidance for the road ahead. You have a great deal to offer the world.

When I used to teach parent education courses, there were many parents who chose to take the courses over and over again, because there were so many things they did not fully "get" the first time through. As they became skilled in one aspect of parenting, their eyes would open to another aspect they needed to learn. This book is designed like a course. You can read its chapters, and do the exercises they contain, over and over again, discovering new things each time. It would make me happy to know you were doing that, because no one could possibly learn all that is in this book in one read-through. Most of this material took me over twenty years to learn. I encourage you to continue to learn from it, as well as from other sources.

This might be your most basic recovery textbook, because it deals specifically with mind control and ritual abuse. However, there are many other helpful books and courses, some specifically directed at the area of life that gives you difficulty. As you explore further learning, remember that your mind is your own, and it is unwise to slavishly follow any other person's method. Accept only what resonates with your deepest parts as true and helpful. Discard the rest. (You can do this with my book, too.)

You have the rest of your life ahead to keep learning and growing. This book has addressed the most difficult parts of the journey. The rest of it can be a wonderful adventure in becoming your true self, and contributing from your own deepest being to the greater whole of humanity and life on this planet.

REFERENCES

Alderman, T., & Marshall, K. (1998). *Amongst Ourselves: A Self-Help Guide to Living with Dissociative Identity Disorder*. Oakland, CA: New Harbinger.

ATW (2005). *Got Parts? An Insider's Guide to Managing Life Successfully with Dissociative Identity Disorder*. Ann Arbor, MI: Loving Healing Press.

Ball, T. (2008). The use of prayer for inner healing of memories and deliverance with ritual abuse survivors. In: R. Noblitt & P. Noblitt (Eds.), *Ritual Abuse in the 21st Century* (pp. 413–442). Bandon, OR: Robert D. Reed.

Bass, E., & Davis, L. (1988). *The Courage to Heal: A Guide for Women Survivors of Child Sexual Abuse*. New York: Harper & Row.

Blume, E. S. (1991). *Secret Survivors: Uncovering Incest and its Aftereffects in Women*. New York: Ballantine Books, 1998.

Boon, S., Steele, K., & van der Hart, O. (2011). *Coping with Trauma-Related Dissociation*. New York: Norton.

Bradshaw, J. (1988). *Bradshaw on: The Family*. Deerfield Beach, FL: Health Communications.

Briere, J., & Runtz, M. (n.d.). Trauma symptoms checklist. www.johnbriere.com/tsc.htm.

Carter, C. (2007). *Science and Psychic Phenomena: The Fall of the House of Skeptics*. Rochester, VT: Inner Traditions.

Carter, C. (2010). *Science and the Near-Death Experience: How Consciousness Survives Death*. Rochester, VT: Inner Traditions.

Carter, C. (2012). *Science and the Afterlife Experience: Evidence for the Immortality of Consciousness*. Rochester, VT: Inner Traditions.

Dissociative Experiences Scale (n.d.). www.serene.me.uk/tests/des.pdf.

Epstein, O. B., Schwartz, J., & Schwartz, R. W. (Eds.) (2011). *Ritual Abuse and Mind Control: The Manipulation of Attachment Needs*. London: Karnac.

Extreme Abuse Survey Results (n.d.). http://eassurvey.wordpress.com/extreme-abuse-survey-final-results/.

Fotheringham, T. (2008). Patterns in mind control: a first person account. In: R. Noblitt & P. Perskin-Noblitt (Eds.), *Ritual Abuse in the 21st Century* (pp. 491–540). Bandon, OR: Robert D. Reed.

Fotheringham, T. (2009). Healing from ritual abuse and mind control: survivor Trish Fotheringham speaks out. Available from: www.endritualabuse.org.

Freyd, J. (1996). *Betrayal Trauma*. Cambridge, MA: Harvard University Press.

Gingrich, H. D. (2013). *Restoring the Shattered Self: A Christian Counselor's Guide to Complex Trauma*. Downers Grove, IL: Inter-Varsity Press.

Gottman, J. M., & Silver, N. (1999). *The Seven Principles for Making Marriage Work*. New York: Three Rivers Press.

Griffin, D., & Bartholomew, K. (1994). Models of the self and other: fundamental dimensions underlying measures of adult attachment. *Journal of Personality and Social Psychology, 67*(3): 430–445.

Guardian (2009). Re. sex trade trafficking: www.guardian.co.uk/world/2009/nov/22/people–trafficking–usa–prostitution–ohio.

Hawkins, T. R. (2010). *Dissociative Identity Disorder. Volume 1, Psychological Dynamics*. Grottoes, VA: RCM.

International Society for the Study of Trauma and Dissociation: http://www.isst-d.org/.

Johnson, S. (2008). *Hold Me Tight: Seven Conversations for a Lifetime of Love*. New York: Little, Brown.

Kluft, R. (2013). *Shelter from the Storm: Processing the Traumatic Memories of DID/DDNOS Patients with the Fractionated Abreaction Technique*. North Charleston, SC: CreateSpace Independent Publishing Platform.

Lacter, E. website: http://ritualabuse.us.

Lacter, E., Karriker, W., Ball, T., Sinason, V., & Somer, E. (2012). Therapists reporting histories of ritual abuse trauma: preliminary results on beneficial and detrimental treatment approaches. 29th Annual Conference of the ISST-D, October.

Lerner, H. (2009a). *The Dance of Anger*. New York: HarperCollins.

Lerner, H. (2009b). *The Dance of Connection*. New York: HarperCollins.

Lerner, H. (2009c). *The Dance of Deception*. New York: HarperCollins.

Lerner, H. (2009d). *The Dance of Fear*. New York: HarperCollins.

Lerner, H. (2009e). *The Dance of Intimacy*. New York: HarperCollins.

LisaBri website: www.dissociatedsurvivor.com.

Los Angeles County Commission for Women's Ritual Abuse Task Force report (1991). http://ritualabuse.us/ritualabuse/articles/report-of-the-ritual-abuse-task-force-los-angeles-county-commission-for-women/.

"Many Voices" (contact www.manyvoicespress.com/newsletter.html.)

McKay, M., & Fanning, P. (1996.) *When Anger Hurts Your Kids*. Oakland, CA: New Harbinger.

Miller, A. (2012). *Healing the Unimaginable: Treating Ritual Abuse and Mind Control*. London: Karnac.

Miller, A., & Rees, A. (2006). *Sidestepping the Power Struggle*. Victoria, BC: LIFE Seminars.

Miller, A., & Rees, A. (2008). *The Parent–Child Connection*. Victoria, BC: LIFE Seminars.

MKUltra declassified document (n.d.). http://abuse-of-power.org/modules/content/index.php?id=31.

Morales, A. L. (1998). Torturers. In: *Medicine Stories: History, Culture and the Politics of Integrity* (pp. 111–116). Cambridge, MA: South End Press.

Noblitt, R., & Perskin-Noblitt, P. (2008). *Ritual Abuse in the 21st Century*. Bandon, OR: Robert D. Reed.

Oglevie, Steve (n.d.). http://truthbeknown2000.tripod.com/Truthbeknown2000/id23/html.

Oksana, C. (1994). *Safe Passage to Healing: A Guide for Survivors of Ritual Abuse*. Lincoln, NE: iUniverse.com.

Patterson, C. H. (2000). Empathy, warmth and genuineness in psychotherapy: a review of reviews. In: *Understanding Psychotherapy: Fifty Years of Client-Centered Theory and Practice* (pp. 431–438). Ross-on-Wye: PCCS Books. See: www.sageofasheville.com/pub_downloads/EMPATHY_WARMTH_AND_GENUINESS_IN_PSYCHOTHERAPY.pdf.

Riseman, J. (n.d.). Simplifying complex programming. www.survivorship.org/resources/articles/programming.html.

Riseman, J. Website: www.ra-info.org. Blog: www.ritualabuse.wordpress.com.

Rose, E. P. (1996). *Reaching for the Light: A Guide for Ritual Abuse Survivors and Their Therapists.* Cleveland, OH: Pilgrim Press.

Ross, C. (2000). *Bluebird: Deliberate Creation of Multiple Personalities by Psychiatrists.* Republished as *The CIA Doctors: Human Rights Violations by American Psychiatrists.* Richardson, TX: Manitou Communications.

Ross, C. A. (1997). *Dissociative Identity Disorder: Diagnosis, Clinical Features, and Treatment of Multiple Personality* (2nd edn). New York: John Wiley.

Rutz, C. (2001). *A Nation Betrayed: The Chilling True Story of Secret Cold War Experiments Performed on Our Children and Other Innocent People.* Grass Lake, MI: Fidelity (http://my.dmci.net/~casey/).

Rutz, C., Becker, T., Overkamp, B., & Karriker, W. (2007). Exploring commonalities reported by adult survivors of extreme abuse: preliminary empirical findings. In: R. Noblitt & P. Noblitt (Eds.), *Ritual Abuse in the 21st Century* (pp. 491–540). Bandon, OR: Robert D. Reed.

Sachs, A. (2012). Boundary modifications in the treatment of people with dissociative disorders. *Journal of Trauma and Dissociation, 14*(2): 159–169.

Sachs, A. (2013). Still being hurt: the vicious cycle of dissociative disorders, attachment and ongoing abuse. *Attachment: New Directions in Psychotherapy and Relational Psychoanalysis, 7*(1): 90–100.

Steinberg, M. (2000). *The Stranger in the Mirror.* New York: HarperCollins.

Survivorship: www.survivorship.org/.

Svali First Series (2000). How the Illuminati Programs People. www.bibliotecapleyades.net/sociopolitica/esp_sociopol_illuminati_svali01a.htm#menu.

INDEX

For Product Safety Concerns and Information please contact our EU representative GPSR@taylorandfrancis.com
Taylor & Francis Verlag GmbH, Kaufingerstraße 24, 80331 München, Germany

www.ingramcontent.com/pod-product-compliance
Lightning Source LLC
LaVergne TN
LVHW080630011026
849160LV00014B/1172
* 9 7 8 1 7 8 2 2 0 0 7 6 5 *